THE
MOOSEWOOD
RESTAURANT
TABLE

The Moosewood Restaurant Cookbook Library

Moosewood Restaurant Favorites

New Recipes from Moosewood Restaurant

Sundays at Moosewood Restaurant (James Beard Award Nominee)

Moosewood Restaurant Kitchen Garden

Moosewood Restaurant Cooks at Home (James Beard Award Winner)

Moosewood Restaurant Cooks for a Crowd (James Beard Award Nominee)

Moosewood Restaurant Low-Fat Favorites (James Beard Award Winner)

Moosewood Restaurant Book of Desserts

Moosewood Restaurant Daily Special

Moosewood Restaurant New Classics (James Beard Award Nominee)

Moosewood Restaurant Celebrates (James Beard Award Nominee)

Moosewood Restaurant Simple Suppers

Moosewood Restaurant Cooking for Health

THE
MOOSEWOOD
RESTAURANT
TABLE

250 Brand-New Recipes from the Natural Foods Restaurant That Revolutionized Eating in America

THE MOOSEWOOD COLLECTIVE

Food Photography by Al Karevy | Food Styling by Patti Harville

ST. MARTIN'S GRIFFIN
NEW YORK

Food photography by Al Karevy
Food Styling by Patti Harville
Endpaper by Al Karevy
Design by Philip Mazzone

www.stmartins.com

The Library of Congress Cataloging-in-Publication Data is available upon request.

ISBN 978-1-250-07433-1 (hardcover)
ISBN 978-1-4668-8597-4 (ebook)

Our books may be purchased in bulk for promotional, educational, or business use. Please contact your local bookseller or the Macmillan Corporate and Premium Sales Department at 1-800-221-7945, extension 5442, or by email at MacmillanSpecialMarkets@macmillan.com.

First Edition: September 2017

10 9 8 7 6 5 4 3 2 1

CONTENTS

MAIN DISH SALADS   131

GRAIN BOWLS   149

ENTREES   161

STEWS & SAUTÉS   207

PASTA   227

BURGERS & BEANS   243

ACKNOWLEDGMENTS

"Let's do a new cookbook!" We said it first in the early '80s, and we've said it thirteen more times since. Arnold and Elise Goodman, our agents, have been with us every step of the way. Thank you, Arnold and Elise, you are true and trusted advocates and friends.

The first cookbook authored by The Moosewood Collective, *New Recipes from Moosewood Restaurant,* published in 1987, featured beautiful photographs taken by Al Karevy and hand-colored by Patti Harville. It is Patti and Al who produced the enticing food photos in this book—Al the photographer and Patti the food stylist. They are a joy to work with and we love how they captured our food. Some of Al's other work can be seen at www.karevy.com.

Michael Aman, a very good friend of Moosewood, toiled long hours back in the '80s typing handwritten recipes for our first manuscript. He caught goofs, inconsistencies, and omissions, and kept us entertained with wry comments. He used a then state-of-the-art electronic typewriter for proofreading and correcting; it had a screen that displayed each line before it was typed by the machine. Wow! Midstream in our work on that manuscript, personal computers came on the scene. Michael learned word processing along with us on an original Macintosh; a computer and small screen all in one box. Wow! It was a whole new world. Michael has stood ready all these years to come to our aid when it's cookbook crunch time. For this one, he once again input handwritten recipes for those among us who prefer the feeling of a pen in the hand. Thanks, Michael.

Since he emerged as a computer and robotics geek in high school, we have relied on Emilio Del Plato to troubleshoot our computer glitches, introduce us to things like file sharing, and perform little miracles here and there. Emilio just turned thirty; he works in IT at RIT and he's the father of a lively toddler, but he'll always be a boy wonder to us. You are dear to us, Emilio. And what would we have done without you?

Next up, Michael Flamini, our editor at St. Martin's. Besides being an astute editor and visionary, Michael cooks and makes us laugh. He tests recipes and sends us wonderful messages that keep us going. We wish there weren't so many miles between us, so we could feed you directly from our kitchens. We love everything about working with you, Michael. Thank you!

Michael's assistant, Vicki Lame, makes everything easier. She has just become an editor at St. Martin's, and just as we appreciate her, we know her new authors will, too. Happy trails to you, Vicki. And now, in the last laps with this book, we're so pleased to work with Gwen Hawkes, Michael's new assistant. Gwen is responsive, efficient, thorough, and personable...pretty much perfect.

At the end of a movie, if you don't need to rush out and you're a speed-reader, you can see the names of the multitude of people who played a part in the production. But you rarely see those vital people named in a book's acknowledgments. Here is a list, not all-inclusive by any measure, of the St. Martin's people who played key roles behind the scenes: Leah Stewart, copy editor; Olga Grlic, jacket designer; Erica Martirano-Red, marketing; Rowen Davis, mechanical designer; Vincent Stanley, production manager; John Karle, publicist; Brant Janeway, team leader; Eric C. Meyer; Jennifer Enderlin; Anne Marie Tallberg; Sally Richardson; and George Witte.

One of our greatest pleasures is creating good food. The whole Moosewood Collective and the restaurant staff have supported and contributed to all of our cookbooks. For their help with this cookbook and for holding down the fort at the restaurant, we especially thank Jenny Wang, Penny Goldin, Sara Robbins, Dave Dietrich, Neil Minnis, Jason Coughlin, Tim Mooney, Karen Sgambati, Lisa Wichman, and Linda Dickinson. Our customers, families, and fans are also an integral part of each cookbook. Their enthusiasm, appreciation, and presence in our lives is reflected throughout this book.

INTRODUCTION

Fourteen books and forty-four years ago, The Vegetable Kingdom, Inc., our founders, brought forth on this land of the Cayuga Nation a new eatery, Moosewood Restaurant, conceived in counterculture idealism and dedicated to the proposition that all people are created hungry and endowed with an innate appetite for real, wholesome, luscious food, and that the people who grow our food, cook our food, and serve our food shall be treated with dignity on this earth. Now we're engaged in a great food revolution, testing whether that notion or any eatery so conceived and so dedicated can long endure.

We weren't the first natural foods restaurant to put the emphasis on natural, plant-based food, and we certainly won't be the last, but Moosewood Restaurant and its cookbooks have influenced how and what a lot of people prefer to eat today—fresh food that travels directly from the garden and the farm to the table and the fork. Somewhere between the farm and your fork is where our recipes, no-nonsense cookery, and a love of culinary adventure fit in. We've never aspired to haute cuisine; everything we've ever cooked up is well within your reach. And yeah, we're still cooking after all these years. Welcome to our table!

Many of us believe that fresh, nutritious food is a human right, and we work to support childhood nutrition and family farms, increase the number of local growers, see agricultural workers make a living wage, turn food deserts into oases with community gardens and regionally sourced foods, and make healthy food affordable and accessible to all people.

People are still uncertain about what to call our restaurant's cuisine. Is it vegetarian, vegan, pescatarian? The answer is yes, and we've published recipes in all of those categories. Is there any orthodoxy here? Without adherence to any doctrine or ideology, we leave the preparation of meat and poultry to other establishments and writers. We decided that this book should focus on what we do best—using our creativity in the vegetable kingdom. So, going back to our roots and the type of food that has made us famous, this is a book of 250 new vegetarian and vegan recipes drawing on multiple ethnic influences. Chapters organize everything into familiar categories: appetizers, dips and spreads, soups, salads, sandwiches, snacks, sides, entrées, sweets, and extras. There are tips and information in the sidebars accompanying some recipes.

We develop recipes for our cookbooks outside the restaurant to make sure they work without the backup of a commercial kitchen. So the Moosewood table extends onto our personal kitchen tables. Before long, every horizontal kitchen surface is covered with competing versions of multiple recipes! Our goal is to make yours the next Moosewood table, maybe a little tidier.

One of our talents, apparently, is to devise vegetarian meals that non-vegetarians like enough that they don't miss the meat. That's also how we approach vegan and gluten-free dishes now—we make them tasty and satisfying enough that most folks won't miss the cheese, or eggs, or wheat flour. Throughout the chapters, we have included a substantial number of vegan and gluten-free vegetarian recipes that can be enjoyed by everyone at the table. Many other recipes can be made vegan by omitting a dairy product or can be made gluten-free with simple substitutions.

Is Moosewood Restaurant a health-food joint? Some people certainly think so when they see fresh-squeezed juices and all the vegetables, herbs, legumes, greens, whole grains, nuts, and tofu we use. We serve folks with a sweet tooth who won't touch sugar. We serve customers who can't consume tree nuts, groundnuts, gluten, any food with meat, any food with wheat, any food that's white, anything with fat, oils, eggs, lactose, glucose, fructose, fish, corn, canola, capsicum, nightshades, nitrates, sugar, honey, hominy, citrus, seeds, shellfish, sulfites, soy, wine, beer, or booze. But they still find things to eat at the Moosewood table.

We've gotten to know our customers and readers pretty well by now. Their tastes and expectations, their curiosity and culinary IQ have grown exponentially and, like us, they don't want to be bored with their food. So, we went on a few adventures while we were developing this book. We've used many new and rediscovered ingredients, tried new combinations, spices, and condiments, and explored a couple of cuisines that are relatively new to us. We dove into working with some less common fruits and vegetables that you might find in your CSA or at the farmers' market: fascinatingly fractal romanesco broccoli, fresh fennel, jicama, watermelon radishes, broccoli rabe, rutabaga, garlic greens, garlic scapes, golden beets, celeriac; fresh shiitake, oyster, enoki, and other mushrooms; microgreens and power greens; heirloom vegetables and fruits, especially apples, carrots, tomatoes. We've gotten more familiar with grains like freekeh, farro, black rice, red rice, millet, red quinoa, flax, and chia seeds. Even though the market has exploded with enticing condiments and seasonings, or maybe because of it (we want to improve on what we can buy), we've experimented with mixing up our own versions of favorite blends, such as za'atar, preserved lemons, harissa, and chermoula sauce; our own garam masala and spice rub; and our own gluten-free flour mix.

We have some new takes on familiar traditional dishes, such as our Nori Rolls with Kale, Burmese Tohu Thoke with tamarind, vegetarian Banh Mi, Cuban Picadillo with tofu, Pasta Carbonara with zucchini and smoked cheese, Spicy Filo Samosas, Butternut Squash Latkes, Power Pesto, Pozole Verde, Sweet Potato Gnocchi, Walnut-Cheddar-

Herb "Meatballs," Ethiopian Greens, and Jamaican Jerk Tempeh Patties. In case you still think we're just a health-food joint, check out recipes for baked goods from Bialys to Apricot Frangipane Tart, and a gluten-free version of a family favorite, Erma Mabel's Fresh Rhubarb Cake.

Whether making food for you, your family, or your friends, cooking at home is self-affirming and empowering on many levels. Among arts and crafts, cooking with wholesome, intriguing ingredients is one of the most emotionally and physically satisfying of creative activities, harnessing all of our senses and intuition. It's not just about filling up the void; being in relationship with the character, sound, color, and aroma of your ingredients, the tasks, the timing, the temperatures, the tools of your trade, and navigating the turf of a kitchen can be as engrossing as carving wood, painting from life, or soloing on your sax. You may read the chart, but you can always improvise or riff on a variation. Recipes are only guidelines.

HOW HOT FOR HOW LONG?

How long it takes to cook, sauté, bake, or roast depends on the size, shape, material, and weight of your pan, the exact temperature, pattern, and source of your heat, and how hot your burner is when you turn it to medium-high (whatever you think medium-high is). Cook the onions on medium heat until translucent, about 5 minutes—but getting to translucence might take 10 minutes or 4 minutes, depending on the pan and stovetop you use. The only place that cooking times can be expected to pretty well match your experience is when boiling and steaming something. Boiling is boiling, but there are still variables—how tender is your kale, how big did you cut the potatoes? How long the liquid takes to come to a boil depends on the size of the pot, the altitude, the size of the burner, and, of course, whether you're watching that pot. Even the time it takes to "purée until smooth" depends on how sharp and fast your blender/food processor blade is, plus the shape of the container. So use what you know about your stovetop and your oven. Use your nose, cool your jets, cook with love, and use the Force.

Multigrain Blueberry Pancakes

If you pick fresh blueberries, this is for you.

Oats, cornmeal, and whole wheat flour give texture and flavor to a breakfast treat that can be made with frozen blueberries, if fresh are not available. If you don't want too sweet a breakfast, try them as is, or with just a dollop of yogurt instead of syrup.

Yields sixteen 4-inch pancakes
Serves 3 or 4
Prep time: 20 minutes
Cooking time: 20 minutes

6 tablespoons (¾ stick) butter
2 large eggs
2 tablespoons pure maple syrup
1¼ cups plain yogurt
1 teaspoon finely grated lemon zest
½ teaspoon pure vanilla extract
½ cup rolled oats
½ cup whole wheat flour
¼ cup cornmeal
1 tablespoon baking powder
½ teaspoon salt
1 cup blueberries, fresh or frozen

Melt 3 tablespoons of the butter and set aside. In a bowl, whisk together the eggs, maple syrup, yogurt, lemon zest, and vanilla. In the bowl of a food processor, whirl the oats for a minute or two until they're crumbly, but not as fine as flour. In a separate bowl, combine the crumbled oats with the flour, cornmeal, baking powder, and salt. Stir the dry ingredients into the wet only until moistened—a few lumps are fine. Whisk in the melted butter, then fold in the blueberries.

If you would like to serve the pancakes all at once, preheat the oven to 200°F and put a baking sheet in it to keep the cooked pancakes warm while the rest are cooking.

Heat a large skillet or griddle on medium heat. Melt some butter on the hot surface and spread it to cover. Pour ¼ cup of batter for each pancake, leaving a bit of space between. After 3 to 4 minutes, when bubbles start to surface and the pancakes are dry around the edges, turn them over and cook for 2 to 3 minutes more, until golden and firm on the bottom. If the pancakes are browning too quickly, lower the heat a little. Serve as they are done, or transfer the pancakes to the warm oven. Add more butter to the pan before making each batch.

SERVING AND MENU IDEAS
Serve with toppings such as maple syrup, fruit preserves, butter, yogurt, or sour cream.

Multigrain Blueberry Pancakes are probably enough for a delicious and satisfying breakfast. If it's a blow-out brunch, add simple fried or scrambled eggs, vegetarian sausage, and maybe a Sweet Fruit Smoothie (page 24).

Gingerbread Pancakes with Lemon Syrup

Your kitchen will smell wonderfully festive while making these delicious pancakes that are like little gingerbread cakes. Great for brunch or holiday gatherings. Double or triple the recipe to feed a crowd.

Yields 18 pancakes; 1⅓ cups syrup
Serves 4 to 6
Time: 40 minutes

LEMON SYRUP
½ cup granulated sugar
1 tablespoon cornstarch
Pinch of freshly grated nutmeg
1 cup water
1 tablespoon butter
1 teaspoon finely grated lemon zest
2 tablespoons fresh lemon juice

DRY INGREDIENTS
2½ cups all-purpose white flour (or 1½ cups white flour and 1 cup whole wheat pastry flour)
1 tablespoon baking powder
1 teaspoon baking soda
¼ teaspoon ground cloves
2 teaspoons ground ginger
2 teaspoons ground cinnamon
¼ teaspoon freshly grated nutmeg
½ teaspoon salt

WET INGREDIENTS
1½ cups buttermilk
⅓ cup molasses
1 cup packed brown sugar
2 large eggs
¼ cup butter, melted and cooled, plus extra butter for the griddle

Make the lemon syrup: In a small saucepan on medium heat, combine the granulated sugar, cornstarch, and nutmeg. Stir in the water until the mixture is smooth. Bring to a boil, lower the heat and cook, stirring until thickened, about 2 minutes. Remove from the heat and stir in the butter, lemon zest, and lemon juice. Cover and set aside.

In a large bowl, sift together the dry ingredients. In another bowl, whisk together the wet ingredients. Add the wet ingredients to the dry and mix until just combined.

Heat the griddle on medium-low heat, and using a spatula, spread a teaspoon of butter over the surface. Pour on ⅓ cup of batter for each pancake. When you can slide the spatula under the pancakes and the bottoms are starting to brown, flip the pancakes over and cook the opposite sides for about half a minute. Keep adding more butter to the griddle between batches.

SERVING AND MENU IDEAS
We think you'll enjoy the easy lemon syrup drizzled on these pancakes, but of course maple syrup is good as well, or even just a dusting of confectioners' sugar. Or top the pancakes with sautéed apples or warmed pitted cherries or peach slices along with the lemon syrup.

Probably the only other thing you might want with this special pancake brunch is cold orange juice or hot apple cider.

So Simple Banana Pancakes

Starting your day with two eggs and a banana? Now there's some fuel. But make those eggs and banana into little pancakes with a drizzle of maple syrup . . . now *there's* delicious! And it's gluten-free. And if you use good-quality margarine instead of butter, it's dairy-free. And if you're going low-carb, it's grain-free.

Some of us are happy to eat these quick little pancakes at any meal, and we make them for breakfast, lunch, or supper. Or as a snack . . . or even a quick little dessert . . . or for no good reason at all!

Yields about twelve 3-inch pancakes
Serves 1 or 2
Time: 10 to 15 minutes

1 ripe banana
2 large eggs
1 teaspoon butter
Sprinkling of salt
1 tablespoon pure maple syrup

In a small bowl, mash the banana with a fork, leaving some lumps. In a separate small bowl, whisk the eggs and stir in the mashed banana, still with lumps.

Warm a skillet on medium heat. Melt the butter in the skillet and spread it over the bottom. The skillet should be hot, but not smoking. Drop tablespoonfuls of the banana-egg "batter" onto the hot surface. After about a minute, when the bottoms have browned a bit and the edges have turned a lighter color, flip the pancakes with a spatula. Cook until the egg is set and the bottom has browned, about half a minute. (Unless you have a very large griddle or skillet, you'll have to cook the pancakes in two or three batches. For better flipping, between batches wipe off the top of the spatula, and you may need to smear the skillet with a little more butter before the last batch.)

Arrange the pancakes on a plate in a single layer. Sprinkle with salt, drizzle with maple syrup, and dig in.

SERVING AND MENU IDEAS
These pancakes are good topped with yogurt and fresh strawberries or raspberries.

Herbed Baked Eggs in a Ramekin

This is a simple technique for baking individual eggs. The eggs emerge like sunny-side-up eggs with softly set yolks and silky whites with crisp edges, seasoned with herbs on the bottom. One of the beauties of baking eggs is that you can make multiple servings all at once and serve them right in the ramekins.

Yields 4 baked eggs
Serves 2 to 4
Baking time: 15 minutes

MEDITERRANEAN
1 teaspoon olive oil or softened butter
2 tablespoons minced fresh chives, parsley, basil, tarragon, marjoram, and/or dill
4 large eggs
2 tablespoons grated Parmesan cheese
Salt and freshly ground black pepper (optional)

ASIAN
1 teaspoon coconut oil
1½ teaspoons peeled and grated fresh ginger
2 tablespoons minced fresh basil or cilantro
4 large eggs
Pinch of cayenne pepper (optional)
Salt

Preheat the oven to 350°F. Brush four 3- to 4-inch ramekins or other ovenproof cups with the oil or butter.

Divide the herbs and/or spices among the ramekins and break an egg into each. Top herbed Mediterranean eggs with ½ tablespoon of Parmesan each and sprinkle with salt and black pepper if you like. Top Asian eggs with a sprinkling of cayenne pepper and salt if you like. Place the ramekins on a baking sheet and bake for about 15 minutes, until the whites are set.

SERVING AND MENU IDEAS
Serve the Mediterranean version with Watermelon Gazpacho (page 108), and the Asian version with Potato Wedges Masala (page 46). Kip's Favorite Scones (page 31) will round out either meal.

Green Tomato Omelet

So it's August and you have lots of firm green tomatoes on hand. . . . Lucky you! The fresh, tart taste of green tomatoes is delicious with eggs. Green tomatoes used to be something you had to figure out how to use at the end of tomato season, but now they are available year-round in many supermarkets because they are so prized.

Serves 4
Time: 30 minutes

1 pound firm green tomatoes
⅓ cup cornmeal
6 large eggs
¼ teaspoon salt
½ teaspoon freshly ground black pepper
3 tablespoons chopped fresh parsley
2 tablespoons snipped or chopped fresh chives
1 teaspoon fresh thyme leaves
3 tablespoons olive oil
2 garlic cloves, minced or pressed

Slice the tomatoes into ½-inch-thick rounds; the tomato rounds will be different sizes. Dredge each slice in cornmeal and set aside. Beat the eggs in a bowl with the salt, pepper, parsley, chives, and thyme.

Warm the oil in a 10- or 12-inch skillet on medium heat. Add the tomatoes and fry for about 2 minutes on each side, until golden but not brown. The tomato slices should be firm; they'll continue to cook in the eggs. Remove from the skillet and drain on paper towels.

Without wiping out the skillet, cook the garlic for less than a minute. Pour in the egg mixture and cook, covered, on medium-low heat for about 2 minutes. Arrange the tomato slices on top and cook for about 5 minutes, until the bottom is firm and browned. At this point you have a choice for how to brown the top. You can finish the omelet under the broiler if your skillet is ovenproof, or you can flip it.

Flipping an omelet this size is challenging, but here's how we do it: Run a spatula around the outside edges and then under the omelet to loosen the bottom. Slide the omelet onto a large plate. Then flip the plate over onto the skillet, depositing the omelet back into the skillet tomato side down. Cook for about 5 minutes, or until the bottom is firm. Position a serving plate, upside down, on top of the skillet and, holding the plate firmly against the skillet with the palm of your hand, flip the skillet over to release the omelet onto the plate tomato side up. Let the omelet sit for a minute or two, then cut into wedges.

Serve hot or at room temperature.

VARIATION
Especially if you have an herb garden, experiment with other herbs. Dill, basil, and cilantro are all good choices.

SERVING AND MENU IDEAS
You can top this omelet with grated Parmesan.

Serve with A Hash of Spuds, Beets, and Greens (page 311) for a special brunch or a homey supper. Green Tomato Omelet also goes nicely with Black Rice Pilaf (page 319).

Asparagus-Mushroom Frittata

Sometimes a traditional ingredient is the traditional ingredient because it is simply the best. Authentic Fontina Valle d'Aosta imported from Italy is a fantastic cheese for melting, and domestic varieties really can't compare. It is a bit more expensive, but because the flavor is so rich, a little goes a long way. It harmonizes beautifully with the asparagus and mushrooms in this impressive frittata. That said, the frittata is fine made with any fontina.

This is a dish you would probably make for a special brunch for family and guests, so it may be helpful to know that most of the preparation can be done in advance; then the frittata should be freshly baked and served puffy and golden. While it bakes, you'll have time to set the table, make coffee, tea, fresh-squeezed orange juice, or mimosas, and enjoy yourselves.

Serves 6 to 8
Prep time: 45 minutes
Baking time: 40 minutes

3 tablespoons olive oil, plus more for the pan
3 cups sliced potatoes (½-inch-thick slices)
2 large garlic cloves, minced or pressed
1 teaspoon smoked paprika
1 teaspoon salt, plus more as needed
1 teaspoon butter (optional)
1½ cups chopped leeks, white and tender green parts (1 large leek)
1 pound asparagus
1½ cups stemmed and sliced fresh shiitake mushrooms★
¼ teaspoon freshly ground black pepper
6 large eggs
3 ounces cream cheese
1½ cups milk
1 cup packed grated Fontina Valle d'Aosta cheese
½ cup shredded Parmesan cheese

★We like the taste and chewy texture of shiitake mushrooms in this dish, but cremini or white mushrooms are also fine to use.

Preheat the oven to 400°F. Lightly oil a 9 x 13-inch baking pan.

In a large mixing bowl, toss together the potato slices, 2 tablespoons of the olive oil, the garlic, ½ teaspoon of the paprika, and ½ teaspoon of the salt. Spread out on the prepared baking sheet and roast for about 20 minutes, until the potatoes are tender and beginning to brown. Set aside.

Meanwhile, in a large skillet, warm the remaining 1 tablespoon olive oil and the butter, if using, and cook the leeks with a sprinkling of salt for a few minutes, until softened. While the leeks cook, prepare the asparagus by snapping off and discarding the tough bottom stem ends. Cut the spears into 1-inch-long pieces and add them to the leeks. Cover and cook for about 3 minutes. Stir in the mushrooms, remaining smoked paprika, and black pepper and cook, covered, for a few minutes more, until all the vegetables are tender. Set aside.

Combine the eggs, cream cheese, milk, and remaining ½ teaspoon salt in a blender and purée until smooth. Layer the roasted potatoes in the prepared baking pan. Spread the leek and asparagus mixture on top and cover with the fontina. Pour the egg custard over all and sprinkle the Parmesan on top.

Bake for 40 minutes, or until the custard is set and the top is lightly browned.

Serve hot or at room temperature.

NOTE: At Moosewood, we roast the seasoned sliced potatoes in the morning (and since we don't have sufficient self-restraint to not snag them right off of the baking sheet, we make a little extra for ourselves). Then we sauté the veggies and grate the cheeses, and assemble the frittatas in oiled baking pans with everything but the custard, and cover and refrigerate them. If kept cold, even the custard can be made in advance. About an hour before serving, we pour on the custard and bake this rich frittata. Chilled frittatas may take an extra 5 minutes to bake.

SERVING AND MENU IDEAS

With this rich frittata, we want a light, refreshing counterpoint such as a vinegary salad or fresh fruit. For a nice spring brunch, also serve something like Watercress Toast (page 53) or Kip's Ginger Scones (page 31), and Greens with Apricots Times Two (page 111) or Greens with Citrus-Date Dressing (page 126). Or you could really do it up with Apple and Fig Galette with Rosemary (page 375).

Baked Eggs with Spinach and Frizzled Sage

Moosewood partner Penny Goldin has long been famous in certain circles for her fabulous brunch parties at which she serves beautiful food, often on her wraparound porch overlooking Cayuga Lake. Almost anything might be an occasion for a brunch—a birthday, a graduation, a new baby, visiting out-of-town friends, or just because it's a long weekend. Penny is always gracious and relaxed, and the crowd is always wowed.

This delicious and uncomplicated dish is a truly elegant way to serve eggs, and it can be expanded to accommodate large families or many brunch guests. You can prep it ahead of time and then about 20 minutes before serving, pop it into the oven.

Serves 2 to 4
Prep time: 15 minutes
Baking time: 20 minutes

Olive oil
Coarse salt
4 cups fresh spinach
4 large eggs
½ cup thinly sliced red, white, or yellow onions
⅛ teaspoon crushed red pepper flakes
½ cup loosely packed fresh sage leaves, cut into strips if large

Preheat the oven to 350°F. Oil an 8-inch square ceramic or glass baking dish with a little olive oil. Sprinkle coarse salt on the bottom of the pan.

In a skillet, heat 1 tablespoon olive oil and sauté the spinach until just limp. Arrange the spinach in the baking dish, making four wells, one for each egg. Crack an egg into each well and top with a scattering of onion slices, a sprinkling of coarse salt, a judicious amount of red pepper flakes, and 1 tablespoon olive oil. Bake for 20 minutes, until the yolks are soft and the whites are firm.

While the eggs bake, wipe the skillet with a paper towel. Warm about 2 teaspoons olive oil on medium heat and cook the sage leaves, stirring frequently, until they're crisp and turn a dark gray-green. Remove and drain on a paper towel.

Serve each baked egg with its bed of spinach, topped with crispy sage leaves.

SERVING AND MENU IDEAS
Serve Baked Eggs with Spinach and Frizzled Sage for brunch, or for supper with a tomato salad or a fruit salad and Asparagus Cacio e Pepe–Style (page 293) along with buttered toast or Bialys (page 278).

Piperade

This recipe for eggs cooked in sautéed peppers with seasonings and tomatoes is a version of *piperade* from the Basque region of France. Variations abound all around the Mediterranean, with different seasonings like cumin or za'atar, and seasonal vegetables like artichokes, zucchini, eggplant, or potatoes. One seeded jalapeño will give a moderate amount of spicy heat; if you like it hot, substitute a hotter fresh hot pepper, or splash on some hot sauce before serving.

Serves 2 to 4
Time: 45 minutes

2 tablespoons olive oil
1 red bell pepper, seeded and sliced into thin strips
1 green, yellow, or orange bell pepper, seeded and cut into thin strips
1 fresh hot pepper, minced, or a pinch of cayenne pepper
1½ cups sliced onions
½ teaspoon salt
3 garlic cloves, minced or pressed
1 teaspoon fresh thyme, or ½ teaspoon dried
1 teaspoon sweet paprika
1 (14-ounce) can diced tomatoes
4 large eggs
2 tablespoons chopped fresh parsley
¼ cup crumbled chèvre cheese (optional)
Crusty baquette or toast, for serving

Warm the oil in a large skillet, add the bell peppers and hot pepper, and sauté on fairly high heat, stirring often, until softened and lightly browned, 5 to 10 minutes. Add the onions, salt, garlic, thyme, and paprika, lower the heat, and cook, stirring often to avoid scorching, for 5 minutes. Stir in the tomatoes and raise the heat until the mixture is bubbling, then lower it to a gentle simmer. Cover and cook until the vegetables in the sauce are quite tender, 5 to 10 minutes.

Break each egg into its own quarter of the pan, sprinkle with the parsley, and cover. Cook on low heat until the egg whites are just set.

Serve at once, topped with cheese if you like, with a crusty baguette or toasted bread.

SERVING AND MENU IDEAS
Piperade simply must be served with some kind of bread. At brunch, Bialys (page 278) would be good. For supper, serve with a baguette and a green vegetable on the side, perhaps Spicy Roasted Broccoli (page 302) or a green salad, such as Kale, Jicama, and Orange Salad (page 128).

Butternut Hash Browns

Colorful, mildly sweet, and simple to prepare, these winter squash "hash browns" are a healthier alternative to the typical potato version. A well-seasoned wok works very well for cooking the squash, and a large heavy skillet does, too.

Serves 4
Time: 25 minutes

1 medium butternut squash, peeled, seeded, and cut into large chunks★
2 tablespoons vegetable oil
1 cup diced onions
1 teaspoon dried thyme, more to taste
Salt and freshly ground black pepper

★If you buy prepped butternut chunks, get about 1¼ pounds.

Using the large-holed shredding blade of a food processor, or on the large holes of a box grater, shred the squash chunks to yield about 5 cups lightly packed.

Warm the oil in a wok or skillet on medium-high heat. Add the onions and cook for 3 or 4 minutes. Add the squash, thyme, and a sprinkling of salt, and lower the heat to medium. Cover and cook, stirring every minute or two, until the squash is tender yet firm, 8 to 10 minutes. Season with salt and pepper to taste.

SERVING AND MENU IDEAS
Serve at breakfast next to eggs or Mushroom Tofu Scramble with Truffle Oil (page 19). For dinner, the hash browns go well with Black Bean and Quinoa Burgers with Chipotle Ketchup (page 246).

Mushroom Tofu Scramble with Truffle Oil

We've done several tofu scrambles in our past cookbooks, but this one features fancier flavors and ingredients: shallots, wild mushrooms, and truffle oil. It's an easy stovetop brunch, lunch, or dinner scramble. Also a delectable invite-friends-over filling for roasted portobellos, zucchini, or squash. Any way you have it, the pervasive flavor of truffle oil adds a seductive touch.

Serves 4
Time: 40 minutes

1 (14- to 16-ounce) block firm tofu
3 tablespoons olive oil
1 cup chopped shallots or onions
3 garlic cloves, chopped
1 pound assorted mushrooms (cremini, shiitake, maitake, oyster, morel, etc.), trimmed and coarsely chopped
½ teaspoon salt
¼ cup chopped fresh parsley
3 tablespoons chopped fresh tarragon
2 teaspoons truffle oil
Coarsely ground black pepper (optional)
½ cup chopped toasted hazelnuts

First, press some water out of the tofu: Put the block of tofu in a shallow bowl in an out-of-the-way place on the countertop. Cover it with a flat plate and balance a heavy can or book on the plate.

In a large heavy skillet, heat the oil on medium heat and cook the shallots and garlic until soft, 3 to 5 minutes. Add the mushrooms and sauté until the mushrooms are soft and chewy. Crumble the pressed tofu and stir it into the mushrooms. Add the salt, parsley, and tarragon. Simmer for about 8 minutes, stirring frequently to help prevent sticking, until the tofu is heated through and well distributed. Add a little water or stock if the scramble sticks too much to the bottom of the pan. Finally, stir in the truffle oil. Taste and add more salt and/or truffle oil, and some coarsely ground pepper if you like.

Serve the scramble with a sprinkling of chopped hazelnuts.

SERVING AND MENU IDEAS

At brunch, Mushroom Tofu Scramble with Truffle Oil goes well with Kip's Favorite Scones (page 31) or Bialys (page 278). For lunch or dinner, serve it with a crusty bread and a tasty salad, such as Belgian Endive Citrus Salad with Gremolata (page 129) or Greens with Apricots Times Two (page 111) and Butternut Hash Browns (page 18).

Tomato-Sesame Tofu Scramble

A super-easy and very satisfying dish that is great for breakfast, lunch, or dinner. We especially love to make tofu scrambles after a busy night at the restaurant when we're craving comfort and need to make something fast. This scramble also serves as a great side dish or as a component on a combo plate. Or roll it up in a warm tortilla or rice paper wrapper for a portable meal.

Serves 2 to 4
Yields 3 cups
Prep time: 30 minutes

1 (14- to 16-ounce) block firm tofu
1 tablespoon olive oil
1 cup diced onions
2 cups chopped fresh tomatoes
½ teaspoon salt
¼ teaspoon freshly ground black pepper
½ cup chopped scallions
3 tablespoons dark sesame oil
2 tablespoons soy sauce
½ teaspoon ground fennel seeds

Wrap the tofu in a couple of paper towels, gently press out some water, and pat dry. Crumble the tofu into a bowl. Set aside.

In a large skillet on medium heat, warm the oil. Add the onions and cook until softened. Add the tomatoes, salt, and pepper and cook, stirring occasionally, until some of the juice released by the tomatoes has cooked off, about 5 minutes.

Add the crumbled tofu, scallions, sesame oil, soy sauce, and fennel to the skillet. Scramble the tofu and other ingredients by stirring occasionally during cooking, until somewhat browned and dry, 15 to 20 minutes.

SERVING AND MENU IDEAS
This is delicious served with Tabasco, Sriracha, or other hot sauce. Nice accompaniment: Snow Peas with Seaweed (page 292) or Jeweled Rice (page 321).

Peppery Green Smoothie, No Pepper

If you're someone who loves the kick of hot green peppers but you have to avoid nightshades, try this smoothie. No pepper, no nightshades, no dairy, no gluten . . . just smooth, hot and sweet, and delicious, *plus* packed with nutrients. It's a good wake-me-up in the morning or pick-me-up in the afternoon.

The mustard green leaves are soft enough to create a velvety smoothie, and they give you that peppery burn at the back of your throat. This recipe has a nice, moderate level of heat; if you want a real blast, do the Hot Hot variation.

Yields about 1½ cups
Time: 20 minutes

4 to 8 dried dates, depending on your penchant
   for sweetness
¾ cup fresh orange juice or apple cider
1 ripe banana, fresh or frozen
½ cup firmly packed stemmed mustard green
   leaves

Soak the dates in hot tap water for about 15 minutes; drain and chop. Put the dates, juice or cider, banana, and mustard leaves into a blender and whirl at high speed for a minute, until smooth. At first, you might think there isn't enough liquid, but give it time to "work." Then, if the finished smoothie is thicker than you like, add some more juice.

VARIATIONS
- Hot Hot: Increase the mustard greens to 1 cup firmly packed and the liquid to 1 cup; yields a generous 2 cups, enough to serve two.
- Use half an avocado instead of a banana.
- In place of dates, use 10 to 12 seedless red or green grapes, fresh or frozen.
- Use other juices, such as pear, cranberry, white grape, etc., or coconut water or milk (dilute coconut milk with half water).

SERVING AND MENU IDEAS
Peppery Green Smoothie, No Pepper is an excellent starter to be followed by eggs and potatoes. End with a bowl of sweet cherries or peaches.

Jenny's Best Breakfast Smoothie

Jenny Wang, a Moosewood cook and one of our partners, starts many days with this smoothie. She jokes that it's a "meal replacement" smoothie, and we think it really is: it will hold you until lunch. Smooth and green, this no-nonsense health-food beverage is bursting with nutrition. The avocado is important for its nutrients, and also for flavor and velvetiness. The kiwi is important for sweetness, but also, its pectin creates a lush note. The grassiness of the greens and the sprightliness of the watermelon will tell you just how good it is for you.

Yields about 2 cups
Serves 2
Time: 10 minutes

1 cup watermelon chunks
½ Hass avocado, pitted and peeled
½ kiwi, peeled
1 cup packed kale or spinach
1 tablespoon almond butter
1 tablespoon flax-chia meal★
½ cup water or apple juice, or more

★You can buy a preground meal of flaxseeds and chia seeds, or grind it yourself in a spice grinder.

Put all the ingredients into the blender and purée. Add more water until the smoothie is the thickness you like.

SERVING AND MENU IDEAS
Accompany this smoothie with Apple-Cinnamon-Oat Breakfast Bars (page 28) or sweet little Sunbutter Bites (page 30).

Sweet Fruit Smoothies

How can something so delicious, refreshing, and satisfying still be so good for you? The fruit is divine blended all together, and the vanilla and maple syrup flavors are just right.

With future smoothies in mind, go ahead and get that beautiful whole melon, even though you know it would take up too much real estate in the refrigerator and you couldn't eat it all before it goes bad. Get a whole honeydew, watermelon, or cantaloupe instead of buying a half or a wedge at about the same price. You can make outstanding fruit smoothies with both fresh and frozen fruit, so eat what you want and freeze the rest (see sidebar). With bags of fruit chunks in your freezer, it's easy to quickly whip up a frosty smoothie without adding ice cubes or crushed ice. A cache of frozen fresh fruit is your friend.

You can make smoothies in advance for the next morning. Refrigerated in a jar or container with a good lid, it will stay delicious, energizing, and fresh-tasting for two days. Just shake it up a little before drinking, morning, noon, or night.

Yields about 3 cups
Time: 10 minutes

1 ripe banana
1 cup watermelon chunks
1 cup orange juice
¼ teaspoon pure vanilla extract (optional)
1 tablespoon pure maple syrup or other sweetener (optional)

1 cup fresh or frozen fruit chunks:
  Red smoothie: red grapes; strawberries; red raspberries; red or Bing cherries; red plums
  Yellow smoothie: green grapes; pineapple; mango; honeydew, Crenshaw, or canary melon
  Orange smoothie: green grapes; cantaloupe; peaches; apricots; nectarines; papaya; guava

Purée all the ingredients in a blender. If your fruit is all or mostly frozen, read the instructions for the frosty variation.

VARIATION
Sweet Fruit Frosties: Make an icy-thick frosty for breakfast, a snack, or dessert, or to spoon into a thermal travel mug and take with you. Use mostly or all frozen fruit in the same proportions as above and purée it in a food processor or a strong blender. If the mix is too thick to purée smoothly, add a little more orange juice . . . or let the frozen fruits defrost a bit. Serve in milk shake glasses or tumblers with a fountain spoon or a fat straw.

SERVING AND MENU IDEAS
We like a sweet fruit smoothie for breakfast with an Avocado Egg Sandwich (page 81) or a Mexican Toasted Cheese Sandwich (page 84). Or blend up a smoothie for dessert after a meal of burgers and potatoes or pizza or Zowee Thai Fried Rice (page 170).

AT-THE-READY SMOOTHIE FRUIT IN YOUR FREEZER

It's easy to freeze fruit for smoothies. Rinsed and stemmed strawberries, grapes, and other berries can go straight into freezer bags and then be stored wherever they fit in the freezer.

Bananas, peaches, pears, or plums ripening too soon? Pop them whole and unpeeled into the freezer; there's no need to wrap them, but store them in freezer bags if you prefer. To peel, rinse them under warm water for a minute and the skins will easily slip off. Then cut the fruit into rough chunks and discard the pits. The bananas won't be pretty, but they taste great in a smoothie, adding body and creamy richness.

Peel and cut chunks of pineapple, melons, and mango. If you have enough freezer space, spread them out on a baking sheet and freeze for about 3 hours or overnight; then loosen from the pan and put into freezer bags. You can also just put the fresh chunks into large freezer bags, pat them into a fairly flat layer, and stack the bags flat in the freezer. After a couple of hours when they've begun to stiffen, bend the bags in your hands to separate the chunks and put back into the freezer. Don't stuff the bags full—you'll use more bags, but you won't have to hack apart massive icebergs of fruit.

Two Granolas

Affectionately, satirically, inextricably, granola and Moosewood have become metaphors for a culture, a lifestyle, even a worldview. Whatever comes to mind, we are celebrating granola's enduring popularity and whole-grain goodness.

For a number of years, Moosewood Collective member Tony Del Plato and his partner Gina Nigro have run a bed and breakfast in their beautiful old farmhouse in Interlaken, New York. Tony creates bountiful breakfasts for their guests, often starting with a lovely parfait of granola, yogurt, and fruit. The guests at A Stone's Throw come from all over the world, and only a few of them are aging hippies . . . but who doesn't like granola?

These granolas are gluten-free if you use gluten-free grains, and vegan if you replace the honey with maple syrup or agave syrup.

PEANUT BUTTER AND HONEY GRANOLA

Yields 4 cups
Prep time: 10 minutes
Baking time: 25 to 30 minutes

2 cups rolled oats
⅓ cup raw sunflower seeds
1 tablespoon unhulled sesame seeds★

¼ cup smooth peanut butter, at room temperature
¼ cup honey or agave or pure maple syrup
¼ cup vegetable oil (sunflower, grapeseed, or olive oil, or other)
1 teaspoon pure vanilla extract
½ teaspoon salt, coarse if you have it
1 cup dried cherries, raisins, currants, or apples, chopped if you like
1 cup chopped roasted salted peanuts

★Unhulled sesame seeds, also called whole sesame seeds, are tan-colored and a significantly better source of iron and calcium than white, or hulled, sesame seeds. Hulled sesame seeds are fine in this recipe, too.

Preheat the oven to 300°F.

In a bowl, combine the oats, sunflower seeds, and sesame seeds. In a separate bowl, whisk together the peanut butter, honey, oil, vanilla, and salt. With a rubber spatula, scrape the peanut butter mixture into the oats bowl. Toss until everything is evenly coated. The mixture will be thick.

Spread out the mixture evenly on a parchment paper–lined baking sheet. Bake for 25 to 30 minutes, stirring every 10 minutes, until the grains are golden brown. The granola may be soft at the end of 30 minutes, but it will crisp up as it cools. Remove from the oven, sprinkle on the dried fruit and roasted peanuts, stir again, and set aside to cool. Store in an airtight container.

MAPLE ALMOND GRANOLA

Yields 4 cups
Prep time: 10 minutes
Baking time: 30 minutes

1 cup rolled oats
1 cup puffed whole grain, such as rice, millet, or kamut
1 cup rolled grain, such as barley, spelt, rye, kamut, or wheat
½ cup chopped almonds
½ cup raw sunflower seeds
¼ cup vegetable oil (sunflower, grapeseed, or olive oil, or other)
½ cup pure maple syrup
1 teaspoon almond extract
½ teaspoon pure vanilla extract
½ teaspoon ground cinnamon
½ teaspoon salt

Preheat the oven to 325°F.

In a bowl, combine the oats, puffed grain, rolled grain, almonds, and sunflower seeds. In a small bowl, whisk together the oil, maple syrup, almond and vanilla extracts, cinnamon, and salt. Pour the liquid mixture over the grains, nuts, and seeds. Use a rubber spatula to combine and evenly coat the grain mixture.

Spread the granola evenly over the surface of a large, un-oiled, shallow-sided baking sheet. Bake for 25 to 30 minutes, stirring every 10 minutes for even baking. When golden, but not browned, remove from the oven. Once cool, store in an airtight container.

SERVING AND MENU IDEAS

Layer granola with yogurt and fresh berries or sliced peaches in parfait glasses. Or just plop some granola into a cereal bowl with some milk or fruit juice for a quick, nutritious breakfast. Out for a hike, keep a baggie of granola in your pocket to nibble on like gorp.

Apple-Cinnamon-Oat Breakfast Bars

At last, here's a crunchy breakfast bar made with simply oats, raisins, and dried apples and flavored with maple syrup, cinnamon, and vanilla. This vegan and wheat-free (gluten-free if the oats are gluten-free) breakfast bar was developed by Moosewood cook Nancy Lazarus for the Cool School Food program in the Ithaca School District. There are hundreds of recipes (or more) for breakfast bars on the Internet, and Nancy read scores of recipes looking in vain for clues to the trick for making vegan and gluten-free bars that are crisp, not gooey, not crumbly. After experimenting with more baking sheets of oat bars than she could find people to give them to, she came up with this maple syrup and raisin purée to hold them together, and found that toasting the oats before mixing them with the liquid makes the texture of the bars crisp and crunchy.

The recipe makes enough for a standard half sheet pan (18 x 12 inches), but you can use a couple of smaller-sized baking sheets that combined are about 200 square inches. Also, the recipe is easily cut in half.

Yields 24 bars (about 4 x 2 inches each)
Prep time: 35 minutes
Baking time: 15 to 20 minutes

8 cups rolled oats
½ cup vegetable oil
1½ teaspoons salt
2 cups pure maple syrup
1½ cups raisins (best at room temperature)
4 teaspoons pure vanilla extract
4 teaspoons ground cinnamon
2½ cups dried apple pieces (½ inch or smaller)
1 cup salted toasted pepitas (pumpkin seeds)

Preheat the oven to 375°F convection, or 400°F conventional.

Put the oats into a bowl, sprinkle with the oil, and stir well to coat evenly. Spread on a sheet pan and sprinkle with the salt. Toast for 10 to 15 minutes, stirring once, until the oats darken somewhat in color.

Meanwhile, in a food processor, purée the maple syrup, raisins, vanilla, and cinnamon until smooth.

In a large bowl, mix together the toasted oats (warm from the oven or cool), maple-raisin purée, dried apple pieces, and pepitas.

Line a half sheet pan, or a couple of smaller baking sheets or pans (see headnote), with parchment paper. Spread the mixture on the baking pan and tamp it down with the back of a spoon to press out any air pockets. Smooth the top and tidy up the edges. Bake for 15 minutes in a convection oven, or a little longer in a conventional oven.

Cool for about 5 minutes and then cut into 24 pieces. If the edges crumble, tamp down while still warm. Cool in the pan. Slice through the cuts again before removing the bars from the pan. Lift the parchment paper to remove them from the pan easily.

VARIATIONS

- Add about a cup of chopped nuts.
- In place of dried apples, use dried cranberries or cherries (whole or chopped) or chopped dried figs or apricots.

SERVING AND MENU IDEAS

These breakfast bars are dense, crisp, and naturally sweet. You'll want a beverage to complete your breakfast. A cup of tea will do, or try one of our smoothies, all different. Jenny's Best Breakfast Smoothie (page 23) is as nutrient-rich as the breakfast bars. The Sweet Fruit Smoothies (page 24) come in red, yellow, or orange versions and are just as they promise—fruity, sweet, and smooth. The Peppery Green Smoothie, No Pepper (page 22) is hot and sweet and unusual, containing mustard greens.

Sunbutter Bites

These very easy-to-make, addictive, little no-bake morsels are delicious, satisfying energy boosters that make a good snack or breakfast. And they are nut- and peanut-free, vegan, gluten-free, and without refined sugar. If you have it, use coarse salt because it makes for interesting little sparks of salt on your tongue. Each Sunbutter Bite is actually two or three bites.

Yields about twenty-four 1-inch balls
Time: 15 minutes

1¼ cups rolled oats
½ cup oat "flour"★
½ cup sunflower seed butter★★
⅓ cup pure maple syrup
1 teaspoon pure vanilla extract
¼ teaspoon salt (coarse salt if you have it)
½ cup toasted pepitas (pumpkin seeds)★★★
½ cup chopped dried cranberries

★Whirl ½ cup rolled oats in the blender until the consistency of cornmeal.
★★Sunflower seed butter is a spread made of whole sunflower seeds. It's a good source of vitamin E, selenium, zinc, and magnesium and its protein contains all the essential amino acids. There are 9 grams of fat in a 1-tablespoon serving, but about 90 percent are unsaturated fats. In Ithaca, there are several good locally produced brands of sunflower butter; the national brand we're familiar with is Sun Butter, which is a perfect consistency for this recipe.
★★★Toasted pepitas are readily available, but if you toast raw pumpkin seeds, do it first, so they can cool before you add them to the mix. In a 350°F oven, pepitas toast in about 10 minutes, and then take 10 minutes to cool.

In a bowl, thoroughly mix the oats, oat flour, sunflower seed butter, maple syrup, vanilla, and salt. Then with a spoon, press and stir until a uniform and somewhat crumbly dough is formed. In the same manner, stir in the pepitas and dried cranberries. Form smooth little balls by squeezing heaping teaspoons of dough in the palm of your hand and then pressing all around with your fingers.

Store in an airtight container in the refrigerator.

VARIATIONS
- Instead of maple syrup, you can use another liquid sweetener such as agave syrup.
- Instead of, or in addition to dried cranberries, try other dried fruits such as cherries, prunes, dates.
- Try with chopped raw or toasted nuts or other seeds such as sunflower, sesame, chia, flaxseeds, or hemp seeds.

SERVING AND MENU IDEAS
Sunbutter Bites have excellent nutritive value as well as being tasty treats. Try a couple for a mid-afternoon pick-me-up with a piece of fresh fruit, or take them on car, bike, or hiking trips. Keep Sunbutter Bites on hand for running-out-the-door breakfasts with a smoothie.

Kip's Favorite Scones: Two Variations

Scones of many persuasions have become commonplace in cafés, farmers' markets, and tea and coffee shops, and they are impossible to resist, especially when still warm just out of the oven. These scones are not too sweet and deliciously studded with dried fruit or crystallized ginger. Eat them while they're hot and falling apart with butter and jam dripping over the edges.

Yields 8 scones
Prep time: 15 to 20 minutes
Baking time: 25 to 30 minutes

TRADITIONAL ENGLISH SCONES WITH SHERRY-SOAKED CURRANTS

Oil, for the baking sheet
½ cup dried currants
¼ cup sherry
¼ cup orange juice (or omit the sherry and use ½ cup orange juice)
2 cups unbleached white all-purpose flour (you can substitute up to 1 cup with whole wheat flour)
3 tablespoons sugar
½ teaspoon salt
2 teaspoons baking powder
½ teaspoon baking soda
5 tablespoons cold unsalted butter
1 large egg
1 cup less 2 tablespoons buttermilk

¼ cup milk, for brushing
A little sugar, for sprinkling

Preheat the oven to 375°F. Oil a baking sheet or line it with parchment paper.

In a small saucepan heat the currants, sherry, and orange juice until hot but not boiling. Set aside to soak.

Sift the flour, sugar, salt, baking powder, and baking soda into a large bowl. Cut the butter into small pieces and, using your fingers or a pastry cutter, rub the butter into the flour mixture until crumbly. Drain the currants and stir them into the flour mixture. Beat the egg and add to the buttermilk. Stir the buttermilk-egg mixture into the flour until just incorporated and you have a soft dough.

Turn the dough out onto a lightly floured cutting board or countertop and pat it into a circle ¾ to 1 inch thick and about 7 inches in diameter. Cut the circle of dough into 8 pie-shaped pieces. Lift each wedge up with a spatula, and arrange on the baking sheet.

Brush the tops of the scones with milk and sprinkle with a little sugar.

Bake for 25 to 30 minutes, until light brown and crisp around the edges. The scones should break open easily and be soft and mottled with small holes throughout.

Serve the scones with butter, marmalade, or jam.

GINGER SCONES

Follow the directions above, omitting the currants, sherry, and orange juice. Increase the buttermilk to 1 cup. Add ½ cup chopped crystallized ginger and about 2 teaspoons grated fresh ginger to the buttermilk and egg mixture before stirring it into the flour.

SERVING AND MENU IDEAS

Just-baked scones in the morning make us very happy. Serve Traditional English Scones with Herbed Baked Eggs in a Ramekin (page 11), and Ginger Scones with Tomato-Sesame Tofu Scramble (page 21). Serve scones for high tea along with Watercress Toast (page 53) and Radish and Herbed Chèvre Spread (page 69) on rye bread.

STARTERS
&
SNACKS

Sweet Potato Croquettes

Green and Yellow Summer Fritters

Nori Rolls with Kale and Egg

Cauliflower Quinoa Bites

Cornmeal Blini

Butternut Squash Latkes

Spicy Filo Samosas with Spinach, Mint, and Cilantro

Potato Wedges Masala with a Cooling Dip

Socca with Three Fillings

Kale Chips

Romaine "Tacos" with Sweet Chili Sauce

Watercress Toast

Cheese Shortbread

Cheesy Garlic Toast

Deviled Eggs

Spiced Nuts

Za'atar Pita Chips

Sweet Potato Croquettes

Moist, colorful, aromatic, flavorful, and vegan, this is one of our most popular small plates, created by our innovative cook and menu planner Jason Coughlin for our occasional tapas menus. At the restaurant, spiced sweet potatoes are rolled in crushed toasted cashews and coconut and served with Fresh Pineapple-Mango Relish, a refreshing fruit salsa that's so simple and perfect with these crunchy croquettes. Dream of the Spice Islands and add a tall iced ginger tea or rum punch.

Yields sixteen to eighteen 2-inch croquettes
Time: 70 minutes

1 tablespoon olive oil, plus more for the pans
2 pounds sweet potatoes
¾ cup cashews (4½ ounces)
¾ cup unsweetened shredded dried coconut
  (3 ounces)
2 tablespoons olive oil
½ teaspoon salt, plus more for sprinkling
2 cups finely chopped onions
¼ teaspoon cayenne pepper, more to taste
1 teaspoon ground coriander
1 teaspoon ground cinnamon
2 tablespoons peeled and grated fresh ginger
1 tablespoon finely grated lemon zest
2 tablespoons fresh lemon juice
Fresh Pineapple-Mango Relish (page 327)

Preheat the oven to 425°F. Lightly oil two baking sheets.

Rinse the sweet potatoes and cut them into large chunks, leaving the skins on. In a bowl, toss the sweet potatoes with the oil and put them on one of the baking sheets. Cover the sheet with aluminum foil and roast the potatoes for 30 to 40 minutes, stirring once or twice, until they are tender and the surfaces are darkly caramelized.

While the sweet potatoes roast, toast the cashews on a small baking sheet until just lightly browned, about 5 minutes. Set aside to cool. When cool, pulse the cashews in a food processor until coarsely ground. In a shallow bowl, stir together the coconut and cashews, and add a sprinkling of salt.

Warm the oil in a heavy skillet and cook the onions with the salt until golden and very soft, about 8 minutes. Add the cayenne, coriander, and cinnamon, and cook for another 3 to 4 minutes, stirring often. Remove from the heat and stir in the ginger, lemon zest, and lemon juice.

When the sweet potatoes are done and cool enough to handle, remove the skins and put the flesh into a bowl. Mash the sweet potatoes with the onions and spices. Season with salt to taste.

Form the mixture into 1½-inch balls (about 2 tablespoons). The mixture is soft, so handle it gently. A small ice cream scoop (#40) is the perfect size and implement for portioning. Roll each ball in the cashew-coconut mixture to generously cover the whole surface. Place the balls a couple of inches apart on the prepared baking sheet and flatten a bit with your fingers. Bake until crisp on the outside, about 15 minutes.

Meanwhile, make the relish.

Allow the croquettes to cool for at least 10 minutes before serving. Serve warm or at room temperature, with the relish on the side.

SERVING AND MENU IDEAS
A great tapas plate or appetizer, but hearty enough to serve as the main dish for lunch or supper.

Green and Yellow Summer Fritters

One of the things that arouse our culinary creativity is a late-summer pile of plenty from the garden or overflowing the CSA basket. Zucchini and yellow summer squash top the list of vegetables that just keep coming in July and August in most of the country. Here's an excellent way to use them. These savory fritters are easy to make, and when you use both zucchini and yellow squash, they look beautiful. We like these fritters with scallions and mint, but if you have fresh dill on hand, add it to the mix by all means.

You can make the mixture ahead of time and keep it in the refrigerator. You can also make the fritters ahead of time and serve them at room temperature. To cook them all at once, use two large skillets.

Yields 8 pancakes
Prep time: 30 minutes
Cooking time: 15 minutes with a single skillet;
  10 minutes with two skillets

1½ pounds zucchini and/or yellow summer squash
1 teaspoon salt
2 large eggs
¼ cup unbleached white all-purpose flour
¼ cup chopped scallions
2 heaping tablespoons chopped fresh mint
Finely grated zest of 1 lemon
2 tablespoons olive oil
1 cup sour cream or plain yogurt, for serving

Using the large-holed shredding blade of a food processor, or on the large holes of a box grater, shred the zucchini and summer squash; you will need about 2 cups. In a bowl, stir the salt into the shredded squash and set aside for about 20 minutes.

Meanwhile, in a mixing bowl, beat the eggs, sprinkle on the flour, and beat again until smooth. Add the scallions, mint, and lemon zest.

When the shredded squash has released liquid, squeeze it by the handful to express as much excess liquid as you can, and add the squash to the bowl with the egg mixture. Stir well to incorporate.

Warm 1 tablespoon of the olive oil in a large heavy skillet on medium heat. Using a large spoon or a small dry measuring cup, drop ¼-cup mounds of the mixture onto the hot surface and flatten slightly. Cook for 2 to 3 minutes on each side, until golden-brown and crisp. Place the cooked fritters on a paper towel–covered plate. Add more oil to the skillet and cook the remaining fritters until the mixture is used up.

Serve hot or at room temperature. Top each fritter with a dollop of sour cream or yogurt.

SERVING AND MENU IDEAS
These fritters are delicious with Fresh Pineapple-Mango Relish (page 327). Serve with Roasted Carrot Gazpacho (page 105) or Wax Bean and Radish Salad with Buttermilk Dressing (page 121).

Nori Rolls with Kale and Egg

Mastering the art of nori rolls just takes a little practice and yields tremendous satisfaction. Your guests will be impressed. These pretty little round bites make a delicious lunch or appetizer. Serve with the traditional little bowls of creamy wasabi and soy sauce for dipping, and pickled ginger for refreshing your palate. Nori rolls are best eaten soon after assembling.

Wasabi is a condiment made from a plant of the *Brassica* family, which also includes cabbages, horseradish, and mustard. It is also called Japanese horseradish. If you're new to wasabi, it is *hot*. For starters, a little dab might do you.

Yields about 32 pieces
Serves 4 to 8 as an appetizer; 3 or 4 as lunch
Time: 45 minutes

1 cup sushi rice
1¼ cups plus 2 tablespoons water
1 tablespoon sugar
1 teaspoon salt
1½ tablespoons rice vinegar
3 tablespoons wasabi powder
4 medium kale leaves
4 scallions
½ medium cucumber
1 avocado
1 tablespoon vegetable oil
2 large eggs
1 teaspoon soy sauce
4 sheets toasted nori seaweed, about 7½ inches square
Pickled ginger (optional)

First, prepare all the ingredients for assembling the rolls, and have everything near at hand when you begin to roll.

Rinse the rice in a sieve until the water runs clear. Shake and set aside to drain. Place the drained rice and 1¼ cups of the water in a small saucepan and bring to a boil. Lower the heat, cover, and simmer gently for about 15 minutes, or until all the water has been absorbed.

Meanwhile, bring a large saucepan of water to a boil for blanching the kale leaves. In a small pan on low heat, dissolve the sugar and salt in the rice vinegar, and set aside.

Make the wasabi cream in a small bowl by mixing the wasabi powder and water until it's the consistency of heavy cream, and set aside.

Strip the kale leaves from their stems and immerse them in the pan of boiling water for 2 minutes. Drain in a colander and rinse under cold running water. Squeeze out the water and lay out the leaves between layers of paper towels.

When the rice is cooked, turn off the heat, place a towel under the lid, and set aside to rest for 10 minutes.

Trim the scallions to 6 inches long and slice them in half lengthwise, or, if they're big scallions, into fourths. Peel the cucumber, cut in half lengthwise, remove the seeds, and cut into narrow strips. Pit, peel, and thinly slice the avocado.

Once the rice has cooled for 10 minutes, gently stir the vinegar-sugar mixture into the rice with a spatula. Set aside, covered with a towel.

Heat the oil in an 8-inch skillet. In a small bowl, whisk the eggs with the soy sauce and pour into the skillet. Carefully tilt the pan and lift the edges of the eggs as they cook allowing the liquid to flow onto the bottom of the skillet. When the thin crepe-like omelet has set, lift it onto a cutting board to cool. Cut into 4 strips.

Now you're ready to assemble the nori rolls. If you're inexperienced at this, we recommend that you watch a few YouTube videos to learn the technique for rolling. You can roll the nori rolls with your hands or with a sushi rolling mat.

To assemble, place a sheet of nori on the countertop or a cutting board with a small bowl of water nearby. Dip your fingers in the water and spread one-quarter of the rice on the nori sheet, leaving ½ inch of the sheet exposed at one end. Lay a kale leaf across the center of the rice, and then about one-quarter of the egg, cucumber, and scallion strips, and finally, a row of avocado slices. With your fingers, spread a little water on the exposed end of the nori. Start by tucking in the filling tightly with your hands or a sushi rolling mat and roll toward the exposed side. When you reach the opposite side, press and roll the nori roll firmly to seal. Set aside on a platter while you prepare three more rolls.

Wrap the rolls separately in plastic wrap and refrigerate until ready to serve.

To serve, cut each roll into 8 pieces with a wet knife. Arrange the pieces on a plate. Serve with little bowls of wasabi cream and soy sauce and a small dish of pickled ginger, if desired.

VARIATIONS
- For more color, add a few thinly sliced carrots or radishes instead of or along with the cucumber and avocado. Do chua, the pickled vegetables for Banh Mi Chay (page 78) are also really good.
- If you'd like to serve nori rolls as appetizers without setting out dishes of wasabi and soy sauce, and utensils for dipping, and the messiness that might result, put some wasabi cream right in the rolls: Mix ¼ cup soy sauce with 1 tablespoon wasabi cream, and when you assemble the rolls, drizzle some on the rice before you add the kale leaf.

SERVING AND MENU IDEAS
For a complete meal, serve with Hot-and-Sour Mushroom Soup (page 97).

Cauliflower Quinoa Bites

Nutrient-rich, high-protein quinoa is usually consigned to the realm of pilafs and cereals—so much potential, so few recipes! Challenged, our experimentation led us to these small, golden, gluten-free croquettes that are easy to prepare, bake, and serve. They are firm and mildly flavored, designed to be perfect little conveyances for flavorful sauces or dollops—the ideal starter or passed appetizer.

The flavor and texture will change with your choice of cheese. For instance, halloumi, a popular Middle Eastern cheese, is a semisoft brined cheese with a high melting point. Unlike cheddar or Parmesan, when halloumi is baked, grilled, or otherwise heated, it becomes softer but doesn't melt.

Yields thirty to thirty-five 2-inch "bites"
Prep time: 30 minutes
Baking time: 30 minutes

¾ cup quinoa (5 ounces)
1½ cups water
2 large eggs
½ teaspoon salt
¼ teaspoon freshly ground black pepper
2 cups grated cauliflower
1½ cups grated halloumi, Parmesan, or sharp ched-
    dar cheese (about 6 ounces)
3 scallions, halved lengthwise and thinly sliced
⅓ cup chickpea flour
½ teaspoon baking soda
2 tablespoons fresh lemon juice

Rinse the quinoa in a fine-meshed sieve under lukewarm running water for about 2 minutes to remove any bitter residue. In a saucepan, bring the rinsed quinoa and the water to a boil. Cover, reduce to a simmer, and cook for 15 minutes. Fluff with a fork and set aside, uncovered, to cool.

While the quinoa cooks and cools, in a bowl, beat the eggs with the salt and pepper until fluffy. Add the grated cauliflower and cheese and the scallions to the bowl and stir well. When the quinoa has cooled to just warm, stir it in. Sprinkle with the chickpea flour and stir well to distribute. In a cup or small bowl, stir the baking soda into the lemon juice and immediately add to the mixing bowl and stir well.

Preheat the oven to 375°F. Line a baking sheet with parchment paper. If you don't have parchment, oil the pan generously with olive oil.

Using a 1-ounce scoop (or otherwise), form balls with 2 tablespoons of the mixture and arrange on the baking sheet. Bake for about 30 minutes, or until firm and golden.

SERVING AND MENU IDEAS
Serve with guacamole, Fresh Pineapple-Mango Relish (page 327), or sour cream with chives, and/or splash on some hot sauce. To move up from a starter to a main dish, serve with Jason's Fresh Fennel and Apple Slaw (page 123) or your favorite green salad.

Cornmeal Blini

Blini conjure up visions of an elegant brunch at the Russian Tea Room, or perhaps a romantic breakfast by a roaring fire while the wild winds blow. . . . But even for every day at home, these golden crepes are a wonderful appetizer, brunch, or breakfast item. Blini can be stacked like pancakes or rolled around a sweet or savory pilling. Add the lemon zest to these pancakes when serving sweet toppings like fruits and syrups.

Yields about twenty-four 3-inch blini
Serves 4 to 6
Time: 45 minutes

1 large egg, separated
1 tablespoon butter melted, plus more butter for the griddle
1½ cups buttermilk
1 cup stone-ground cornmeal
⅓ cup unbleached white all-purpose flour
1¼ teaspoons baking powder
¼ teaspoon baking soda
1 teaspoon sugar
½ teaspoon salt
2 teaspoons finely grated lemon zest (optional)

Beat the egg white until stiff peaks form. In a separate bowl, whisk together the buttermilk, egg yolk, and cooled melted butter.

In a large bowl, sift together the cornmeal, flour, baking powder, baking soda, sugar, and salt. Gently fold the buttermilk mixture into the dry ingredients until just combined. Gently fold in the egg whites and lemon zest, if using, until everything is well combined, but be careful not to overmix the batter.

Heat the griddle. Using a spatula, spread a teaspoon of butter over the surface. For each blini, add 2 tablespoons of batter and, using the back of a spoon, quickly spread them into 3-inch circles. When bubbles appear on the surface and the bottom is starting to brown, flip the blinis over and cook the opposite sides for about half a minute. Keep adding more butter to the griddle between batches. You should be able to cook 5 or 6 blini at a time. If need be, keep the cooked blini warm in a 200°F oven.

SERVING AND MENU IDEAS
Top or fill the blinis with diced fresh fruit, preserves, or maple syrup . . . or a fruit sauce. Make a quick fruit sauce by briefly heating mango chunks, blueberries, and sliced strawberries or whatever is in season. Drizzle with maple syrup and garnish with a dollop of yogurt. Make the blinis savory with chunks of avocado, diced sweet peppers, thinly sliced jicama, and pepper Jack cheese. Or how about refried beans and green salsa . . . get creative!

Butternut Squash Latkes

These savory squash pancakes are a lighter variation on the traditional Jewish potato latkes and a favorite at Moosewood. Because the demand for them is high and we need to be ready when the orders come rolling in, we prebake the latkes and then finish them off quickly on the stovetop. The baked latkes are firm and cooked through, and then it takes only a couple of minutes in a hot skillet with a small amount of oil to crisp the outside.

For lunch, we serve latkes with sour cream or yogurt and a side of applesauce. Smaller latkes make a nice appetizer. This recipe is gluten-free.

Yields 12 latkes
Serves 4 to 6
Hands-on time: 30 minutes
Baking time: 25 minutes
Total time: about 1 hour

1 butternut squash (about 3 pounds)
1 medium Spanish onion
3 large eggs, beaten
¼ cup minced fresh sage leaves
1½ teaspoons salt
½ teaspoon freshly ground black pepper
¾ cup brown rice flour
Vegetable oil or olive oil, for pan-frying

Preheat the oven to 325°F. Line two baking sheets with parchment paper.

Peel and seed the squash. Using the grater blade of a food processor, grate the squash and the onion. You should have about 6 cups of grated squash and about ¾ cup of grated onions. Drain in a colander, squeezing the mixture by hand or with the back of a spatula to remove excess moisture. In a bowl, thoroughly mix the drained squash and onions with the eggs, sage, salt, pepper, and brown rice flour. Add more flour if the mixture seems watery.

Using a ⅓-cup measure, scoop the batter. Drop the batter for 6 latkes, evenly spaced out, on each lined baking sheet. Flatten each latke somewhat with a spatula or the back of a spoon. Bake for 12 minutes, flip the latkes, and bake for another 12 minutes.

When ready to serve, heat a small amount of oil in a cast-iron skillet or griddle on high heat. Sear both sides of each baked latke until lightly brown, a minute or less per side, adding more oil to the pan as needed. Serve right away, hot from the skillet.

SERVING AND MENU IDEAS

Serve with yogurt or sour cream and applesauce and/or Za'atar Yogurt and Cucumber Salad (page 122). At the restaurant, we often serve them with Jason's Fresh Fennel and Apple Slaw (page 123). Beetroot Sticks (page 313) are nice, too.

Spicy Filo Samosas with Spinach, Mint, and Cilantro

Samosa filling wrapped with filo dough makes for a delicate, flaky, baked version of this beloved Indian snack. Easily made ahead and refrigerated (or even frozen), filo samosas can then be baked just before serving. You can use regular filo dough or whole wheat filo dough.

Yields 8 samosas
Serves 8 as an appetizer; 4 as an entrée
Prep time: 30 minutes
Baking time: 40 minutes

2 quarts water
½ teaspoon salt
3 cups peeled and chopped potatoes
1 cup diced carrots
4 cups packed spinach leaves (either baby spinach or chopped mature leaves)
3 tablespoons plue ⅓ cup oil★, plus more as needed
½ cup finely chopped onions or scallions
2 tablespoons minced garlic
½ fresh hot pepper, seeds and membrane removed (use more or less according to taste)★★
2½ teaspoons cumin seeds
¼ teaspoon crushed cardamom seeds
2 teaspoons peeled and grated fresh ginger
1 teaspoon garam masala★★★
2 tablespoons chopped fresh mint
2 tablespoons chopped fresh cilantro
8 leaves filo dough★★★★
⅓ cup oil or oil/butter mixture
mustard seeds, for garnish

★Coconut, olive, or vegetable oil, or oil/butter combination
★★If you'd rather use dried red pepper flakes, add ¼ to ½ teaspoon with the cardamom and cumin.
★★★See our recipe for garam masala in Potato Wedges Masala recipe page 46, or if you use commercial garam masala mix, add ¼ teaspoon ground turmeric.
★★★★For this recipe, you need only part of a package of filo dough, so tightly roll and wrap the leftover and refrigerate or freeze for use later.

Pour the water and salt into a soup pot. As you prep the potatoes and carrots, add them to the pot. Bring to a boil and cook for about 7 minutes.

While the potatoes and carrots are cooking, wash the spinach and set aside in a colander to drain. Heat the oil in a heavy skillet until it shimmers. Add the onions, garlic, and hot peppers and sauté for about a minute. Add the cumin, cardamom, and ginger and stir for about 30 seconds. Stir in the garam masala and immediately add the spinach leaves. Sauté the spinach until wilted. Turn off the heat.

When the potatoes and carrots can be easily pierced with a fork, drain, and then mash them in the pot. Stir the mashed potatoes into the spinach-spice mixture. Taste and add more salt as needed. Stir in the mint and cilantro.

To wrap the filling in filo, lightly oil two baking sheets or line with parchment paper. Locate your pastry brush. Heat the remaining ⅓ cup oil mixture. Unfold a stack of 8 filo leaves on a large cutting board. Cut the stack lengthwise into thirds (or in half, depending on the width of your filo) so you have long strips about 4 inches wide. Divide the potato filling into 8 portions (about ¼ cup per samosa). Each samosa is made with 2 strips of filo. Using a pastry brush, lightly oil the top strip of filo. Place a portion of filling on one end of the oiled strip and pick up a corner of 2 leaves and fold the filo over the filling. Keep folding to the right to the left, like a flag, to make a triangular pastry. Tuck any short ends under at the finish. Place the samosa on the baking sheet. Repeat the steps for seven more samosas. Brush the top and bottom of each samosa with the remaining oil and sprinkle a few mustard seeds on each one.

Bake for about 40 minutes, until the edges turn brown and crisp.

SERVING AND MENU IDEAS
Serve with a fruit chutney, or Cooling Dip (see page 47).

Potato Wedges Masala with a Cooling Dip

Does anyone not like roasted potatoes? Add an intoxicating blend of spices that will perfume your kitchen and wake up your taste buds, then make a refreshing sauce to dip the spicy, crisp potato wedges into, and it's roasted potatoes taken to a new level.

Garam masala is a spice blend that varies across the Indian continent from region to region and household to household. Garam masala, made of roasted spices, has a rich, heady, yet mellow flavor and is usually added toward the end of a dish's preparation to punch up the flavor. Once you gather the spices, you can easily make your own garam masala to have on hand in the cupboard, and you can customize it to your taste in the future. Homemade garam masala will keep for six weeks in a tightly lidded clean glass jar in a cool, dark place; for four months if refrigerated; and indefinitely if stored in the freezer. But for convenience, we've found that Kohinoor and Frontier Herbs and Spices both make tasty commercial garam masalas.

Yields ½ cup garam masala
Serves 4
Garam masala prep time: 5 minutes
Garam masala baking time: 30 minutes
Potato wedges and dip prep time: 15 to 20 minutes
Potato roasting time: 40 minutes
Total time: about 80 minutes

GARAM MASALA*

1 (3-inch) cinnamon stick
2 tablespoons coriander seeds
1 tablespoon cumin seeds
2 teaspoons black peppercorns
1 teaspoon cardamom seeds
1 teaspoon whole cloves
1 teaspoon fennel seeds
1 tablespoon ground turmeric

POTATOES

Oil, for the baking sheet
½ pound white potatoes
½ pound sweet potatoes
2 teaspoons crushed or minced garlic
2 tablespoons coconut oil, warmed briefly to liquefy
¾ teaspoon salt

COOLING DIP
½ cup plain Greek yogurt
1½ tablespoons finely chopped fresh mint
1 tablespoon chopped scallions

*For this recipe, if using commercial garam masala, combine 2½ teaspoons garam masala with ½ teaspoon ground turmeric.

Make the masala: Crush the cinnamon stick with a rolling pin into small pieces. Scatter all the spices, except the turmeric, on a pie plate or small baking pan. Roast at 200°F for 30 minutes. Shake or stir the spices once or twice during roasting. Remove from the oven, let cool briefly, and pulverize in a spice grinder until smooth. Stir in the turmeric.

Increase the oven temperature to 450°F. Lightly oil a baking sheet.

While the spices are roasting, scrub the potatoes; there is no need to peel if the skins are smooth and unblemished. Cut both white and sweet potatoes into ½-inch-wide wedges. Place the potato wedges in a large bowl and toss them with the minced garlic. In a small bowl, whisk the coconut oil with the salt and 1 tablespoon of the garam masala. (Store the remaining garam masala for future use.)

Pour the spiced oil over the potatoes and toss with a rubber spatula to evenly coat.

Transfer the potatoes to the prepared baking sheet, separating any potatoes that are touching. Place on the middle rack of the oven and bake for 40 minutes; gently stir and turn over the potato wedges once or twice. When done, the potatoes will be crisp on the outside.

While the potato wedges are roasting, make the dip. Combine the yogurt, mint, and scallions in a small bowl, and refrigerate until ready to serve.

Serve the potato wedges with the dip on the side.

SERVING AND MENU IDEAS
These potato wedges would share a table nicely next to the Asian version of Herbed Baked Eggs in a Ramekin (page 11), or after Chilled Curried Pea and Coconut Soup (page 106), with Monsoon Pickles (page 339) nearby. Or they can be the star of a light meal accompanied by a refreshing salad, such as Greens with Citrus-Date Dressing (page 126) or Sugar Snap Peas with Coconut and Lime (page 113).

Socca with Three Fillings

Known as *socca* in Provence and *cecina*, *torta di ceci*, and *farinata* in Italy, these thin pancakes are made from chickpea flour batter.

You can make the batter ahead and keep it in the refrigerator for up to 24 hours. Chickpea flour is available in the gluten-free section and Indian foods section of well-stocked supermarkets and specialty stores.

Yields 12 small crepes
Time: 30 minutes

2 tablespoons olive oil, plus more for the pan
1 cup chickpea flour
1 cup water
½ teaspoon salt
¼ teaspoon cracked black pepper
Pinch of saffron (optional)
¼ cup sliced scallions
1 tablespoon chopped fresh rosemary, thyme, or
   oregano

By hand or in a blender, mix the olive oil, chickpea flour, water, salt, pepper, and saffron until smooth and the consistency of heavy cream. Add a little more water if the batter is too thick. Stir in the scallions and herbs.

Heat a teaspoon of oil in a small crepe pan or cast-iron skillet on medium heat. Pour 2 generous tablespoons of the batter into the pan and quickly swirl the batter to make a small crepe. After about 30 seconds, when the crepe is set, flip it over and briefly cook the opposite side. Transfer the crepe to a plate and proceed with the next one, repeating until all the batter has been used.

To serve, add fillings and roll the crepes into small tubular finger appetizers and arrange on a platter. A sprig of fresh herbs, such as dill, cilantro, or basil, rolled up inside the crepe and peeking out from the ends is an especially pretty presentation.

PESTO FILLING
Garlic Scape Pesto (page 331) is a perfect filling . . . or almost any pesto. Spread the pesto thinly on the crepes, insert a sprig of dill or a basil leaf, and roll into a narrow tube.

HERB AND FETA FILLING
A thin slice of feta and a sprig of dill, cilantro, or basil rolled up inside each crepe is a simple delicious filling.

TOMATO-CILANTRO RELISH FILLING
Spoon about a tablespoon of Tomato-Cilantro Relish onto a crepe, squeeze a little lime juice over it, and roll up. Or, serve the relish in a small bowl on a plate of socca with thin lime wedges on the side of the plate, and use the socca to scoop up some relish, or spoon relish onto a socca, roll it up, and pop it into your mouth.

1 cup chopped grape or cherry tomatoes
¼ cup minced red onions
2 tablespoons chopped fresh cilantro
½ fresh hot pepper, seeded and minced
salt to taste

Drain juice from the chopped tomatoes in a strainer or colander for about 5 minutes. In a small bowl, mix together all the ingredients.

SERVING AND MENU IDEAS
These versatile crepes go well with any of our three other Pestos (pages 328 to 331). Hummus with Preserved Lemon (page 66) and Walnut and Roasted Pepper Spread (page 68) are good fillings also.

Kale Chips

This may be the ultimate healthy chip: kale leaves simply toasted with a little olive oil and a dusting of salt and red pepper flakes or ground cumin. The transformation from chewy kale to a delicate chip that simply melts in your mouth is amazing. Put your feet up for a good movie and some guilt-free munching. You could probably eat the whole batch yourself and still be just fine, but they keep well.

Yields about 8 cups
Serves 4 as a snack
Prep time: 15 minutes
Baking time: about 12 minutes

8 large kale leaves (any variety)
1 tablespoon olive oil
½ teaspoon salt
¼ teaspoon crushed red pepper flakes (optional)
½ teaspoon ground cumin (optional)

Preheat the oven to 325°F. Cover two large baking sheets with parchment paper or spray with oil.

Strip the kale leaves from their ribs, place in a colander or salad spinner, and rinse under cold water. Shake or spin to remove water and roll leaves on a clean dish towel to absorb any water still clinging to the leaves. Tear the leaves into bite-size pieces (about 2 or 3 inches across) and place in a large bowl.

Drizzle the olive oil over the leaves, and with your hands, lightly massage the leaves until they are coated with the oil. Spread the leaves on the baking sheets; avoid overlapping as much as possible. Sprinkle lightly with salt and crushed red pepper flakes and/or cumin, if you like.

Bake until the kale chips are dry and crisp. Check after 12 minutes and bake a little longer, if necessary.

Cool on the baking sheets and then store in a closed container or plastic bag. Handle the chips gently to prevent crushing or breaking. Kale chips will keep for a week if kept dry.

SERVING AND MENU IDEAS

Serve Kale Chips next to a burger or a sandwich, such as White Bean and Olive Sandwich (page 83). Serve them alongside hummus and crudités as an appetizer, although they are probably too delicate to serve as dippers themselves. Crumble tasty bits of the kale chips over a pilaf or over Kale, Jicama, and Orange Salad (page 128) to contrast with the soft, rubbed kale.

Romaine "Tacos" with Sweet Chili Sauce

Fresh leaves of romaine lettuce are smeared with a gooey, intensely flavored paste of ground cashews, ginger, and Asian seasonings. Then the lettuce leaves function like a taco shell to hold your choice of crunchy fillings. Put a platter of romaine leaves in front of your guests with a bunch of fillings and it's a party—especially if you're sampling craft beers.

The Sweet Chili Sauce is a sweet and slightly spicy Southeast Asian–inspired dipping sauce that can accompany lettuce wraps, dumplings, spring rolls, samosas, tempura, baked tofu, etc. Use whatever sugar you like and have on hand. The sugar you choose to use will affect the color of the sauce somewhat: with brown sugar or coconut sugar (available in the natural foods section of well-stocked supermarkets), it will be darker than with granulated white sugar. The optional red bell pepper makes it more reddish.

Serves 8 as a snack or appetizer
Yields 1¼ cups Sweet Chili Sauce
Time: 45 minutes

FLAVOR PASTE

2 tablespoons peeled and grated fresh ginger
1½ cups salted roasted cashews
2 tablespoons brown sugar
1 tablespoon sesame oil
1 tablespoon soy sauce
2 tablespoons hoisin sauce
1 teaspoon Chinese chili paste, or a few squirts of hot sauce
½ cup fresh cilantro leaves
1 jalapeño pepper, stemmed and coarsely chopped

SWEET CHILI SAUCE

⅓ cup rice vinegar
½ cup sugar
1 tablespoon crushed or minced garlic
2 teaspoons minced red fresh hot pepper (Fresno, jalapeño, etc.)
1 teaspoon hot sauce or Chinese chili paste
¾ cup water
¼ red bell pepper, seeded and minced (optional)
¼ teaspoon salt
2 tablespoons cornstarch dissolved in 2 tablespoons cold water

FILLINGS (choose 2 or 3, or more)

Bean sprouts (mung, soybean, alfalfa, mixed peppery-spicy sprouts)
Grated carrots (cut into very thin matchsticks or grated into long threads)
Cucumber sticks (peeled and seeded, and cut into thin matchsticks)
Cilantro leaves (rinsed, patted dry, and coarsely chopped)
Mint leaves (rinsed, patted dry, and chopped)
Scallions (sliced diagonally)
8 romaine lettuce leaves

Make the flavor paste: In the bowl of a food processor, pulse the ginger, cashews, and brown sugar until the cashews are coarsely chopped. Add the sesame oil, soy sauce, hoisin, chili paste, cilantro, and jalapeño. Process until you have a dark brown paste about the consistency of crunchy peanut butter.

Make the sweet chili sauce: In a small saucepan on medium heat, combine the vinegar, sugar, garlic, hot peppers, hot sauce, water, bell pepper (if using), and salt, and bring to a simmer. Stir in the cornstarch and water mixture. Bring back to a simmer and stir until the sauce has thickened and coats a spoon. Allow it to cool enough to taste it. It should be sweet, spicy, and with a little taste of salt. If you'd like it spicier, add another squirt of hot sauce or more minced hot peppers.

Rinse and dry the romaine leaves. Spread about 1½ tablespoons of the flavor paste over about 2 inches on both sides of the inner spine of each leaf. Pile on two or three or more of the fillings. Either drizzle on some Sweet Chili Sauce or serve it in small shallow dipping dishes. To eat, hold the filled lettuce like a taco.

SERVING AND MENU IDEAS
Aside from being a good companion to these "tacos," the Sweet Chili Sauce is also good with Sweet Potato Croquettes (page 35) and Jamaican Jerk Tempeh Patties (page 200).

Watercress Toast

This compellingly delicious dish is so simple: just peppery-flavored watercress quickly sautéed and served on top of toasted bread. And with the first bite, you can tell that watercress is a healthful boon to your body; in fact, it's an antioxidant superfood. In a recent study of nutrient values of forty-seven fruits and vegetables, watercress was rated number 1 (kale is number 15). It's extremely high in vitamins A, C, and K and has more calcium than milk.

Watercress often appears at farmers' markets tied in bunches, and lately, we're finding organic watercress still attached to its roots in supermarkets.

Serves 4 as an appetizer; 2 as sandwiches
Time: 15 minutes

8 to 10 ounces watercress (chopped, about
  4 lightly packed cups)
3 or 4 garlic cloves, minced or pressed
2 tablespoons extra-virgin olive oil
Salt and freshly ground black pepper
4 thick slices of bread

Rinse the watercress and shake or pat it dry. Holding a bunch at the base, cut the leaves and stems crosswise every inch until you get to the thick stems without leaves; discard these. Pour the olive oil into a heavy skillet and have the garlic, watercress, salt, and pepper close at hand because the cooking process goes very quickly.

Lightly toast or grill the bread. Warm the skillet on medium heat and cook the garlic, stirring constantly, until golden, about a minute. Add the watercress and toss until bright green and wilted, probably less than a minute. Sprinkle with salt and pepper.

Pile the watercress on the toast and serve immediately.

SERVING AND MENU IDEAS

To tame the peppery sharpness of this dish and to make it a more substantial sandwich, top the watercress with slices of fresh mozzarella. Watercress Toast is a jolt of green goodness as an appetizer before Cheesy Risotto with Grapes (page 176), Fettuccine with Caramelized Onions and Yogurt (page 235), or Mushroom Barley Salad (page 147). Or enjoy it as an accompaniment and counterpoint to Celery or Celeriac Soup Two Ways (page 100) or Roasted Carrot Gazpacho (page 105).

Cheese Shortbread

Waiting for a table at the Moosewood bar, you might take the edge off your hunger with a couple wafers of cheese shortbread and a glass of red wine or ale. You'd pass the time talking to our affable and knowledgeable partner and bartender, Neil Minnis. While you won't be able to take Neil home with you, you will be able to reproduce this gluten-free shortbread recipe at home in about 5 minutes. The dough can be baked right away, or chilled to bake later, or frozen to bake even later.

Yields 24 to 30 small wafers
Prep time: 10 to 15 minutes
Baking time: 15 minutes

½ cup (1 stick) butter, at room temperature
1 cup grated Pecorino Romano cheese
1 cup Moosewood's Gluten-Free All-Purpose Flour Mix (page 351) or other gluten-free flour mix
1¼ teaspoons cracked black pepper
¼ teaspoon salt, if you used unsalted butter

Preheat the oven to 350°F.

Put the butter, grated cheese, flour, pepper, and salt (if using) into the bowl of a food processor and pulse a few times until the dough sticks together. Scrape the dough onto a lightly floured flat surface. With your hands, roll the dough to form two 6-inch logs about 1½ inches in diameter. If you want to bake the shortbread wafers later, wrap the logs in waxed paper and twist the ends tightly closed before refrigerating or freezing. Allow a frozen roll of dough to defrost a few minutes before cutting.

Cut each log crosswise into rounds about ½ inch thick. You should get 12 to 15 rounds per log. Place the rounds 1 inch apart on an ungreased baking sheet.

Bake until firm and fragrant, about 15 minutes. Reset the oven to turn on the broiler. Place the baking sheet under the broiler for just a minute until the wafers become golden brown—watch closely and take care not to burn them.

Serve warm or at room temperature. Cool thoroughly before storing in an airtight container.

VARIATIONS
- Roll the logs of dough in finely chopped pecans (you'll need about ¼ cup) before slicing into rounds. Bake the same as above but don't broil.
- This recipe works fine substituting the same amount of regular unbleached white flour.

SERVING AND MENU IDEAS
At Moosewood, cheese shortbreads are a bar snack because they pair well with a glass of wine or a beer. At home, they can serve this function also, or make a fine appetizer, perhaps served with other pre-meal nibbles such as Walnut and Roasted Pepper Spread (page 68) with crudités. The shortbreads are tasty alongside a bowl of soup or chili, or as an after-school treat with apple slices.

Cheesy Garlic Toast

Use the best-quality artisan baguette you can find because this deluxe flavorful preparation will glorify a good crusty bread, which can elevate a simple meal into something special. The garlic paste, which is easily made in a food processor, can be made ahead, so at mealtime you'll only wait 3 or 4 minutes for this hot crusty treat. Cheesy Garlic Toast is also an excellent snack to serve with a glass of wine or a mug of hot cider.

Serves 4 to 8
Time: 25 minutes

About 12 peeled garlic cloves (one head)
½ cup extra-virgin olive oil
1 cup grated Pecorino Romano or Parmesan
  cheese
1 tablespoon chopped fresh parsley
1 teaspoon finely grated lemon zest
½ teaspoon crushed red pepper flakes
1 baguette

In a small saucepan on very low heat, cook the garlic cloves in the olive oil until they are soft and just golden, about 10 minutes. Be careful not to allow the garlic to brown too much or it could become bitter.

Place the garlic and oil in a food processor and whirl for 5 or 6 seconds. Add the cheese, parsley, lemon zest, and red pepper flakes and process for a few more seconds to make a rough paste.

Cut the baguette in half lengthwise and then in half crosswise. Arrange the 4 pieces of bread cut side down on an aluminum foil–lined baking sheet and broil for a couple of minutes until warm and golden. Flip the pieces over and spread the garlic paste on the cut side. Broil for a couple of minutes until bubbling and crusted on top. Slice into smaller pieces if you like and serve hot.

SERVING AND MENU IDEAS

Serve with Pasta with Spinach and Apricots (page 230) or Spring Greens and Vegetables with Shallot Vinaigrette (page 139). Cheesy Garlic Toast is a great accompaniment for soup, such as Roasted Fennel and Leek Tomato Soup (page 98), and it makes a terrific bar snack with a glass of red wine.

Deviled Eggs

Deviled eggs seem like one of the most retro of foodstuffs. We think of a 1950s housewife flouncing through a cocktail party with crinolines puffing out her skirt and a plateful of deviled eggs balanced on her outstretched open palm. But in fact, this dish dates back to ancient Rome and has been perennially popular ever since.

Deviled eggs work as appetizers, bar snacks, kid-pleasers, breakfast on the run, or a protein-rich accompaniment to soup or salad. We propose a few different variations here. Colorfully garnished, two or three, or even all four kinds together, displayed on a big platter, are an attractive, pretty surefire party food. Flounce on.

Older eggs, at least one week old, peel more easily. To help prevent eggs from cracking during cooking, bring them to room temperature before cooking. You may want to add a few extra eggs just in case one or two crack during cooking or peeling. Those can be samplers for the cook and all the eggs for presentation to diners will be silky smooth and perfect.

Yields 12 deviled eggs
Serves 4 to 6
Time: 25 minutes

HARD-COOKED EGGS
6 large eggs

Arrange the eggs in a pot large enough to accommodate them in a single layer. Add cold water to cover by an inch or so and bring to a rapid simmer on medium-high heat. Simmer for 5 minutes; do not allow the eggs to knock about in a rapid boil. Turn off the heat and let the eggs rest in the hot water for another 10 to 15 minutes. Drain the eggs and cover them with cold water to stop the cooking. When the eggs are cool enough to handle, gently crack the shell all over and peel the egg. It may be easier to peel them under water.

Choose one of the following:

BUFFALO-STYLE DEVILED EGGS
2 tablespoons mayonnaise
3 tablespoons crumbled blue cheese
¼ cup minced celery
¼ teaspoon salt
Freshly ground black pepper
Celery leaves and hot sauce, for garnish

DILLY DEVILED EGGS
2 tablespoons mayonnaise
1 teaspoon Dijon mustard
3 tablespoons minced cornichon or small dill
  pickles
2 tablespoons finely chopped fresh dill
Salt and ground black pepper
Dill sprigs or cornichon pickles halved lengthwise,
  for garnish

CHIPOTLE DEVILED EGGS

2 tablespoons mayonnaise
1 roasted red bell pepper, a few thin slices set aside
   for garnish and the rest minced
1 to 2 teaspoons adobo sauce from canned
   chipotles in adobo
1 small chipotle pepper from canned chipotles in
   adobo, minced
Salt

BLACK OLIVE DEVILED EGGS

2 tablespoons extra-virgin olive oil or
   mayonnaise
1 teaspoon red wine vinegar
1 garlic clove, minced or pressed
Salt and freshly ground black pepper
3 tablespoons minced pitted black olives
Sprigs of fresh oregano, large pitted black olives
   cut in half lengthwise, and/or a sprinkling of
   crushed red pepper flakes, for garnish

Slice the peeled hard-boiled eggs in half length-wise. Pop the yolks into a bowl and thoroughly mash with a fork. Add the mayonnaise or olive oil and vinegar, depending on which flavoring you're using, and mix into a smooth paste. Fold in the rest of the ingredients, except the garnish. Fill the whites with the yolk mixture and decorate the tops with the garnish. Cover loosely with plastic wrap and refrigerate until serving time.

SERVING AND MENU IDEAS

Deviled eggs can add that little bit of filling protein to a thrown-together CSA-inspired vegetable meal. Imagine a meal of corn on the cob, Mediterranean Potato Salad (page 124), Jason's Fresh Fennel and Apple Slaw (page 123), sliced tomatoes, and, rounding it all out, a big platter of assorted deviled eggs.

Spiced Nuts

These spiced and roasted mixed nuts have a crisp, light texture, and flavors that are a little sweet, a little spicy, and salty. People have found them an addictive snack with drinks, and they add dimension and elegance sprinkled on salads or garnishing a creamy soup.

If you can, take a little extra time to make our Laura's Spice Rub and keep enough on hand to add a couple of teaspoons to these nuts.

Yields 3 cups
Prep time: 15 to 20 minutes
Baking time: 25 to 30 minutes

3 cups raw nuts: cashews, hazelnuts, pecans, and/or walnuts and/or salted roasted peanuts
3 tablespoons coconut oil, melted, or olive or vegetable oil
1 tablespoon mild curry powder, or more if desired
Dash of cayenne pepper
¼ teaspoon salt, or more if desired
3 tablespoons pure maple syrup

Preheat the oven to 350°F. Lightly oil a baking sheet.

Combine the nuts in a bowl and toss with the oil. Then add the curry powder, cayenne, salt, and 1 tablespoon of the maple syrup and stir thoroughly.

Spread the nuts evenly in one layer on the baking sheet, and bake for 10 to 15 minutes. Turn the nuts over with a spatula, stir, and return to the oven for another 10 to 12 minutes, until brown.

Lower the over temperature to 225°F. Toss the nuts with the remaining 2 tablespoons maple syrup and return them to the oven to dry for a few minutes, or turn off the heat and let them dry in the oven as it cools.

When the nuts are at room temperature, remove them from the pan. They should be toasted and crisp, with all the syrup and oil absorbed. Taste them, and sprinkle lightly with a little more curry powder or salt, if you like.

VARIATION
Use 2 teaspoons curry powder plus 2 teaspoons Laura's Spice Rub (page 333).

SERVING AND MENU IDEAS
Spiced Nuts are a very nice garnish on Pumpkin Cheesecake (page 370).

Za'atar Pita Chips

Pita chips are easy and quick to make. Za'atar is a complex, compelling flavor—sour, herbal fruity, and sometimes a bit smoky—and this recipe is another very good reason to always have za'atar in the pantry. See page 334, for both a recipe to make your own and recommendations for the commercial za'atars we like best.

For the best chips, start with a plain wheat pita bread so the za'atar will shine through. Either whole wheat or white pita work, though we find whole wheat pita makes for a crisper chip. Baking time depends on the thickness of the bread.

Yields 48 thick pita chips or 96 thin pita chips
Prep time: 10 minutes
Baking time: 12 to 15 minutes

¼ cup olive oil, plus more for the pans
1 package pita bread (6 rounds)
¼ cup za'atar (page 334)
Coarse salt (optional)

Preheat the oven to 350°F. Lightly oil two baking sheets or line them with parchment paper.

For thin pita chips, run a paring knife around the edge of each pita round to separate it into two rounds; leave the pita rounds whole for thicker chips. Brush each round with olive oil and cut into eight triangles. Spread out the wedges in a single layer on the prepared baking sheets. Sprinkle with za'atar and a little coarse salt (more or less depending on how salty the za'atar is).

Bake until the chips are crisp and lightly browned, 12 to 15 minutes. Cool on the baking sheets.

Store in an airtight container.

SERVING AND MENU IDEAS
Roasted Carrot Hummus (page 67) is our favorite dip for these za'atar-flavored pita chips. They are also good next to a bowl of soup or a green salad.

SPREADS
&
DIPS

Roasted Beet and Walnut Dip

Color and vitamins! This is a light, beautiful fuschia-colored dip. The sweetness and depth of roasted beets and walnuts are offset by refreshing mint and tart Greek yogurt. What a gorgeous dip to show off in a simple or decorative clear glass bowl.

Yields 2 generous cups
Prep time: 15 minutes
Roasting time: 45 to 60 minutes

1½ pounds raw beets
¾ cup plain Greek yogurt
2 large garlic cloves, minced or pressed
2 tablespoons olive oil
2 tablespoons red wine vinegar
1 teaspoon salt
Dash of cayenne pepper
3 tablespoons chopped fresh mint
¾ cup toasted walnuts
Thinly sliced scallions, for garnish

Preheat the oven to 400°F.

Rinse the beets and place them on a roasting pan. Roast until a knife can easily pierce the beets; the oven time will depend on the size and age of the beets, usually between 45 and 60 minutes. Allow the beets to cool enough to handle and then rub the peel off with your hands or peel with a knife. Cut the beets into chunks.

Place the beets, yogurt, garlic, oil, vinegar, salt, cayenne, mint, and walnuts in the bowl of a food processor and whirl until smooth.

Serve garnished with scallions.

SERVING AND MENU IDEAS
Try serving this gorgeous dip surrounded by an assortment of vegetable crudités and toasted pita triangles, pita chips, or savory crackers. Multicolored nasturtiums would further bejewel the platter. The dip is tasty on sliced cucumbers, crisp apples, or Bosc pears.

Spicy Butternut Squash Dip

This dip is light and flavorful, and can be varied for the amount of spiciness you like. The flavor of butternut squash is naturally sweet. Frozen squash is usually flash-frozen at peak ripeness and it certainly is convenient: however, the robust flavor and vivid color of fresh squash are hard to beat.

Serve warm as a side dish, or at room temperature or chilled as a dip with crudités and pita chips or wedges, or spread on warm cornbread.

Yields about 2 cups
Time: 30 minutes

1 medium butternut squash, seeded, peeled, and diced (or two 10-ounce packages frozen butternut squash chunks)
3 tablespoons extra-virgin olive oil
1½ teaspoons ground caraway
1½ teaspoons ground coriander
3 garlic cloves, minced or pressed
½ teaspoon salt
2 tablespoons fresh lemon juice
2 teaspoons Harissa (page 338)

Cook the squash in water to cover until tender. Drain and mash well.

Warm the oil in a small skillet or pan on low heat, add the caraway, coriander, and garlic and cook on low heat just until the garlic sizzles, a minute or two. Stir the oil and spices into the mashed squash. Add the salt, lemon juice, and harissa and mix well. Add more salt, lemon juice, and harissa to taste.

VARIATION
Instead of harissa, use ⅛ teaspoon cayenne pepper, or more to taste. Cook it with the caraway, coriander, and garlic.

SERVING AND MENU IDEAS
Serve with crudités and Za'atar Pita Chips (page 60), a good starter before Fennel and Chickpea Stew with Saffron and Prunes (page 213).

Edamame Hummus

We had some fusion fun with this fresh, creamy spring-green dip. We started with Asia, where many things are soy originated, then turned to the Middle East, home of hummus and tahini, and last added some bite from eastern Europe with prepared horseradish. *Namaste.*

Yields 2 cups
Time: 20 minutes

2 cups edamame, fresh or frozen (10 ounces)
1 teaspoon minced or pressed garlic
1 tablespoon chopped scallion
2 tablespoons tahini
1 teaspoon finely grated lemon zest
¼ cup fresh lemon juice
1 tablespoon extra-virgin olive oil
1½ tablespoons prepared white horseradish, more to taste
1 teaspoon salt
½ cup water
1 tablespoon finely chopped fresh dill (optional)

Cook fresh edamame in boiling water until tender, about 6 minutes, and frozen edamame according to the package directions. Drain, rinse with cold water to cool, and drain well.

Transfer the edamame to the bowl of a food processor. Add the garlic, scallion, tahini, lemon zest, lemon juice, olive oil, horseradish, salt, and water and process until smooth. Spoon the hummus into a bowl and stir in the dill, if using. Add more horseradish and/or salt to taste.

SERVING AND MENU IDEAS

To create a festive spread, serve as a dip with toasted pita bread wedges, rye crackers, roasted potato wedges, or sliced apples or pears, and also put some assorted olives, capers, spiced or toasted nuts, or thickly sliced ripe tomatoes on the table. For sandwiches, include crisp lettuce, sliced red onions, and cucumber slices.

Hummus with Preserved Lemon

Preserved lemons give hummus a deep undertone of lemony essence without acidity, and lemon juice imparts a bright, slightly sharp sensation. You can certainly serve the hummus without the spice swirl, but the spice swirl is kind of amazing, and addictive. Sometimes we double the amount because we want to keep spooning it on.

Yields 1¾ cups
Time: 20 minutes

HUMMUS
1 (15-ounce) can chickpeas, drained and rinsed
¼ cup hot water
¼ cup tahini
1½ tablespoons preserved lemon peel (see Note)
1 tablespoon minced or pressed garlic
2 tablespoons fresh lemon juice
Dash of crushed red pepper flakes
½ teaspoon salt
2 tablespoons olive oil

SPICE SWIRL
1 tablespoon olive oil
1 teaspoon za'atar (page 334)
¼ teaspoon paprika

To make the hummus, put the chickpeas in the bowl of a food processor. Add the hot water and whirl until fluffy. Add the tahini, preserved lemon, garlic, lemon juice, red pepper flakes, and salt, and whirl until smooth and creamy. While the processor is on, drizzle in the olive oil. Scrape the hummus into a serving bowl.

For the spice swirl, heat the olive oil, za'atar, and paprika in a small skillet. Simmer for about 1 minute. Swirl it into the hummus and add salt to taste.

The hummus will keep refrigerated for up to 5 days.

NOTE: We give directions for making preserved lemons on page 344. To use them, rinse the lemon, remove the pulp and use only the peel. If you don't have preserved lemons, add another tablespoon of lemon juice to the hummus.

SERVING AND MENU IDEAS
A classic appetizer served with pita or crostini, it also pairs nicely with Quinoa Tabouli with Pomegranates and Pistachios (page 145) or Cracked Freekeh with Dried Cherries and Almonds (page 137).

Roasted Carrot Hummus

This unusual hummus is a pretty brick orange color. Very richly flavorful and complex: the sweetness of the roasted carrots, the spicy heat of garam masala, and the zing of lemon and vinegar create a sweet-spicy-tart sensation. Experiment and vary the amount of spices according to your taste.

Yields 2 cups
Hands-on time before roasting: 15 minutes
Roasting time: about 25 minutes
Puréeing time: 10 minutes

1 teaspoon cumin seeds
1 teaspoon coriander seeds
1 pound carrots
3 to 5 garlic cloves
1 teaspoon salt
3 tablespoons olive oil, plus more for topping
½ teaspoon hot garam masala, or mild garam masala and crushed red pepper flakes
¼ teaspoon ground cinnamon
1 cup drained and rinsed chickpeas
3 tablespoons fresh lemon juice
2 teaspoons apple cider vinegar
2 to 4 tablespoons water

Preheat the oven to 425°F. Lightly oil a large baking sheet, or line it with parchment paper or aluminum foil.

In a small, dry skillet on low heat, toast the cumin and coriander seeds until fragrant. Set aside to cool.

Cut the carrots and cut into ¼-inch-thick chunks. Put in a bowl. Stir the garlic into the carrots. In a spice grinder, whirl the cooled cumin and coriander seeds until powdered. Add the ground cumin and coriander and ½ tablespoon of the salt, and 1 tablespoon of the olive oil to the carrots and toss well. Spread out on the prepared baking sheet and cover with aluminum foil. Roast for 15 minutes and then remove the foil and return to the oven. After 10 minutes, sprinkle the garam masala and cinnamon on the carrots, stir lightly, and continue roasting until tender, about 5 minutes.

Transfer the carrots to the bowl of a food processor and add the chickpeas, lemon juice, vinegar, salt, and remaining 2 tablespoons olive oil. Purée, adding just enough water to make a smooth consistency. Scoop the hummus into a serving bowl and drizzle on a little olive oil.

SERVING AND MENU IDEAS
Serve as a dip for cucumber spears, celery sticks, bell pepper strips, green beans, and cauliflower florets and/or Za'atar Pita Chips (page 60). For a refreshing meal, top the hummus with yogurt and serve with toasted naan or pita and Chilled Curried Pea and Coconut Soup (page 106).

Walnut and Roasted Red Pepper Spread

Originally from Aleppo, Syria, where it's called *muhammara*, versions of this spread or dip can be found throughout the Levant. The flavor is richly delicious, mildly sweet, and slightly spicy. Muhammara has an appealing terra cotta orange color. And it's very easy to make!

Pomegranate molasses (or syrup) has a very tart but fruity flavor and slight sweetness, and it adds an authentic and unique touch to this dish, but in case you can't find it, we give you a substitute. Roast red bell peppers yourself, or save time by using jarred roasted red peppers. If you like spicier dishes, go for the higher amount of red pepper flakes.

Yields 2 cups
Time: 15 minutes

1 cup walnut halves or pieces
2 garlic cloves, minced or pressed
2 large roasted red peppers, drained if using
    canned (about 1½ cups, coarsely chopped)
1 tablespoon fresh lemon juice
4 teaspoons pomegranate molasses★
¼ cup extra-virgin olive oil
1 teaspoon ground cumin
¼ teaspoon crushed red pepper flakes
¼ teaspoon salt
⅓ to ½ cup bread crumbs

★Well-stocked supermarkets may have pomegranate molasses (or syrup) with other Middle Eastern specialties. If it's not available where you live, double the lemon juice and add 1 teaspoon brown sugar or honey.

Toast the walnuts in a conventional or toaster oven at 350°F for about 5 minutes, until fragrant and lightly browned. Set aside to cool for a few minutes before processing.

Place the walnuts in the bowl of a food processor and process until the nuts are well chopped. Add the garlic, roasted red peppers, lemon juice, pomegranate molasses, oil, cumin, red pepper flakes, salt, and ⅓ cup of the bread crumbs and process until smooth. Add more bread crumbs if you want the spread to be thicker. Season with more salt and/or red pepper flakes to taste.

This spread will keep in the refrigerator for at least 1 week.

SERVING AND MENU IDEAS

For a simple appetizer, serve with toasted pita or other flatbreads, crackers, or crostini. On crostini, you could garnish with a cornichon, sliced red or orange cherry or grape tomatoes, a toasted walnut half, sliced seedless grapes, or a dab of chèvre. It also makes a flavorful topping for simple steamed vegetables, grains, or stews. Serve alongside roasted potatoes, asparagus, carrots, sweet potatoes, onions, or other vegetables.

Radish and Herbed Chèvre Spread or Dip

Red radishes have a little bite and are very pretty contrasted with the mild white cheeses. This spread is delicious on toast or in a sandwich with arugula, or on little pumpernickel rounds decorated with cucumber slices or sprigs of dill.

Yields 1¼ cups radish spread
Time: 20 minutes

½ cup finely chopped red radishes
4 ounces goat cheese
2 ounces cream cheese
¼ cup minced scallions
¼ cup chopped fresh parsley
2 tablespoons chopped fresh dill
½ teaspoon finely grated lemon zest
½ teaspoon cracked black pepper
Dash of salt

To press out some of the moisture, spread the radishes between two paper towels and top with a heavy skillet or pan for a few minutes.

In a medium bowl, combine the goat cheese and cream cheese. Stir in the scallions, parsley, dill, lemon zest, and pepper. Squeeze the chopped radishes in the paper towels and add to the bowl with a sprinkling of salt.

SERVING AND MENU IDEAS
Top sandwiches with a thin slice of tomato, sliced black olives, alfalfa sprouts, or thinly sliced cucumber. For a complete meal, serve with a bowl of soup, such as Golden Cauliflower Soup (page 89) or Smoky Split Pea Soup (page 96), or next to a salad, such as Spring Greens and Vegetables with Shallot Vinaigrette (page 139) or Mushroom Barley Salad (page 147).

Easy Labneh Dip

Labneh is a fresh soft cheese that has been a staple in the Middle East for centuries. Tangy and somewhat salty, nutritious and full of probiotics, labneh is made by straining most of the whey from yogurt. It's thicker than sour cream, but not as thick as cream cheese. You can buy labneh, also spelled labne and labna, in well-stocked supermarkets or online. Or make it yourself by draining dairy yogurt made from cow's, sheep's, or goat's milk, or vegan yogurt.

For an appetizer, snack, or party food, spread labneh on a plate, sprinkle and drizzle it with a few simple toppings, and you have a quick, attractive, and delicious dip to serve with warm sliced flatbread, toasted pita wedges, or bread sticks to swipe across the plate of labneh. Or scoop up the labne with crudites or slices of fruit.

Serves 4 to 6
Time: 5 to 15 minutes, depending on the topping

Spread about 2 cups of labneh on a flat plate, pushing it out to the edges with the back of a spoon. Sprinkle and/or drizzle with a topping.

OLIVE OIL AND ZA'ATAR TOPPING

Drizzle up to ¼ cup of a fruity extra-virgin olive oil over the top. Sprinkle with a tablespoon or two of za'atar (page 334) and a few pinches of coarse salt.

FRESH HERBS AND LEMON TOPPING

Drizzle the labneh with a couple of tablespoons of extra-virgin olive oil and a tablespoon of lemon juice. Sprinkle with a teaspoon of lemon zest, about ¼ cup of minced fresh herbs, and some coarse salt and cracked black pepper. We like Italian parsley and chives with some combination of basil, thyme, dill, oregano, and mint.

POMEGRANATE SEED, PISTACHIO, AND OLIVE TOPPING

After drizzling with olive oil, sprinkle with 2 tablespoons of chopped parsley and/or fresh mint, a tablespoon of chopped black olives, such as kalamata, 2 tablespoons of chopped toasted pistachios (or walnuts), and ¼ cup of pomegranate seeds. A pinch of red pepper flakes will add a little bite.

MORE IDEAS:

- Chopped dried fruit such as figs or cherries; toasted pine nuts or chopped toasted nuts such as almonds, hazelnuts, or walnuts; a drizzle of honey.
- Olive oil; finely chopped black garlic; chopped chives or scallions; black sesame seeds; coarse salt.
- Olive oil; tiny cubes of cooked red and golden beets; chopped fresh dill; coarse salt and cracked black pepper.
- Olive oil; minced sun-dried tomatoes; chopped green olives; toasted pine nuts; minced fresh garlic; salt and pepper.

Fresh Mozzarella Sandwich with Grilled Onions and Greens

Philly Portobello Steak Sandwich

Tofu Fillets with Onion and Fresh Herb Relish

Banh Mi Chay Sandwich

TLT Sandwich

Avocado Egg Sandwich

Denver Omelet Sandwich

White Bean and Olive Sandwich

Mexican Toasted Cheese Sandwich

A Big Fat Tomato Sandwich

Singapore Sliders with Tropical Slaw

Fresh Mozzarella Sandwich with Grilled Onions and Greens

Often it's the combination of just a few of the right ingredients that makes a terrific sandwich. The texture and flavor contrasts of the creamy, mild cheese, sweet onions, sharp greens, and classic tomato on a big fresh roll make this one just right. You can make it with a crusty bread like ciabatta or French or Italian bread or rolls, but then you'd better tuck a big linen napkin under your chin and hold the sandwich over a dinner plate to catch the juices and pieces of the generous filling that may slide out. So roll up your sleeves, grab hold of this stack of deliciousness, and open wide! And serve with a pile of extra napkins.

Yields 4 sandwiches
Time: 30 minutes

4 tablespoons extra-virgin olive oil
1 tablespoon chopped fresh parsley or basil and oregano
1 garlic clove, minced or pressed
8 ounces fresh mozzarella cheese, cut into ¼-inch-thick slices
1 large red onion, sliced into ¼-inch-thick rounds
6 cups loosely packed fresh greens, such as chard, arugula, or spinach (large stems removed and leaves coarsely chopped)
Salt and freshly ground black pepper
2 teaspoons white balsamic vinegar or apple cider vinegar
2 tomatoes, sliced
4 big sandwich rolls

In a bowl large enough to hold the cheese, combine 2 tablespoons of the olive oil with the herbs and garlic. Add the cheese, coat with the seasoned oil, and set aside. Prep the other ingredients.

Warm a griddle or large heavy skillet to medium-high. Add 1 tablespoon of the oil and the onion slices, arranged in a single layer, and sprinkle with salt. Cook for 2 to 3 minutes on each side until just tender and browned but not scorched. Using a large enough spatula to keep the rounds intact, remove the onions from the skillet. Add the remaining 1 tablespoon oil and the chopped greens and stir until wilted, just a minute for arugula or spinach, a bit longer for chard. Transfer the greens to a bowl and toss with the vinegar and a little salt and black pepper.

Assemble the sandwiches: onion slices, greens, cheese, and tomato. Drizzle the inside surface of the top pieces of the rolls with whatever is left of the seasoned oil from the cheese.

SERVING AND MENU IDEAS
This mild cheese sandwich goes well with a soup that has a touch of smoky hotness, such as Sopa Verde de Elote (page 90) or Smoky Split Pea Soup (page 96).

Philly Portobello Steak Sandwich

Moosewood's Wynnie Stein grew up in Philly, home of the famous Pat's Steaks. Her dad, Milt, has been eating steak sandwiches at Pat's for at least seventy-five years and he still loves to go there. He remembers in his youth playing cards until the wee hours and then heading over to Pat's so he could end the night eating his favorite sandwich. It cost fifteen cents. He would always eat two.

So, when Wynnie was asked to create a vegetarian version of this classic sandwich, she knew she'd better get it right. Milt thinks she did.

Serves 4
Time: about 1 hour

MARINADE
¼ cup olive oil
2 tablespoons soy sauce
2 teaspoons ground fennel seeds
1 tablespoon minced or pressed garlic
¼ teaspoon crushed red pepper flakes
2 teaspoons dried oregano
¼ teaspoon paprika
¼ teaspoon freshly ground black pepper
½ teaspoon salt

FILLING
4 medium portobello mushrooms (about 5 inches in diameter)
2 tablespoons olive oil
4 cups thinly sliced onions
Salt
1 large red or green bell pepper
2 tablespoons all-purpose flour
4 ounces grated sharp cheddar, mozzarella, or provolone cheese

ASSEMBLY
4 Italian rolls or Italian bread, split and cut into 4 servings
2 tablespoons butter
Mustard
Hot cherry peppers (optional)

In a large bowl, whisk together the marinade ingredients. Set aside.

Remove and discard the stems from the portobellos and, using a teaspoon, scrape out and discard the gills on the undersides of the caps. Place the caps, gill side down, on a cutting board and cut into 1-inch-thick slices. Place the slices in the bowl and use your fingers to gently rub them with the marinade. Set aside.

Warm the oil in a large skillet on medium heat. Add the onions, sprinkle with salt, and cook until the onions begin to soften. Lower the heat and cook, stirring occasionally, until the onions have caramelized, at least 20 minutes. While the onions cook, seed the bell pepper and cut it into ¼-inch-thick slices.

When the onions have caramelized, raise the heat to medium, add the bell pepper and the marinated mushroom slices, and cook until the pepper is soft and the mushrooms have released some juice, about 10 minutes. Drain a couple of tablespoons of the cooking liquid into a small bowl and whisk in the flour. Stir the flour mixture back into the vegetables and continue to cook, stirring constantly, until thickened. Add more soy sauce to taste. Sprinkle the grated cheese on top and let it melt.

Assemble the sandwiches: Spread the butter on the rolls or bread and toast lightly. Then spread mustard (or ketchup, if you want to horrify folks from Philly) on the bread and divide the hot vegetables and cheese among the four sandwiches.

If you like, serve Philadelphia-style with hot cherry peppers on the side.

SERVING AND MENU IDEAS
Traditionally, folks eat their sandwiches outside their favorite joint, standing up and leaning over a little to let the juice drip onto the pavement. But at home, sitting at a table for your meal, you may want to add a soup, like Celery or Celeriac Soup Two Ways (page 100), or a little salad on the side, like Jason's Fresh Fennel and Apple Slaw (page 123). Then you'll be fortified in case you play cards until the wee hours.

Tofu Fillets with Onion and Fresh Herb Relish

Invited to a vegan picnic and want to take something to grill? Tofu fillets will be a welcome addition. These fillets are very easy to throw together and make a good appetizer, small plate, or sandwich filling.

Yields 8 pieces
Serves 4
Prep time: 15 minutes
Marinating time: 30 minutes or more
Broiling time: 12 minutes

1 (16-ounce) block of firm tofu

RELISH
1 small onion or large shallot
1 large garlic clove
5 tablespoons extra-virgin olive oil
½ cup packed fresh basil, oregano, and/or cilantro (any combination, but all three is best)
½ teaspoon salt
¾ teaspoon ground fennel seeds
3 tablespoons red wine vinegar

Dry the tofu by wrapping it in folded paper towels and gently pressing out the excess water, then patting it dry. Cut the block of tofu in half, and then each half into fourths to make 8 slabs. Lay out these fillets in a single layer on a nonreactive baking sheet or in a couple of baking pans.

In a food processor, whirl the onion and garlic until somewhat liquefied. Add the rest of the relish ingredients and pulse a few times until everything is well combined. Transfer the relish to a bowl.

Slather half the relish on both sides of the tofu slabs and refrigerate the remaining relish. Refrigerate the tofu for at least 30 minutes. The longer it marinates, the better, but if you're pressed for time, 30 minutes will do it.

Broil the marinated tofu fillets for 6 minutes on each side, until lightly browned. Or grill the tofu fillets in a grill pan or on an outside grill.

For a nice fresh herb flavor, serve topped with a dollop of the reserved relish.

SERVING AND MENU IDEAS
For a delicious sandwich, stuff a ciabatta roll with two fillets, some relish, a slice of juicy tomato, and some Giardiniera (page 342) or one of our other pickles on the side. Or serve the sandwich with a soup, such as Purée of Parsnip, Carrot, and Celeriac (page 91). Or serve as an entrée along with Basmati Rice Pilaf (page 318) and Lemony Roasted Beets (page 297).

Banh Mi Chay Sandwich

Banh mi means "bread" in Vietnamese. The sandwich that in the United States we call banh mi is a Vietnamese-French fusion food popularized first in Saigon, and then in the 1980s by Vietnamese in California. Banh mi sandwiches are usually made with airy, crisp Vietnamese baguettes, which are made with both rice and wheat flour. A regular baguette will do when you can't find the Vietnamese variety. Although most banh mi sandwiches include a filling of sliced meat or pâté, there is also *banh mi chay*, a vegetarian banh mi sandwich, and our inspiration.

So many luscious sandwiches comprise savory, creamy, crunchy, and tangy elements, and this sandwich meets all these criteria. The elements of almost any banh mi sandwich are a savory filling, pickled carrots and daikon (*do chua*), cilantro or mint, cucumbers, mayonnaise, and thinly sliced jalapeños or other hot peppers. Do chua is often only carrots and daikon, but we like to add red onions for both the color and flavor. In this recipe, we give you three filling options (good either warm or chilled): baked tofu; eggs; roasted, grilled, or pan-fried portobello or other mushrooms.

The pickled vegetables, herbed mayonnaise, and baked tofu all keep for several days, and can be made ahead of time.

Yields four 6-inch sandwiches
Serves 4
Sandwich assembly time (with all elements prepped): 10 minutes

Do Chua prep time: 15 minutes
Do Chua pickling time: at least 1 hour, up to several days
Herbed Mayo prep time: 5 minutes
Herbed Mayo chilling time (for flavor to develop): at least 30 minutes, or up to several days
Prep time for the Filling Options and the remaining ingredients: 20 to 30 minutes

PICKLED VEGETABLES (*DO CHUA*)
1 cup carrot matchsticks
1 cup daikon matchsticks
½ cup thinly sliced red onions
½ cup white vinegar
½ cup fresh lime or lemon juice
2 tablespoons sugar
½ teaspoon salt
⅛ teaspoon freshly ground black pepper

HERBED MAYO
1 cup mayonnaise
2 tablespoons fresh lime or lemon juice
½ cup chopped fresh cilantro, mint, and/or basil

FILLING OPTIONS
Maple Baked Tofu (see page 80)
or
4 large eggs
1 tablespoon soy sauce
1½ teaspoons oil
or
2 portobello mushrooms
2 tablespoons dark sesame oil
Sprinkling of salt

SANDWICH ASSEMBLY

1 cucumber, peeled and thinly sliced crosswise

1 cup shredded lettuce, or baby greens

Fresh cilantro, mint, and/or basil, whole leaves or cut into chiffonade (optional)

1 or 2 thinly sliced jalapeños or other hot peppers (optional)

4 small or two 12-inch baguettes★

★Baguettes are traditional, but you can use any crusty, porous bread, such as batard, a wide Italian loaf, focaccia, even toasted sliced bread.

Once you have all the elements of a banh mi sandwich on hand, it's a snap to assemble. The do chua needs at least an hour of marinating time, and it keeps for 3 to 4 days. The herbed mayonnaise is fine right away, and it will keep well for about a week. If you want Maple Baked Tofu for the sandwiches, plan on getting that into the oven at least 90 minutes before you want to serve the sandwiches, but it's good either warm or cold and it keeps for days. So you can make all of these ahead of time.

Make the do chua: Put the carrot and daikon matchsticks and the onion slices into a heatproof bowl. Bring the vinegar, lime juice, sugar, salt, and black pepper to a boil in a small saucepan, and then pour it over the vegetables. As the vegetables soften a bit, in just a minute or two, press them down into the brine with the back of a spoon. Cover and refrigerate for at least an hour.

Make the herbed mayonnaise: Stir the lime juice and chopped herbs into the mayonnaise, cover and refrigerate.

Prepare one or more of Maple Baked Tofu (page 80), eggs, portobellos. To make the eggs, warm the oil in a large skillet. Beat the eggs with the soy sauce and pour into the pan. Tilt the pan and lift the edges of the eggs as they cook allowing the liquid to flow into the bottom and cook until firm and beginning to brown. Transfer to a plate. Cut into 2-inch-wide strips. To cook the mushrooms, slice the portobello caps into ½-inch-wide strips. Brush the cut sides of the strips with sesame oil, sprinkle with salt, and grill, pan fry, or broil or roast in a 400°F oven.

When ready to assemble the sandwiches, prep the cucumber, lettuce, fresh herbs, and hot pepper. Slice the baguettes and toast them if you like. Generously spread herbed mayonnaise on both cut sides of the baguettes. From the bottom up, layer tofu, eggs, and/or mushrooms, do chua, cucumbers, lettuce, fresh herbs, sliced hot peppers. Press the baguette top onto the fillings.

Cut the sandwich into smaller pieces if you like.

SERVING AND MENU IDEAS

This is a big sandwich, but you can serve it with a light soup, such as Vietnamese Lemongrass Vegetable Soup (page 101) or Chilled Pineapple-Mango Soup (page 104) for a more complete meal. Then, maybe a couple little Peanut-Ginger Cookies (page 352) to end on a sweet note.

TLT Sandwich

There's nothing else quite like a ripe summer tomato sandwich. When we find ourselves craving one on a dreary winter day, or even during summer before the tomatoes have ripened, slices of flavorful baked tofu can go a long way toward compensating for a less-than-luscious supermarket tomato. And when the tomatoes are glorious, so is this classic sandwich.

One block of tofu makes enough dense, chewy baked tofu for four sandwiches. For the tofu, we especially like maple syrup, but you can also use other sweeteners, such as agave syrup or brown sugar. Double the recipe if you'd like to have Maple Baked Tofu on hand for easy sandwiches or snacks.

Yields baked tofu for 4 sandwiches
Serves 4
Prep time for tofu: 10 minutes
Tofu baking time: about 1 hour
Sandwich prep time: 10 minutes

MAPLE BAKED TOFU
1 (16-ounce block) firm or extra-firm tofu
2 tablespoons pure maple syrup
2 tablespoons brown mustard
2 tablespoons soy sauce
2 tablespoons olive oil or vegetable oil

Mayonnaise
Sliced bread
Slices of ripe tomatoes
Lettuce
Salt

Prepare the baked tofu: Preheat the oven to 400°F. In a small bowl, combine the maple syrup, mustard, soy sauce, and oil. Cut the block of tofu horizontally into 4 slabs. Place the tofu pieces in a 9 x 12-inch baking pan; they should fit without overlapping and with a little space between. Put about a teaspoon of the sauce on top of each slab and, using the back of the spoon, spread it over the top surfaces. Flip the tofu over and spread on more sauce. Bake for about an hour total. After about 30 minutes in the oven, flip the tofu slabs and cover the tops with sauce. Return to the oven for 10 to 15 minutes, and then flip, cover with sauce again, and return to the oven for another 10 minutes. Cool to room temperature and then refrigerate.

To assemble a sandwich, spread mayonnaise on two slices of bread. Cut a slab of tofu to fit the shape of the bread and put it on the bottom slice. Cover with tomato slices and lettuce. Sprinkle with salt if you like. Put the top slice on, and eat it leaning over a plate to catch the drips.

VARIATIONS
- Add avocado slices or guacamole, thinly sliced cucumbers, and/or sprouts.
- Shred the lettuce and toss with chopped fresh herbs, such as basil or cilantro.
- Use herbed mayonnaise.

SERVING AND MENU IDEAS
Raspberry-Carrot Pickles (page 340) or Kale Chips (page 49) are tasty little sides for a sandwich. Or make a full meal of a TLT Sandwich by adding a soup, such as Aigo Bouido (page 102) or Celery or Celeriac Soup Two Ways (page 100), or by pairing it with a salad like Jason's Fresh Fennel and Apple Slaw (page 123) or Wax Bean and Radish Salad with Buttermilk Dressing (page 121).

Avocado Egg Sandwich

With whole grain, fiber, protein, and healthful fat, this tasty sandwich for breakfast will keep you satisfied all morning. Or later in the day, for lunch or supper, a soup would round out the meal.

Yields 2 or 3 open-faced sandwiches (depending on size of bread)
Serves 2 or 3
Time: 25 minutes (with already-boiled eggs)

½ cup plain Greek yogurt
1 small cucumber, peeled, seeded, and finely chopped
¼ cup minced scallions
1 tablespoon chopped fresh dill
½ teaspoon ground cumin
1 tablespoon minced cornichon or dill pickle (optional)
2 teaspoons plus 1 tablespoon fresh lemon juice
Salt and freshly ground black pepper

2 or 3 hard-boiled eggs★ (1 egg for each slice of bread)
1 avocado
2 or 3 slices of rye or pumpernickel bread

★If you don't have hard-boiled eggs on hand, cook them first, before prepping the other ingredients.

In a small bowl, combine the yogurt, cucumbers, scallions, dill, cumin, pickle, if using, and 2 teaspoons of the lemon juice. Season with salt and pepper to taste.

Cut each hard-boiled egg lengthwise into about 6 slices. Peel, pit, and slice the avocado and drizzle it with the remaining 1 tablespoon lemon juice.

Toast the bread and assemble the sandwiches: top each slice of bread with the cucumber-yogurt mixture and then slices of avocado and egg. Sprinkle a little salt and pepper on top.

VARIATIONS
- The pickle is optional but does add a little jolt of piquancy. To ramp it up a little, substitute pickle juice from the jar for the lemon juice.
- Instead of hard-boiled eggs, fry eggs in olive oil. It won't be as pretty, but it will be a little less messy.

SERVING AND MENU IDEAS
Avocado Egg Sandwich is pretty much a square meal of a breakfast on its own, but a smoothie such as Peppery Green Smoothie, No Pepper (page 22) goes well with it. For a brunch spread, a bowl of fresh cherries or raspberries would be nice, along with Sweet Potatoes with Bitter Orange (page 303) and Lemon Zucchini Cake with Thyme (page 363) or Sunbutter Bites (page 30). For lunch or dinner, pair with Roasted Fennel and Leek Tomato Soup (page 98) or Celery or Celeriac Soup Two Ways (page 100).

Denver Omelet Sandwich

Here is a simple Denver-style omelet served between two bronco-sized slices of your favorite bread, toasted and buttered for one mile-high sandwich. If you've only had a Western omelet at a diner or breakfast café, try this at home. There's nothing new about an omelet with a side of toast, but putting it all together as a big, hot, and hefty sandwich is pretty darn satisfying. Classic Western omelets feature diced ham, peppers, and onions, but (surprise!) we leave out the ham and "beef up" the onions and bell peppers with a few other doo-dads like Jack cheese.

You can add your favorite salsa, ketchup, or hot sauce for a little zing. For colts and calves who want less, you can split it and serve two. The Denver can be wrapped up and stowed in your saddle bag, and come chow time just open wide and you'll be Rocky Mountain high in no time. Then git along little doggie, git along.

Serves 1 or 2
Time: 15 minutes

2 teaspoons butter
½ cup finely chopped onion
Salt and freshly ground black pepper
½ cup finely diced green, red, or orange bell peppers
2 large eggs
1 tablespoon water
1 teaspoon minced fresh parsley
⅓ cup grated Monterey Jack or sharp cheddar (optional)
Tomato salsa or hot sauce (optional)
2 slices of a large loaf of bread (or 4 regular-size slices of bread or 2 rolls)
Butter or mayonnaise
Tomato slices (optional)

In an 8-inch skillet or omelet pan, heat the butter over medium heat. Add the onion, sprinkle with salt and black pepper, and cook, stirring frequently, until translucent. Stir in the bell peppers and cook for another 3 to 4 minutes, until the peppers soften and the onion is golden on the edges.

In a small bowl, beat the eggs with the water and parsley.

Gather the onion and bell peppers into a circle an inch or so from the edge of the skillet and pour the eggs and parsley over them. As the eggs begin to set around the edges, using a spatula, gently lift an edge and tilt the pan so that the uncooked egg runs out to the edges of the skillet. When the eggs are mostly set, sprinkle with the cheese and/or salsa, if using, and fold the omelet in half. The omelet should be lightly golden and set, but not dry. Sprinkle with salt and black pepper to taste.

Toast the bread and spread with butter or mayonnaise. Place the omelet on one piece of toast and add the tomato slices, if using. Cover with the second slice of toast, cut the sandwich in half, and serve hot or at room temperature.

SERVING AND MENU IDEAS
Slather this sandwich with whatever condiments you like—mayo, ketchup, hot sauce or salsa, pickles. Then put some potato chips or Kale Chips (page 49) on the plate, or even fancier, Butternut Hash Browns (page 18). How about a Whole-Grain Blondie (page 359) for dessert?

White Bean and Olive Sandwich

This very quick and easy recipe yields a generous amount of an interesting topping for hearty open-faced sandwiches for a satisfying lunch, or elegant crostini for appetizers or party food, especially good served with a fruity red wine.

Pop leftover topping into a covered container in the refrigerator, where you'll be glad to find it in a couple of days when you're looking for a midnight snack or something extra for a meal. It keeps well for about a week.

Yields about 3 cups
Time: 15 minutes

1 (15-ounce) can cannellini beans, drained and rinsed
2 cups pitted black olives (a combination of mild Greek olives and oil-cured Kalamatas is nice)
1 (15-ounce) can butter beans, drained and rinsed
¼ cup extra-virgin olive oil, plus more to drizzle on the bread
2 tablespoons white wine vinegar
2 teaspoons garlic chili paste or sauce*
Salt and freshly ground black pepper

½-inch-thick slices of bread
Chopped fresh basil or mint (optional)

*Any garlicky chili paste or sauce is fine. We like Vietnamese-style chili garlic sauce from Huy Fong Foods.

Put the cannellini beans into a bowl and set aside. In the bowl of a food processor, whirl the olives until chopped but not puréed, 3 or 4 seconds, and add them to the cannellini beans in the bowl. In the bowl of the food processor (no need to rinse it), put the butter beans, oil, vinegar, and chili paste and purée until smooth. Stir into the cannellini beans and olives in the bowl and mix well. Season with salt and pepper to taste.

Lightly toast or grill slices of bread and drizzle or brush the tops with olive oil. Spread the bean and olive topping on each slice, and sprinkle with the basil or mint if you like.

SERVING AND MENU IDEAS
Bread and this spread is good by itself, or top the sandwiches with slices of fresh mozzarella and/or tomato slices. Strips of roasted red peppers are also nice.

This sandwich goes well with Watermelon Gazpacho with Feta-Yogurt Crema (page 108). Zucchini Slaw with Toasted Buckwheat and Feta (page 119) works as a side dish when this sandwich is the main course. For appetizers, spread the topping on toasted baguette rounds, nice before Kale and Walnut Risotto (page 173) or Pasta Carbonara with Zucchini (page 229).

Mexican Toasted Cheese Sandwich

A couple of simple additions give this easy grilled cheese sandwich a kick. With soup or salad, this is a good casual meal.

Yields 4 open-faced sandwiches
Serves 4
Prep time: 20 minutes
Broiling time: 5 to 8 minutes

½ teaspoon adobo sauce (from a can of chipotle
   peppers in adobo sauce), or more to taste
½ cup mayonnaise
4 slices whole wheat or other bread
1 cup shredded cheddar cheese
4 large tomato slices
Thinly sliced red onions
Chopped fresh cilantro (optional)

Turn the broiler on. Stir the adobo sauce into the mayonnaise and set aside. Put the slices of bread on a baking sheet. Spread each bread slice with the adobo mayonnaise. Sprinkle with cheese. Top with a tomato slice and some red onions.

Broil until the cheese is bubbling and the edges of the toast have browned, 5 to 8 minutes. Check after about 5 minutes and reposition the sandwiches, as necessary, for even browning. Remove from the pan. Sprinkle with cilantro, if you like, and serve immediately.

VARIATION
Substitute chopped scallions for the red onions.

SERVING AND MENU IDEAS
Mexican Toasted Cheese Sandwich is delicious with any or all of these dishes: Sopa Verde de Elote (page 90), Winter Chopped Salad (page 130), Rich Vegan Chocolate Pudding (page 380).

A Big Fat Tomato Sandwich

August is the moment in the northeast when the tomatoes ripen. It's suddenly time for bruschetta, gazpacho, tomatoes and fresh mozzarella, panzanella, fried green tomatoes, and roasted tomato sauce. Here's a tomato sandwich that's a cross between pan bagnat and old-fashioned tomato-and-mayo-between-two-slices-of-bread. If you have some yellow or heirloom tomatoes in your garden or farmers' market, this is a great way to give them center stage. Fresh, local tomatoes have an incomparable scent, juiciness, and flavor so superior to their tough, hard-traveling cousins who ripen in the back of a semi, far away from their sunny homes.

Our Herb and Olive Mayonnaise is packed with three different fresh herbs and chopped green olives. We think you'll love it as much as we do.

Yields 4 sandwiches
Serves 4
Time: 15 minutes

1 loaf Foccacia Pugliese (page 277) or a ciabatta or
   other crusty, porous loaf
2 big ripe tomatoes
Pickled Sweet Peppers (page 341; optional)
Lettuce or arugula

HERB AND OLIVE MAYONNAISE
½ cup mayonnaise
1 teaspoon finely grated lemon zest
2 teaspoons fresh lemon juice or vinegar
¼ cup minced fresh parsley
¼ cup minced fresh chives
¼ cup minced fresh oregano
½ cup chopped green olives

Preheat the oven or toaster oven to 350°F.

In a small bowl, mix the mayonnaise, lemon zest, lemon juice, herbs, and olives.

Slice the bread horizontally and heat in the oven until just warm inside and a little crisp on the outside. Slice the tomatoes, put the slices on the bottom half of the bread, and push them gently into the bread with a fork. Layer some pickled peppers and lettuce or arugula on the tomatoes. Spread the herb and olive mayonnaise on the top half of the bread. Put the two halves together, slice into four sandwiches, and serve with big, absorbent napkins.

SERVING AND MENU IDEAS
Serve A Big Fat Tomato Sandwich with one of the soups made with Italian Cheese Broth (page 94), a few olives or Raspberry-Carrot Pickles (page 340), and maybe a cookie or two, such as Orange Oatmeal Cookies with Dark Chocolate Chips (page 356), and you'll be big, fat, and happy.

Singapore Sliders with Tropical Slaw

These easy little sandwiches slide right down, so to speak, in two or three flavorful bites. They can be the main dish for a casual meal, or fun appetizers or party food.

Serves 4 to 8
Hands-on time: 20 minutes
Marinating time: 30 minutes
Baking time: 60 minutes

1 (16-ounce) block firm tofu

MARINADE
1 tablespoon vegetable oil or grapeseed oil
3 tablespoons soy sauce
1 tablespoon dark sesame oil
2 tablespoons tomato ketchup, or 1 to 2 tablespoons Chinese chili paste
1 tablespoon peeled and grated fresh ginger
½ teaspoon ground fennel seeds

TROPICAL SLAW
Finely grated zest and juice of 1 lime
½ cup peanut butter
¼ cup coconut milk
1 tablespoon light brown or coconut sugar
1 tablespoon rice vinegar
1 teaspoon Sriracha, Tabasco, or other hot sauce, or less or more to taste
2 cups shredded cabbage (a mix of green and red is nice)
½ cup grated carrots

8 slider buns

Cut the block of tofu lengthwise into 8 slices. Halve the slices to yield 16 pieces.

In the bottom of a glass baking dish, whisk together the marinade ingredients. Turn the tofu pieces in the marinade until well coated and refrigerate for 30 minutes or more.

Preheat the oven to 400°F. Lay out the tofu in a single layer in an oiled baking pan. Bake, uncovered, for 45 minutes to an hour, gently turning the tofu about every 15 minutes, until firm, browned, and crisp around the edges.

Make the slaw: In a bowl, whisk together the lime zest and juice, peanut butter, coconut milk, sugar, and vinegar until creamy. Add hot sauce to taste. Thin if necessary with more coconut milk. Toss the cabbage and carrots with the dressing and refrigerate.

To assemble the sliders, fill each bun with two pieces of baked tofu and ¼ cup of the slaw.

SERVING AND MENU IDEAS
Singapore Sliders pair well with Thai Corn Chowder (page 93) or Vietnamese Lemongrass Vegetable Soup (page 101) for a soup and sandwich meal. Or like most burger-type sandwiches, they have an affinity for potatoes, such as Potato Wedges Masala with a Cooling Dip (page 46). A jar of Monsoon Pickles (page 339) would not be out of place.

Golden Cauliflower Soup

Sopa Verde de Elote

Purée of Parsnip, Carrot, and Celeriac

Thai Corn Chowder

Italian Cheese Broth

Smoky Split Pea Soup

Hot-and-Sour Mushroom Soup

Roasted Fennel and Leek Tomato Soup

Celery or Celeriac Soup Two Ways

Vietnamese Lemongrass Vegetable Soup

Aigo Bouido

Chilled Pineapple-Mango Soup

Roasted Carrot Gazpacho

Chilled Curried Pea and Coconut Soup

Watermelon Gazpacho with Feta-Yogurt Crema

Golden Cauliflower Soup

This attractive soup is quick and easy to make. It has a beautiful golden color, just enough body, a lovely fragrance, and a little hint of heat from the curry powder. Make sure the turmeric and curry powder are fresh; if too old, they can add bitterness to the soup.

Yields 9 cups
Serves 6
Time: about 50 minutes

3 tablespoons olive oil or coconut oil
1½ cups chopped onions
1½ teaspoons salt, plus more as needed
2 tablespoons curry powder
1 teaspoon ground turmeric
2 cups chopped carrots
7 cups chopped cauliflower
6 cups vegetable stock
¼ cup unsweetened shredded coconut
1 (14-ounce) can coconut milk
¼ cup fresh lime juice
⅓ cup minced fresh cilantro (with stems)

In a soup pot on low heat, warm the oil. Add the onions and a dash of salt. Cover and cook for about 10 minutes, until the onions are golden. Add the curry powder and turmeric and cook for 2 minutes. Add the carrots, cauliflower, vegetable stock, shredded coconut, and salt. Cover and bring to a boil. Lower the heat and simmer until the carrots and cauliflower are tender, about 20 minutes.

Remove from the heat. Stir in the coconut milk. Purée with an immersion blender or in batches in a blender. Add the lime juice and cilantro. Reheat before serving.

VARIATIONS
• This recipe is vegan, but butter or ghee (see sidebar, page 287) can be used in place of olive or coconut oil for a richer soup.
• For textural contrast, set aside some of the cooked cauliflower florets to add to the finished soup before serving.

SERVING AND MENU IDEAS
For extra flavor and a nice color contrast, top each serving with a dollop of yogurt and some chopped cilantro or spinach chiffonade. Toasted shredded coconut also makes a great topping.

Sopa Verde de Elote

This is a lovely, lime-colored herbaceous purée with the subtle tang of tomatillos. Most of the vegetables are cooked as minimally as possible to preserve flavors, color, and nutrition. In winter, thawed frozen corn and peas work fine. Thanks to Diana Kennedy, via Heidi Swanson, for introducing this Mexican soup north of the border, and beyond. This is our version, enjoy.

Yields 8 cups
Serves 4 to 6
Time: 40 minutes

1 poblano pepper
3 tablespoons butter
1 cup diced onions
2 garlic cloves, minced or pressed
1½ teaspoons salt
1 small zucchini, diced (about 1 cup)
2 medium tomatillos, husked and diced
  (about 1 cup)
4 cups corn kernels, fresh or frozen
⅔ cup green peas, fresh or frozen
3½ cups water
½ cup packed coarsely chopped fresh cilantro

Place the poblano pepper on a small baking sheet and broil until it has blistered on all sides. Or place on a wire rack over a gas flame and roast until tender, turning to char all sides. Put it in a small bowl, cover tightly with foil or plastic wrap, and set aside.

Melt the butter in a soup pot. Stir in the onions, garlic, and salt and cook on medium-low heat until the onions are soft, about 10 minutes. Stir in the zucchini and tomatillos, cover, and cook for about 10 minutes, until the zucchini is tender. While the vegetables cook, remove the charred skin, stem, and seeds of the poblano.

Add the poblano, corn, peas, and water to the pot and bring to a boil. Remove from the heat and stir in the cilantro. Purée with an immersion blender, or in a blender, working in batches. Season with additional salt to taste.

SERVING AND MENU IDEAS

Serve this soup as soon as possible and kick it up a notch by topping each bowl with a dollop of crème fraîche or sour cream, or grated cheddar cheese, and more fresh cilantro. A few crumbled corn tortilla chips and a squeeze of fresh lime juice are good additions as well. Stay in a *verde* or "green" mode by pairing this with a Kale, Jicama, and Orange Salad (page 128).

Purée of Parsnip, Carrot, and Celeriac

A lovely soup—creamy without dairy or potatoes. The first spoonful is so good; then you taste all the different flavors as they unfurl on your palate.

These three sturdy root vegetables have become common winter fare in farmers' markets, CSAs, and supermarkets. They are excellent keepers when kept cool and dry, and combine well as a satisfying stick-to-your-ribs winter soup. This soup is vegan, but if you're not, you might like the richness that a couple tablespoons of butter added at the end give it. We advise prepping all the ingredients before you begin to cook the soup.

Yields 8 cups
Serves 4 to 6
Time: 1 hour

2 tablespoons olive oil
2 cups coarsely chopped onions
2 tablespoons chopped garlic
2 teaspoons ground coriander
¼ teaspoon freshly ground black pepper
1½ teaspoons salt
1½ teaspoons dried basil
2 cups diced carrots
1½ cups peeled and diced parsnips
2 cups peeled and chopped celeriac
½ cup peeled and chopped apples
5 cups water

Warm the oil in a soup pot on medium heat. Then add the onions, garlic, coriander, pepper, salt, and dried basil and cook, stirring occasionally, until the onions are soft and translucent, about 6 minutes. Add the carrots, parsnips, celeriac, and apples and cook, stirring occasionally, for another 5 to 10 minutes. Add a splash of water if the vegetables stick to the bottom of the pan. Pour in the water and bring the soup to a boil. Lower the heat and simmer until the vegetables are soft, about 20 minutes.

In a blender or food processor, purée the soup until smooth. Add more water if the soup is too thick.

SERVING AND MENU IDEAS
Serve with Mushroom Barley Salad (page 147), or Mediterranean Potato Salad (page 124), or Farro Pilaf with Cannellini and Arugula (page 317).

Thai Corn Chowder

Ithaca has been carrying on a hot love affair with elegant Thai cuisine for almost thirty years. It's inspired some of our most popular dishes, but we attempt to emulate Thai-style dishes with great humility. This simple, naturally vegan and gluten-free chowder features classic ingredients like potatoes and sweet corn, but simmered with coconut milk, fresh ginger, and aromatic Thai basil and sparked with jalapeño. This soup is good without the cilantro or mint garnishes, but with them, it's divine.

Yields about 8 cups
Serves 4
Time: about 1 hour

1 tablespoon coconut oil or vegetable oil
1½ cups chopped onions
1 fresh hot pepper, minced and seeded for a milder "hot," or ¼ teaspoon cayenne pepper
1 cup chopped red bell peppers
½ teaspoon salt, plus more as needed
2 tablespoons peeled and grated fresh ginger
2½ cups diced potatoes
3 cups vegetable stock
3½ cups fresh or frozen corn kernels (one 1-pound bag frozen)

1 (14-ounce) can unsweetened coconut milk
2 tablespoons fresh lime juice
3 tablespoons chopped fresh basil (Thai basil is best, but Italian basil is fine, too)
Hot pepper sauce or Chinese chili paste (optional)
Chopped fresh cilantro, and/or mint, for garnish (optional)

Warm the oil in a soup pot on medium heat. Add the onions and hot pepper and cook for a couple of minutes. Add the bell peppers and salt and cook, stirring often, until the vegetables soften, about 6 minutes. Add the ginger, potatoes, and stock. Cover and bring to a boil. Reduce the heat and simmer until the potatoes are almost tender, about 5 minutes. Add the corn and simmer for 5 minutes. Add the coconut milk, lime juice, and basil and remove from the heat.

Using a blender or an immersion blender, purée about half the soup. Stir the purée back into the pot. Season with salt to taste, and, if you want it spicier, add some hot pepper sauce or Chinese chili paste.

Garnish with lime, fresh cilantro, and/or mint, if desired.

SERVING AND MENU IDEAS
Serve with Kelp Noodle Salad (page 143) for a nice meal.

Italian Cheese Broth

It's such a waste to throw out the Parmesan and Pecorino Romano rinds left over from grating. These two cheeses are not waxed and the rinds can easily be saved in the freezer in a plastic bag until you have enough collected to make broth. Check with the cheese department of your grocery store or supermarket—many will sell their leftover cheese rinds at an economical price, which can give you a head start with your collection.

This cheese broth has an enticing aroma and a rich taste with lots of depth, and it can be the versatile base for any number of easy and delectable soups. . . . We give you three ideas.

Yields about 10 cups
Prep time: 20 minutes
Simmering time: 1½ hours

1 tablespoon olive oil
1 large onion, coarsely chopped
1 head garlic, cut in half horizontally to expose the cloves
1 cup dry white wine
Handful of fresh thyme sprigs
Handful of fresh parsley sprigs
3 bay leaves
1 teaspoon whole black peppercorns
1 pound Parmesan and/or Pecorino Romano cheese rinds
12 cups water

In a large soup pot on medium heat, warm the olive oil. Add the chopped onions and halved garlic head and cook for 5 to 6 minutes, stirring frequently, until the onion is translucent and the exposed sides of the garlic are browned. Add the wine and cook for about 5 minutes, scraping the bottom of the pot to loosen any browned onion. Add the thyme, parsley, bay leaves, peppercorns, cheese rinds, and water.

Bring the water to a near boil, then reduce the heat, cover the pot, and simmer gently for about 1½ hours. Stir once in a while to prevent the cheese rinds from sticking to the bottom of the pot. The broth will reduce by a couple of cups.

Strain the broth through a colander, pressing on the solids to release all the tasty liquid. Use the broth to make one of the suggested soups below, or use it in a fabulous soup you invent.

CHEESE BROTH SOUPS

- **With pasta, peas, and spinach:** Start with about 4 cups cheese broth. Add some filini pasta (*filini* means "little cat whiskers" in Italian) or other small, fine pasta (about 1 cup, 4 ounces dry). You can cook the pasta first in water as usual, or cook the pasta in the broth (the pasta will thicken the broth and reduce the amount of liquid a bit), or add about 2 cups leftover pasta. Add about 1 cup green peas, 2 cups baby spinach, and a tiny pinch of nutmeg. Season with salt and pepper to taste. Serve sprinkled with a little grated Parmesan or Pecorino Romano cheese.

- **With potatoes and cabbage:** In a couple of teaspoons of olive oil, sauté a thinly sliced small onion and a potato, peeled and cut into thin bite-size pieces, for a few minutes, until the sliced onions are translucent. Add about 4 cups cheese broth and simmer until the potato pieces are tender. Meanwhile, add half a small mild red hot pepper, seeded and minced, and some shredded cabbage (a cup or two—you can use packaged slaw mix for convenience). Season with salt and pepper to taste and sprinkle a little grated Parmesan or Pecorino Romano cheese on top.

- **With rice and greens:** Sauté a thinly sliced small onion and about 2 cups finely chopped endive or escarole in 2 teaspoons olive oil. Add about 4 cups cheese broth and a cup or two of cooked rice. Season with salt and pepper to taste. Serve sprinkled with a little grated Parmesan or Pecorino Romano cheese.

SERVING AND MENU IDEAS

Any of the Cheese Broth Soups make a satisfying easy meal with White Bean and Olive Sandwich (page 83) and a crisp salad, such as Spring Greens and Vegetables with Shallot Vinaigrette (page 139) or Kale, Jicama, and Orange Salad (page 128). Finish your meal Italian style with fresh fruit and Easy Lemon Butter Cookies (page 353) or Espresso Shortbread (page 355).

Smoky Split Pea Soup

This beautiful, unconventional soup is thick, dense, full of vegetables, and deeply flavorful: all the features of a hearty wintertime favorite to sustain you on a chilly day. This is an East-West soup made with exquisitely smooth yellow split peas, and gets its smoky character from spicy chipotle peppers in adobo sauce, toasted cumin, and heady smoked paprika. We recommend using *chana dal*, Indian yellow split peas, found in the international section of the supermarket or in an Indian specialty shop, which have a buttery, silky texture when puréed.

A squeeze of lemon juice and chopped fresh cilantro will finish each bowl of soup with a perfect piquancy.

Serves 6
Hands-on time at start: 20 minutes;
  at end: 15 minutes
Simmering time to cook split peas: 1 hour;
  to finish the soup: 20 minutes
Total time: 1 hour, 30 minutes

1½ cups yellow split peas or chana dal, rinsed
2 bay leaves
8 cups water or vegetable stock
2 tablespoons vegetable oil
2 cups coarsely chopped onions
2 tablespoons chopped garlic
1 teaspoon salt
1½ cups chopped celery
1½ cups sliced carrots
½ teaspoon ground turmeric
2 to 3 teaspoons smoked paprika
1 teaspoon chipotle peppers in adobo sauce, chopped
2 teaspoons toasted and ground cumin seeds
Freshly ground black pepper
Lemon wedges, for garnish
Chopped fresh cilantro, for garnish

In a large pot, cook the split peas and bay leaves in the water or stock until soft, about 1 hour.

In a separate large heavy-bottomed pot on medium-high heat, warm the oil, add the onions, garlic, and salt, and sauté until the onions are soft and translucent, about 6 minutes. Add the celery and carrots and a splash of water, cover, lower the heat, and cook for several minutes. Stir in the turmeric, smoked paprika, chipotle, and cumin and remove from the heat while the peas cook.

When the split peas are soft, add them to the vegetables along with the cooking water. Remove and discard the bay leaves. Simmer the soup for about 20 minutes, making sure the vegetables are thoroughly cooked. Remove 2 cups of the soup from the pot and purée it in a food processor or blender, taking care not to splatter the hot liquid. Stir the purée back into the pot and season the soup with additional salt and black pepper to taste.

Serve with lemon wedges and chopped fresh cilantro.

SERVING AND MENU IDEAS
Serve this soup with a light salad with some fruity element, such as Greens with Citrus-Date Dressing (page 126) or Mango-Spinach Salad with Spicy Dressing (page 118).

Hot-and-Sour Mushroom Soup

Warming, piquant, and fortifying, this is our elixir for cold, cold nights or when you feel your resistance to colds and flu wavering.

The key to this lovely soup is the stock, which will smell heavenly as it simmers. We decided to ramp up the mushroom flavor and aromatics by using a quartet of mushrooms—dried shiitake in the stock and a blend of fresh cremini, shiitake, and oyster mushrooms in the finished soup—however, any group of fresh mushrooms will do. Today there were button, brown beech, and hen-of-the-woods mushrooms at the market. Happy foraging!

Yields 8 cups
Serves 4 to 8
Time: 1 hour to prep and simmer the stock,
  30 minutes to finish the soup

STOCK
3 cups coarsely chopped onions
2 tablespoons vegetable oil
4 cups thickly sliced carrots
1 cup sliced celery
10 whole garlic cloves
⅓ cup sliced fresh ginger (from about a 3 x 1-inch piece)
½ teaspoon salt
2 large bay leaves
2 star anise pods (up to 4 if you love anise flavor)
½ ounce dried shiitake mushrooms
8 cups water

SOUP
12 ounces sliced fresh mushrooms; use a blend of three types
¼ teaspoon ground white pepper★
¼ cup soy sauce
¼ cup rice vinegar
2 tablespoons cornstarch (optional)

2 cups thinly sliced bok choy or napa cabbage (slice both green and white parts horizontally)

TOPPING IDEAS
Cubed silken tofu
Sliced scallions
Bean sprouts

★White pepper is quite hot. We call for a very moderate amount—add more at the end to taste. It is also quite expensive if purchased in a jar in the spice section of the market. However, some supermarkets and food co-ops carry it in bulk at a fraction of the price.

Make the stock: Sauté the onions in the oil until they begin to brown, about 10 minutes. Add the carrots, celery, garlic cloves, and ginger and sauté for another 5 to 7 minutes. Add the salt, bay leaves, star anise, shiitakes, and water and bring to a boil. Reduce the heat and simmer for 45 minutes.

When the stock is finished, strain it through a colander and return the clear stock to the pot. You should have a little over 6 cups of strained stock. Stir in the sliced fresh mushrooms, white pepper, and soy sauce and simmer for 20 minutes. Add the vinegar, or if you'd like the stock to be thickened a bit, whisk the cornstarch into the rice vinegar until it dissolves and then stir it into the soup and heat until the soup thickens slightly. Avoid boiling the soup once you've added cornstarch, because cornstarch will thin out at a boil. Stir in the bok choy just before serving so it will stay bright green and crunchy.

Serve the soup with one or more toppings, if you'd like.

SERVING AND MENU IDEAS
Serve with Jeweled Rice (page 321) for an eclectic but satisfying combination of flavors.

Roasted Fennel and Leek Tomato Soup

Here is a smooth, flavorful soup, especially interesting because of the roasted vegetables. We could have called this "waste not, want not" soup. One of the frustrations of working with fresh fennel and leeks is that less than half of each vegetable winds up in the pot. We thought it a pity to once again have to toss away those flavorful and aromatic stalks, leaves, and fronds. On a bit of a mission, we found ways to use pretty much the whole plant, arriving at this light, full-flavored puréed soup.

Some of us like to make a gremolata (see sidebar, page 99) to garnish this soup with and consider it an integral part, giving an extra burst of flavor. Others prefer the creamy, smooth soup just as it is.

Yields 8 cups
Serves 4 to 8
Time: 90 minutes

2 or 3 fennel bulbs
2 fat leeks
10 unpeeled garlic cloves, smashed
2 bay leaves

6 cups water
3 tablespoons olive oil
1½ teaspoons salt
1 teaspoon ground fennel seeds
¼ teaspoon freshly ground black pepper
6 plum tomatoes, sliced in half
1 (15-ounce) can chopped tomatoes

Thinly slice the fennel bulbs (about 6 cups sliced) and set aside in a large bowl. Roughly chop the stalks, stems, cores, and bottoms and put into a stockpot.

Rinse the leeks very well to remove any sand. Slice the white bulb and tender part of the green stalks crosswise (about 4 cups) and add to the large bowl. Coarsely chop the root ends and tough, dark green leaves and add to the stockpot.

Put the garlic into the stockpot with the bay leaves and water and bring to a rapid boil. Reduce to a simmer and cook for about 40 minutes.

While the stock simmers, roast the vegetables: Preheat the oven to 400°F. Toss the sliced fennel and leeks with 2 tablespoons of the olive oil and the salt, ground fennel, and black pepper. Spread out on a baking sheet.

Toss the sliced plum tomatoes with the remaining 1 tablespoon olive oil and sprinkle with the salt. Spread out on a separate baking sheet or pan.

Place both baking sheets in the oven and roast for 30 minutes, or until the fennel and leeks begin to brown, and the tomatoes start to dry and pucker.

When the roasted vegetables are done, strain the stock. Working in batches, purée the roasted vegetables in a blender with the canned tomatoes and about 3 cups of the stock. Purée until very smooth. Reheat the soup on the stovetop just before serving.

SERVING AND MENU IDEAS
Serve as a first course with Pasta with Spinach and Apricots (page 230) or Pasta Carbonara with Zucchini (page 229).

GREMOLATA

A dollop of this quick little gremolata on each bowl of soup gives it an extra bit of interest and flavor.

  ½ cup finely chopped fresh fennel fronds or fresh basil leaves

  2 tablespoons finely grated lemon or orange zest

In a small bowl, mix the chopped fennel fronds with the lemon or orange zest. Serve each bowl of soup topped with about a teaspoon of Gremolata.

Celery or Celeriac Soup Two Ways

Here are two simple and lovely soups. First, you make the basic soup with either celery or celeriac. And then you finish it in one of two ways. The Gorgonzola and lemon soup has a distinctive, delicate flavor and an elegant fragrance. The rosemary and cheddar version tastes heartier, but is an uncomplicated and comforting treat for anyone who loves potatoes and cheese.

Celeriac, also called celery root, is a gnarly, hairy, bulbous root that looks like it might be cultivated by Professor Sprout as a remedy for Hogwarts mischief. But once peeled and trimmed, it has a subtle flavor and perfume similar to celery, but also unique.

Different cheeses vary in saltiness, so taste the soup and adjust for salt at the end. If you purée in a blender, these soups will be velvety-smooth. If you use an immersion blender, the texture will be smooth with little bits to chew on.

Yields 8 cups
Serves 4 to 8
Time: 55 minutes

2 cups chopped onions
4 cups thinly sliced celery or peeled, diced celeriac
  (1½ pounds whole)
1 teaspoon salt
1 tablespoon olive oil
4 cups water
3 cups peeled cubed white or yellow potatoes

ROSEMARY AND CHEDDAR

1 tablespoon minced fresh rosemary leaves
4 ounces cream cheese
6 ounces extra-sharp cheddar cheese, shredded
  (about 1½ cups)
Freshly ground black pepper

GORGONZOLA AND LEMON

4 ounces cream cheese
6 ounces Gorgonzola or blue cheese, crumbled
Finely grated zest of 1 lemon (about 1 teaspoon)
1 tablespoon fresh lemon juice (add more to taste
  to the finished soup)
Freshly ground black pepper

In a covered soup pot on medium heat, cook the onions, celery or celeriac, and salt in the olive oil for 15 minutes, stirring occasionally. If you're making the rosemary-cheddar variation, add the rosemary for the last 5 minutes. You want the onions to stay pale. Golden is good, but if the onions begin to brown, reduce the heat. When the onions have softened, add the water and potatoes, cover, and bring to a simmer. Cook for about 20 minutes, or until the potatoes and celery or celeriac are tender.

When the vegetables in the soup pot are tender, purée the soup until smooth. For a silky smooth soup, purée in batches in a regular blender; for a smooth-with-little-bits-of-vegetables soup, purée with an immersion blender. Add the ingredients of the version you're making, and purée until smooth. Reheat until hot, but not boiling, stirring frequently. Season with black pepper and more salt to taste, and more lemon juice if you'd like the lemon version to be more lemony.

SERVING AND MENU IDEAS
Serve with a light salad such as Belgian Endive Citrus Salad with Gremolata (page 129), or Microgreens Salad with Sweet Carrot Dressing (page 117).

Vietnamese Lemongrass Vegetable Soup

Lemongrass adds a fragrant citrus flavor to many Southeast Asian dishes. Here it provides a subtle yet noticeable background for vegetables and aromatic mint. Reminiscent of vegetable *pho*—but without the signature rice noodles—this light, refreshing soup has complex but distinct flavors and stimulating aromas. The stock is a medium tan color, and the mushrooms look handsome with the carrots and green snow peas, celery, mint, and scallions. It's substantial and filling and you won't miss the noodles.

Yields 9 cups
Serves 4 to 6
Time: 45 minutes

4 fresh lemongrass stalks
2 quarts water
2 tablespoons vegetable oil
2 garlic cloves, minced or pressed
1 tablespoon peeled and grated fresh ginger
1 cup chopped onions
1 cup chopped celery
2 cups chopped carrots
1 teaspoon salt
3 cups sliced mushrooms★
2 cups sugar snap or snow peas, strings and stem ends removed, cut in half
½ to 1 teaspoon chili paste (optional)
⅓ cup fresh mint leaves, torn or cut in half
4 teaspoons fresh lime juice
⅔ cup chopped scallions

★Fresh shiitake or enoki mushrooms are tasty here, but regular white ones work well, too. Leave enoki or other small mushrooms whole and remove and discard the stems of fresh shiitakes.

Cut each lemongrass stalk in half lengthwise, lay on a cutting surface, and press with the side of your chef's knife to help release the fragrant oils. Cut the stalks crosswise into 3- to 4-inch segments so they will more easily fit your pot. Put the lemongrass segments in the pot with the water, cover, and bring to a boil. Lower the heat, and simmer for 30 minutes.

While the stock is simmering, prep and cook the soup vegetables and seasonings. In a soup pot, warm the oil and cook the garlic and ginger for a moment before adding the onions, celery, carrots, and salt. Cook, stirring often, until the vegetables are just tender, about 6 minutes. Add the mushrooms and continue to cook for a minute or two.

When the stock has simmered for 30 minutes, strain it, add it to the soup pot, and bring to a simmer. Add the peas and the chili paste, if using, and cook until the peas are crisp-tender, 2 to 3 minutes. When you are ready to serve the soup, stir in the mint, lime juice, and scallions.

Bowls of this soup are pretty garnished with mint leaves.

SERVING AND MENU IDEA
Serve with Banh Mi Chay Sandwich (page 78) for a Vietnamese-style meal.

Aigo Bouido

Aigo bouido (literally "boiled water" in Provençal, and also called *aigo boulido*) is a simple soup full of generosity. Not only do you use 6 whole heads of garlic, but also a generous mix of herbs and spices. No need to be tidy and precise; measurements don't have to be exact. Roasting the garlic makes for a more mellow flavor, but there is no doubt that this is a garlic lover's soup.

A healing and comforting soup for whatever ails you, aigo bouido is also a perfect first course for a more formal occasion.

Serves 4
Time: 1 hour, 10 minutes

ROASTED GARLIC
4 heads garlic
1 tablespoon olive oil
Sprinkling of salt

STOCK
1 teaspoon salt
2 tablespoons olive oil
2 cups coarsely chopped onions
1 cup coarsely chopped celery
1 cup coarsely chopped carrots
2 heads garlic, outer papery skin removed, sliced in
  half crosswise
½ cup coarsely chopped parsley with stems
4 sprigs fresh thyme
½ teaspoon whole black peppercorns
¼ teaspoon ground turmeric
1 teaspoon ground coriander
⅛ teaspoon crushed red pepper flakes
6 cups water

2½ cups cubed potatoes (½-inch cubes)
1 rounded tablespoon minced fresh thyme
¼ cup chopped fresh parsley leaves

Preheat the oven to 400°F. Remove the loose outer papery skins of the garlic and cut off just the tips of the cloves. Toss the garlic with the olive oil and salt.

Wrap the garlic in aluminum foil and roast in the oven for 30 to 40 minutes. After 30 minutes, check for doneness. A sharp knife should easily pierce the garlic and the outer skin will have begun to loosen. When done, set the garlic on a cutting board to cool.

While the garlic is roasting, make the stock. In a large soup pot, sauté the onions and salt in the olive oil for a few minutes. Add the celery, carrots, garlic, parsley, and thyme. Stir in the peppercorns, turmeric, coriander, and red pepper flakes. Increase the heat and add the water. When the stock comes to a rapid simmer, reduce the heat to maintain a simmer and cook for 30 minutes.

Prep the potatoes and set aside, covered with water, in a bowl. Mince the thyme and chop the parsley and set aside.

When the stock has simmered for 30 minutes, strain it through a sieve into a separate pot, pressing on the vegetables to extract the maximum liquid. Set aside 2 cups of stock, and pour the rest back into the soup pot. Drain the potatoes and add them to the pot and bring to a boil. Reduce to a simmer and cook until the potatoes are tender, 7 to 10 minutes.

While the potatoes are simmering, remove the roasted garlic from its skin. This is the most labor-intensive part of making the soup. Press the skins to squeeze out the soft garlic. Some cloves may pop out easily, while you may need to press others down on one end with a knife and push out the garlic. Place the soft garlic in a blender with the reserved stock. When the potatoes are tender, scoop out a cupful and add to the blender. Purée until thick and smooth. Pour into the soup pot. Stir in the minced thyme and additional salt, if needed.

Garnish each bowl of soup with chopped parsley.

SERVING AND MENU IDEAS

For a simple meal, serve Aigo Bouido with a crisp baguette, cheese, and salad. Or serve with Lentil Salad with Baby Greens and Oranges (page 142), Baby Arugula Salad with Crusted Chèvre and Pears (page 114), Pizza with Greens (page 275), or Asparagus with Fried Eggs and Sizzled Shallots (page 183).

Chilled Pineapple-Mango Soup

This oh-so-refreshing soup is a lovely start for any summer meal, a cooling intermission between courses, or an accompaniment to spicy entrées. This is a rich soup; a good serving size is ⅔ cup.

The art of muddling is easily learned, just be careful not to overmuddle delicate leaves like mint and basil, because the end result will be bitter. Press the leaves, don't shred them.

Yields 4 cups
Serves 6
Prep time: 20 minutes
Chilling time: at least 20 minutes

1 ounce fresh mint, stemmed (about 1½ cups)
1 ounce fresh basil, stemmed (about 1½ cups)
1 cup coconut water★
2 cups fresh pineapple chunks
1 cup chopped fresh mango (preferably the small yellow, champagne variety)
½ cup unsweetened coconut milk

★Look for pure coconut water, without any flavorings or additives. The package ingredient list should read: fresh coconut and water.

Place the herbs and coconut water in a bowl. Using a wooden spoon, muddler, or pestle, press the herbs into the coconut water and against the side of the bowl until the herbs wilt and shrink in volume. The goal is to infuse the coconut water with the flavor and aroma of mint and basil. Be gentle: the coconut water may turn cloudy, but there should not be any green bits floating in the solution. Set the bowl aside while you prepare the fruit.

Put the pineapple and mango pieces and the coconut milk into a blender. Strain the muddled coconut water into the blender, gently squeezing the herbs to extract the maximum amount of flavored liquid. Purée until smooth. Refrigerate for at least 20 minutes before serving; the purée will thicken as it chills.

SERVING AND MENU IDEAS
Serve with Burmese Tohu Thoke (page 194) or Two Potato Tomato Curry with Yellow Split Pea Dal (page 194).

Roasted Carrot Gazpacho

The main essence of this soup is carrots sweetened by roasting and blended into a gorgeous orange purée. Mint, cilantro, jalapeño, garlic, red wine vinegar, and olive oil each contribute to its complexity of flavors. The topping of diced raw veggies and herbs gives the soup a contrast of smooth and crunchy textures and flavors.

Gazpacho is a summertime favorite because chilled soup is so refreshing. Of course, at Moosewood, ovens are on year-round, but roasting carrots in summer may be a challenge if your kitchen isn't cool. No wonder people in rural areas built outdoor summer kitchens. It takes a couple of hours to chill the gazpacho thoroughly, so make it far enough ahead to serve it cold.

Serves 4 to 6
Time: 55 minutes, including roasting time
Chilling time: 2 hours

SOUP
4 cups carrots cut into 2-inch chunks
4 tablespoons olive oil
1 teaspoon salt
¼ teaspoon freshly ground black pepper
1 cup chopped red cherry or grape tomatoes
¼ cup chopped fresh mint
¼ cup chopped fresh cilantro
1 tablespoon seeded and chopped jalapeño or
 other hot pepper, or more to taste
1 garlic clove, chopped
2 tablespoons red wine vinegar or fresh lemon
 juice
2 cups water

TOPPING
1 cup chopped cucumbers
1 avocado, pitted, peeled, and chopped
2 tablespoons chopped fresh mint
2 tablespoons chopped fresh cilantro
Fresh lemon juice
Olive oil

Preheat the oven to 425°F. In a medium bowl, toss the carrots with 2 tablespoons of the olive oil, the salt, and the black pepper. Spread the carrots in a roasting pan, cover with aluminum foil, and roast for 20 minutes. Remove the foil, stir, and return to the oven for 15 to 20 minutes, until the carrots are tender and can be easily pierced with a paring knife.

Place the remaining soup ingredients in a blender. When the carrots have finished cooking, add them to the blender and whirl until smooth. Add more water if the purée is too thick. (It may be best to do this in two batches.)

Chill for at least 2 hours, less if you have room in your refrigerator to chill the soup more quickly in a large flat baking pan.

In a small bowl, mix together the topping ingredients with a squirt of lemon juice and a drizzle of olive oil.

Serve the soup in cups or small bowls, topped with the avocado-cucumber mixture.

SERVING AND MENU IDEA
Perfect on a warm day with Spring Greens and Vegetables with Shallot Vinaigrette (page 139).

Chilled Curried Pea and Coconut Soup

This chilled soup blends the sweet flavors from an early summer garden: peas, cilantro, basil, scallions, and spinach. It's a beautiful green soup, rich but light, full-flavored but not heavy-handed, and with a great synergy where no one ingredient dominates. Of course, if it actually is early summer when you make this soup and you have sweet peas in your garden, use fresh. It's also lovely served warm.

Don't be daunted by all the stemming, chopping, toasting, and grinding required; you'll have time to keep prepping during cooking. If using an immersion blender to purée the soup, for the smoothest consistency, chop the chard or spinach into fairly small pieces.

This soup will stay fresh for a few days in the fridge, so it can be made ahead of time.

Serves 4 to 8
**Preparation time: 60 minutes (includes
  15 minutes cooling time before puréeing)**
Chilling time: at least 3 hours

2 tablespoons vegetable oil
2 cups chopped onions
1 teaspoon salt
1½ teaspoons coriander seeds★
2½ teaspoons curry powder
1½ tablespoons raw white jasmine or basmati rice
¼ cup chopped scallions
1 cup water
1 quart light vegetable stock★★
1 pound frozen green peas (about 3 cups)
4 cups chopped spinach or green chard, large
  stems removed
1 cup unsweetened coconut milk
½ cup loosely packed coarsely chopped fresh
  cilantro leaves
½ cup loosely packed coarsely chopped fresh basil
  leaves

★Use about the same amount of preground coriander. Although ground spices are denser than whole seeds, preground spices are less flavorful.
★★An easy, homemade stock made from vegetable scraps of onions, carrots, scallion tops, parsley, and cilantro stems simmered in a quart of water for about 30 minutes is a light stock that's perfect for this soup. If you use a packaged stock, dilute it so its flavor won't overpower the delicate and fresh flavor of the soup: use half stock, half water.

In a large soup pot on medium heat, warm the oil for a minute or two. Add the onions and salt and sauté for about 6 minutes until the onions become translucent. While the onions cook, toast the coriander seeds lightly in a small skillet on low heat for about a minute, shaking the skillet once or twice so the spices don't burn. Grind the coriander and stir it into the onions along with the curry powder, rice, and scallions.

Add the water and simmer for about 10 minutes, until the rice is cooked. Pour in the vegetable stock and bring to a simmer. Add the peas. When the stock returns to a simmer, cook the peas for a minute or two until just tender. Remove the pot from the heat. Stir in the spinach or chard, coconut milk, cilantro, and basil.

Cool for about 5 minutes. If you have an immersion blender, you can purée the soup at this point. If you use a container blender, to avoid "eruptions," cool the soup for 15 to 20 minutes before puréeing. Purée until very smooth. Season with salt to taste.

The soup is good warm, but we prefer it cold. Refrigerate, uncovered, for 3 hours or overnight until the soup is thoroughly chilled.

Pour into soup cups or bowls and garnish with fresh basil or cilantro leaves.

SERVING AND MENU IDEAS
A nasturtium floating on top is gorgeous against the green soup. This is a perfect starter for a summer meal or component of an Indian, Southeast Asian, or Caribbean dinner. Pack it up in a thermos for a picnic or lunch.

Watermelon Gazpacho with Feta-Yogurt Crema

This chilled soup is a light fruity purée with diced vegetables. It's a great way to cool off on a hot summer day. Gazpacho is sometimes defined as a fruit soup. With sweet and refreshing watermelon, it's perfect for the first course of a sunny brunch or supper.

Yields 5 cups
Serves 4
Prep time: 35 minutes
Chilling time: at least 1 hour

PURÉE
2½ cups coarsely chopped seedless watermelon
1 cup chopped ripe tomatoes
1½ cups peeled, seeded, and chopped cucumbers
¼ cup chopped fresh hot peppers, seeded for a
   milder "hot"
1 teaspoon apple cider vinegar
1 tablespoon balsamic vinegar
½ teaspoon salt
¼ teaspoon freshly ground black pepper

DICED VEGETABLES
3 cups diced seedless watermelon
1 cup peeled, seeded, and diced cucumbers

CREMA
½ cup crumbled feta cheese
¼ cup plain Greek yogurt or sour cream
3 tablespoons milk

Toasted almonds, coarsely chopped, for garnish

In a blender, purée the watermelon, tomatoes, cucumbers, hot peppers, vinegars, salt, and black pepper until smooth. Add more salt to taste and chill the soup for at least an hour before serving.

In a small bowl, mix together the diced watermelon and cucumber and set aside in the refrigerator.

Prepare the crema: In a small bowl, mash together the feta and the Greek yogurt or sour cream. Whisk in the milk. Refrigerate.

When you're ready to serve, spoon diced watermelon and cucumbers into individual bowls and pour the purée over them. Top each portion with some of the crema and sprinkle on the almonds, or serve the toppings on the side and let each person garnish their own soup.

SERVING AND MENU IDEAS
Garnish with chopped fresh cilantro and/or mint. To continue the theme of summer abundance, serve with Summer Squash and Tomato Tian (page 306).

Greens with Apricots Times Two

Sugar Snap Peas with Coconut and Lime

Baby Arugula Salad with Crusted Chèvre and Pears

Microgreens Salad with Sweet Carrot Dressing

Mango-Spinach Salad with Spicy Dressing

Zucchini Slaw with Toasted Buckwheat and Feta

Wax Bean and Radish Salad with Buttermilk Dressing

Za'atar Yogurt and Cucumber Salad

Jason's Fresh Fennel and Apple Slaw

Mediterranean Potato Salad

Roasted Eggplant Salad with Chermoula Sauce

Greens with Citrus-Date Dressing

Roasted Cauliflower Salad with Lemon-Tahini Sauce

Kale, Jicama, and Orange Salad

Belgian Endive Citrus Salad with Gremolata

Winter Chopped Salad

Greens with Apricots Times Two

If you're a fan of apricots, check out this salad that combines the concentrated flavor and sweetness of the dried fruit with the succulence and tanginess of the fresh. Mixed greens are a good foil and contrast in texture, as are the toasted nuts. The thick dressing has a chutney-like quality.

Serves 4
Time: 30 minutes

8 dried apricots
4 ripe fresh apricots (more if your apricots are small)
1 tablespoon chopped shallots
Juice of 1 lemon (2 to 3 tablespoons)
½ teaspoon salt
½ teaspoon Dijon-style mustard
1 teaspoon apple cider vinegar or white wine vinegar
¼ cup water or apricot soaking liquid
3 tablespoons hazelnut oil or olive oil
2 teaspoons chopped fresh tarragon, or 1 teaspoon dried
Freshly ground black pepper

6 cups mixed salad greens (about 5 ounces)
⅓ cup coarsely chopped toasted hazelnuts (optional)

Preheat the oven to 400°F. Place the dried apricots in a small bowl and cover with boiling water. Set aside.

Cut the fresh apricots into halves or quarters and roast on a baking sheet until soft but not falling apart. Depending on the firmness and size of the apricots and the directness of the heat, it takes between 15 and 25 minutes to roast the apricots.

In a blender, combine the softened dried apricots, the shallots, lemon juice, salt, mustard, vinegar, water, oil, and tarragon and purée until smooth. Season with more salt and/or vinegar and some pepper to taste.

In a serving bowl, toss the greens with dressing (there may be more dressing than you want for this dish; leftover dressing will keep in the refrigerator for a couple of weeks). Slice the roasted apricots and arrange them on top of the greens. Sprinkle with toasted nuts, if desired.

SERVING AND MENU IDEAS
Serve this warm weather salad with Summer Stir-Fry with Halloumi (page 215), Pasta Carbonara with Zucchini (page 229), or Summer Squash and Tomato Tian (page 306).

Sugar Snap Peas with Coconut and Lime

Green, green, and green—we love pea season! Edible podded peas, like sugar snap or snow peas, are the basis for a quickly prepared salad with a distinctive crunch and the fragrance of coconut, lime, and mint. Sugar snaps are still good when the peas inside have fattened up a bit, while snow peas are best when the pods are flat. Snap peas are usually sweeter than snow peas, so they tend to be our first choice, but snow peas are so tender and satisfying. Pea shoots add another shot of pea flavor, and an interesting texture. If you want green color and garden freshness with your meal, this is another quick, easy, and tasty side dish.

Yields 4 cups
Serves 3 or 4
Time: 15 to 20 minutes

1 pound sugar snap peas or snow peas, stem ends and strings removed
2 tablespoons coconut oil
⅓ cup unsweetened coconut flakes★
3 tablespoons chopped scallions
3 tablespoons chopped fresh mint
1 tablespoon finely grated lime zest
½ teaspoon salt
2 to 3 tablespoons fresh lime juice
2 cups pea shoots (optional)

★Coconut flakes are heftier than shredded coconut. Look for them in the bulk section of supermarkets and natural food stores.

Steam the peas for about 2 minutes until tender, but still crisp. In a bowl large enough to accommodate all the ingredients, toss the steamed peas with the coconut oil and set aside.

Toast the coconut flakes in a dry pan, stirring often, until the edges are just lightly browning, 2 to 3 minutes. Transfer to a dish to cool.

Stir the scallions, mint, lime zest, and salt into the peas. Just before serving, add the lime juice; start with the smaller amount and add more to taste. Top with the toasted coconut and, if using, the pea shoots.

SERVING AND MENU IDEAS
A good side for Tomato-Sesame Tofu Scramble (page 21), Jamaican Jerk Tempeh Patties (page 200), or Asian Filo Rolls (page 198).

Baby Arugula Salad with Crusted Chèvre and Pears

This salad is a delightful ensemble of crunchy, creamy, smooth, sweet, peppery, and tart. The sharp flavor of arugula is mellowed by sliced pears and a simple lime and Dijon vinaigrette. Savory balls of chèvre baked in panko crumbs and a drizzle of olive oil pull everything together.

You can easily make your own sweet spiced nuts to top this salad, and you'll be happy you've done it. You'll find a recipe in the sidebar on page 115, or try Laura's Spiced Nuts (page 59). Make the nuts in advance, or get them into the oven first and prep the crusted chèvre while they bake; remove the nuts to let them cool, then raise the oven temperature to bake the crusted chèvre.

Serves 4
Time: 30 minutes; if preparing nuts, 45 minutes

CRUSTED CHÈVRE
8 ounces plain chèvre
¾ cup plain panko bread crumbs
1 tablespoon olive oil

DRESSING
¼ cup fresh lime juice
1 teaspoon Dijon mustard
½ cup extra-virgin olive oil
½ teaspoon salt
½ teaspoon freshly ground black pepper
6 cups rinsed and dried baby arugula
1 ripe Bosc, Bartlett, or Anjou pear, thinly sliced
1½ cups spiced nuts (see sidebar, opposite)

First, prepare the crusted chèvre. Preheat the oven to 400°F. Lightly oil a baking sheet.

Roll heaping teaspoons of chèvre in the panko to fully cover each 1-inch ball and place on the baking sheet; it should yield 16 to 20 balls. Drizzle each with a bit of olive oil. Bake for 8 to 10 minutes, until the chèvre is warm and the panko lightly crisp.

While the chèvre is baking, make the dressing: Whisk together the lime juice, mustard, olive oil, salt, and pepper. In a bowl, toss the arugula and sliced pears with the dressing. Portion the salad onto individual salad plates, if you like.

Serve the salad topped with the warm crusted chèvre and spiced nuts.

SERVING AND MENU IDEAS
A salad this versatile and lovable can be served with all manner of main dishes, or by itself for lunch.

SPICED NUTS

$\frac{1}{8}$ cup water

$\frac{1}{4}$ cup sugar

$\frac{1}{8}$ teaspoon ground cardamom

$\frac{1}{4}$ teaspoon ground cinnamon

$\frac{1}{4}$ teaspoon salt

$\frac{1}{4}$ teaspoon freshly ground black pepper

$1\frac{1}{2}$ cups pecans or walnuts

Preheat the oven to 350°F. In a small saucepan, bring the water, sugar, cardamom, cinnamon, salt, and pepper to a boil. Stir at a simmer for a minute until the sugar has dissolved. Add the nuts and stir gently to coat well with the syrup. With a slotted spoon, lift out the nuts and spread them on an oiled baking sheet. Bake for 10 to 15 minutes, until browned. Stir once after about 5 minutes of baking. Stir again when you remove them from the oven. Cool to room temperature.

Microgreens Salad with Sweet Carrot Dressing

The tiny, very young leaves of tender microgreens can be a bit pricey, but they are intensely flavored and nutrient-rich, the pure expression of new growth and the essence of spring. They have a good mix of textures and are lovely looking.

The carrot dressing is thick so it will cling to delicate greens and sprouts and is a bit sweet to contrast with the sharpness of radishes and some of the sprouts.

Yields about 1 cup dressing; about 8 cups salad
Serves 4 to 6
Time: 30 minutes

SWEET CARROT DRESSING

1 cup shredded carrots
1 tablespoon soy sauce
1 teaspoon dark sesame oil
1 tablespoon peeled and grated fresh ginger
2 tablespoons rice vinegar or apple cider vinegar
2 tablespoons chopped scallions
¼ cup vegetable oil
½ teaspoon salt
2 teaspoons brown sugar
2 tablespoons mirin (optional)★

SALAD

2 cups microgreens (about 1 ounce)
1 cup pea shoots
4 cups tender lettuce, such as Boston, Bibb, or oak leaf lettuce mixed with watercress or mesclun
1 cup small sprouts, such as radish, alfalfa, sunflower, or a mixture
4 thinly sliced radishes

★Mirin is optional, but we highly recommend it for the way it smoothes out the dressing and kicks up the flavor a notch.

Put all the dressing ingredients into a blender and whirl until smooth and thick.

Prepare the salad greens. The microgreens are perfect as they are. You may wish to cut the pea shoots in half if they are too long to be bite-size. Lettuce should be cut or ripped to bite-size pieces. The small sprouts should be pulled apart so they are not in clumps and can be distributed through the salad. Toss everything together.

Heap the salad onto individual plates, top with sliced radishes, and pass the dressing.

SERVING AND MENU IDEAS
Microgreens Salad goes nicely with Kale and Walnut Risotto (page 173), Pizza with Roasted Eggplant and Plum Tomatoes (page 274), or Spring Potpie (page 168).

Mango-Spinach Salad with Spicy Dressing

We love summer and feel at our most inventive when we're thinking up new salads. Presented with a bounty of vegetables so fresh, we often think that the simplest preparation is the best. Chili powder colors this dressing a lovely warm red-orange, creating a festive dish that's also fast and easy to prepare.

Serves 2 as an entrée salad; 4 as a side salad
Time: 20 minutes

SPICY DRESSING
1 teaspoon chili powder
1 garlic clove, minced or pressed
½ cup olive oil
2 tablespoons fresh lemon juice
Pinch of salt
Dash of freshly ground black pepper

4 cups baby spinach and/or arugula
1 ripe mango, peeled and sliced
½ cup lightly toasted pepitas (pumpkin seeds)

Put all the dressing ingredients into a blender and whirl until smooth.

Arrange the greens on individual plates. Top with the mango slices and pepitas. Drizzle some dressing on top and pass the remaining dressing at the table.

VARIATIONS
- In place of pepitas, you can use toasted pine nuts or other nuts.
- The salad is also delicious with this very simple dressing: Whisk together ½ cup olive oil, 1½ tablespoons white vinegar, 2 teaspoons Tabasco, a pinch of salt, and a dash of black pepper.

SERVING AND MENU IDEAS
Serve as a refreshing counterpoint to Pozole Verde (page 223), Award-Winning Chili with Chocolate and Stout (page 264), or other hearty, spicy dishes.

HOW TO CUBE A MANGO

What is more delicious than a ripe mango? But the pulp is slippery and it's hard to cut it away from the pit. Here's what we do: Using a sharp knife, slice off one of the broad sides, cutting as close to the pit as you can. Slice off the other side, leaving a strip of pulp and peel attached to the pit. Without cutting into the peel, score each of the halves into a cross-hatch pattern. Bend each half back and the cubes will separate from one another and stand out, and then you can easily slice the cubes off the peel. Cut or pull off the strip of peel left on the pit, and then cut away the pulp.

Zucchini Slaw with Toasted Buckwheat and Feta

You might feel healthy just looking at this love-ly zucchini dish. This colorful salad is refreshing and quickly put together. Make it even prettier by using a mix of green and yellow zucchini or summer squash. The toasted buckwheat adds a nice crunch—take a bite, and you will want more!

Yields 3½ cups
Serves 4 to 6
Time: 20 minutes

¼ cup buckwheat groats
2 tablespoons fresh lemon juice
3 tablespoons extra-virgin olive oil
¼ cup finely chopped red onions
¼ cup chopped fresh mint and/or parsley
1 teaspoon dried oregano
½ teaspoon salt
⅛ teaspoon freshly ground black pepper
2 medium green and/or yellow zucchini
   (about 3½ cups shredded)
⅓ cup crumbled feta cheese

In a dry cast-iron skillet on low heat, toast the buckwheat groats for 4 to 5 minutes, stirring frequently and taking care not to scorch them. Set aside to cool.

In a salad bowl, whisk together the lemon juice, olive oil, onions, mint, oregano, salt, and pepper. Shred the zucchini on the large holes of a box grater and add it to the bowl. Toss well.

Just before serving, stir in the cooled, toasted buckwheat groats and top with the crumbled feta.

VARIATIONS
- You can substitute scallions or chives for the red onions.
- Use shaved Parmesan or farmers' cheese instead of feta. Use chopped toasted almonds in place of the toasted buckwheat.

SERVING AND MENU IDEAS
Serve this light salad with Pasta with Spinach and Apricots (page 230) or Persian Kuku (page 192).

Wax Bean and Radish Salad with Buttermilk Dressing

A quick, easy, and healthy side dish, this salad is invitingly attractive.

Serves 5
Time: 20 minutes

BUTTERMILK DRESSING
¼ cup buttermilk
¼ cup plain Greek yogurt
3 tablespoons chopped fresh parsley
1½ tablespoons fresh lemon juice
1½ tablespoons minced onion
1½ tablespoons Dijon-style mustard
¼ teaspoon salt
Dash of freshly ground black pepper

8 cups water
1 pound fresh yellow wax beans or green beans or a mix
1 cup thinly sliced radishes
1 tablespoon extra-virgin olive oil

Make the dressing: Place the buttermilk, yogurt, parsley, lemon juice, onion, mustard, salt, and pepper in a bowl. Whisk until smooth. Refrigerate.

Meanwhile, bring about 8 cups of water to a boil. Trim the ends of the beans. Cook the beans until tender but not too soft, about 7 minutes. Drain.

In a serving bowl, combine the beans and the sliced radishes. Drizzle with the olive oil and toss. Drizzle all the buttermilk dressing on top and let it flow down through the beans and radishes.

VARIATION
Top with crumbled blue cheese, grated Parmesan, or any shredded cheese.

SERVING AND MENU IDEAS
Serve this salad with A Big Fat Tomato Sandwich (page 85), Roasted Carrot Gazpacho (page 105), Scalloped Potatoes and Mushrooms (page 202), Pasta Carbonara with Zucchini (page 229), or a gazillion other dishes.

Za'atar Yogurt and Cucumber Salad

If you keep za'atar on hand, this simple and tasty dish is so quick and easy. Although it's almost not a salad, we serve it as one. And it's not exactly a sauce or a condiment, but we like to top our burgers with it, serve it dolloped on toasted pita, or dip it up with pita chips (page 60).

We think it's especially good made with fresh herb za'atar (page 334). Sometimes we add chopped fresh dill or roasted or pressed garlic.

In Ithaca, the season for fresh cucumbers is not long. Out of season, our choice is those crisp, seedless, thin-skinned English or Lebanese cucumbers, usually individually wrapped in taut plastic.

Yields about 2 cups
Serves 4
Prep time: 10 minutes
Sitting time: 30 minutes

2 tablespoons za'atar (page 334), plus more for
  garnish.
7 ounces plain Greek yogurt
2 medium cucumbers
Salt

In a serving bowl, stir the za'atar into the yogurt and set aside. Peel and seed the cucumbers. Shred one of the cucumbers on the coarse holes of a box grater. Put it in a sieve and, using the back of a large spoon, press out as much water as possible. Finely chop the other cucumber. Stir the cucumbers into the yogurt. Set aside for at least 30 minutes for the flavors to develop. Season with salt to taste.

Just before serving, sprinkle a little more za'atar on top . . . because it looks so pretty.

SERVING AND MENU IDEAS

One needn't limit the use of this salad to Mediterranean or Middle Eastern menus. Za'atar Yogurt and Cucumber Salad adds zing and creaminess to simple green salads, and alongside burgers, frittatas, and grain-based dishes.

Jason's Fresh Fennel and Apple Slaw

Fresh, pure flavors. This is the simplest slaw. Make it in minutes and serve it right away as a side with anything that will taste better with a refreshing counterpoint. The combination of thinly sliced fennel and shredded apples gives it both a crunchy and a soft mouthfeel. We make it over and over again in the restaurant because of all of the above.

Jason Coughlin, Moosewood chef and kitchen manager, has developed many dishes in the Moosewood kitchen, and this has got to be the simplest, but keeping it pure and simple is sometimes the mark of a great cook. Thank you, Jason.

Yields about 3 cups
Serves 4 to 6
Time: 10 minutes

2 tablespoons fresh lemon juice
1 fresh fennel bulb (about 8 ounces after
   trimming)
2 tart-sweet apples
2 tablespoons olive oil
¼ teaspoon salt

Put the lemon juice into a bowl. Trim and core the fennel bulb, slice it thinly crosswise, and then cut the slices into pieces about 1 inch long. Toss the fennel with the lemon juice. Peel and shred the apples. Toss with the fennel and lemon juice. Add the olive oil and salt and toss well.

Delicious served right away, but this can be made a couple of hours ahead, and still tastes good the next day.

SERVING AND MENU IDEAS

When we're looking for a quick-and-easy light side salad, one with flavor and texture to provide appealing contrast to richer and more complex dishes, we often turn to this tasty slaw.

Mediterranean Potato Salad

Everyone enjoys potato salad, but it can be a bit boring, bland, and business as usual. This handsome and healthful potato salad is new and interesting with a unique piquancy from the Middle Eastern seasoning mix called za'atar and an unusual combination of ingredients.

Common in the Mediterranean and the Middle East, za'atar is a mixture of sumac, sesame, and herbs that has a sour, citrusy taste. Make your own za'atar (page 334) or find it with spices in a well-stocked supermarket or in the aisle with Middle Eastern specialty goods.

Serves 4 to 6
Time: 30 minutes

3 pounds small Yukon Gold potatoes or other
   yellow potatoes
½ cup extra-virgin olive oil
¼ cup red wine vinegar
1 tablespoon Dijon-style mustard
2 garlic cloves, minced or pressed
1 teaspoon salt
1 teaspoon cracked black pepper
1 tablespoon za'atar (page 334)
½ cup large black pitted olives
1 (14-ounce) can quartered artichoke hearts in
   brine (about 1⅓ cups)
¼ cup minced scallions

Bring a large covered pot of salted water to a boil. Cut small potatoes into quarters and the larger ones into roughly 1½-inch chunks. When the water boils, add the potatoes and cook until just tender, 10 to 15 minutes. Drain in a colander and set aside to dry for about 5 minutes.

Meanwhile, in a large serving bowl, whisk together the olive oil, vinegar, mustard, garlic, salt, pepper, and za'atar. Slice the olives in half lengthwise and add them to the bowl. Drain the quartered artichoke hearts and add them to the bowl along with the minced scallions. Add the potatoes to the bowl and stir gently to coat with the vinaigrette. Taste for salt, pepper, and za'atar, and add more if needed.

Serve warm, at room temperature, or chilled.

SERVING AND MENU IDEAS

This is an intensely flavored potato salad, so serve it with a mildly flavored soup, sandwich, or main dish.

Roasted Eggplant Salad with Chermoula Sauce

If you want to like eggplant but haven't quite felt the love, try this salad. We think you'll enjoy the rich colors and savory and caramelized flavors of oven-roasted vegetables tossed with the zesty spices of North African chermoula sauce—a lemon and olive oil dressing with the exotic and aromatic seasonings of cumin, cilantro, and paprika.

Serves 6 as a side
Prep time: 15 minutes
Roasting time: 30 minutes
Sitting time: 15 minutes
Total time: 1 hour

ROASTED VEGETABLES
2 garlic cloves, pressed
1 teaspoon ground cumin
2 tablespoons olive oil
7 to 8 cups cubed eggplant (peeled or not; ¾-inch cubes, from 1 large or 1 medium and 1 small eggplant)
3 cups chopped red, orange, or yellow bell peppers (1-inch pieces)
2 cups chopped sweet onions
Salt and freshly ground black pepper

CHERMOULA SAUCE
¼ teaspoon cayenne pepper
1 teaspoon ground cumin or roasted cumin
¾ cup extra-virgin olive oil
½ cup chopped fresh parsley
¼ cup chopped fresh cilantro
½ teaspoon sweet Hungarian paprika or roasted paprika
3 garlic cloves, pressed
Finely grated zest of 1 lemon
⅓ cup fresh lemon juice
½ teaspoon salt
2 tablespoons minced preserved lemon (page 344; optional)
Pinch of crumbled saffron threads (optional)

SUGGESTED GARNISHES
2 large scallions, sliced
Chopped fresh parsley
Sprinkling of capers
Lemon slices

Preheat the oven to 375°F. Lightly oil two baking sheets.

In a large bowl, mix together the garlic, cumin, and olive oil. Add the eggplant, bell peppers, and onions and toss well. Spread evenly in one layer on the prepared baking sheets and sprinkle with salt and black pepper. Roast for 15 to 20 minutes, then turn the vegetables with a spatula and return to the oven for 10 to 15 minutes to brown on the other sides. When the eggplant is tender and the peppers and onions have browned a little, remove from the oven and set aside to cool for 5 to 10 minutes.

While the vegetables are roasting, mix together all the ingredients for the chermoula sauce. Taste and adjust the seasonings if needed.

In a bowl, thoroughly dress the roasted vegetables with half the sauce, and then add more sauce to taste.

Serve the salad at room temperature in a colorful bowl. Top with scallions, parsley, and/or capers and decorate with slices of lemon, if you wish. Serve any extra sauce on the side.

SERVING AND MENU IDEAS
Serve with toasted pita wedges, Focaccia Pugliese (page 277), or a simply cooked grain like rice or bulgur. Any extra chermoula sauce would be good on other roasted or steamed vegetables, plain boiled potatoes, or grains.

Greens with Citrus-Date Dressing

This delightful salad will awaken and refresh a winter palate. The dressing is an inspiration. Just when you think there is nothing to eat but root vegetables, the citrus family migrates north, and fresh, sprightly greens appear in local hoop houses.

Vary the salad ingredients as you like: try orange sections or pomegranate seeds instead of kumquats, green onions instead of red, and hazelnuts instead of almonds.

Serves 6
Yields about 1 cup dressing
Prep time: 20 minutes

CITRUS-DATE DRESSING
½ cup pitted dates
1 cup water
¼ cup fresh lemon juice
2 tablespoons white wine vinegar
¼ teaspoon salt
⅓ cup olive oil

6 to 8 kumquats, coarsely chopped, or 3 oranges, sectioned
½ cup thinly sliced red onions
1 cup thinly sliced radishes
8 cups watercress, arugula, baby kale, or mixed salad greens
⅓ cup toasted sliced almonds

Make the dressing: Place the dates and water in a small saucepan. Bring to a simmer and cook for about 15 minutes, until the water has been absorbed and the dates are soft and can be mashed with a fork. Put the dates into a blender with the lemon juice, vinegar, and salt. Turn on the blender and pour in the olive oil in a steady stream. Blend until smooth. If the dressing is too thick, add a little more water.

While the dates are simmering, prepare the kumquats or oranges, red onions, and radishes, and rinse and dry the greens.

Put the greens in a large serving bowl. Toss in the kumquats or oranges, onions, and radishes. Serve with a drizzle of the dressing and top with the toasted almonds.

SERVING AND MENU IDEAS
This intensely flavorful and nutritious salad is a delicious contrast for a mildly flavored entrée, such as Cheesy Risotto with Grapes (page 176) or Sweet Potato Gnocchi (page 236). It's a natural fit with Middle Eastern dishes, such as Mujadara (page 258), Persian Kuku (page 192), or Cracked Freekeh with Dried Cherries and Almonds (page 137).

Roasted Cauliflower Salad with Lemon-Tahini Sauce

Cauliflower has become so popular as a side dish, sometimes served a quarter of a head per person, sometimes grilled, fried, sautéed, or, our favorite, oven-roasted. It gets tender and nicely browned in 20 minutes or less, and absorbs oils and seasonings beautifully. Here the florets are roasted with olive oil and za'atar, then tossed with fresh green herbs and dipped in a rich, thick tahini sauce. The walnuts and fresh herbs are perfect with the flavor and texture of cauliflower.

Serves 6 as a side dish
Prep time: 10 minutes
Roasting time: about 20 minutes

4 cups cauliflower florets★
½ teaspoon ground cumin
2 teaspoons za'atar (page 334)
½ teaspoon salt
2 tablespoons extra-virgin olive oil

¼ cup chopped fresh parsley
¼ cup thinly sliced scallions
1 cup chopped toasted walnuts

Lemon-Tahini Sauce (page 325)

★An average head of cauliflower yields about 4 cups florets. If your cauliflower is large and you want to use it all, increase the amounts of oil, cumin, and za'atar.

Preheat the oven to 400°F. Lightly oil a baking sheet.

Put the cauliflower florets into a large bowl. Combine the cumin, za'atar, and salt in a small cup. Toss the florets with the oil. Sprinkle the dry seasonings over all the florets and toss again to distribute well. Spread out the florets evenly on the prepared baking sheet and roast for 10 minutes. Turn the florets and roast until tender and brown, 5 to 10 minutes more. Remove from the oven and set aside to cool for 5 minutes.

In a serving bowl, toss the cooled, roasted cauliflower with the parsley, scallions, and walnuts. If the herbs don't cling to the florets, drizzle on a little olive oil and toss again.

Serve the cauliflower with Lemon-Tahini Sauce to dip the florets into, or spoon some of the sauce onto each serving.

SERVING AND MENU IDEAS
A salad with lots going on needs only some ciabatta or other fresh bread to accompany. Roasted Fennel and Leek Tomato Soup (page 98) or Socca with Three Fillings (page 48) could be added for a fuller menu.

Kale, Jicama, and Orange Salad

Raw kale salads have taken off and appear everywhere. This one, a combination of fresh-tasting crunchy jicama, sweet and tart oranges, dried fruit, and vividly green kale, is unique and appealing. There's a lot of healthy crunch to chew on, and we like it!

Serves 4 to 6
Yields about 4 cups
Time: 40 minutes

2 navel oranges
1½ tablespoons extra-virgin olive oil
1½ tablespoons fresh lemon juice
½ teaspoon salt
1 garlic clove, minced or pressed
6 cups shredded kale★
1 cup ¼-inch matchsticks peeled jicama
½ cup raisins or Craisins
⅛ teaspoon freshly ground black pepper

★We like to use heirloom dinosaur, or Lacinato kale, but you can also use Red Russian kale. Baby kale works, but because it's so tender and shrinks once you massage it in the dressing, increase the amount to about 8 packed cups (one 11-ounce package) for the same yield. To shred the kale, remove the tough central stem from each kale leaf. Stack the stemmed leaves and roll up along the length. Cut across the roll to yield very thin strips about ⅛ inch wide. You will probably need to do this in batches.

Zest and juice one of the oranges. Combine the orange zest and juice with the oil, lemon juice, salt, and garlic and set aside. Peel and section the other orange. Cut each section in half and set aside.

Here's the fun part: In a large bowl, add the juice and oil dressing to the shredded kale and massage the dressing into the shredded kale with your fingers for about 3 minutes. This "softens" the kale by breaking down the plant fibers. Stir in the jicama, raisins, pepper, and orange pieces.

Serve right away or within a few hours. Refrigerate anything that's left over because it's just as tasty the next day.

VARIATION
Kale and Fennel Slaw: You can make a very simple yet satisfying slaw of shredded kale, very thin slices of fennel bulb, and the dressing above. A few orange sections make a tasty garnish.

SERVING AND MENU IDEAS
A garnish of toasted pine nuts or toasted chopped almonds would be nice. Serve this salad with something creamy, such as Scalloped Potatoes and Mushrooms (page 202), Fettuccine with Caramelized Onions and Yogurt (page 235), or Celery or Celeriac Soup Two Ways (page 100).

Belgian Endive Citrus Salad with Gremolata

With crisp leaves, juicy citrus, and tasty gremolata, this light, refreshing cool-weather salad is gorgeous to look at. It's a lovely salad to serve guests because it's easy to make and a little out of the ordinary.

Serves 4
Time: 25 to 30 minutes

GREMOLATA
¼ cup walnuts, toasted and cooled
1 garlic clove, minced or pressed
½ cup coarsely chopped fresh parsley
1 teaspoon finely grated lemon zest
2 tablespoons fresh lemon juice
2 tablespoons extra-virgin olive oil
½ teaspoon salt Freshly ground black pepper

2 Belgian endives★ (about 12 ounces)
2 navel oranges
1 pink or red grapefruit

★Belgian endive is relatively expensive because it is difficult and time-consuming to grow. The last stages of growth are in the dark so that the leaves will be very crisp and very pale, just barely green.

Whirl all the ingredients for the gremolata in a food processor until well combined.

Trim the root end of the endives, but leave enough attached to hold the leaves together. Slice them lengthwise into eighths and then crosswise on a severe diagonal into manageable lengths, 2 to 3 inches. Peel the oranges and grapefruit, removing all of the white pith, and cut into "clean" sections (without the separating membranes); work over a bowl to save the juices.

Either toss the endive pieces and citrus sections with the gremolata, or compose the salad on individual salad plates: first a bed of endive, then orange and grapefruit sections (drizzle with the juice that has collected), and a dollop of gremolata on top.

SERVING AND MENU IDEAS
This light salad complements richer dishes such as Paella de Verduras (page 177), Squash Polenta with Mushroom and Kale Stew (page 196), Scalloped Potatoes and Mushrooms (page 202), or White Bean Stew with Rosemary (page 217).

Winter Chopped Salad

This colorful, fresh-tasting salad is good any time of year, and the ingredients are all usually available even in winter when the richness of the avocado and the juicy bursts of sweetness from the oranges and pomegranate seeds are most appreciated.

Serves 4 to 6
Time: 20 minutes

DRESSING
2 tablespoons extra-virgin olive oil
1 tablespoon red wine vinegar
1 teaspoon Dijon mustard
¼ teaspoon salt
Sprinkling of cracked black pepper

SALAD
2 Hass avocadoes
2 tablespoons fresh lemon juice
3 oranges
1 head romaine lettuce, chopped (about 4 cups)
1 head radicchio, chopped (about 3 cups)
¾ cup pomegranate seeds★

★Pomegranate seeds are sold in many supermarkets. See page 309 for the easiest way to remove seeds from a whole pomegranate.

In a small bowl, whisk together all the ingredients for the dressing. Set aside.

Pit, peel, and cube the avocadoes and toss with the lemon juice in a separate bowl. Segment and set aside.

Arrange the chopped romaine and chopped radicchio on a platter and drizzle with the dressing. Top with the avocado cubes, orange sections, and pomegranate seeds.

SERVING AND MENU IDEAS
With a bowl of soup, this salad makes a meal. Try Sopa Verde de Elote (page 90), Purée of Parsnip, Carrot, and Celeriac (page 91), or Smoky Split Pea Soup (page 96). Or serve the salad with Butternut Squash Latkes (page 43) or Mexican Toasted Cheese Sandwich (page 84) for an easy and pleasing supper.

MAIN DISH SALADS

Herbed Quinoa Salad

Black Rice and Spinach Salad

Cracked Freekeh with Dried Cherries and Almonds

Spring Greens and Vegetables with Shallot Vinaigrette

Italian Couscous and Vegetable Salad

Lentil Salad with Baby Greens and Oranges

Kelp Noodle Salad

Quinoa Tabouli with Pomegranates and Pistachios

Mushroom Barley Salad

Spinach Salad with Blueberries and Corn

Herbed Quinoa Salad

Quinoa salad is a perfect side dish or luncheon main course. This particular version combines coriander and cumin along with plentiful amounts of fresh dill, mint, cilantro, and scallions.

Quinoa is not a grain, but rather a seed from an annual plant first cultivated 5,000 years ago by the Incas. It has high protein content and contains all the essential amino acids. To remove the natural bitter coating that protects quinoa seeds from insects and foraging birds, before cooking, rinse in a sieve until the water runs clear.

Yields about 7 cups
Serves 6
Time: 45 minutes

1 cup quinoa
2 cups water
½ teaspoon salt, plus more as needed
4 tablespoons olive oil
2 garlic cloves, minced or pressed
1 teaspoon ground coriander
1 teaspoon ground cumin
1 (15-ounce) can chickpeas, drained and rinsed

½ cup chopped dried apricots
½ cup chopped green olives
1 cup thinly sliced celery
2 tablespoons chopped preserved lemon peel (see page 344), or 1 tablespoon lemon zest
¼ cup chopped scallions
¼ cup chopped fresh dill
¼ cup chopped fresh mint
¼ cup chopped fresh cilantro
3 tablespoons fresh lemon juice
Freshly ground black pepper

Put the quinoa in a fine-mesh strainer and thoroughly rinse under cool water to remove any bitter residue. Drain well. In a small saucepan, bring the 2 cups water and salt to a boil. Add the quinoa and simmer for 15 minutes until the water has been absorbed and the grains of quinoa are soft. Remove from the heat, place a tea towel over the saucepan, and set aside to steam for 10 minutes.

Heat 1 tablespoon of the oil in a heavy skillet. Add half the garlic and sizzle, stirring constantly, for about a minute. Stir in the coriander and cumin and cook for another minute. Add the chickpeas and cook, stirring constantly, until they are warm and coated with the spices. Remove from the heat and set aside.

In a bowl, combine the apricots, olives, celery, preserved lemon, scallions, dill, mint, and cilantro. Set aside.

Whisk together the lemon juice, remaining garlic, remaining 3 tablespoons olive oil, and a pinch of salt.

When the quinoa has steamed, fluff the grains with a fork and add to the apricots and herbs. Stir in the lemon-olive oil dressing and mix well. Season with salt and pepper to taste.

SERVING AND MENU IDEAS
Serve with Roasted Winter Squash Agrodolce (page 309), or Spice-Crusted Roasted Carrots with Harissa-Yogurt Sauce (page 294).

Black Rice and Spinach Salad

Nutrient-rich and high in antioxidants, black rice and fresh green spinach combine beautifully with rouge-colored radishes, pastel-green avocado and edamame, and a handsome flavorful carrot dressing. Attractive, healthful, and so satisfying served as a main dish, this salad is also gluten-free and vegan.

Yields 12 cups
Serves 3 as a main dish, 6 as a side salad
Time: 1 hour

1¾ cups water
1 cup black rice★ (see sidebar page 136)
4 packed cups baby spinach leaves (about
  5 ounces)
1½ cups fresh or frozen shelled edamame
1 cucumber
1 cup thinly sliced radishes★★
1 Hass avocado, pitted, peeled, and diced
¼ cup thinly sliced pickled ginger★★★
1 TABLESPOON TOASTED SESAME
SEEDS
CARROT-WASABI DRESSING
1 small carrot, grated (about ½ cup packed)
1 small shallot, minced (about 2 tablespoons)
1 tablespoon peeled and grated fresh ginger
1 teaspoon wasabi paste, or more to taste
¼ cup sunflower or vegetable oil
3 tablespoons rice wine vinegar
2 tablespoons soy sauce
1 teaspoon dark sesame oil
1 tablespoon prepared mustard
Salt

★We've found that different brands and batches of black rice absorb more or less water and take more or less time to cook; however, the cooking procedure we describe works for us every time.
★★When available, we favor watermelon radishes in this salad.

★★★ The Ginger People makes a delicious brand of jarred, organic Pickled Sushi Ginger, found in the condiment or Asian specialty section of many grocery stores.

Bring the water to a boil in a saucepan with a tight-fitting lid. Add the rice and when the water returns to a boil, reduce the heat to low. Stir well, cover, and simmer until the rice is tender, about 45 minutes. Check it at about 35 minutes to see that the water hasn't completely evaporated, and if it has, add a little more hot water. When the rice is almost tender, turn off the heat (if there's any water in the bottom of the pan, drain it off) and let the rice steam, tightly covered, for about 10 minutes. Fluff with a fork and spread out on a baking sheet to cool.

While the rice is cooking, prepare the other salad ingredients. Cook the edamame in water to cover until tender, then drain and set aside to cool. Peel the cucumber and halve it lengthwise. Scrape out and discard the seeds. Slice each half into ½-inch crescents (about 1½ cups).

Make the dressing: Whirl all the dressing ingredients in a blender or food processor until smooth and thick. Season with salt to taste.

When the rice has cooled to room temperature, assemble the salad. In a large serving bowl, toss together the rice, spinach, avocado, cucumber, pickled ginger, edamame, and three-quarters of the dressing. Decorate the top of the salad with the radish slices, drizzle on the rest of the dressing, and sprinkle sesame seeds over everything.

SERVING AND MENU IDEAS
This earthy salad is complemented by a light fruity soup, such as Chilled Pineapple-Mango Soup (page 104) or Watermelon Gazpacho with Feta-Yogurt Crema (page 108). You might like a tasty bread alongside, perhaps Bialys (page 278) or Carrot Cornbread (page 281). If the salad is served alone, you'll have room for Fresh Pineapple Upside-Down Cake (page 369).

BLACK RICE

How many times lately have we heard "black rice is the new brown"? Lots. But the thing is, it's true! Its deep purple hue signals that it's rich in the antioxidants called anthocyanins that have unique antiaging and health-boosting properties. Ten spoonfuls of cooked black rice have about the same amount of anthocyanins as a serving of blueberries. It's also rich in iron, making it probably the healthiest rice of all.

Sometimes, black rice is called "forbidden rice" or "Emperors' rice" because at various times during the long history of imperial China, black rice was so rare that only royalty was allowed to consume it.

It has a texture similar to brown rice, and a nuttier flavor. You cook it about the same as brown rice. But be careful: its purple hue will dye almost anything it comes into contact with, including brown or white rice it's mixed with, your T-shirt, the tablecloth, a light-colored enamel pan . . . almost anything.

1 cup raw black rice = $3\frac{1}{2}$ cups cooked

Cracked Freekeh with Dried Cherries and Almonds

Freekeh means "to rub" in Arabic. The legend of this ancient grain has it that over two thousand years ago a Middle Eastern village was attacked and their field of green wheat set on fire. Trying to rescue their crop, resourceful cooks rubbed off the chaff and prepared a delicious roasted grain.

In this tabouli-like salad, developed by Moosewood's Wynnie Stein, freekeh's interesting, nutty flavor is complemented by the refreshing bite of mint and the sweetness of dried cherries. Wynnie loves to cook Middle Eastern-style food and to seek out authentic ingredients. She first heard about freekeh years ago while discussing ancient grains with a local farmer. Then, during a visit to Manhattan, Wynnie went with Michael Flamini, our St. Martin's editor and an avid cook, to the marvelous specialty store Kalustyan's, where she found freekeh and a whole suitcase-full of other goodies to bring home to Ithaca. Happily, freekeh can now be found in most natural foods stores and supermarkets.

Serves 4
Time: 25 to 50 minutes, depending on how coarsely your freekeh is cracked

1 cup roasted cracked freekeh★ (see sidebar page 140)
2 cups water
1 cup loosely packed finely chopped fresh parsley
¼ cup chopped fresh mint
¼ cup chopped or slivered toasted almonds
½ cup coarsely chopped dried sour cherries
½ teaspoon salt

DRESSING
¼ cup extra-virgin olive oil
Finely grated zest and juice of 1 lemon
1 large garlic clove, minced
½ teaspoon salt
¼ teaspoon ground black pepper

★For this dish, we like cracked freekeh, which comes in a wide range of sizes. Cracked freekeh is whole grains broken into pieces, sometimes almost as large as the grains themselves, giving it a chewy texture, and sometimes quite small, giving it a more delicate texture. You can also use whole-grain freekeh, which is firm and chewy with a texture something like wheat berries.

Place the freekeh and water in a saucepan and bring to a boil. Cover, reduce the heat to a simmer, and cook gently until tender. If you have packaged freekeh, follow the cooking directions on the package. If you bought bulk freekeh, keep an eye on it: it may be tender when all the water has been absorbed, but if not, add a little more boiling water, and if there is still water in the pan when it's done, drain off the liquid. The cooking time varies: about 15 minutes for small, finely cracked freekeh, and 45 minutes or more for coarsely cracked and whole-grain freekeh.

In a serving bowl, toss together the cooked freekeh, parsley, mint, almonds, cherries, and salt. Whisk together the dressing ingredients and toss with the freekeh mixture. Season with more salt and pepper to taste.

SERVING AND MENU IDEAS
Serve this on a Mediterranean buffet or combo plate that includes dips such as Roasted Carrot Hummus (page 67), Edamame Hummus (page 65), or Walnut and Roasted Red Pepper Spread (page 68) and assorted olives and marinated vegetables or artichoke hearts.

Spring Greens and Vegetables with Shallot Vinaigrette

This salad is lovely with shades of green and yellow: the colors of spring in our neck of the woods. It is a celebration of the hopeful days when fresh salad greens, sugar snaps, asparagus, and fragrant herbs are bountiful. Green and yellow pole or bush beans may not be ready to pick in our local gardens, but they're being harvested not too far away. We think you'll love the taste of fresh-picked salad greens topped with carefully blanched tender-crisp garden vegetables, plus a satisfying bit of protein, all dressed with a lively shallot vinaigrette. Food like this restores our faith in the good earth.

Serves 4
Time: 30 minutes

4 ounces salad greens, baby spinach, arugula, mesclun, or a combination (about 4 cups)
1 cup fresh parsley leaves, no stems
2 tablespoons chopped fresh tarragon or dill (optional)
6 ounces green beans (a combination of green beans and yellow wax beans is pretty)
6 ounces sugar snap peas
12 asparagus spears

SHALLOT VINAIGRETTE

¼ cup plus 2 tablespoons extra-virgin olive oil
1½ cups peeled and chopped shallots (about 8 ounces)
¼ cup rice vinegar
⅓ cup water
1 tablespoon Dijon mustard
2 tablespoons fresh tarragon leaves
1 tablespoon sugar
1 teaspoon salt

4 or 5 quartered hard-boiled eggs, or 2 cups Simple Seasoned Tofu cubes (page 346, optional)

Rinse and dry the salad greens, parsley, and tarragon or dill, if using, and put into a serving bowl.

Bring a saucepan of salted water to a boil. Fill a large bowl with ice cubes and cold water and set close to the stovetop. Trim the beans and slice each diagonally into 2 or 3 pieces. When the water boils, blanch the beans until just tender and bright green, 3 to 5 minutes. Remove with a slotted spoon or strainer and plunge them into the bowl of ice water.

Trim the sugar snap peas and remove and discard the tough strings. Bring the water back to a boil and blanch the sugar snap peas for 2 to 3 minutes, then remove with a slotted spoon or strainer and add them to the ice water. Break off and discard the tough ends of the asparagus and slice the spears diagonally into pieces about 2 inches long.

Bring the water back to a boil and blanch the asparagus pieces for 3 minutes, then remove them with a slotted spoon or strainer and plunge into the ice water. When the blanched vegetables are cool, drain them.

Make the vinaigrette: Heat ¼ cup of the oil in a skillet or saucepan on medium heat. Add the shallots with a sprinkling of salt, cover, and cook, stirring a few times, until the shallots are translucent and soft, 3 to 5 minutes. Don't allow them to brown. Put the cooked shallots, vinegar, water, mustard, tarragon, sugar, remaining 2 tablespoons oil, and salt into a blender. Whirl until smooth. Taste and add more salt if needed.

Arrange the vegetables on the salad greens and top with the hard-boiled eggs or tofu cubes, if using. Drizzle on some of the shallot vinaigrette and pass more at the table.

SERVING AND MENU IDEAS

Serve with Spaghetti with Olives and Lemon (page 241) or Pizza with Roasted Eggplant and Plum Tomatoes (page 274).

FREEKEH

Freekeh is a staple food in northern Africa and in Middle Eastern cuisines, especially in Lebanon, Jordan, Egypt, and Syria. It has also become extremely popular in Australia, where modern processing of freekeh originated. Freekeh is wheat that is harvested while green and moist, and then the grains are parched, roasted, dried, and rubbed to remove the chaff, leaving pale green kernels. Cracked freekeh is then broken into pieces.

Freekeh is not gluten-free, but because the grains are harvested when green, the gluten structure is slightly different from regular wheat, and the grain may lack an amino acid called gliadin, which acts as a trigger to gluten intolerance. Also, the grain is roasted, which denatures the gluten.

Because it's harvested at an earlier stage of development, freekeh contains higher levels of fiber, protein, and certain minerals than more mature, typically processed wheat. And the process for making freekeh keeps the raw wheat's high protein and mineral content largely intact. Freekeh is higher in fiber than brown rice and even quinoa. It also has a relatively low glycemic index compared to many other grains.

Italian Couscous and Vegetable Salad

We love the nutty taste of whole wheat couscous, and because it is just slightly more substantial than refined couscous, it holds its own when mixed with a variety of ingredients. This satisfying main dish salad can be the centerpiece of a lunch or light supper, or part of a Mediterranean spread.

Yields 8 cups
Serves 4 to 6
Time: 35 minutes

COUSCOUS
1½ cups whole wheat couscous
1 teaspoon salt
½ teaspoon ground black pepper
1 teaspoon ground fennel seeds
1 tablespoon extra-virgin olive oil
1½ cups boiling water

SALAD
1 cup diced bell peppers (a mix of red, yellow, and orange is nice)
1 cup halved grape or cherry tomatoes
1 cup diced zucchini
½ cup diced fresh fennel bulb
1 teaspoon minced or pressed garlic
1 tablespoon extra-virgin olive oil
½ teaspoon salt

1 (15-ounce) can cannellini beans, drained and rinsed
½ cup coarsely chopped fresh basil
½ cup coarsely chopped fresh parsley
½ to ¾ cup crumbled or grated ricotta salata, feta, or chèvre cheese (optional)

DRESSING
3 tablespoons extra-virgin olive oil
3 tablespoons balsamic vinegar
½ teaspoon salt

Make the couscous: Put the couscous, salt, black pepper, ground fennel, olive oil, and boiling water in a large bowl and stir to combine. Immediately cover the bowl with aluminum foil, plastic wrap, or a plate and set aside to steam. After 10 minutes, fluff the couscous with a fork.

Make the salad: Preheat the broiler. In another bowl, mix together the bell peppers, tomatoes, zucchini, fresh fennel, garlic, oil, and salt. Spread out on a shallow rimmed baking sheet and broil close to the heat source for 10 minutes, stirring after 5 minutes. Set aside to cool.

Stir the cooled vegetables into the couscous along with the beans, basil, and parsley. If you're adding cheese, either stir it into the salad, or sprinkle it on top just before serving.

Make the dressing: In a small cup or bowl, whisk together the oil, vinegar, and salt. Pour it over the salad and mix thoroughly.

Serve the salad at room temperature or chilled.

SERVING AND MENU IDEAS
With grain, vegetables, and beans, this hearty salad just needs a stocky soup such as Aigo Bouido (page 102) to make a flavorful meal. We like to create a combo plate with this salad and either Spicy Butternut Squash Dip (page 64) or Radish and Herbed Chèvre Spread (page 69).

Lentil Salad with Baby Greens and Oranges

This salad will hold your interest from the first bite to the last. French lentils are smaller than regular lentils and have a nice mouthfeel because they retain their shape when cooked.

Serves 6
Time: 50 minutes

1 cup French lentils
1¾ cups water
1¼ cups fresh orange juice
1 teaspoon salt

1½ cups quartered and thinly sliced red onions
2 celery stalks, thinly sliced diagonally
½ cup chopped fresh parsley
3 tablespoons chopped fresh basil
2 or 3 navel oranges or 4 clementines or tangerines, segmented
½ cup chopped toasted walnuts or pistachios, or sliced toasted almonds

DRESSING

2 tablespoons orange juice
¼ cup extra-virgin olive oil
1 tablespoon fresh lemon juice
4 cups baby greens, mesclun, or spinach and radicchio
1 tablespoon olive oil

Sliced red radishes, for garnish (optional)

In a covered saucepan, bring the lentils, water, orange juice, and salt to a boil. Lower the heat and simmer until the lentils are tender but not mushy, about 30 minutes. Drain the lentils.

While the lentils cook, put the onions, celery, herbs, oranges, and nuts in a mixing bowl. Set aside.

Make the dressing: Whisk together the orange juice, olive oil, and lemon juice.

Add the warm drained lentils and the dressing to the mixing bowl and toss well. Add salt and/or more lemon juice to taste. In a separate bowl, toss the salad greens with the olive oil.

Arrange the greens on a platter or individual plates and spoon on the lentil mixture. Garnish with sliced radishes, if using.

SERVING AND MENU IDEAS
Focaccia Pugliese (page 277) or your favorite flatbread goes well with this salad.

Kelp Noodle Salad

This salad is so refreshing, light, and versatile. You'll be amazed that you're eating something made of kelp! The crisp, clear, cool noodles are rich in minerals, taste a bit like cucumber, and have a crunchy texture. Their flavor is mild—sort of like rain on your tongue.

A generous platter with piles of various toppings for the diners to choose from makes this a fun, informal meal. We give you a multitude of ideas for toppings, and we think you'll think of more. Mix and match fresh vegetables and fruits, mushrooms, seasoned tofu, beans, toasted seeds and nuts . . . anything that appeals to you.

The dressing is substantial, rich, and spicy sweet. The dressing thickens when refrigerated, but it is easily thinned out with a little water.

Serves 4
Prep time: 20 minutes (or more with more toppings to prep)

SALAD
12- to 16-ounce package of kelp noodles★
6 cups greens sliced into chiffonade (lettuce, spinach, savoy cabbage, Asian greens, or frisée)

TOPPINGS (choose several or many)
Julienned carrots
Cucumber matchsticks
Sliced snow peas
Quartered grapes
Pickled daikon and onions (see page 78)
Simple Seasoned Tofu (page 346)
Beans (adzuki, garbanzo, cannellini, cranberry)
Roasted or pan-fried quartered cremini mushrooms
Fresh basil leaves sliced into chiffonade
Coarsely chopped fresh cilantro
Sliced scallions
Toasted chopped cashews, peanuts, almonds, sesame or sunflower seeds

DRESSING
½ cup nut butter (cashew, peanut, or almond)
3 tablespoons fresh lime juice
2 teaspoons sugar
2 tablespoons soy sauce
2 teaspoons peeled and grated fresh ginger
1 minced jalapeño pepper, ¼ teaspoon crushed red pepper flakes, or hot sauce to taste
¼ to ⅓ cup water

★Look in the supermarket, natural foods store, or Asian grocery store on the shelf near other Asian noodles for ready-to-eat kelp noodles in 12- to 16-ounce aseptic or plastic packages. The Sea Tangle Company makes konaberry kelp noodles that boast powerful antioxidants.

Soak the noodles for 10 minutes in a bowl of warm water to separate the strands. Rinse and drain. (You may need to cut the long strands.) Portion the greens into four wide, shallow bowls. Top with a tangle of kelp noodles.

Prepare the toppings you like for the salad and arrange on a platter to be served at the table.

Place all the ingredients for the dressing except the water in a blender. Whirl on low speed and add water until the dressing is smooth and as thick as heavy cream. Top each bowl of salad with dressing, or serve the dressing in a small bowl or pitcher at the table.

Put the platter of toppings in the center of the table for individuals to choose from, give everyone a bowl of greens and noodles, and let the feast begin.

SERVING AND MENU IDEAS
Serve with Thai Corn Chowder (page 93) or Chilled Curried Pea and Coconut Soup (page 106).

Quinoa Tabouli with Pomegranates and Pistachios

Toasted quinoa, beautiful pomegranate seeds, and toasted pistachios—that's a whole lotta crunch. Not just a workout for the jaws, this salad is also a refreshing, healthful treat with the traditional tabouli seasonings of olive oil, parsley, lemon, and mint, plus the high-protein benefits of gluten-free quinoa! Toasting the quinoa is really worth the extra ten minutes because it yields a wheat-like aroma and adds warmth, a nutty richness, and a lovely light brown color to the salad.

Yields 6 cups
Serves 6
Time: 50 minutes

1½ cups quinoa
2½ cups water
½ teaspoon salt, plus more as needed
1 pomegranate
⅓ cup extra-virgin olive oil
2 scallions, sliced
2 tablespoons finely minced fresh mint, or
   1 tablespoon crushed dried mint
1½ cups finely chopped parsley
2 tablespoons minced preserved lemon
   (see page 344), or 1 tablespoon finely grated
   lemon zest
3 to 4 tablespoons fresh lemon juice
1 garlic clove, minced or pressed
Freshly ground black pepper
½ cup coarsely chopped pistachios

In a fine-mesh strainer, rinse and drain the quinoa. In a dry skillet on medium heat, toast the quinoa, stirring frequently, until it darkens to a golden brown and gives off a pleasant fragrance, about 10 minutes. Meanwhile, in a saucepan, bring the water and salt to a boil. Carefully pour in the toasted quinoa (not all at once because it will bubble up and sputter). Simmer, covered, until the water has been absorbed, about 20 minutes.

While the quinoa cooks, cut open the pomegranate and remove the seeds (see ingredient note on page 309). Set the seeds aside.

When the quinoa is done, fluff it with a fork and put it in a mixing bowl. Stir in the oil, scallions, mint, parsley, preserved lemon or lemon zest, 3 tablespoons of the lemon juice, the garlic, and the pomegranate seeds. Season with salt and pepper and additional lemon juice to taste. Just before serving, stir in the chopped pistachios or sprinkle them on top.

SERVING AND MENU IDEAS

Good choice for a soup-and-salad meal with Celery or Celeriac Soup Two Ways (page 100) or Watermelon Gazapacho with Feta-Yogurt Crema (page 108). Or an interesting mezze meal with Hummus with Preserved Lemon (page 66) and Spice-Crusted Roasted Carrots with Harissa-Yogurt Sauce (page 294). Or serve this tabouli beside a burger, such as Roasted Red Pepper, Black Olive, and Tofu Burgers (page 249), no bun.

Mushroom Barley Salad

Grain salads have been part of the international and gourmet vegetarian repertoire for decades. But until recently, barley as a salad grain has been overlooked. Well, it's time to think beyond soup! Barley is a great foundation for salads. It holds its shape, even over days, without becoming mushy or dry. This is a hearty, good-looking winter salad. We use pearled barley for quicker cooking.

Yields 6 cups
Serves 4 to 6
Time: 45 minutes

¾ cup pearled barley
4 cups water

1 (15-ounce) can small red beans, rinsed and drained
4 tablespoons extra-virgin olive oil
2 teaspoons balsamic vinegar
½ teaspoon salt, plus more as needed

1 heaping cup sliced shallots
1½ teaspoons minced garlic
8 ounces mushrooms, sliced★
1 tablespoon soy sauce
⅛ teaspoon freshly ground black pepper

2 tablespoons fresh lemon juice, plus more to taste
½ cup chopped fresh parsley
3 tablespoons chopped fresh cilantro
2 tablespoons chopped fresh dill

½ cup chopped toasted walnuts (optional)

★We like to use a variety of mushrooms for depth of taste and visual interest, but if you go with one, make it cremini.

In a covered saucepan, bring the barley and water to a boil. Reduce the heat and simmer, covered, until the barley is soft but chewy, about 30 minutes. Check the water level periodically and add additional water if needed. Drain well and spread out on a baking sheet to cool.

While the barley cooks, put the beans in a small bowl and toss them with 2 tablespoons of the oil, the vinegar, and the salt. Cover the bowl and refrigerate.

Warm the remaining 2 tablespoons oil in a skillet on medium heat, add the shallots and garlic, and cook until the shallots are translucent, about 6 minutes. Add the mushrooms and cook for another 5 minutes. Add the soy sauce and pepper and cook, stirring frequently, until the mushrooms are juicy.

In a serving bowl, combine the mushrooms, cooled barley, and marinated red beans. Toss with the lemon juice, parsley, cilantro, and dill. Add salt and more lemon juice to taste.

Serve at room temperature or chilled, topped with toasted walnuts, if using. If you are making this salad ahead, taste before serving and add lemon juice and salt to taste.

SERVING AND MENU IDEAS
We like the melding of flavors when the salad is served with Purée of Parsnip, Carrot, and Celeriac Soup (page 91).

Spinach Salad with Blueberries and Corn

The earthy taste of spinach is perfectly complemented by the natural sweetness of blueberries,
corn, and basil in this fresh, healthful summer salad.
With walnuts and goat cheese, it's all you need for
a simple summer meal. Every time we serve this
salad, people rave about it. So delicious!

Yields about ¾ cup dressing
Serves 4, more as a side salad
Prep time: 20 minutes

BLUEBERRY DRESSING
½ cup fresh blueberries★
2 tablespoons extra-virgin olive oil
2 tablespoons fresh lemon juice
2 tablespoons coarsely chopped fresh basil leaves,
  packed
1 teaspoon Dijon mustard
¼ teaspoon salt
Pinch of sugar
⅛ teaspoon cracked black pepper

½ small red onion
4 ears fresh sweet corn
6 ounces baby spinach or arugula
  (about 8 cups, moderately packed)
Fresh blueberries★

OPTIONAL EXTRAS
1 (4-ounce) log goat cheese, sliced into 8 rounds
½ cup walnuts, toasted

★One pint of blueberries is a good amount for both
the dressing and for sprinkling on the salad.

Make the dressing: Place the blueberries in a
blender or food processor along with the olive oil,
lemon juice, basil, mustard, salt, sugar, and pepper.
Whirl until fairly smooth. Set aside. The dressing
will thicken as it sits. Stir it before drizzling on
the salad. This dressing keeps for several days in an
airtight container in the refrigerator.

Thinly slice the red onion. Cut the corn kernels
off the cobs; you'll have about 2 cups. If you're
adding goat cheese, slice it into 8 rounds.

To assemble the salad, divide the spinach among
the serving plates and top each with red onion
slices. Drizzle about 2 tablespoons of the thick,
purple dressing over each salad. Arrange blueberries and the corn kernels on top. Add goat
cheese slices and walnuts, if you like.

SERVING AND MENU IDEAS
Finish this summer meal with Cherry Tomato
Upside-Down Cake (page 365) or Lemon-
Zucchini Cake with Thyme (page 363).

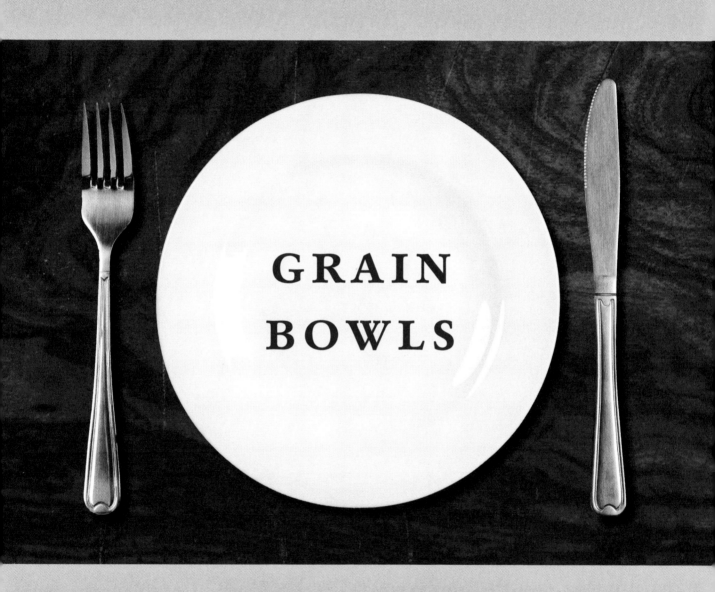

Italian Grain Bowl

Middle Eastern Grain Bowl

African Bowl

Mexican Rice Bowl

Asian Noodle Bowl

Indonesian Rice Bowl

Italian Grain Bowl

Israeli couscous or orzo serves as a vehicle for a garlicky, quick sauté of tomatoes, mushrooms, wilted greens, and fresh mozzarella. The radicchio or arugula is an assertive counterpoint to the mildly flavored couscous.

Serves 4
Time: 40 minutes

2 cups Israeli couscous★ or whole wheat orzo
1 teaspoon salt, plus more as needed
2 tablespoons olive oil
6 garlic cloves, minced or pressed
3 cups chopped plum tomatoes
4½ cups sliced mushrooms
¼ teaspoon crushed red pepper flakes
3 packed cups chopped greens, such as radicchio, arugula, chicory, or escarole
3 tablespoons chopped fresh basil
3 tablespoons chopped fresh parsley
1 cup cubed fresh mozzarella cheese (about 6 ounces)
¼ cup grated Pecorino Romano cheese

★Israeli or pearl couscous is a wheat pasta shaped in small spheres and toasted. Often found in supermarkets in the international foods section with Jewish or Israeli foods, it has the advantage of being available in whole wheat.

Prepare the couscous or orzo: Bring a large pot of water with a pinch of salt to a boil.

Add the couscous or orzo to the boiling water, stir, and simmer until tender, usually 8 to 10 minutes, but follow the package instructions. Drain and set aside until the vegetables have cooked.

Heat the olive oil in a large skillet on medium-high heat and briefly sauté the garlic until it just begins to turn golden and fragrant. Add the tomatoes and sauté for 3 to 4 minutes. Add the mushrooms, salt, and red pepper flakes and cook, stirring often, for a couple of minutes to soften the mushrooms. Stir in the greens and cook until just wilted; depending on the type, this should take 3 to 5 minutes. Add the drained couscous and stir in the fresh herbs. Spread the fresh mozzarella cubes on top and push them into the mixture; to avoid long strings of cheese, do not stir. To incorporate any juices and melt the cheese, cover the pan, turn off the heat, and let it sit for a couple of minutes before serving.

Serve in individual bowls and top with the grated Pecorino Romano, or pass the cheese and a grater at the table.

SERVING AND MENU IDEAS
Think Mediterranean. You could start with Giardiniera (page 342) and/or serve a simple green salad or an easy side vegetable, such as Spicy Roasted Broccoli (page 302). After all those vegetables, you might want Espresso Shortbread (page 355) served with fresh fruit.

Middle Eastern Grain Bowl

With lots of colorful and nutritious ingredients, this tasty grain bowl is quick and easy enough for a weeknight supper.

Serves 4
Time: 30 minutes

1 to 1¼ cups boiling water
1 cup whole-grain bulgur wheat or whole-grain Israeli couscous

2 tablespoons olive oil
1 large onion, minced (about 2 cups)
2 small zucchini, cut lengthwise into quarters, then chopped into ½-inch chunks (about 2 cups)
1 teaspoon ground cumin
1 teaspoon ground coriander
½ teaspoon salt, plus more as needed
2 garlic cloves, minced
2 tomatoes, cut into ½-inch cubes (about 2 cups)
1 (15-ounce) can chickpeas, drained and rinsed
4 cups packed baby spinach or arugula (about 5 ounces)
Freshly ground black pepper

1 cucumber, peeled, seeded, and diced
½ cup plain Greek yogurt (5 ounces)
¼ cup minced fresh parsley, dill, and/or mint
Sprinkling of cracked black pepper

To cook the bulgur: Pour 1 cup boiling water over the bulgur in a bowl or pot and let sit for 20 minutes. Fluff with a fork. The yield of cooked bulgur will be about 2½ cups. To cook Israeli couscous: Add the couscous to 1¼ cups boiling water in a small saucepan. Cover, turn the heat to low, and simmer for 8 to 10 minutes until the couscous is al dente and the water has been absorbed. The cooked couscous yield should be about 2 cups. Set the cooked couscous aside until the toppings are done.

In a large pan, sauté the onion and zucchini in the oil for about 5 minutes, or until golden and tender. Add the cumin, coriander, salt, and garlic. Add the chopped tomatoes and cook for 1 minute. Add the chickpeas and spinach, cover, and cook until heated through and the spinach has wilted. Season with salt and ground black pepper to taste.

Meanwhile in a small bowl, combine the diced cucumbers, yogurt, and parsley or dill. Season with salt and ground black pepper to taste.

Serve the stew over the bulgur or couscous in individual serving bowls, topped with dollops of cucumber yogurt and a sprinkling of cracked black pepper

SERVING AND MENU IDEAS
Grain bowls sort of have it all in one bowl, but if you want to add more to the meal, try an appetizer of Roasted Beet and Walnut Dip (page 63) with pita triangles or crudités, or serve a light refreshing salad such as Belgian Endive Citrus Salad with Gremolata (page 129), and then Turkish Coffee Brownies (page 358) for dessert.

A WORD ABOUT GRAIN BOWLS

Meals in a bowl have been gaining traction and sophistication during the last few years and have been a great source of inspiration for us. They are the new "TV dinner," though no tray table is needed and they usually call for a single utensil for eating.

Successful bowls are all about balance of nutrition, taste, and texture, unified and elevated by a dressing or sauce. The formula—a grain; a protein; cooked, raw, or pickled vegetables; and nuts, seeds, or fruit—offers a fantastic canvas of possibilities, and easily adapts to what's in season and what you want to eat for the season you're in.

We've discovered a few tips for making grain bowls easy: when you have more ingredients at the ready, less time stopping at the store, and less time at the stove.

- When you make a grain or pasta for an entrée or salad, deliberately make more.
- Stock a variety of canned beans.
- Hard-boil some eggs and refrigerate.
- Pick up a couple of bags or boxes of greens, lettuces, or slaw.
- Have nuts, seeds, and dried fruit on hand.
- Stock sharp and mellow, hard and crumbly cheeses.

African Bowl

A millet pilaf with cilantro, scallions, and soy sauce is the supporting grain for this bowl's layers of shredded greens, roasted sweet potatoes, chopped fresh tomatoes, and roasted peanuts. A drizzle of our coconut-lime dressing brings it all together. It's an interesting combination of flavors and textures.

We like a mixture of spinach and romaine: spinach for the color and flavor, romaine for the crunch. But it's fine with one or both.

Serves 4 to 6
Time: 50 minutes

8 cups peeled sweet potato chunks (1½-inch
  pieces; about 2 pounds whole)
1 tablespoon olive oil
1 teaspoon salt
1½ cups millet (see sidebar, opposite)
2¼ cups water
¼ cup packed minced fresh cilantro
½ cup chopped scallions
2 tablespoons soy sauce

COCONUT MILK-CILANTRO-LIME DRESSING
½ cup coconut milk
¼ cup packed fresh cilantro
¼ cup chopped scallions
¼ cup fresh lime juice
¼ teaspoon salt
⅓ cup olive oil
1 teaspoon sugar (optional)

1 cucumber
4 to 6 cups thinly sliced spinach and/or romaine
3 cups chopped fresh tomatoes
1 cup salted roasted peanuts

Preheat the oven to 425°F. Oil a baking sheet.

In a bowl, toss the sweet potato chunks with the olive oil and ½ teaspoon of the salt. Spread them out on the prepared baking sheet and roast for 15 minutes. Remove from the oven and stir. Return to the oven and roast until tender and lightly browned, 5 to 10 minutes.

While the sweet potatoes roast, cook the millet. In a saucepan on medium-high heat, dry-roast the millet, stirring continually for about 4 minutes, or until it becomes golden brown and aromatic with a scent something like popcorn. Add the water and remaining ½ teaspoon salt and bring to a boil. Reduce the heat to low, cover, and simmer without disturbing for 15 minutes. Uncover and don't stir, but using a spoon, push aside the millet in the middle of the pan to see if the water has been absorbed. If there's little or no water on the bottom of the pan, remove it from the heat; if there's more than ½ inch of water in the bottom of the pan, drain it off. Cover and let stand, off the heat, for 10 minutes. Fluff with a fork. Stir in the cilantro, scallions, and soy sauce.

While the millet cooks, in a blender, whirl the coconut milk, cilantro, scallions, lime juice, and salt until smooth. With the blender running, slowly pour in the olive oil. Add the sugar if you'd like the dressing to be a little less tart. Peel and seed the cucumber. Slice lengthwise into ¼-inch-wide strips and then cut the strips every ¼ inch or so.

To serve in individual bowls, layer millet, greens, cucumber, roasted sweet potatoes, and then tomatoes. Drizzle on some dressing and top with peanuts.

SERVING AND MENU IDEAS

If you'd like something to munch on while you prepare dinner, look to lightly curried Spiced Nuts (page 59) or piquant Pickled Sweet Peppers (page 341). Of course, after an African Bowl you don't really need dessert. . . . No, of course you don't, but if you do, we recommend Custard and Pear Pie (page 376), or easiest of all, freeze some banana slices and then purée them in a food processor last minute for a creamy-seeming sorbet.

MILLET

Millet is an African grain, also widely eaten in China and India. It's gluten-free, has about the same protein content as wheat, and is a good source of vitamins and minerals. Its flavor is distinct but mild, making it a good carrier of other flavors.

One cup raw millet makes about 3½ cups cooked. Invariably, online recipes for cooking millet call for 2 cups water for each cup of millet, but when we make it, that's always too much water. Several things probably affect it: size and heaviness of the pan, how tight the lid is, how low your low heat is. Maybe it's the millet itself—the conditions when it was harvested, how it has been stored (different "batches" may be more or less dehydrated), and how fresh it is when you cook it. When we use 1½ cups of water for each cup of raw millet, it usually works fine, although occasionally, we need to add a little more boiling water, say ¼ cup, near the end of cooking.

When you want fluffy millet, it's important to leave it alone while it cooks: don't stir it until it's done.

Mexican Rice Bowl

This lime-infused grain bowl brings together rice, richly flavored black beans, and a colorful roasted corn and radish salad. It is topped off with an easily prepared avocado-tomatillo dressing.

Serves 4
Time: 50 minutes

1½ cups white or long-grain brown rice
Vegetable oil
Salt
3 cups water

BEANS
2 tablespoons vegetable oil
2 cups chopped onions
1 tablespoon minced or crushed garlic
1 teaspoon salt
2 teaspoons ground coriander
2 teaspoons ground cumin
2 (15-ounce) cans black beans, undrained
1 cup fresh orange juice
½ teaspoon freshly ground black pepper

CORN AND RADISH SALAD
2 cups corn kernels, fresh or thawed frozen
2 tablespoons vegetable oil
1 teaspoon ground cumin
½ teaspoon salt
4 thinly sliced red radishes
4 thinly sliced scallions (white and green parts)
¼ cup fresh lime juice

DRESSING
½ cup water
2 cups chopped tomatillos
1 Hass avocado
¼ to ½ seeded jalapeño
2 tablespoons fresh lime juice
½ teaspoon salt, or more to taste
¼ cup chopped fresh cilantro

To prepare the rice: If using brown rice, sauté the grains in a little vegetable oil with a pinch of salt and add 3 cups of water. Bring to a boil, lower to a simmer, and cook for 40 minutes. If using white rice, which cooks in half the time, start it later, when the beans come to a simmer.

To prepare the beans: Warm the oil in a heavy-bottomed pot or Dutch oven. Add the onions and garlic along with the salt and sauté for about 5 minutes. Add the coriander and cumin and cook for another 5 minutes, stirring to prevent sticking, until the onions are translucent. Stir in the black beans and their liquid, the orange juice, and the pepper and bring to a boil. Reduce the heat to a simmer, cover, and cook for 20 minutes. Stir intermittently and scrape the bottom of the pot if needed.

If using white rice, start it at this point so that it and the beans will be done at about the same time.

While the rice and beans cook, make the corn salad: Preheat the broiler. In a medium bowl, toss the corn kernels with the oil, cumin, and salt. Spread out in an even layer on a baking sheet and broil for 5 to 10 minutes, until the kernels just begin to pucker and turn brown. Return the corn to the bowl. Add the radishes and scallions and toss with the lime juice. Set aside.

Make the dressing: Put all the ingredients into a blender and purée until smooth.

Divide the rice among four shallow bowls. Position each of the other components next to one another on the rice. Pour a ribbon of dressing over each bowl, and sprinkle generously with chopped fresh cilantro.

SERVING AND MENU IDEAS
You might like a simple salad like Jason's Fresh Fennel and Apple Slaw (page 123) or Mango-Spinach Salad with Spicy Dressing (page 118). If the meal isn't over until you've had dessert, try Rich Vegan Chocolate Pudding (page 380), which is made smooth and thick by avocado.

Asian Noodle Bowl

There is a lot going on at once in this colorful bowl, but when you see that it's going to work, what fun! The secret to creating this satisfying meal is in the prep and the timing. Start by having all the ingredients and equipment at the ready: a pot with water for boiling the noodles, a wok or large skillet for the vegetables, and a smaller skillet for the eggs. The recipe begins with the sauce and toppings to set aside, so the other components can go piping hot from the stovetop into the serving bowls.

Serves 4
Prep time: 40 minutes

SAUCE
¼ cup soy sauce
2 teaspoons finely grated lime zest
¼ cup fresh lime juice
¼ cup brown sugar
½ teaspoon minced jalapeño or other hot pepper (or Chinese chili paste or hot sauce)
2 teaspoons crushed or minced garlic

TOPPINGS
¼ cup chopped or thinly sliced fresh basil
¼ cup chopped fresh cilantro
1 cup roasted peanuts, whole or chopped

¼ cup vegetable oil
2 cups sliced scallions (cut into 1-inch pieces)
6 cups thinly sliced broccoli or Chinese broccoli
2 cups chopped fresh tomatoes
2 tablespoons peeled and grated fresh ginger

8 ounces rice stick noodles
1 tablespoon dark sesame oil
4 large eggs, beaten

Make the sauce: In a small bowl, whisk together all the ingredients for the sauce. Put the toppings into individual serving dishes and set the sauce and toppings on the table.

Bring 3 quarts water to a boil.

Meanwhile, heat the vegetable oil in a wok or large skillet. Add the scallions and sauté until they soften. Stir in the broccoli and cook until its color deepens, about 3 minutes. Stir in the tomatoes and ginger, cover, lower the heat, and cook for about 7 minutes, or until the broccoli is tender and the tomatoes juicy.

While the vegetables cook, add the rice noodles to the boiling water. Cook according to the package directions until tender, and then drain.

Meanwhile, heat the dark sesame oil in a skillet. Pour in the beaten eggs and cook until the edges are set, then flip to cook the opposite side. Remove the eggs from the heat and slice into thin strips.

Serve each person a large bowl filled with a bed of noodles, topped with the broccoli and tomatoes, and strips of fried egg. At the table, top with the sauce, fresh herbs, and peanuts.

Congratulations! After all that juggling, you're an iron chef.

SERVING AND MENU IDEAS
If you want a side dish for this generously portioned meal, choose Sugar Snap Peas with Coconut and Lime (page 113) just for the fresh crunch it adds. Coconut-Pineapple Sorbet (page 382) is a refreshing dessert, or just serve a bowl of tangerines or some Asian pears.

Indonesian Rice Bowl

This is a nutritious and delicious meal. It all comes together by layering the rice with sautéed spinach and shallots, a colorful slaw, seasoned tofu or hard-boiled eggs, and a sweet and citrusy peanut dressing. A topping of roasted peanuts is always a treat. Mung bean sprouts are also a good crunchy garnish.

Serves 4
Time: 45 minutes

RICE
1½ cups rice★
1 tablespoon oil, if using brown or red rice
2¼ cups water for white rice; 3 cups water for brown or red rice

PROTEIN (choose one or more)
4 large eggs
1 cup Simple Seasoned Tofu (page 346)
1 cup salted roasted peanuts

SLAW
1 cup shredded or thinly sliced red cabbage
1 cup grated carrots
1½ cups chopped juicy fruit, such as mango, papaya, pineapple, or peaches
2 heaping tablespoons chopped fresh cilantro

DRESSING
¼ cup fresh lime juice
2 tablespoons soy sauce
2 tablespoons pure maple syrup
3 tablespoons no-sugar-added smooth peanut butter
2 tablespoons peeled and grated fresh ginger
½ teaspoon Vietnamese or Chinese chili paste or 2 teaspoons chopped jalapeño

SPINACH
3 tablespoons vegetable oil
1 cup chopped shallots or red onions
½ teaspoon salt
8 cups packed baby spinach

★Use a quick-cooking white rice, like Carolina or basmati, or long-grain brown rice or Bhutanese red rice.

Cook the rice: If using white rice, bring the rice and water to a boil. Reduce the heat to low, cover, and cook for about 20 minutes. If using long-grain brown rice or red rice, sauté the rice grains in the oil for a minute or two until the grains become aromatic. Add the water, bring to a boil, and simmer, covered, for about 45 minutes.

While the rice cooks, prepare the protein you've chosen. For hard-boiled eggs: Cover the eggs with water in a medium pot, bring the water to a boil, then cover the pot and remove it from the heat for 12 minutes. Drain and rinse the eggs in cool water. Peel the eggs, then slice or crumble and set aside in a small bowl. Cut the seasoned tofu into strips or bite-size pieces.

Make the slaw: Combine the slaw ingredients in a bowl and set aside.

Make the dressing: Whirl all the ingredients for the dressing in a blender until smooth.

Cook the spinach: Warm the oil in a saucepan on medium-high heat, add the shallots and salt, and sauté until soft but not browned. Add the spinach in batches, stirring after each addition, and cook until the spinach has wilted and is hot.

Serve in individual bowls: Divide the rice among the bowls and top with wilted spinach, then eggs or tofu, and then slaw. Drizzle some dressing over all. Sprinkle the peanuts on top.

SERVING AND MENU IDEAS
For dessert, sprinkle fresh pineapple slices with brown sugar and broil.

Autumn Potpie

Winter Potpie

Spring Potpie

Zowee Thai Fried Rice

Kale and Walnut Risotto

Spring Risotto

Cheesy Risotto with Grapes

Paella de Verduras

Stuffed Poblano Peppers

Mushroom-Stuffed Winter Squash

Asparagus with Fried Eggs and Sizzled Shallots

Black Sesame–Coated Tofu and Udon Noodles

Scallion Crepes with Chinese Greens

Cuban Picadillo

Pineapple-Lime Glazed Tofu with Spicy Cucumber Salad

Persian Kuku

Korean Noodle Pancake

Burmese Tohu Thoke

Squash Polenta with Mushroom and Kale Stew

Asian Filo Rolls

Jamaican Jerk Tempeh Patties

Scalloped Potatoes and Mushrooms

Walnut-Cheddar-Herb "Meatballs"

Vegetable "Noodles"

Autumn Potpie

Potpies are warming and consoling. This is the perfect dish to steam up the kitchen windows on an icy night. This New England–style pie topped with a cheddar pastry crust is an impressive vegetarian dish for the holidays.

Yields one 9 x 13 x 2-inch potpie
Serves 6
Prep time: 1½ hours
Baking time: 45 minutes

CHEDDAR PASTRY
2 cups unbleached white all-purpose flour
½ teaspoon salt
½ cup (1 stick) cold butter, diced
1 cup chilled grated sharp cheddar cheese
4 to 5 tablespoons ice water

VEGETABLE FILLING
1 tablespoon vegetable oil
4 cups chopped leeks★
2 bay leaves
1 teaspoon dried thyme, or 1 tablespoon fresh
1 teaspoon dried sage, or 1 tablespoon fresh
½ teaspoon salt
2 cups green beans (cut into 1-inch lengths)
¾ cup vegetable stock (see Note)
3 cups chopped green cabbage
3 cups cubed butternut squash
3 cups sliced mushrooms

CHEESE SAUCE
3 tablespoons butter
¼ cup unbleached white all-purpose flour
1½ cups warmed vegetable stock (see Note)
½ teaspoon Dijon-style mustard
½ cup grated cheese (Gruyère, Asiago, and/or Parmesan)
Salt and freshly ground black pepper

★Use the well-rinsed white and light green parts of 2 medium leeks

First, make the cheddar pastry: Using a food processor, briefly pulse the flour, salt, and butter until the mixture has lumps about the size of peas. Add the cheddar and pulse a few times until the mixture resembles a coarse meal. Add the water, a tablespoon at a time, pulsing briefly to incorporate. Press the dough into a ball. Wrap in waxed paper or plastic wrap and refrigerate until ready to roll out.

Make the filling: In a large saucepan or pot, warm the oil briefly on medium-high heat and then add the leeks, bay leaves, thyme, sage, and salt and sauté for 3 minutes. Add the green beans and the stock and simmer for 5 minutes. Add the cabbage and squash and cook for 8 to 10 minutes until the vegetables are becoming tender. Add the mushrooms and cook for 3 minutes. Remove from the heat and cover. The goal at this stage is barely tender vegetables that will hold their shape in the baked potpie.

Make the cheese sauce: In a small saucepan, melt the butter and whisk in the flour. Cook, whisking, for a couple of minutes to "cook" the flour, and then continue whisking while you slowly add the vegetable stock and it thickens into a sauce. Add the mustard and cheese and whisk until smooth. Stir the sauce into the vegetable filling. Season with salt and pepper to taste. Pour the filling into a 9 x 13-inch baking dish.

Preheat the oven to 375°F.

On a lightly floured surface, roll out the dough to fit over the baking dish. Cut a few slits in the crust to allow steam to vent for a crisper crust. Place the crust on top of the filling and trim the edges.

Bake the potpie for 40 to 50 minutes until the crust is golden. Let sit for 10 minutes before serving.

NOTE: The squash peels and the tough parts of the leeks make a tasty stock to use in the filling and the cheese sauce. To give the stock time to simmer, prep the leeks and squash before starting the pastry dough. Simmer covered in a large saucepan with about 4 cups water and ½ teaspoon salt. As you need it, dip simmering stock out of the pan.

SERVING AND MENU IDEAS
For a festive fall meal, serve with Jason's Fresh Fennel and Apple Slaw (page 123) and Pumpkin Cheesecake (page 371).

Winter Potpie

On a cold dark night, nothing beats a warm succulent potpie with fresh biscuits just out of the oven. For this potpie, let the oven roast the vegetables while you prepare the other ingredients. While the biscuits are baking on top of the pie, set the table and make a crisp, cool salad. Light some candles and sit down to a cozy dinner reminiscent of days gone by.

The root vegetables do not need to be measured in exact amounts, and you can use more of one than another, according to the amount you have on hand or your own preferences. Aim for about 7 cups prepped.

You can prepare the vegetable filling ahead of time. When the filling is in the baking dish, cover it and refrigerate. Then, about 45 minutes before you want to eat, put the dish of filling into a 425°F oven and make the biscuit batter. When the filling is hot and bubbling, about 25 minutes, spoon on the biscuit batter and bake until the biscuits are golden brown.

Serves 6
Time: about 1 hour 45 minutes

VEGETABLES
1 head garlic
1 cup French lentils, rinsed★
3 cups water
3 bay leaves
2 tablespoons chopped fresh rosemary
1 medium carrot, sliced (1 heaping cup)
1 small parsnip, sliced (1 heaping cup)
1 small rutabaga, cut into chunks (1 heaping cup)
1 small celeriac, cut into chunks (1 heaping cup)
1 medium sweet potato, cut into chunks (about 2 cups)

4 tablespoons olive oil
Salt
Crushed red pepper flakes
1 medium onion, chopped (about 2 cups)
3 cups chopped kale

ROUX
2 tablespoons olive oil
2 tablespoons unbleached white all-purpose flour
2 cups vegetable stock or water (see Note)
1 tablespoon soy sauce
1 teaspoon chopped fresh rosemary

BISCUITS
2½ cups unbleached white all-purpose flour (or up to half whole wheat)
1 teaspoon sugar
½ teaspoon salt
1 teaspoon baking soda
2 teaspoons baking powder
8 tablespoons cold butter, cut into small pieces
2 tablespoons minced scallions
2 tablespoons fresh thyme leaves
1½ cups buttermilk

★Brown lentils aren't as pretty, but if you have them on hand, go ahead and use them.

Preheat the oven to 450°F. Have ready two baking pans or one large baking sheet for roasting the vegetables, and for the potpie, a deep 10-inch pie plate or a 9 x 13-inch baking dish. Separate and peel the garlic cloves.

Place the lentils in a small pot with the water, a few cloves of garlic, 1 bay leaf, and 1 tablespoon of the chopped rosemary. Simmer on low heat until the lentils are al dente and still maintain their shape, about 20 minutes. Drain and set aside.

Peel the root vegetables and cut into bite-size (1- to 1½-inch) chunks. In a bowl, toss the carrots, parsnips, rutabaga, celeriac, and most of the remaining garlic cloves with 2 tablespoons of the olive oil, ½ teaspoon of salt, about ¼ teaspoon red pepper flakes, 1 bay leaf, and 2 teaspoons of the rosemary. Put the vegetables into one of the baking pans or on half of the baking sheet. Cover with aluminum foil.

In the same bowl, toss the sweet potatoes with 1 tablespoon of the olive oil, about ¼ teaspoon salt, a few red pepper flakes, the remaining garlic cloves, and 1 teaspoon of rosemary. Place in the second baking pan or on the other half of the baking sheet (don't cover).

Bake the root vegetables and the sweet potatoes for 15 minutes. Remove the aluminum foil and stir the vegetables and sweet potatoes. Roast for 10 to 15 minutes more, until easily pierced with a fork. When you take the roasted vegetables out of the oven, reduce the temperature to 425°F.

While the vegetables roast, cook the onions and kale and make the roux.

In a skillet on medium heat, cook the onions in the remaining 1 tablespoon olive oil and a little salt until translucent. Stir in the kale. Add a little water, cover, and steam until the kale has softened, but is still bright green. Remove from the heat and set aside uncovered.

Make the roux: In a small heavy skillet, heat the olive oil and stir in the flour. Whisk for about 30 seconds and add the stock, soy sauce, and rosemary. Simmer until the sauce thickens to the consistency of heavy cream. Remove from the heat.

Toss the roasted root vegetables and sweet potatoes with the kale and onions and the drained lentils. Gently fold in the roux. Pour the filling into the pie plate or baking dish and bake until hot and bubbling, 10 to 15 minutes.

Meanwhile, make the biscuits: Sift the flour, sugar, salt, baking soda, and baking powder into a bowl. Using your fingertips or a pastry cutter, work in the butter until thoroughly distributed and crumbly. Stir in the scallions and thyme. Stir in the buttermilk just until well incorporated.

When the filling is bubbling hot, remove the baking dish from the oven and spoon 6 large dollops of the biscuit batter on top of the vegetables. Return to the oven and bake for 10 to 15 minutes until the biscuits are cooked through and golden brown on top. Let rest for about 5 minutes before serving.

NOTE: You can make stock for the roux with the trimmings from the vegetables. While the vegetables are roasting, in a small covered pot, simmer the trimmings in water to cover.

SERVING AND MENU IDEAS
Some applesauce or a simple salad is all you really need with this hearty potpie: however, Baby Arugula Salad with Crusted Chèvre and Pears (page 114) is a delicious match.

Spring Potpie

Potpies have taken on many new fashionable looks since the traditional two-crust pies of yesteryear, but these contemporary pies have not lost their warm, comforting, familiar allure. Here is a spring herb, vegetable, and bean pie enveloped in filo that welcomes warmer, lighter, softer weather that arrives at the end of winter. You can vary the herbs (dill, thyme, or tarragon) and choose a mix of mushrooms.

Although the recipe has several parts, each one is "as easy as pie" to make, and those who have baked with filo dough before will find the pie a cinch to assemble. If you haven't had much experience with filo dough, follow the steps and don't worry about making a mistake. You will have plenty of extra sheets of dough on hand.

Serves 6
Prep time: 45 minutes
Baking time: 35 to 40 minutes

BREAD CRUMBS
⅓ cup bread crumbs
½ cup grated Parmesan cheese
Pinch of freshly ground black pepper

VEGETABLE LAYER
2 tablespoons olive oil
2 cups chopped onions
½ teaspoon salt
¾ pound mushrooms, sliced (about 3 cups)★
1 pound asparagus, stemmed and cut into 1-inch
    pieces (about 2 cups)
⅓ cup chopped fresh dill, tarragon, or thyme
⅓ cup chopped fresh chives or scallions

BEAN LAYER
1 tablespoon olive oil
2 tablespoons chopped garlic
¼ teaspoon crushed red pepper flakes
1 (15-ounce) can navy beans, drained and rinsed
2 tablespoons water
¼ teaspoon salt
Pinch of freshly ground black pepper
2 generous tablespoons chopped fresh dill,
    tarragon, or thyme

FILO "CRUST"
2 tablespoons olive oil, plus more for the baking
    dish
2 tablespoons butter
1 package filo dough
½ cup grated Parmesan cheese

★Cremini, maitake, shiitake, chanterelle, porcini, or white button mushrooms.

Make the bread crumbs: In a small bowl, mix together the bread crumbs, Parmesan, and black pepper and set aside.

Prepare the vegetable layer: Warm the olive oil in a large heavy skillet on medium heat. Add the onions along with the salt and cook for about 5 minutes until soft and translucent. Add the mushrooms and cook for 5 minutes, stirring often. Add the asparagus and cook until the moisture evaporates, the mushrooms are limp and soft, and the asparagus is tender, about 5 minutes. Stir in the fresh herb of your choice and the chives, remove from the heat, and set aside.

Prepare the bean layer: In a small heavy skillet, warm the olive oil. Add the garlic and red pepper flakes and cook for about 30 seconds. Stir in the beans and cook for 5 minutes. Place the beans, water, salt, and black pepper in a food processor and purée until smooth. Briefly whirl in the herbs and set aside.

Preheat the oven to 350°F. Thoroughly oil a deep 10-inch pie plate or 9 x 13-inch baking dish.

Assemble the potpie: Heat the butter and olive oil. Unroll the filo dough on a flat, clean surface and cover it with a tea towel to keep it from drying out. Place a sheet of filo in the prepared pie plate or baking dish, allowing the extra to drape evenly over the sides. Using a pastry brush, brush the filo with the oil-butter mixture and sprinkle with 2 generous tablespoons of the bread-crumb mixture. Repeat until you have 5 layers.

Spread the bean mixture evenly over the top filo layer. Sprinkle with the grated cheese. Add the vegetable layer. Using scissors, trim the filo to about 1½ inches of overhang. Carefully fold this overhang over the vegetables and brush with the oil-butter mixture. Sprinkle the rest of the bread crumbs over the top. Add 4 more layers of filo, two sheets at a time (8 sheets total). Brush the oil-butter mixture between each layer and allow the extra filo to drape evenly over the sides. Trim the edges and use the pastry brush to tuck the filo in around all sides.

Bake the potpie until golden brown, 35 to 40 minutes.

If you prefer to make the potpie ahead, cover it with plastic wrap and refrigerate. A chilled pie will take about 10 minutes longer to bake.

VARIATIONS
- For a vegan option, use olive oil in place of the butter and omit the cheese.
- To the vegetable layer, add 1 cup green peas and/or crumbled feta cheese or dots of creamy goat cheese.

SERVING AND MENU IDEAS
Spring Potpie pairs nicely with a green spring salad, such as Greens with Apricots Times Two (page 111) or Microgreens Salad with Sweet Carrot Dressing (page 117).

Zowee Thai Fried Rice

This dish has lots of ingredients and is a bit of a production, but with protein, nutritious grain, plenty of colorful vegetables and fruits, and a hot and sour bite, it is a tasty meal all in itself.

It's best to use chilled leftover rice or make it ahead. Just-cooked hot rice won't fry as well and may steam into soft clumps. Have all the ingredients prepped and close at hand before you start cooking because the stir-frying goes quickly and requires some theatrical stirring and tossing.

Yields 12 cups
Serves 6 to 8
Time: 50 minutes

1 (16-ounce) block firm tofu, cut into ½-inch cubes
3 tablespoons soy sauce
2 teaspoons dark sesame oil
½ cup cashews or peanuts
4 tablespoons vegetable oil
8 ounces green beans, cut into 1-inch lengths
Salt

1 red onion, diced (about 1½ cups)
1 red bell pepper, seeded and diced (about 1½ cups)
3 celery stalks, thinly sliced (1½ cups)
1 tablespoon peeled and grated fresh ginger
2 tablespoons minced garlic
2 teaspoons ground coriander
6 cups chilled cooked short-grain brown rice
1 tablespoon Chinese chili paste or Sriracha or other hot sauce
1 tomato, diced (about 1 cup)
1 large mango, pitted, peeled, and diced into ½-inch cubes (see sidebar page 118)
¼ cup fresh lime juice
½ cup minced scallions
About 20 fresh basil leaves, cut into thin strips

Put the tofu cubes into a bowl. Add the soy sauce and sesame oil and use a rubber spatula to stir gently to coat. Set aside.

If the nuts are already roasted, set them aside. If not, dry-roast them in a wok or heavy skillet for about 3 minutes until slightly browned, and set aside.

Heat 1 tablespoon of the vegetable oil in a large wok or a large heavy skillet on medium-high heat.

Add the green beans along with a sprinkling of salt and sear for 4 to 5 minutes until bright green with some scorch marks. Set aside.

Add 2 tablespoons of the vegetable oil to the pan and stir-fry the onions, peppers, and celery for a couple of minutes. Add the ginger, garlic, and coriander and the tofu and its marinade. Cook for about 3 minutes, or until the vegetables are tender. Add half the rice and toss to coat. Add the remaining tablespoon of vegetable oil and the rest of the rice and toss again. Cook for 2 to 3 minutes, stirring and tossing to heat through. Add the hot sauce, tomatoes, green beans, and nuts and cook, stirring for a couple of minutes until the tomatoes have slightly softened. Add the mango, lime juice, scallions, and basil and cook until the basil has wilted and the mango hot. Season with salt to taste.

Serve hot immediately.

VARIATIONS

- Instead of tofu, cook a couple of beaten eggs in oil until browned on both sides. Cut into thin strips and add to the rice at the end.
- Top each serving of fried rice with a fried egg.
- Leftover Zowee Thai Fried Rice is a great omelet filling.

SERVING AND MENU IDEAS

This elaborate rice is probably enough on its own, but you could start with Chilled Curried Pea and Coconut Soup (page 106). If you want something crisp and refreshing on the side, perhaps serve with cucumber or watermelon slices.

Kale and Walnut Risotto

Kale and Walnut Risotto is nutritious, satisfying, and quite attractive. Pale green and fresh-tasting, it has quickly become one of our favorites.

If you're new to making risotto, we recommend that you make the pesto before you start sautéing the onions, so you can be relaxed during the stock-adding and stirring process. We think this risotto is best served right away; if you have leftovers, think about making Risotto Cakes (see sidebar, page 175).

Yields 6 cups
Serves 4
Prep time: 35 minutes

½ cup walnuts
1 quart vegetarian no-chicken stock or vegetable
  stock

PESTO
2 garlic cloves
4 cups packed baby kale (8 ounces)
1 cup chopped fresh parsley
½ teaspoon salt
2 tablespoons olive oil
¼ cup water

2 tablespoons extra-virgin olive oil
1½ cups finely chopped onions
1½ cups Arborio rice
½ cup dry white wine
1 cup finely grated Pecorino Romano or
  Parmesan cheese

Toast the walnuts until fragrant and turning darker; set aside to cool. Bring the stock to a simmer in a covered saucepan.

Make the pesto: In a food processor, pulse half of the toasted walnuts with the garlic until ground. Add 2 cups of the kale (put the remaining cup of kale aside). Add the parsley, salt, olive oil, and the water. Process until a paste forms. With a knife, coarsely chop the other half of the walnuts and set aside.

In a large, heavy-bottomed saucepan (nonstick works well for risotto) on medium heat, warm the extra-virgin olive oil. Add the onions and sauté until softened, about 4 minutes. Add the rice and stir, using a wooden spoon to avoid breaking the rice kernels, for a minute to thoroughly coat the rice with oil. Add the wine and cook, stirring constantly, until it has been absorbed.

Add simmering stock, about a cup (a ladleful or two) at a time, stirring after each addition. The liquid should come to a simmer, but don't let it come to a rolling boil. Continue adding stock as the rice absorbs it, every few minutes, stirring frequently.

When you add the last ladleful of stock to the rice, stir in the pesto, the remaining kale, and about half the cheese. Stir and cook for a couple of minutes more until the kale has wilted and the cheese has melted.

Serve hot, topped with the rest of the cheese and the chopped walnuts.

SERVING AND MENU IDEAS
Begin supper with Spicy Butternut Squash Dip (page 64) with crudités. Or accompany this creamy risotto with a salad such as Wax Bean and Radish Salad with Buttermilk Dressing (page 121), Microgreens Salad with Sweet Carrot Dressing (page 117), or sliced tomatoes sprinkled with olive oil, salt, pepper, and chopped fresh basil. Because risotto demands last-minute attention, choose a side that can be made ahead.

Spring Risotto

Packed with tender green vegetables and protein-rich edamame, this elegant risotto is a spring tonic.

Yields 6 cups
Serves 4 to 6
Time: 45 minutes

1½ cups packed chopped arugula
4 tablespoons extra-virgin olive oil
1 teaspoon salt, plus more as needed
1 cup grated Pecorino Romano or Parmesan cheese
12 ounces asparagus spears
4 cups vegetable stock
1 cup water
1 cup frozen shelled edamame, or 1½ cups green peas (petits pois)
1 cup diced onions
1½ cups Arborio or Carnaroli rice
½ cup dry white wine
2 tablespoons minced fresh mint, thyme, or oregano
1 tablespoon butter (optional)
Freshly ground black pepper

Place the arugula, 2 tablespoons of the oil, the salt, and the grated cheese in the bowl of a food processor and whirl for a few seconds. Set aside. Snap off the fibrous tough ends of the asparagus spears and discard. Cut off the tips and set aside. Slice the stalks into 1-inch-long pieces.

Bring the stock and the water to a boil in a saucepan. Lower the heat to maintain a simmer. If using edamame, add them to the stock.

Meanwhile, in a large heavy-bottomed pot (nonstick works well for risotto) on medium heat, cook the onions in the remaining 2 tablespoons oil, stirring occasionally, until translucent but not browned, about 4 minutes. Add the rice and stir, using a wooden spoon to avoid breaking the rice kernels, to thoroughly coat the rice with oil.

Add the wine and stir constantly until the wine has been absorbed.

Add the simmering stock about ½ cup at a time, stirring after each addition. (The edamame will continue to cook whether in the stock or in the rice.) Continue adding stock as the rice absorbs it, every 2 or 3 minutes, stirring frequently. (It will take about 25 minutes to add all the stock and cook the rice until loose but thick and creamy. As the rice nears completion, it requires more frequent stirring.)

When about half the stock has gone into the rice, add the sliced asparagus spears. When there is only about ½ cup of stock left, add the asparagus tips and the green peas, if using. With the last

½ cup of stock, add the reserved arugula and cheese mixture. Stir well and remove from the heat. Gently beat in the fresh herbs and the butter, if using. Season with additional salt and pepper to taste.

SERVING AND MENU IDEAS

Start with Watercress Toast (page 53) or Deviled Eggs (page 57). Lemony Roasted Beets (page 297) are a lovely side dish. Fresh strawberries are the perfect dessert.

LEFTOVER RISOTTO CAKES

Leftover risotto of any kind can be easily turned into crisp golden risotto cakes that are tasty snacks or appetizers, or serve them on a bed of sautéed greens for another meal.

Start with 2 cups cold leftover risotto. Add 1 beaten egg and about ½ cup coarsely shredded cheese and stir until the egg is evenly distributed. Then form into patties (4 large ones or more smaller ones) and coat with bread crumbs or panko (about 1 cup). Cook in a skillet on medium heat in about 1 tablespoon olive oil until golden brown, about 4 minutes per side. Sprinkle with salt and pepper and eat hot.

Cheesy Risotto with Grapes

With more wine and onions than is usual in risotto, this creamy dish is punctuated with bursts of fresh juicy grapes. If risotto is not yet in your repertoire, this is a great recipe for your first experience.

Yields about 8 cups
Serves 4 as a main dish; 8 as a starter
Time: about 45 minutes

1 quart vegetable stock or vegetarian no-chicken stock
2 tablespoons extra-virgin olive oil
1½ cups finely diced onions
1½ cups Arborio or Carnaroli rice
1½ cups dry white wine, such as chardonnay
1 cup grated flavorful creamy cheese, such as aged Gouda, Gruyère, or Fontina Valle d'Aosta
1½ cups seedless red or purple grapes, cut in half if large
Salt and ground black pepper

Bring the stock to a simmer in a covered saucepan.

Meanwhile, warm the olive oil in a heavy-bottomed pot or large saucepan (nonstick works well for risotto) on medium heat. Add the onions and cook for 3 to 4 minutes until translucent but not browned. Add the rice and stir, using a wooden spoon to avoid breaking the rice kernels, to thoroughly coat the rice with oil.

Add half the wine and stir constantly until it has been absorbed. The liquid should come to a simmer, not a rolling boil. Add the rest of the wine and stir until nearly absorbed. Add simmering stock, a ladleful or two at a time, stirring after each addition. Continue adding stock as the rice absorbs it, about every 2 minutes, stirring frequently. (It will take about 25 minutes to fully cook the rice.) With the last ladleful of stock, add the cheese and grapes, and season with salt and pepper to taste. Remove from the heat. Stir to evenly distribute the cheese and grapes and serve immediately.

VARIATION
Stir in some chopped fresh tarragon with the last ladleful of stock.

SERVING AND MENU IDEAS
In Italy, risotto is often served in modest portions as a first course to be followed by an entrée and perhaps a side vegetable. For this style of meal, we suggest Cheesy Risotto with Grapes, followed by Roasted Red Pepper, Black Olive, and Tofu Burgers (page 249) accompanied by a slightly bitter green vegetable, such as Spicy Broccoli Rabe with Sun-Dried Tomatoes and Almonds (page 288) or Beet Greens with Raisins and Pine Nuts (page 290). Or follow the risotto with a substantial salad, such as Spring Greens and Vegetables (page 139).

In this country, risotto is more often served as the main dish and goes well with an interesting green salad, such as Kale, Jicama, and Orange Salad (page 128) or Greens with Citrus-Date Dressing (page 126).

Paella de Verduras

Paella is a comfort meal-in-a-skillet, along the lines of other rice and vegetable pilafs like Indian biryani, Asian fried rice, Creole jambalaya, and West African *theboudienne*.

Our vegetable paella includes the traditional Valencian ingredients white rice, artichokes, white beans, saffron, and rosemary and not-so-traditional leeks, fennel, sweet peppers, and bay. No need to invest in a paella pan; a 10-inch cast-iron or other heavy skillet or Dutch oven works fine. If you are a beginner cook, this is a good dish to try; you'll be rewarded with a tasty, bountiful meal to feed your family and friends.

Serves 4 to 6
Yields about 7 cups
Time: about 1 hour

3 tablespoons extra-virgin olive oil
2 cups chopped leeks, white and tender green parts
1 tablespoon minced or pressed garlic
1 teaspoon ground fennel seeds
1 teaspoon sweet paprika
1½ teaspoons salt, plus more as needed
1½ cups diced red, orange, or yellow bell peppers, or a combination
⅓ cup dry sherry
1 (14-ounce) can artichoke hearts, drained and quartered
1 cup diced fresh tomatoes, or 1 (15-ounce) can diced tomatoes, drained
1 (15-ounce) can butter beans or cannellini beans, drained
¾ cup medium-grain white rice
¼ teaspoon saffron
1 bay leaf
1 sprig fresh rosemary
1½ cups water
1 cup green peas, fresh or frozen (optional)

In a paella pan, large cast-iron or other heavy skillet, or Dutch oven on medium heat, warm the oil and add the leeks, garlic, fennel, paprika, and salt. Cover and cook until the leeks soften. Add a few splashes of water if needed to prevent sticking. Stir in the bell peppers and sherry and cook for 5 minutes. Stir in the artichoke hearts, tomatoes, beans, rice, saffron, bay leaf, and rosemary. Pour in the water and stir well. Cover with a tight-fitting lid or aluminum foil and bring to a boil. Reduce the heat and simmer, covered, for 25 minutes, or until the rice is tender and the liquid has been mostly absorbed. Remove the lid, sprinkle on the green peas if using (frozen straight from the freezer works), cover, and steam the peas for about 5 minutes. If all the liquid has not been absorbed, remove the pan from the heat, remove the lid, and cover the pan with a clean dishtowel. Replace the lid on top of the towel and set aside for 10 minutes.

Just before serving, remove and discard the bay leaf and rosemary sprig. Stir to fluff the rice and distribute the vegetables and beans. Season with additional salt to taste.

SERVING AND MENU IDEAS
A meal unto itself: Start with a bowl of Spiced Nuts (page 59) to generate excitement.

Stuffed Poblano Peppers

Dark green poblanos are mild to medium hot and have a complex flavor, especially when roasted. And they are sturdy, so they work well for stuffing. Happily, they have become much more widely available in grocery stores and at farmers' markets.

The delicious filling can be used to stuff other vegetables, too. Try it in bell peppers, winter squash, tomatoes, sweet potatoes, or zucchini.

Serves 4 to 6
Yields 6 stuffed peppers
Time: about 1 hour 10 minutes

6 medium fresh poblano peppers
2 teaspoons olive oil or olive oil spray

FILLING

2 cups chopped onions
½ teaspoon salt, plus more as needed
2 tablespoons olive oil
2 large garlic cloves, minced
2 teaspoons ground cumin
1 teaspoon dried basil
1 teaspoon chili powder
1 cup fresh or frozen corn kernels
1 tablespoon cream cheese
1 cup cooked brown rice★
1 tomato, cored and diced
3 tablespoons chopped fresh cilantro
1 cup shredded Monterey Jack cheese
Freshly ground black pepper

★If you don't have leftover rice, the first thing to do is cook some.

Preheat the oven to 475°F. Line a roasting pan with parchment paper or brush with oil. Rub or spray the poblano peppers with oil. Roast the peppers for about 20 minutes, turning halfway through the roasting time, until the peppers are soft and the skin is somewhat blackened.

Meanwhile, make the filling: In a large skillet on medium heat, cook the onions along with the salt in the olive oil until softened. Add the garlic and cook for a few minutes more until lightly browned. Add the cumin, basil, chili powder, corn, and cream cheese. Stir until everything is heated through and the cream cheese has melted.

In a large bowl, combine the rice, tomato, cilantro, and ½ cup of the cheese. Stir in the cooked onions and corn mixture. Season with additional salt and black pepper to taste.

When you take the peppers out of the oven, place them in a bowl and cover with plastic wrap or a plate and set aside until cool enough to handle. If any juice has accumulated in the sheet, add it to the filling. Reduce the oven temperature to 350°F.

Remove and discard any blistered poblano skin. Keeping the stem intact, make a lengthwise slit in each pepper. Gently open the pepper and scrape out the seeds. Pack about ½ cup of the filling into the cavity of each pepper; the slit should be open about ½ inch. Sprinkle the remaining ½ cup cheese on top of the filling, place the peppers back on the baking sheet, and return to the oven for about 10 minutes.

SERVING AND MENU IDEAS

With Stuffed Poblano Peppers as the centerpiece, there are so many good dishes you can add to make a feast. Start with a soup, such as Sopa Verde de Elote (page 90) or Roasted Carrot Gazpacho (page 105). Maybe a salad, such as Belgian Endive Citrus Salad with Gremolata (page 129) or Mango-Spinach Salad (page 118), or a side vegetable like Sweet Potatoes with Bitter Orange (page 303) or a gorgeous platter of Roasted Winter Squash Agrodolce (page 309). Surely, Carrot Cornbread (page 281) should be on the table and a few Tomatillo Pickles (page 343). Then for dessert, how about Coconut-Pineapple Sorbet (page 382).

Mushroom-Stuffed Winter Squash

Butternut and delicata are probably the favorite varieties of winter squash at Moosewood because they are beautiful and delightfully sweet. We've been stuffing them in various ways for decades. Here they are stuffed with a simple layering of onions and mushrooms seasoned with herbs and sherry or wine.

If you have various types and sizes of winter squash to choose from, we recommend 4 to 6 smallish delicata because they're usually so sweet and their skin is tender and edible. But you can make this dish with whatever squash you have—just layer more or less of the onions and mushrooms depending on the size of the cavities. If you have one large butternut, scoop out some of the flesh along the neck to make a longer space for the filling. Two large acorn squash or 4 to 6 smaller ones will work. You could even stuff a medium-size Hubbard. Be creative and practical about how you "stuff" whatever squash you have.

Serves 4
Time: about 1 hour, 15 minutes

1 large butternut squash, or 2 large or 6 small
  delicata squash, etc. (see headnote)
olive oil
½ cup water
Splash of dry sherry or wine

ONION LAYER
2 tablespoons olive oil
2 cups chopped onions
2 large garlic cloves, pressed or minced
¼ teaspoon salt
¼ teaspoon freshly ground black pepper
½ teaspoon dried thyme
1 teaspoon dried tarragon
⅓ cup minced fresh parsley

MUSHROOM LAYER
2 tablespoons olive oil
4 cups thickly sliced white or cremini mushrooms
Salt and freshly ground black pepper
1 tablespoon soy sauce
2 tablespoons red wine
1 tablespoon chopped fresh tarragon
3 tablespoons dry sherry or wine

2 tablespoons butter or olive oil, microwaved with
  an optional chopped garlic clove

Preheat the oven to 350°F. Lightly oil a baking sheet.

Wash the squash and cut it in half lengthwise. Remove the seeds. Place the squash halves, cut side down, on the baking sheet and brush the skin with oil. Sprinkle the squash with the water and sherry. Cover with aluminum foil and bake until the flesh is beginning to soften and the bottom surface has browned. Turn the squash over and continue to bake, covered, until tender and done. The baking time depends on the squash you're using.

Make the onion layer: Heat the oil in a large skillet and sauté the onions, garlic, salt, pepper, thyme, and tarragon until the onions are translucent and beginning to brown. Transfer to a bowl and stir in half the parsley. Cover and set aside.

Make the mushroom layer: Add the oil to the same skillet. Add the mushrooms, sprinkle with salt and pepper, and sauté for 3 to 4 minutes until they release moisture and begin to brown. The mushrooms will shrink in volume a lot; keep stirring to brown on all sides. When browned, sprinkle with the soy sauce, red wine, and tarragon and sauté for 2 to 3 minutes more. Transfer the mushrooms to a bowl and set aside. Deglaze the skillet with the sherry and any juices remaining in the baking pan and reserve. (If there was no liquid left in the baking pan, add a teaspoon of olive oil and some water.)

Arrange the baked squash on a serving platter. Score and loosen the flesh a little with a fork, and drizzle with the heated butter or olive oil. Sprinkle lightly with salt and pepper. Spread some of the sautéed onions on each squash half, and then mushrooms. Drizzle with the juices from the skillet. Neatly mound the remaining onions and mushrooms on the squash and sprinkle with the remaining parsley.

SERVING AND MENU IDEAS
Great served with fresh applesauce, cranberry sauce, or a fruity relish.

Asparagus with Fried Eggs and Sizzled Shallots

Easy and elegant looking, this classic Italian dish has been a favorite of ours for a long time, and we shared it with you in one of our cookbooks years ago. But then we tried a simple little recipe by Deborah Madison in which she recommends a sizzling vinegar and shallot sauce for fried eggs, which gives them a "new personality." It is a great combo.

This dish is good for brunch or a special supper, especially in spring when the first beautiful asparagus spears appear at the farmers' market or in your garden.

Serves 2
Time: 15 to 20 minutes

Salt and freshly ground black pepper
1 pound fresh asparagus
2 large shallots
3 teaspoons extra-virgin olive oil
2 tablespoons red wine vinegar
2 or 4 large eggs
2 tablespoons shaved Pecorino Romano cheese

In a wide pot, bring several inches of salted water to a boil. While the water heats, snap off and discard the fibrous tough ends of the asparagus spears and peel and finely slice or dice the shallots. Set aside.

When the water boils, cook the asparagus spears until just tender, 5 to 8 minutes.

While the asparagus cooks, heat 2 teaspoons of the olive oil in a heavy skillet on medium-high heat. Sizzle the shallots until golden brown, a minute or two. Transfer to a cup and stir in the vinegar. Set aside.

Add the remaining 1 teaspoon olive oil to the hot skillet and crack the eggs into the skillet. Cover and cook until the whites are firm and crisp around the edges and the yolks are partially cooked but not hard.

Arrange the drained, hot asparagus on serving plates and top with the fried eggs. Top the fried eggs with the shallots. Sprinkle on the cheese and salt and pepper and serve immediately.

SERVING AND MENU IDEAS
Serve after Watercress Toast (page 53) or Green and Yellow Summer Fritters (page 37) or Edamame Hummus (page 65) with crudités. At brunch, this goes well with Focaccia Pugliese (page 277) and Sweet Fruit Smoothies (page 24).

Black Sesame-Coated Tofu and Udon Noodles

Fried tofu coated with black sesame seeds is flavorful and has an interesting texture. Baby bok choy is juicy and fresh, and the udon noodles are long, slippery strands. We think you'll be happy.

Serves 4
Time: 60 minutes

1 (16 ounce) block firm tofu

MARINADE
⅓ cup soy sauce
¼ cup apple cider vinegar
2 tablespoons vegetable oil
¼ teaspoon freshly ground black pepper

1 (8-ounce) package udon noodles
14 to 16 ounces baby bok choy, coarsely chopped
4 scallions, chopped

TOFU TRIANGLES
¼ cup whole wheat flour
¼ cup black sesame seeds
Pinch of salt

3 tablespoons vegetable oil (canola, olive, grapeseed, or peanut) for frying
Salt and freshly ground black pepper

Blot the tofu with paper towels. Cut the block into 8 slabs, about ½ inch thick, then cut the slabs in half diagonally into triangles. Place the triangles in a single layer in a large baking dish. Combine the marinade ingredients. Drizzle half the marinade over the tofu triangles and set the other half aside. Set the triangles aside to marinate for at least 15 minutes, turning them over once to coat both sides with marinade.

Meanwhile, cook the noodles until almost done. In a colander, run the noodles under cold water and drain. Prep the bok choy and scallions.

Coat the tofu triangles: Mix the flour, black sesame seeds, and salt and spread on a plate. Coat the tofu triangles on both sides. Press firmly with your fingers to be sure the seeds stick to the tofu. Place the coated triangles on a dry plate. Reserve any marinade.

In a large skillet on medium-high heat, warm 2 tablespoons of the oil and fry the tofu until crisp, in several batches.

In a large saucepan on medium-high heat, stir-fry the bok choy and scallions in the remaining 1 tablespoon oil until barely tender. Add the drained noodles and reserved marinade, and cook on medium heat for about 5 minutes, tossing frequently, until hot. Season with salt and pepper to taste.

Mound the noodles and bok choy on a serving platter, arrange the tofu triangles on top, and serve.

VARIATIONS
- All-purpose flour could be used instead of whole wheat.
- Add matchstick-cut carrots when cooking the bok choy.

SERVING AND MENU IDEAS
Some of us like to drizzle a little dark sesame oil on the mound of noodles and bok choy before topping with the tofu triangles. If you'd like a salad with this, Microgreens Salad with Sweet Carrot Dressing (page 117) is a good choice, or maybe Gingered Radish Pickles (page 336) on the side would do it. Finish with slices of watermelon and cups of green tea.

Scallion Crepes with Chinese Greens

Rolling your own crepes is a fun way to start a meal. Or these crepes can be the meal.

Light, pale yellow scallion crepes are tasty and have a delicate texture. Making crepes is surprisingly easy. The batter is whirled in a blender, and the crepes flip over obediently. The crepes are also good with other fillings, as long as the ingredients are thinly sliced and soft enough not to tear the delicate wrappers.

The medley of Chinese greens is an excellent filling for these crepes, and is also good on rice or in an omelet.

Yields 10 to 12 crepes; about 3 cups Chinese greens
Serves 4 to 6
Prep and cooking time for the crepes:
   30 minutes
Prep and cooking time for the greens:
   20 minutes

SCALLION CREPES

1½ cups water
3 large eggs
1 tablespoon dark sesame oil
1 tablespoon soy sauce
1 tablespoon vegetable oil, plus more for frying
1 cup unbleached white all-purpose flour
6 scallions

CHINESE GREENS

4 ounces mushrooms (about 1 cup sliced)
1 pound yu choy★ or baby bok choy (about 9 cups sliced)
4 ounces snow peas (about 1 cup sliced)
1 tablespoon vegetable oil
2 tablespoons water
1 tablespoon soy sauce
¼ teaspoon salt

GARNISH SUGGESTIONS

Chopped roasted peanuts
Toasted sesame seeds
Sliced scallions
Chiffonade of fresh basil
Simplest Sauce (see page 193) or other light sweet-sour Asian condiment

★Yu choy is a green, leafy Chinese cabbage with a delicate sweet flavor. Yu choy, also called yau choy, has long, slender stalks with dark green flat leaves and small yellow flowers. The flowers are cooked along with the leaves and stems; they are not bitter and do not mean the plant is past its prime.

Make the crepes: Put the water, eggs, sesame oil, soy sauce, and vegetable oil into the blender. Whirl at high speed briefly. Add the flour and whirl again. Scrape down the sides and whirl briefly. Set aside. Pull off any dried outer layers of the scallions and cut off the roots and all but about 3 inches of the green tops. Wash and blot dry. Slice very thinly on a diagonal. You should have about ½ cup after slicing. Place in a small bowl next to the stovetop.

Preheat the oven to 250°F. Warm about a tablespoon of vegetable oil in an 8- or 9-inch crepe pan on medium heat. Brush the oil over the bottom and keep the oil-soaked brush next to the pan. When the pan is hot, but not smoking, pour ⅓ cup of the crepe batter into the middle of the pan and tilt the pan to spread the batter evenly over the bottom surface of the pan all the way to the edges. Scatter some chopped scallions over the top and cook for about a minute, until the bottom is golden. Run a spatula around the outside of the crepe and flip it over. Cook until dry, less than a minute, and slide the crepe onto a plate. Continue making crepes, sliding each onto the top of the stack, until all the batter has been used. Between every few crepes or if a crepe sticks, brush more oil on the bottom of the pan. Wrap the stack of crepes in aluminum foil and keep warm in the oven.

Prepare the Chinese greens: Remove the mushroom stems and slice each cap in half horizontally, then slice in the usual way, from the top down. You'll have about a cup of roughly rectangular mushroom pieces. Slice the greens crosswise, starting at the leaf end. Cut into 1-inch lengths and then into shorter pieces as you go, slicing the thicker stalks into ¼-inch pieces. Slice the snow peas crosswise into pieces about ¼ inch wide.

Heat the vegetable oil in a wok or large skillet on medium-high heat. Add the mushrooms and stir-fry for 2 minutes. Add the yu choy or bok choy and stir-fry until just wilted, about 3 minutes. Add the sliced snow peas and stir-fry for a minute or two. Add the water, soy sauce, and salt and stir-fry briefly. Cover, reduce the heat to medium, and steam until just tender-crisp, about 3 minutes. Transfer to a serving bowl.

Put the stack of crepes, the bowl of greens, and small bowls of whichever garnishes you're serving in the middle of the table, so that each person can put a crepe on their plate, put a spoonful of greens in the middle of the crepe, sprinkle with garnishes, and fold the crepe over or roll it up. Serve with knives and forks or chopsticks.

SERVING AND MENU IDEAS

Filled crepes make a light meal by themselves, but also go well with Vietnamese Lemongrass Vegetable Soup (page 101).

Cuban Picadillo

Picadillo is served throughout Central and South America and the Caribbean. It is one of Latin America's staples. Each country, even each household, has its favorite version. Picadillo is traditionally served with rice and beans or used as a filling in tacos or empanadas. Most picadillos are ground beef simmered with a *sofrito* of tomatoes, onions, peppers, herbs, and spices. Sometimes regional vegetables and ingredients are added. We think frozen and thawed tofu gives this picadillo the chewy texture of classic picadillos.

Our friend Ian Irvin's picadillo, which he learned to make as a child in Cuba, is the inspiration for our vegetarian (and vegan) version.

Yields 6 cups
Time to freeze and thaw the tofu: at least
  12 hours
Time: 1 hour

1 (16-ounce block) tofu, frozen and thawed★

SOFRITO
1½ cups diced onions
3 garlic cloves, minced or pressed (1 tablespoon)
2 tablespoons olive oil
1¼ teaspoons salt

1 cup diced green bell peppers
1½ teaspoons ground cinnamon
2 teaspoons ground cumin
1 large bay leaf
¼ teaspoon ground black pepper
1 (28-ounce) can diced tomatoes
⅓ cup raisins

⅓ cup coarsely ground almonds
2 tablespoons soy sauce
⅓ cup sliced stuffed Spanish olives or
  Castelvetrano olives

★When tofu is frozen, the water within it separates into little cells and leaves the tofu like a sponge. After it has thawed, it has a chewy texture, and you squeeze out the water and crumble or shred the tofu. To freeze, put the block of tofu on a plate in the freezer until frozen solid, about 4 hours in most freezers. If you're going to keep the tofu in the freezer longer than a day, put it in a freezer bag to prevent freezer burn. Thaw the frozen block of tofu in the refrigerator for at least 8 hours. Or you can thaw it at room temperature, usually in a few hours. When we've forgotten to take it out of the freezer, we've even thawed it in a 250°F oven for about 30 minutes, turning it over every 10 minutes. Drained, thawed tofu will keep well wrapped in the refrigerator for a day, but it should be used soon.

Make the sofrito: In a heavy-bottomed saucepan, sauté the onions and garlic in the olive oil along with the salt for 5 minutes, until the onions are translucent. Add the bell peppers, cinnamon, cumin, bay leaf, and black pepper and cook for another 5 minutes, stirring often and scraping the bottom of the pan to prevent the spices from sticking or scorching. Stir in the tomatoes and raisins, cover the pan, and bring to a boil. Reduce the heat and simmer for 20 minutes.

While the sofrito simmers, toast the almonds and set aside to cool. When the almonds have cooled to room temperature, whirl them in a food processor just until coarsely ground. Hold the thawed tofu over a colander and squeeze out as much water as you can. The colander will catch any pieces of tofu that may fall. Crumble or grate the tofu into a mixing bowl. Toss with the soy sauce and ground almonds.

When the sofrito has simmered for 20 minutes, stir in the tofu-almond mixture. Add the sliced olives (or serve them later at the table). Simmer for another 10 minutes. The mixture will be quite thick; stir frequently to prevent sticking and add a little water if needed.

SERVING AND MENU IDEAS

Use as a filling for tacos, burritos, or empanadas. Or serve on yellow rice and top with chopped fresh parsley or cilantro and a dollop of sour cream. Add a side of fried plantains, a tangy slaw, and sliced tropical fruit, such as mango, papaya, or pineapple for a very satisfying meal.

Pineapple-Lime Glazed Tofu with Spicy Cucumber Salad

This dish has so much going on. With an amazing variety of textures and flavors—sweet shallots and pineapple, tangy lime, cool cucumbers, salty hot-and-sour dressing, chewy tofu, crunchy salad, and toasted peanuts—this is a perfect dish for summer lunch or supper. Pan-frying the tofu is a quick way to brown it and give it a crisp skin. Then the tofu and pineapple chunks finish in a pineapple-lime marinade that reduces to envelop them in a shiny glaze. Doesn't this sound good?

Serves 4
Prep time: about 1 hour

SPICY CUCUMBER SALAD
3 cucumbers
½ teaspoon salt, plus more as needed
1 red or orange bell pepper

DRESSING
2 tablespoons sunflower oil, peanut oil, or
   vegetable oil
½ cup thinly sliced shallots or red onions
½ cup rice vinegar
2 tablespoons brown sugar
2 tablespoons soy sauce
¼ teaspoon crushed red pepper flakes or Chinese
   chili paste

MARINADE
2 tablespoons coconut oil or vegetable oil
3 tablespoons soy sauce
2 tablespoons minced lemongrass, tender part only
   (optional)
½ teaspoon ground turmeric
1 teaspoon finely grated lime zest
¼ cup fresh lime juice
¾ cup pineapple juice
¼ teaspoon crushed red pepper flakes or Chinese
   chili paste with garlic, more to taste

1 (16-ounce) block firm tofu
2 tablespoons coconut oil
2 cups fresh pineapple chunks
Salt
½ head lettuce, shredded
½ cup grated carrots
¼ cup toasted peanuts, coarsely chopped
¼ cup chopped fresh cilantro

Make the salad: Peel, halve lengthwise, and seed the cucumbers, then cut each half into 1-inch-thick crescents. Put the cucumber crescents into a colander, sprinkle with the salt, and place a weight on top, such as a zip-top bag filled with water or a heavy plate. Set aside to drain for about 30 minutes.

Meanwhile, halve, seed, and stem the bell pepper and cut into ½-inch-long strips. Set aside.

Make the dressing: In a small saucepan, warm the sunflower oil and cook the shallots with a sprinkle of salt until just wilted. Add the vinegar, sugar, soy sauce, and red pepper flakes and simmer for about 3 minutes. Set aside.

When the cucumbers have drained, rinse, pat dry, and toss in a bowl with the bell pepper strips and the dressing. Set aside.

Make the marinade: In a small bowl, whisk together the coconut oil, soy sauce, lemongrass (if using), turmeric, lime zest and juice, pineapple juice, and red pepper flakes. Set aside.

Dry the tofu by wrapping it in folded paper towels, gently pressing out excess water, and patting it dry. Cut the block of tofu into three equal horizontal slices, stack them, and cut into 1-inch cubes.

In a large skillet on medium-high heat, warm the coconut oil until fairly hot. Add the tofu cubes in a single layer (be careful not to be splattered by the hot oil). Fry the tofu until it is brown on the bottom, about 5 minutes, then carefully turn over the cubes and fry until brown on the other sides, about 5 minutes. The browned tofu forms a crisp skin. Lower the heat to medium and pour the marinade over the tofu. Stir in the pineapple chunks. Gently toss the tofu and pineapple as the marinade cooks, thickens, and is absorbed, about 10 minutes. When finished, the tofu and pineapple will be coated with a shiny glaze. Sprinkle with salt. Set aside.

Compose the dish on a large, colorful platter or on individual salad plates. Make a bed of shredded lettuce, mound on cucumber salad and tofu, side by side. Sprinkle grated carrots, peanuts, and cilantro on top.

VARIATIONS
- Also good served on a bed of brown rice instead of lettuce.
- You can use unsweetened canned pineapple chunks instead of fresh pineapple. Drain it and reserve the juice for the marinade. If you don't have ¾ cup of juice, add water to make that amount.

SERVING AND MENU IDEAS
Your meal is taken care of, but Coconut Rice Pudding with Mangoes (page 379) would be a lovely finish.

Persian Kuku

Try this if you enjoy green veggies in your omelets. *Kuku* is a traditional Persian egg dish made with lots of fresh greens and herbs. There are many variations of kuku throughout the Middle East. This version has a fluffy texture from the flavorful sharp and mild cheeses. Some recipes include toasted walnuts and a garnish of barberries for color. Crimson pomegranate seeds work beautifully as well, as do sliced red or yellow cherry tomatoes.

Serves 6
Prep time: 30 minutes
Baking time: 50 to 55 minutes

3 tablespoons olive oil, plus more for the baking dish
1 large garlic clove, minced or pressed
8 packed cups fresh baby spinach or baby kale (one 10- or 11-ounce package)
2 medium leeks, cleaned, white and tender green parts finely chopped (about 2 packed cups)
¼ teaspoon salt, plus more as needed
½ cup finely chopped scallions
¼ cup finely chopped fresh cilantro
¼ cup finely chopped fresh dill
6 large eggs, beaten
½ cup crumbled feta cheese
1 cup cottage cheese
½ cup grated kasseri or Pecorino Romano cheese
¼ teaspoon freshly grated nutmeg
¼ teaspoon freshly ground black pepper

Preheat the oven to 350°F. Oil a 2-quart baking dish, 9 x 7-inch baking pan, or an ovenproof skillet.

In a soup pot on medium-high heat, warm 1 tablespoon of the olive oil, add the garlic, and cook briefly. Stir in the baby greens, cover, and steam until just wilted. Drain in a colander, pressing out any excess liquid. Turn the greens out onto a cutting board, chop coarsely, and transfer to a large mixing bowl.

In a small skillet or sauté pan on medium-high heat, warm the remaining 2 tablespoons olive oil, add the leeks, and sauté along with a sprinkling of salt until softened. Transfer to the bowl of cooked greens. Stir in the scallions, cilantro, dill, eggs, feta, cottage cheese, kasseri or Pecorino Romano cheese, nutmeg, pepper, and salt and mix well.

Pour the mixture into the prepared baking pan. Smooth the top and cover the pan with aluminum foil. Bake for 20 minutes. Remove the foil and bake uncovered for 30 to 35 minutes more, until the kuku is browned around the edges and golden on top.

VARIATION

This recipe can be made dairy-free by omitting the cheeses and doubling the quantity of scallions and herbs. Although denser in texture and flavor, the kuku will be closer to a time-honored recipe. Both versions are delicious.

SERVING AND MENU IDEAS

Serve hot or at room temperature as a main dish, side dish, or as an appetizer (cut small). It pairs wonderfully with Roasted Beet and Walnut Dip (page 63) and Sweet Potatoes with Bitter Orange (page 303).

Korean Noodle Pancake

This homey pancake—simply lots of thinly sliced, finely chopped, or shredded vegetables held together by eggs and strands of noodles—is a great thing to make for lunch, supper, appetizer, or snack. It's so full of vegetables that it won't hold together like an omelet (less eggy), but that's part of what makes it so good. Our Simplest Sauce is more delicious than you might guess.

When you're scrounging around in your refrigerator and find a couple of baby bok choy, the last inner stalks of a head of celery, an ear of corn, or one carrot, don't keep passing them by until they're fit only for the compost pile, just turn to this recipe. Other vegetables are also delicious: mushrooms, spinach, broccoli, cabbage, red or green bell peppers, carrots, zucchini, and bean sprouts. Use about 2½ cups of finely sliced, chopped, or shredded vegetables total.

Yields one 10- or 12-inch pancake
Serves 2 to 4
Time: 35 minutes

3 ounces Korean sweet potato vermicelli★ or other Asian noodles (1 cup cooked)
4 large eggs
¼ teaspoon salt
⅓ cup thinly sliced scallions or chopped fresh chives
⅓ cup thinly sliced celery
1 cup fresh corn kernels or thawed frozen corn kernels
1 cup thinly sliced yu choy★★ or baby bok choy leaves and stems

SIMPLEST SAUCE
¼ cup pure maple syrup
¼ cup apple cider vinegar
¼ cup soy sauce

1 tablespoon olive oil
Sliced scallions

★Korean sweet potato noodles are translucent with a unique texture—pleasant, light, and springy. They're always used in the Korean stir-fry dish, *Jap Chae*. *Dang-myeon* in Korean, sometimes called glass noodles in English, they're made from sweet potato starch.
★★Yu choy is a flowering brassica with flat leaves, slender stalks, and small yellow flowers, usually picked when 9 to 12 inches long. Its flavor is fresh and mild, a little grassy.

Cook the noodles according to the package directions. Drain and set aside to cool.

In a mixing bowl, beat the eggs until evenly colored. Mound the cool cooked noodles on a cutting board and cut every 2 inches or so, for pieces 2 to 4 inches long. Add the noodles, salt, scallions, celery, corn, and yu choy to the bowl and stir well.

Make the sauce: In a small bowl, mix together the maple syrup, vinegar, and soy sauce. Set aside.

Warm the olive oil in a 10- or 12-inch skillet on medium heat. Pour the egg-noodle-vegetable mixture into the skillet and spread it out evenly. After about 4 minutes, when the bottom is beginning to brown, cut the pancake into wedges and flip each over. The pancake is full of veggies and some may break loose at the edges—that's OK.

When the pancake is cooked through and both sides have browned, serve the wedges straight from the skillet. Pass the sauce at the table. Garnish with sliced scallions.

SERVING AND MENU IDEAS
Hot-and-Sour Mushroom Soup (page 97) or Chilled Pineapple-Mango Soup (page 104) nicely complements this dish.

Burmese Tohu Thoke

Tohu thoke is a chilled Burmese salad (*thoke*) composed of *tohu* (similar in texture to both tofu and polenta, but made with chickpea flour) tossed with a tamarind–hot pepper–herbed dressing and topped with crisp fried shallots. Intrigued by this curious array of ingredients? Try this refreshing salad for something different. You can serve it plain, or with some of the extras that we think make it most interesting and delicious.

Chickpea flour is available in the gluten-free and Indian foods sections of well-stocked supermarkets. A thermometer is a useful tool for deep-frying the shallots, but we also give you directions for deep-frying in two batches without a thermometer.

Serves 4 to 6
Prep time: 30 minutes
Cooling and chilling time: 1½ hours

TOHU
2 cups vegetable stock
1 cup chickpea flour
¼ teaspoon ground turmeric
1 cup cold water

CRISP FRIED SHALLOTS
2 cups vegetable oil (peanut, canola, sunflower, coconut, or safflower oils)
2 cups thinly sliced shallots

TAMARIND DRESSING
2 tablespoons tamarind concentrate
3 tablespoons water
2 garlic cloves, pressed or minced
1 fresh hot pepper, seeded and minced
1 tablespoon fresh lime juice
2 teaspoons brown sugar
1 teaspoon oil from cooking the shallots★
½ cup chopped fresh cilantro, mint, and/or Thai or regular basil
Salt
Hot sauce

OPTIONAL EXTRAS
4 cups chopped romaine lettuce
2 cups chopped cucumbers
¾ cup sliced radishes
2 cups steamed green beans
½ cup sliced scallions
⅓ cup chopped fresh cilantro

★Or a mild vegetable oil if you opt to not make the shallots.

Make the tohu: Bring the vegetable stock to a rolling boil. In a bowl, whisk together the chickpea flour, turmeric, and cold water until smooth. Stir the chickpea flour mixture into the boiling stock, lower the heat to its lowest, and stir vigorously for 5 minutes. Pour into a 9-inch square pan and spread evenly. Cool to room temperature, then chill in the refrigerator for at least 1 hour.

Fry the shallots: Heat the oil in a saucepan on medium heat until it shimmers and a slice of shallot bubbles and sizzles when dropped in (275°F). Fry the shallots, stirring often, for 8 minutes, until lightly golden. Using a skimmer or strainer, transfer the shallots to a plate. Increase the heat to medium-high (350°F). Set up a strainer over another saucepan or a heatproof bowl. Carefully pour the shallots into the hot oil and sizzle for just 2 or 3 seconds to brown and crisp, and then immediately pour the hot oil and shallots into the strainer to drain the oil from the shallots. When well drained, empty the crisp shallots onto a paper towel–lined plate. Lightly salt the cooked shallots and set aside at room temperature, uncovered, for use the same day. (Cool the shallot-infused oil to room temperature and then refrigerate to use in future cooking.)

Make the dressing: In a bowl, dilute the tamarind concentrate with the water. Add the remaining ingredients and whisk until smooth. Season the dressing with salt and hot sauce to taste.

Assemble the tohu: At serving time, cut the tohu into strips about ½ inch wide by 2 to 3 inches long and remove from the pan with a spatula. Place the tohu strips in a bowl and toss gently with about three-quarters of the dressing. Top with the fried shallots and serve with the remaining dressing. Or serve on a bed of greens topped with any or all of the suggested extras. Serve with the remaining dressing.

NOTE: Plain tohu keeps refrigerated for 4 to 5 days; drain the liquid that gathers in the bottom of the container. The cooled shallots will keep in an airtight container until the next day.

SERVING AND MENU IDEAS
Another excellent opportunity to employ those Monsoon Pickles (page 339) waiting in your fridge.

Squash Polenta with Mushroom and Kale Stew

A deeply flavored, rich, and woodsy stew is an ideal solace on a chilly evening, especially when served over soft and comforting polenta. This polenta is especially sunny with the addition of puréed winter squash, which gives it a subtle vegetable sweetness that works really well with the cheese, and also gives it a smooth, creamy texture.

When you make this stew with portobellos, it looks its best immediately after cooking, while it is still colorful. If you make it ahead and it sits, it will turn a bit dark and gothic . . . and there's nothing wrong with that.

Serves 4
Time: 45 minutes

POLENTA

1 cup cornmeal★
1 teaspoon salt
2½ cups cold water
1½ cups puréed cooked winter squash (a 12-ounce package of frozen is fine)
½ cup grated Pecorino Romano or Parmesan cheese

STEW

2 cups diced onions
1 red bell pepper, stemmed, seeded, and diced (about 1¼ cups)
3 tablespoons extra-virgin olive oil
1½ pounds mushrooms★★ (8 to 10 cups chopped)
1 teaspoon dried thyme
½ cup red wine or marsala
1 tablespoon soy sauce
2 cups baby kale
Salt and cracked black pepper

★You can use coarse or fine cornmeal for polenta, but the cooking time varies significantly depending on the grind (15 to 35 minutes).
★★Choose a variety of mushrooms. Start with about ½ pound of portobellos for meatiness and bulk, and then choose a pound of mushrooms such as shiitake, morels, oyster mushrooms, or golden trumpets, or wild or exotic varieties. Or just use the more economical cremini or white button mushrooms, which also work fine in this stew.

Make the polenta: In a heavy-bottomed 2-quart saucepan, stir together the cornmeal, salt, and cold water. Bring to a boil on high heat, stirring constantly with a wooden spoon. Reduce the heat to a simmer. If the polenta starts spitting, lower the heat or loosely cover the pan. Stir the polenta every few minutes to prevent sticking, and cook until it is soft and thick, pulls away from the sides of the pot when stirred, and tastes done. Depending on the grind and kind of your cornmeal, you might need to add a little more water, and the simmering time can range between 15 and 30 minutes. Add the puréed squash and stir to incorporate. Turn off the heat and stir in the cheese.

Make the stew: In a stew pot on medium heat, warm the oil and cook the onions and bell peppers for about 5 minutes. Gently wipe off any grit clinging to the mushrooms with a soft brush or a damp towel; avoid immersing or rinsing them in water. Chop portobellos into 1-inch pieces. Cut other mushrooms lengthwise into halves or quarters. Separate oyster mushrooms or other mushrooms that grow in clumps into smaller bunches. Add the tougher mushrooms, like portobellos, porcini, cremini, or shiitake to the onions and peppers in the stew pot and stir to coat with oil. After 4 to 5 minutes, add the more tender mushrooms and the thyme and cook for another 4 to 5 minutes. Add the red wine and soy sauce, stir in the baby kale, and cook for a couple of minutes more, until the kale has wilted. Season with salt and cracked black pepper to taste.

To serve, spoon polenta into individual wide, shallow bowls and top with stew.

SERVING AND MENU IDEAS
Serve with Jason's Fresh Fennel and Apple Slaw (page 123) or a crisp lettuce salad with Shallot Vinaigrette (page 139) or Sweet Carrot Dressing (page 117).

Asian Filo Rolls

These baked rolls are a fusion of what we like best in summer rolls, egg rolls, spring rolls, and mu shu pancakes. They are delightful: crisp filo pastry wrapped around succulent stir-fried vegetables, slippery cellophane noodles, and a blend of fresh herbs, with a spicy hoisin dipping sauce to punctuate the flavors. Serve as a main dish, appetizer, side dish, or snack.

Yields 6 rolls; about ½ cup sauce
Prep time: about 1 hour
Baking time: 30 minutes

FILLING
2 ounces bean threads (cellophane noodles)★
2 tablespoons peanut oil or other vegetable oil
1½ cups thinly sliced onions
1½ cups thinly sliced red bell peppers
2 cups shredded cabbage
Salt
1 tablespoon peeled and grated fresh ginger
3 garlic cloves, minced or pressed
1½ cups shredded carrots
¼ cup chopped fresh basil (if you have Thai basil, so much the better)
1 tablespoon chopped fresh cilantro or mint, or a mixture of both
2 tablespoons soy sauce
½ teaspoon Chinese chili paste, plus more as needed

FILO ROLLS
¼ cup peanut oil or other vegetable oil
1 tablespoon dark sesame oil
12 sheets filo dough, cut to about 12 x 7 inches

HOISIN DIPPING SAUCE
¼ cup hoisin sauce
1 tablespoon water
2 tablespoons rice vinegar
1 teaspoon dark sesame oil
½ teaspoon Chinese chili paste (or more or less to taste)

★To separate the dried bean threads from the block without littering 10 square feet of the kitchen with little pieces, do it gingerly over a large bowl.

Make the filling: Soak the bean threads in a bowl of warm water until softened, 10 to 15 minutes. Meanwhile, prepare the rest of the filling ingredients and have them near at hand before beginning to stir-fry.

Heat the peanut oil in a wok or large skillet on high heat. Add the onions and bell peppers and stir-fry for about 4 minutes. Add the cabbage and a sprinkling of salt and stir-fry for another 3 minutes. Stir in the ginger, garlic, and carrots, reduce the heat to medium, and cook for a minute, until the vegetables have softened but are still firm. Remove from the heat.

Drain the softened bean threads and cut them into 3- to 4-inch lengths with scissors or a knife. Combine the stir-fried vegetables with the herbs, soy sauce, chili paste, and bean threads. Add additional salt and chili paste to taste.

Preheat the oven to 350°F.

Assemble the rolls on a dry work surface. Combine the vegetable oil and sesame oil in a small bowl, and locate your pastry brush. Place the filling and a baking sheet nearby. Lay down 2 sheets of the filo with a short edge nearest you, and lightly brush with oil. Mound about a cup of the filling a couple of inches from the bottom of the filo, and spread it in a line to about an inch from the sides. Lift the bottom of the filo sheets over the filling and roll it up to about 4 inches from the top. Fold over the right and left sides and then roll all the way to the top. Transfer the roll to the baking sheet, placing it seam side down, and brush all over with

oil. Proceed to make 5 more rolls. Bake for about 30 minutes, until crisp and golden.

While the rolls bake, whisk together the ingredients for the dipping sauce.

Serve hot or warm. At serving time, drizzle the rolls with some sauce, or serve the sauce on the side.

SERVING AND MENU IDEAS

Sprinkle sesame seeds and/or sliced scallions on top of the rolls for a nice garnish. For a full meal, serve with rice, a crisp green salad with Sweet Carrot Dressing (see page 117), and Simple Seasoned Tofu (page 346).

Jamaican Jerk Tempeh Patties

In Jamaica, "patties" are beef-filled pastries shaped like turnovers, with a flaky dough similar to piecrust. Some say that savory Caribbean patties may have been inspired by Cornish pasties, the sturdy meat turnovers from the British Isles.

Jamaican patties are often seasoned with curry spices, but not always. In this recipe, we went for a spicy jerk seasoning with allspice, onions, scallions, and thyme. To really part from tradition, this recipe has no meat. The ground tempeh filling and the crust are vegan, and the patties can be baked or deep-fried. Patties are often brushed with beaten egg to give them a golden color. A traditional alternative to egg wash is to sift a teaspoon of turmeric into the flour for a nice golden tint.

You can buy small jars of prepared all-natural jerk seasoning among the Caribbean specialty foods in a supermarket or gourmet/specialty food market. Jerk seasoning comes in mild, medium, and hot varieties, and it is often very salty; a little goes a long way, so there is no salt needed in the filling. But a little salt in the crust gives it flavor.

Yields 8 large patties or more smaller patties
Serves 4 to 8
Prep time: 1 hour
If frying the patties: the time depends on your skillet and how many batches you do
If baking the patties: about 25 minutes

CRUST
2 cups unbleached all-purpose flour (white or whole wheat)
1 teaspoon ground turmeric (optional)
½ teaspoon salt
½ cup vegetable oil
4 to 6 tablespoons cold water (or more if needed)

FILLING
8 ounces tempeh
½ teaspoon dried thyme, or 1 teaspoon minced fresh thyme
½ teaspoon ground allspice
2 teaspoons vegetarian Worcestershire sauce
1 teaspoon soy sauce
2 tablespoons Jamaican jerk seasoning
1 teaspoon sugar or agave syrup
2 tablespoons vegetable oil (canola, sunflower, peanut, safflower, corn, or olive oil)
1 cup minced onions
2 garlic cloves, crushed
½ cup finely diced red bell peppers
½ cup finely sliced scallions

Oil, for frying or baking

Make the crust: In a food processor or by hand in a bowl, mix the flour, turmeric (if using), and salt together, then drizzle in the oil. When the oil is well distributed and the mixture is crumbly, sprinkle in the water a tablespoon at a time and mix thoroughly until the dough pulls away from the sides of the bowl and can be formed into a ball. Wrap the dough ball in plastic wrap and chill it while you make the filling.

Make the filling: In a bowl, finely crumble the tempeh. Add the thyme, allspice, Worcestershire sauce, soy sauce, jerk seasoning, and sugar and mix well. Set aside.

In a large skillet, warm the vegetable oil on medium heat, add the onions and garlic, and cook until translucent. Stir in the bell peppers and sauté for 3 minutes. Stir in the scallions and the reserved seasoned tempeh and cook until the tempeh darkens and becomes crisp on the bottom. Turn the mixture over and brown it for another few minutes. Add a little more oil if it begins to stick. Put the filling into a bowl and set it aside while you roll out the pastry crust.

Cut the ball of dough into 8 to 12 pieces. On a lightly floured surface, roll each piece into a thin round roughly 4 to 5 inches in diameter. Divide the filling into 8 to 12 equal portions and put a portion of filling on the lower half of each pastry round. Fold over the top to make a half-moon. Fold over the edges to make a little seam and pinch the round edge with the tines of a fork to seal the pastry.

Fry or bake the patties: To fry the pastries, fill a skillet with vegetable oil to a depth of ½ inch and heat over medium-high heat. When the oil is hot enough that a little ball of dough dropped into it sizzles, or a light sprinkle of flour scoots away, carefully lower as many patties into the oil as fit in the skillet without touching each other. Fry until they turn golden brown on the bottom side. Turn them over and fry on the other side. When they are golden brown and crisp, drain briefly on paper towels and then transfer to a platter. Keep them in a warm oven until all the patties are fried and you're ready to serve them.

To bake the patties, preheat the oven to 350°F and arrange the patties on a well-oiled baking pan. Brush the tops with oil. Bake until golden brown and crisp, 20 to 25 minutes, depending on the size of the patties.

SERVING AND MENU IDEAS
Serve with Fresh Pineapple-Mango Relish (page 327) or your favorite fruit chutney or fruit salsa on the side. Mango-Spinach Salad (page 118) provides a colorful and refreshing counterpoint as well.

Scalloped Potatoes and Mushrooms

This satisfying, homey dish has plenty of rich flavor without the usual butter and cream of scalloped potatoes.

Yields one 9 x 13-inch casserole
Serves 6 to 8
Prep time: 40 minutes
Baking time: about 1 hour

1 tablespoon olive oil
1 large onion, thinly sliced (about 2 cups)
1 red bell pepper, seeded and minced (about 1½ cups)
1 pound mushrooms, sliced (heaping 4 cups)
¼ teaspoon dried thyme
½ teaspoon salt
¼ teaspoon cracked black pepper
3 pounds Yukon Gold potatoes
2 tablespoons unbleached white all-purpose flour
2 cups mushroom stock (packaged, or see the sidebar on page 203)
1½ cups grated Gruyère cheese

Coat a 9 x 13-inch baking dish with cooking spray or brush it with oil and set aside.

In a large pot on medium-high heat, warm the oil. Add the onion and bell pepper and sauté for 5 to 6 minutes, stirring frequently, until the onion starts to become translucent. Add the mushrooms, thyme, salt, and black pepper and stir to coat the mushrooms in oil. Cook for a few minutes, until the mushrooms are browned and slightly reduced, then turn off heat.

Preheat the oven to 400°F. Prepare the potatoes by peeling, slicing lengthwise into halves or quarters, and then slicing crosswise as thinly as you can; you want about 6 cups.

Layer half of the sliced potatoes in the prepared baking dish and sprinkle with 1 tablespoon of the flour. Spread all the vegetable and mushroom mixture over the potatoes and sprinkle with one-third of the grated Gruyère. Next, layer in the rest of the potatoes and sprinkle with the remaining 1 tablespoon flour. Pour the mushroom stock over everything and top with the rest of the cheese.

Cover the baking pan tightly with aluminum foil and bake for 30 minutes. Uncover and bake for another 30 minutes, until the potatoes are tender and the top is crusty and golden brown. Remove from the oven and let stand for at least 10 minutes before serving.

SERVING AND MENU IDEAS

Good dishes to pair with Scalloped Potatoes and Mushrooms are a bit piquant and have some crispness. Start with a pickled vegetable mix, such as Giardiniera (page 342), or Watercress Toast (page 53). For a salad, try Kale, Jicama, and Orange Salad (page 128), Microgreens Salad with Sweet Carrot Dressing (page 117), or Wax Bean and Radish Salad with Buttermilk Dressing (page 121).

MUSHROOM STOCK

Commercially prepared mushroom stock in aseptic quart boxes is quite tasty and very convenient, but you can also make a flavorful mushroom stock this way: Pour 2 1/2 cups boiling water over 1/2 cup dried sliced mushrooms, such as shiitake, and let them soak for at least 20 minutes. Strain the liquid through a fine-mesh sieve or a sieve lined with a coffee filter to remove all traces of grit.

Start soaking the dried mushrooms when you begin with the recipe, so the stock will be ready when you assemble the baking dish. The soaked dried mushrooms can be rinsed, sliced, and added as well.

Walnut-Cheddar-Herb "Meatballs"

Once you assemble all the ingredients, these rich and delicious "meatballs" are easy to make. The fresh herbs and the dried spices in this recipe are important. The dried herbs provide traditional Italian flavors, while the green herbs give everything a fresh lift. The amount and combination of fresh herbs is flexible. It's hard to make a mistake.

Seasoned walnuts, cheddar, and a crisp crust make these a tempting appetizer, served plain or with marinara or Roasted Red Pepper Sauce (see page 258). This recipe makes about 16 to 18 balls between 1½ and 2 inches in diameter. Make smaller balls for appetizers. Larger ones can be used any way meatballs are served.

Yields 16 larger balls; 32 smaller ones
Serves 4 to 6 as a main dish with pasta;
** 8 to 12 as an appetizer**
Time: about 1 hour

2 cups shredded extra-sharp cheddar cheese
⅓ cup grated or shredded Parmesan and/or
   Pecorino Romano cheese
2 cups walnuts, coarsely ground★
¼ cup minced fresh basil
1 tablespoon minced fresh parsley
1 tablespoon minced fresh oregano and/or
   marjoram (optional)

1 tablespoon olive oil
1 cup finely chopped onions
4 garlic cloves, crushed
1 teaspoon dried oregano
½ teaspoon dried marjoram
½ teaspoon ground fennel seeds
½ teaspoon ground coriander

½ teaspoon salt
¼ teaspoon freshly ground black pepper
¼ teaspoon crushed red pepper flakes

2 large eggs, beaten
⅔ cup dry bread crumbs
2 to 3 tablespoons olive oil and/or walnut oil

★Coarsely grind the walnuts in a food processor, or spread the walnuts in a paper bag or between sheets of parchment paper and crush them well with a rolling pin. Leave some pieces the size of grains of rice to give the meatballs more texture.

Toss the cheddar, Parmesan, walnuts, basil, parsley, and fresh oregano together in a bowl and set aside.

Heat the oil in a skillet, add the onions and garlic, and lightly sauté for 2 minutes. Stir in the dried marjoram, dried oregano, fennel, coriander, salt, black pepper, and red pepper flakes and sauté for another 2 minutes. Remove from the heat.

Stir the cooked onions and spices into the walnuts and cheese mixture. Add the beaten eggs and stir well. Stir in ⅓ cup of the bread crumbs and mix well.

To form the "meatballs," either divide the mixture into the number of balls you want, or use 2 to 3 tablespoons of the mixture for each ball until all the mixture has been used up. Press each portion between your palms and roll it into a ball, coat the ball with the remaining dry bread crumbs, and set on a plate.

Heat 2 tablespoons of fresh oil in the skillet on medium-low heat. Working in two or three batches, place 5 or 6 balls in the skillet and fry for 6 to 7 minutes. As they brown, turn them with a long-handled spoon or tongs to brown all over. As the cheese softens inside, they probably won't retain a round shape, but turn the balls to brown thoroughly and develop a nice crust. Remove with a slotted spoon and drain on paper towels. Continue to cook the remaining batches, adding more oil as necessary.

NOTE

These balls reheat nicely in a microwave, with or without sauce. Cover the dish with a paper towel if microwaving with sauce.

SERVING AND MENU IDEAS

Serve Walnut-Cheddar-Herb Meatballs hot, either plain or with pasta and a zesty tomato sauce or roasted red pepper sauce, and top with a little shredded or grated Parmesan. Or serve with sauce accompanied by Mediterranean Potato Salad (page 124).

MAKE A "MEATBALL" PITA

"MEATBALL" PITA

Toast pita bread pockets. Line the pockets with some romaine lettuce, stuff with a few smaller-sized hot "meatballs," top with marinara sauce, and add a sprinkle of grated Parmesan if you like.

"MEATBALL" SUB

Heat the oven or toaster oven to 375°F. On a baking pan, spread marinara or pizza sauce on an open Italian sub roll and add a couple of slices of mozzarella. Arrange 3 or 4 larger "meatballs" on one half and toast the sub in the oven until the cheese melts and the bread is crisp. Fold the halves together, wrap in aluminum foil or waxed paper to keep the filling in, and cut it in half. Serve with 2 or 3 pepperoncini or a little green salad on the side.

Vegetable "Noodles"

C'mon baby, let's spiralize! This craze is sweeping the nation like doing the Twist in the early '60s. Folks are using fancy spiralizers, or a gadget called a Vegetti, or a mandoline to make "noodles" from vegetables. We like creating these nutritious noodles as a great way to put a dent in that huge pile of zucchini that inevitably accumulates in August. They're also delicious and less filling than pasta.

As the seasons change, you can spiralize different vegetables or a combination of vegetables: summer squash, carrots, beets, sweet potatoes, and winter squash. Cook them in one of our recommended sauces, or boil the "noodles" in water until just tender, drain, and top with a sauce.

Vegetable noodles can be the center of the plate or a side dish, and they're another way of slipping vegetables into the kids.

Serves 4 as a main dish; 6 to 8 as a side dish
Time: 35 minutes

3 medium zucchini and/or yellow squash
  (2 to 3 pounds)
½ teaspoon salt

SIMPLE SUMMER SAUCE
1 small onion, diced
1 tablespoon olive oil, plus 2 teaspoons butter
  (or use 2 tablespoons olive oil)
1 garlic clove, minced
2 cups chopped fresh tomatoes, or 1 pint cherry
  tomatoes, halved
½ cup packed chopped fresh basil
Splash of white wine (optional)
½ cup grated cheese (sharp cheddar, fontina,
  Gorgonzola, or your favorite)
¼ teaspoon freshly ground black pepper

Grated or shredded Parmesan cheese

Spiralize the zucchini: Make long strands using a spiral vegetable slicer or a mandoline. While prepping the sauce ingredients and cooking the sauce, dry the zucchini noodles (summer squash is full of water, and would otherwise release a lot of liquid into the sauce). Lay out a clean dish towel and cover it with three layers of paper towels. Spread the spiralized zucchini on the towels and sprinkle with the salt. Put two layers of paper towels on top and press down every once in a while as the zucchini drains water into the towels. After about 20 minutes, roll up the dishtowel like a jelly roll and twist the water out over the sink. The "zoodles" are now ready to add to the sauce.

Make the summer sauce: In a large skillet on medium-high heat, sauté the onions in olive oil and butter for a couple of minutes until softened. Add the garlic and stir briefly before adding the tomatoes, basil, wine (if using), grated cheese, and black pepper. Cover and cook, stirring occasionally, for about 5 minutes, until saucy and bubbling.

Add the zucchini noodles and cook them submerged in the sauce until just tender but still firm, 3 to 5 minutes. Season with salt to taste.

Serve right away, topped with grated Parmesan.

VARIATIONS
Cook the vegetable noodles in boiling water for 3 minutes, drain, and top with one of the following, or your favorite sauce:
  • Brown Butter Sauce with Sage (see page 237)
  • Roasted Red Pepper Sauce (see page 258)
  • Grandma Anne's Pasta with Navy Beans (page 238) without the pasta

Japanese Curry

Two Potato Tomato Curry with Yellow Split Pea Dal

Fall Root Vegetable Stew

Fennel and Chickpea Stew with Saffron and Prunes

Summer Stir-Fry with Halloumi Cheese

White Bean Stew with Rosemary on Orecchiette with Goat Cheese Toast

Tofu Noodles with Mushrooms and Bok Choy

Rainbow Carrot Stir-Fry

Pozole Verde

Winter Squash and Red Bean Mole

Five-Spice Tofu with Napa Cabbage and Shiitakes

Japanese Curry

Japanese curry is a staple comfort food that is a hybrid of British, Indian, and Japanese cuisines. A thick, warm, and slightly sweet stew, this curry is more reminiscent of classic beef stew than of Indian curry, but definitely has an Eastern flavor. Other root vegetables, such as parsnips and rutabagas, could also be added to this classic dish.

Serves 4
Time: about 1 hour

3 tablespoons olive oil
1½ cups coarsely chopped onions
3 garlic cloves, minced
½ teaspoon salt
1 cup bite-size pieces of carrots
1 cup bite-size pieces of potatoes
2 teaspoons curry powder
1 tablespoon peeled and grated fresh ginger
Pinch or more crushed red pepper flakes
2 tablespoons unbleached white all-purpose flour
¾ cup diced tomatoes, canned or fresh
½ cup grated peeled apples
1¾ cups water or vegetable stock
2 generous cups coarsely chopped spinach or kale
¾ cup fresh or frozen shelled edamame
2 teaspoons apple cider vinegar
2 tablespoons soy sauce
Brown rice, for serving
¼ cup chopped fresh parsley
½ cup chopped scallions

Warm the oil in a large skillet on low heat. Add the onions and cook for about 10 minutes. Stir in the garlic and salt and cook for a couple of minutes. Add the carrots and potatoes and cook for about 5 minutes. Stir in the curry powder, ginger, red pepper flakes, and flour and cook for 2 to 3 minutes. If the mixture sticks to the bottom of the skillet, add a little water or stock. Stir in the tomatoes, grated apples, and water or stock and bring to a simmer. It will thicken and bubble. Cover and simmer for about 30 minutes, or until the potatoes and carrots are tender. Stir frequently and add more water if necessary to prevent sticking. After 20 minutes of simmering, stir in the edamame. For the last 5 minutes of cooking, stir in the spinach or kale. When all the vegetables are tender, stir in the vinegar and soy sauce.

Serve the curry with brown rice, topped with the parsley and scallions.

SERVING AND MENU IDEAS
Rice is a good choice with this curry, but rolls or crusty bread would work well, too. This vegetable-rich stew might only need a salad like Sugar Snap Peas with Coconut and Lime (page 113).

Two Potato Tomato Curry with Yellow Split Pea Dal

Yellow split peas (*chana dal*) cook into a delicious, comforting texture, smoother and less mealy than green or red lentils. This is a thick, hearty dish. The two potatoes in this curry are sweet potatoes and white potatoes simmered with tomatoes, onions, and aromatic curry spices.

Usually, we serve the curried vegetables on top of or alongside the dal, and it looks very nice, especially when garnished with yogurt, freshly minced herbs, and toasted cashews. But sometimes we combine the vegetables and split peas—it looks a little "humbler" that way, but it sure tastes good.

Serves 4 to 6
Time: 1 hour, 15 minutes

DAL
1 pound yellow split peas (about 2⅓ cups)
6 cups water
1 teaspoon salt, plus more as needed
Freshly ground black pepper
3 tablespoons vegetable oil
1 teaspoon curry powder
2 teaspoons ground coriander
2 teaspoons whole or ground cumin

CURRIED VEGETABLES
3 tablespoons vegetable oil
1 cup chopped onions
2 large garlic cloves, minced or pressed
1 small fresh hot pepper, minced (seeded for a "milder hot")
1 teaspoon salt, plus more as needed
2 teaspoons curry powder, or 1 teaspoon garam masala and 1 teaspoon curry powder
½ teaspoon ground cumin
½ teaspoon ground coriander
Pinch of ground cinnamon
2 cups diced white potatoes (peeled or unpeeled)
2 cups peeled, diced sweet potatoes
1 (15-ounce) can diced tomatoes
1 to 2 teaspoons sugar or agave syrup (optional)
Freshly ground black pepper

Make the dal: Rinse the split peas and combine them in a 2-quart pot with the water and salt. Cover and bring to a boil, then reduce to a simmer and cook on low heat until very soft, about 1 hour. The cooking time may vary depending on the freshness and dryness of the split peas, so keep checking. Split peas can bubble up and overflow the pot and make a mess on your stovetop, so lower the heat as soon as they begin to boil, and keep them just barely simmering. Stir occasionally to prevent sticking or scorching. When soft, remove from the heat and season with salt and black pepper to taste. Set aside.

While the split peas are cooking, in a small skillet, warm the oil and cook the curry powder, coriander, and cumin for about 2 minutes. Set aside until the split peas are done.

Prep and cook the curried vegetables: Heat the oil in a soup pot or large skillet on medium heat. Add the onions, garlic, hot pepper, and salt, cover, and cook, stirring occasionally, until the onions are transparent. Stir in the curry powder, cumin, coriander, and cinnamon, lower the heat, and cook, covered, for 5 minutes. Stir in the white potatoes and sweet potatoes, cover, and cook for about 8 minutes, stirring occasionally.

Drain the canned tomatoes into a measuring cup, reserving the tomatoes and adding water as needed to the juice to make 1½ cups of liquid. Add the tomato juice to the cooking vegetables, cover, and bring to a boil. Reduce the heat and simmer until the potatoes are just tender, about 20 minutes. Stir in the reserved diced canned tomatoes and heat, uncovered. When the potatoes are done, stir in the sugar or agave syrup if you want that touch of sweetness, and season with salt and black pepper to taste.

Stir the reserved spices and oil into the dal.

Serve the curried vegetables on top of or beside the dal. Or stir the dal into the vegetables.

SERVING AND MENU IDEAS
Serve with warm naan bread or basmati brown rice. We like the following garnishes: plain yogurt, chopped fresh cilantro, chopped fresh mint, chutney, and toasted cashews.

Fall Root Vegetable Stew

In the film *The Hundred Foot Journey*, Indian restaurateur Mr. Kadam clashes across cuisines with his traditionalist French neighbor and rival restaurateur, Madame Mallory. To impress their differences upon her, he yells in exasperation, "If you have a *spice*, use it! *Don't sprinkle it. Spoon it in!*" *Vive la difference!* Moosewood fell in love with curries over forty years ago, and *mise en place* for us means curry spices are ready at hand in soup cups. But you may not need so much.

Parsnips, carrots, celeriac, and sweet potatoes make this a sweet, cold-weather root vegetable stew with hot-climate spices. Use a little more cayenne pepper to suit your taste. At the end, a squeeze of tart lemon juice and dollop of tangy yogurt are perfect contrasts to the hearty, spicy curry.

Yields about 8 cups
Serves 4
Time: about 1 hour

4 cups vegetable stock
2 cups chopped onions
1 tablespoon vegetable oil
4 garlic cloves, minced or pressed
1 tablespoon peeled and grated fresh ginger
1½ teaspoons ground coriander
2 teaspoons ground cumin
½ teaspoon ground cinnamon
¼ teaspoon cayenne pepper, plus more to taste
1 teaspoon ground turmeric
1½ cups peeled and chopped parsnips
2 cups chopped carrots
2 cups peeled and chopped sweet potatoes
1½ cups diced celeriac
1 teaspoon Dijon mustard
¼ cup raisins
1 apple, peeled, cored, and finely chopped
2 tablespoons chopped fresh parsley (optional)

Plain yogurt
Lemon wedges

Heat the vegetable stock in a small saucepan so it will be hot when you add it to the stew.

In a large pot on medium heat, cook the onions in the oil for 8 minutes, stirring often. Stir in the garlic, ginger, coriander, cumin, cinnamon, cayenne, and turmeric. Cook, stirring continually for a minute. Add the hot vegetable stock and the parsnips, carrots, sweet potatoes, and celeriac, cover, and bring to a boil. Reduce to a simmer. Stir in the mustard, raisins, and apples and simmer, covered, until the vegetables are tender, about 15 minutes. Stir in the parsley if using. Season with salt to taste.

Serve with yogurt and lemon wedges.

SERVING AND MENU IDEAS

Try this stew served with fluffy millet (see page 155), brown rice, naan bread, papadums, or whole wheat couscous. Mango-Spinach Salad with Spicy Dressing (page 118) is an excellent accompaniment.

Fennel and Chickpea Stew with Saffron and Prunes

Savory vegetable stews and slowly braised tagines with added dried fruits are a delicious tradition throughout the Middle East and North Africa. Some of us make the hour's drive to Syracuse where Samir's Imported Foods carries some of the most luscious dates, unsulphured apricots, figs, prunes, olives, and other delicacies too numerous to list.

This colorful, aromatic North African–style stew is satisfying but not too heavy. Saffron is a pricey seasoning, but a small amount makes a big difference. The anise flavor of fresh fennel, the sweetness of minced prunes, and the intriguing tang of preserved lemon make this a fragrant, hearty, and complex dish.

Roasted cumin and coriander are available in most supermarkets, and their flavor is very nice in this stew, although plain ground cumin and coriander are fine, too. If you have a little more time, for an earthier and fuller flavor and fragrance, try toasting whole cumin, coriander, and fennel seeds yourself (see sidebar page 247), and then grind them in a spice grinder for this recipe.

Yields 8 cups
Serves 4 to 6
Time: 45 minutes

3 tablespoons olive oil
2 cups chopped onions
2 garlic cloves, minced or pressed
1 cup chopped carrots
1 teaspoon ground cumin
1 teaspoon ground coriander
½ teaspoon ground cinnamon
½ teaspoon salt
½ teaspoon crumbled saffron threads
½ teaspoon ground turmeric
⅔ cup minced dried prunes
2 cups chopped fresh fennel
1½ cups water or vegetable stock
1 (15-ounce) can chickpeas, undrained
3 tablespoons finely diced preserved lemon (page 344), or 1 to 2 tablespoons lemon zest
1 (15-ounce) can tomatoes
1 tablespoon fresh lemon juice (optional)
⅓ cup finely chopped fresh parsley

Heat the oil in a soup pot on medium heat. Add the onions and garlic, stir, cover, and cook for 5 minutes. Stir in the carrots, cover, and cook for 4 minutes. Stir in the cumin, coriander, cinnamon, salt, saffron, and turmeric. Add the prunes, chopped fennel, water or stock, chickpeas, and preserved lemon, stir well, and bring to a boil. Reduce the heat and simmer, covered, until the prunes have rehydrated and the fennel is tender-crisp. Stir in the tomatoes and lemon juice (if using). Cover and simmer until the vegetables are tender. Stir in the parsley.

VARIATIONS

- Just before serving, stir in 2 to 3 cups of stemmed and coarsely chopped spinach or whole baby spinach leaves, or put some in each serving bowl and ladle the hot stew on top.
- If you'd like the stew to have some hot spiciness, when you add the other spices, add Harissa (page 338) or cayenne pepper to taste.
- For color, add diced yellow, orange, or red bell peppers to the stew with the tomatoes.

SERVING AND MENU IDEAS

Serve on brown rice or couscous and top with Greek yogurt or feta cheese and/or a spoonful of Harissa (page 338). Greens with Citrus-Date Dressing (page 126) goes nicely with the North African flavors of the stew.

Summer Stir-Fry with Halloumi Cheese

This is a beautiful and very simple vegetable dish for any season, but when the garden or the market has tender fresh zucchini, bell peppers, big ripe tomatoes, and fresh basil and oregano, it's everything a lover of Mediterranean food could desire.

Halloumi cheese is a traditional sheep's milk cheese from Cyprus that looks like mozzarella but comes packaged in salty brine. The fascinating thing about halloumi is that when it is grilled or pan-fried, it immediately turns a gorgeous golden brown while staying chewy on the inside without melting in a messy way. Halloumi has a meaty texture and its flavor is rich, heady, a little reminiscent of some sheep's milk feta but not crumbly. If you can't find halloumi, substitute little balls of fresh mozzarella stirred into the hot vegetables, or for the more ambitious, breaded and fried mozzarella sticks.

Serves 4 to 6
Time: 30 minutes

1 large onion
3 garlic cloves
2 medium zucchini
2 bell peppers, red and yellow
1 large fresh tomato
4 tablespoons olive oil
¼ teaspoon crushed red pepper flakes
½ teaspoon salt, plus more as needed
½ teaspoon freshly ground black pepper
¼ cup chopped fresh basil, or more if desired
¼ cup chopped fresh parsley, or 1 tablespoon
   minced fresh oregano
4 ounces halloumi cheese
2 teaspoons vegetarian Worcestershire Sauce

Your favorite pitted black olives, for garnish
   (optional)

Prepare the vegetables: Chop the onion (you will need about 2 cups chopped), mince or press the garlic, cut the zucchini and the bell peppers into pieces about ½ x 2 inches, and cut the tomato into 12 wedges. Chop the herbs and cut the cheese into ¼-inch-thick pieces about ½ x 1 inch. Have all the ingredients near the stove before you start to cook.

In a large skillet or a wok, heat 3 tablespoons of the oil. Stir-fry the onions for 2 minutes and add the garlic. When the onions are translucent, add the zucchini and bell peppers and stir-fry until just barely tender. Stir in the tomato wedges, red pepper flakes to taste, salt, black pepper, and half the fresh herbs. Cover and cook for a minute or two until the tomatoes have softened.

In a separate small skillet, heat the remaining 1 tablespoon oil. Add the halloumi and fry on medium-high heat until golden brown on all sides.

Stir the fried halloumi and the Worcestershire sauce into the hot vegetables. Season with additional salt and pepper to taste.

Serve garnished with the remaining fresh herbs and with black olives, if you like.

SERVING AND MENU IDEAS
Serve with Orzo Risotto (page 322), a simple rice pilaf, or Focaccia Pugliese (page 277) or similar bread to soak up some of the stir-fry juices.

White Bean Stew with Rosemary on Orecchiette with Goat Cheese Toast

This is a stew full of flavor and texture: mellow cannellini beans, chewy bursts of sun-dried tomatoes, pungent rosemary. Served on al dente orecchiette and topped with the crusty baguette pieces spread with creamy goat cheese, it's a complete meal. Karen Sgambati, a treasured and respected longtime staff member at Moosewood, loves full-flavored stews. We had Karen—and stew lovers everywhere—in mind when we created this cross between a rich rustic stew and a pasta. Truly something for everyone!

Time the prepping of the pasta and toasts to fit with when you'll serve the meal. The stew is great both freshly cooked and made ahead and reheated.

Yields 6 cups stew
Serves 6
Time: 1 hour, 20 minutes

STEW
3 tablespoons olive oil
2 cups coarsely chopped onions
4 to 6 garlic cloves, minced or pressed
1 teaspoon salt, plus more as needed
2 or 3 celery stalks, coarsely chopped (about 1 cup)
2 large carrots, coarsely chopped (about 1 cup)
¼ cup chopped sun-dried tomatoes
2 tablespoons chopped fresh rosemary
⅛ teaspoon crushed red pepper flakes
1½ cups vegetable stock
1½ cups water
1 (15-ounce) can diced tomatoes or 3 cups chopped fresh tomatoes
1 (15-ounce) can cannellini beans or other white beans, drained and rinsed
1½ cups trimmed and cut green beans (1-inch lengths)
1 cup chopped kale leaves
½ cup chopped fresh parsley

GOAT CHEESE TOASTS
1 baguette
½ to ¾ cup chèvre or other soft mild goat cheese

PASTA
½ teaspoon salt
2 cups orecchiette
Olive oil

Making the stew: In a soup pot, heat the oil, add the onions, and cook for 5 minutes. Add the garlic and salt. When the onions have softened, add the celery and carrots and cook for about 10 minutes, stirring occasionally. Add a splash of water or stock if needed to prevent sticking. Stir in the sun-dried tomatoes, rosemary, red pepper flakes, stock, water, tomatoes, and white beans. Simmer for about 20 minutes. During the last 5 minutes of cooking, add the green beans and kale. Cook until the green beans are tender-crisp and the kale is tender and limp but still bright green. Remove from the heat and stir in the parsley. Season with salt to taste.

About 30 minutes before the meal will be served, prepare the goat cheese toasts: Preheat the

(continued)

oven to 350°F. Split the baguette in half lengthwise and then cut it (on a diagonal is nice) into the number of slices that will give each diner at least a couple of pieces. Arrange, cut side up, on a baking sheet. Bake until crisp, about 20 minutes. Remove from the oven and set aside. When you're ready to serve the stew, spread the chèvre on the toasted baguette slices.

Start the pasta about 20 minutes before you're ready to serve the meal: Salt 1 quart water and bring to a boil. Add the pasta and cook until al dente, about 10 minutes. Drain. In a bowl, toss the pasta with a little olive oil and set aside.

To serve the stew, divide the cooked pasta among large, individual bowls, ladle the stew over the pasta, and serve topped with Goat Cheese Toasts.

SERVING AND MENU IDEAS
Walnut and Roasted Red Pepper Spread (page 68) with crudités is a good appetizer to nibble on before this lavish stew.

Tofu Noodles with Mushrooms and Bok Choy

Here's a quick, gluten-free and low-carb weeknight meal of chewy mushrooms, slippery noodles, and greens. This noodle dish is stocky, not quite a soup, but stockier than a pasta. Best eaten with chopsticks or a fork . . . then use a spoon for the tasty clear brown stock.

Our editor, Michael Flamini, first told us about tofu noodles and how popular they are in NYC. We requested them at our supermarket in Ithaca, and they showed up a couple of weeks later. So if you don't find them, ask your market to stock them, and maybe they'll appear.

Serves 2
Time: 30 minutes

6 dried shiitake mushrooms
Boiling water
Salt
8 ounces tofu noodles★
2 to 3 teaspoons vegetable oil
1 garlic clove, minced or pressed
1 tablespoon peeled and grated fresh ginger
6 ounces fresh mushrooms, such as white, cremini, oyster, or shiitake, but not portobello (about 2 cups sliced)
About 2 cups sliced bok choy, leaves and stems separated
2 tablespoons dry sherry
2 tablespoons soy sauce
1 tablespoon rice vinegar
1 cup water or vegetable stock
1 scallion, sliced

★The Japanese name for tofu noodles is *shirataki*. Tofu noodles are firmer and chewier than wheat pasta and are available in several forms, such as spaghetti or fettuccine. Look for shirataki in a plastic bag, squishy with water, in the refrigerator case at Asian or natural foods stores or the supermarket.

Place the dried mushrooms in a bowl and add just enough boiling water to cover. Set aside. Bring a medium pot of salted water to a boil for cooking the tofu noodles. Prep the other ingredients and have them close at hand before you begin to stir-fry.

Boil the tofu noodles for 2 to 3 minutes, drain, and set aside.

In a soup pot or wok on medium-high heat, warm the oil. Add the garlic and ginger, stir-fry briefly, then add the fresh mushrooms and bok choy stems and stir-fry for a minute. Add the sherry, soy sauce, and vinegar and continue stir-frying for another minute before adding the water or stock. Simmer, covered, for 3 minutes.

Meanwhile, drain the softened dried shiitakes, reserving the soaking liquid. Remove and discard the woody stems and thinly slice the caps. Add the sliced shiitakes and liquid to the pot and simmer for about 3 minutes. Add the bok choy greens and cook for a minute, then add the drained noodles.

Serve in bowls, garnished with the scallion.

VARIATION
This dish could be made with other sorts of noodles, but then you don't get the same nutritional value, nor the fun of eating noodles made of tofu.

SERVING AND MENU IDEAS
This dish has an intense *umami* and no starch, so you could serve it with Sweet Potatoes with Bitter Orange (skip the feta) (page 303). For dessert, you'll want something light, fruity, and refreshing, such as Coconut-Pineapple Sorbet (page 382) or a citrus salad.

Rainbow Carrot Stir-Fry

This is a lovely, lively vegetable stir-fry seasoned with sesame, lemon, and anise.

Talking to venders at the farmers' market, we found it fascinating to learn that not so very long ago, carrots were various colors: yellow, red, purple, and white. The orange flesh we naturally associate with "carrot" is actually a hybridization of red and yellow carrots. Happily, with heirloom carrots, we're getting back to where we started. We are also learning that different carrot pigments can confer different health benefits. Heirloom carrots of different colors are showing up increasingly at farmers' markets and well-stocked neighborhood markets; even, conveniently, in pre-peeled baby carrot form. Or you can grow your own. Who can resist names like Purple Haze, White Satin, Atomic Red, or Yellow Sun?

Serves 4
Time: 60 minutes

VEGETABLES
1 tablespoon hijiki (aka hiziki; optional)
12 ounces firm tofu, diced into bite-size pieces (about 2 cups)
3 tablespoons dark sesame oil
3 cups julienned carrots★ (¼-inch-wide matchsticks, 2 inches long)
3 cups trimmed and snapped green beans (1-inch pieces)
2 teaspoons peeled and grated fresh ginger
2 teaspoons minced or pressed garlic
2 star anise pads

SAUCE
¼ cup soy sauce
1 teaspoon finely grated lemon zest
1½ tablespoons fresh lemon juice
2½ tablespoons pourable honey
2 teaspoons cornstarch
2 tablespoons cold water

★If available, use a colorful mix of orange, yellow, red, purple, and ivory carrots.

If using hijiki, soak it in about ½ cup water. It will soften and expand by the time it's ready to add to the stir-fry.

Transfer the tofu cubes to a paper towel–lined plate or baking sheet and put another couple of paper towels on top; pat occasionally to dry the tofu. Meanwhile, prep the vegetables and ingredients for the sauce. Stir-fries move pretty fast. They are time-sensitive and demand attention, so it is best to have everything prepped before you start to cook.

In a wok or slope-sided sauté pan on high heat, heat 1 tablespoon of the sesame oil and stir-fry the tofu for about 3 minutes. Move the tofu around continuously until it no longer sticks to the bottom of the pan because it is beginning to release water. Transfer the tofu to a plate or bowl.

Heat the remaining 2 tablespoons sesame oil and stir-fry the carrots for a couple of minutes. Add the green beans, ginger, garlic, and star anise. Continue to stir-fry for a few more minutes. Then add about ¼ cup water to the pan, cover, lower the heat, and simmer until the carrots and green beans are tender-crisp and brightly colored. Stir in the tofu and the drained hijiki (if using).

Whisk together all the ingredients for the sauce. Pour the sauce over the vegetables, turn up the heat, and repeatedly fold the sauce over the vegetables until the sauce thickens. Serve at once, on rice or noodles.

SERVING AND MENU IDEAS
Serve the stir-fry on soba, udon, or ramen noodles, or any variety of rice. The colorful drama of this dish is heightened when served on black rice or black rice noodles.

Rainbow Carrot Stir-Fry,
previous page, on black rice

Pozole Verde

Pozole verde is a traditional Mexican hominy stew with pre-Columbian origins. *Pozole* means "hominy," the large cooked kernels of maize. The simple hominy stew is seasoned with a distinctive salsa verde of raw tomatillos, cilantro, green chiles, and fresh oregano blended with pepitas (pumpkin seeds). This vividly green vegetarian version is hearty and surprisingly easy to make once you've gathered the ingredients. The toppings add crunch, freshness, and pizazz, and each person can choose exactly the garnishes they like best.

Serves 4 to 6
Yields 8 cups
Time: 45 minutes

SALSA VERDE
1 cup packed chopped fresh cilantro leaves and stems
¼ cup fresh oregano leaves
1½ cups coarsely chopped tomatillos
2 fresh green hot peppers, seeded for a "milder hot" (about ½ cup)★
½ cup water
¼ cup fresh lime juice
¾ cup pepitas (pumpkin seeds)

STEW
2 tablespoons vegetable oil
¾ cup chopped onions
4 to 6 garlic cloves, minced or pressed
1 teaspoon ground cumin
2½ cups diced red or white potatoes (½-inch cubes)
1½ cups water
1½ teaspoons salt
¼ teaspoon ground black pepper
2 (15-ounce) cans white and/or yellow hominy, drained and rinsed

TOPPINGS
1 ripe avocado, pitted, peeled, and diced
Thinly shredded romaine lettuce
Thinly sliced red radishes
Wedges of lime
Toasted salted pepitas (pumpkin seeds)
Thin, crisp tortilla chips

★We like to use a combination of jalapeños and poblano peppers.

In a blender or food processor, combine all the ingredients for the salsa verde and purée until smooth. Season with salt to taste. Set aside.

Heat the oil in a soup pot on medium heat. Add the onions and garlic, cover, and cook, stirring frequently, for 5 minutes. Stir in the cumin, potatoes, water, salt, and black pepper. Cover and bring to a boil. Lower the heat and simmer for about 10 minutes.

While the stew simmers, prepare any or all of the toppings and set them aside to serve with the stew.

When the potatoes are tender but still firm, add the hominy and the salsa verde and simmer, covered, for 5 minutes.

Serve the stew in shallow soup bowls with the toppings on the side.

SERVING AND MENU IDEAS
A piece of Golden Cornbread (page 280) or Carrot Cornbread (page 281) is a natural with this stew.

Winter Squash and Red Bean Mole

This is a hearty variation on traditional chili. Chock-full of sweet and hot peppers and creamy squash and beans, we've added more body and depth with some classic mole ingredients: ground pepitas, sesame seeds, and bittersweet chocolate. Choose poblano peppers for their flavor and mild heat, but for a spicier chili, add a jalapeño or another favorite hot pepper to the pot.

Yields 8 cups
Serves 4 to 6
Time: 1 hour

2 tablespoons olive oil
1½ cups chopped onions
1 tablespoon minced or crushed garlic
1 teaspoon ground fennel seeds
1 teaspoon ground cinnamon
1 tablespoon chopped fresh thyme, or 1 teaspoon dried
1½ teaspoons salt
½ teaspoon freshly ground black pepper
⅓ cup chopped celery
½ cup seeded and chopped poblano peppers
1½ cups seeded and chopped red, yellow, or orange bell peppers
3 cups diced butternut squash (bite-size cubes)
1 (14-ounce) can diced tomatoes
1⅓ cups water
3 tablespoons pepitas (pumpkin seeds)
1 tablespoon sesame seeds
1 (15-ounce) can red kidney beans, drained
1 tablespoon finely chopped chipotle peppers in adobo sauce
1½ ounces bittersweet chocolate (70% cocoa solids)
½ cup chopped fresh cilantro

In a heavy-bottomed pot on medium heat, warm the oil. Add the onions, garlic, fennel, cinnamon, thyme, salt, and black pepper and cook for 5 to 7 minutes until the onions soften, stirring often to prevent sticking. Add the celery, poblano peppers, and bell peppers and cook for another 5 minutes until the peppers brighten and become fragrant. Stir in the squash and cook for a minute or two more. Add the tomatoes and water to the pot, cover, bring to a boil. Reduce the heat and simmer for about 20 minutes, or until the squash is tender.

Using a spice grinder, mini food processor, or, if you have the patience and upper body strength, a mortar and pestle, finely grind the pepitas and sesame seeds. When the squash is tender, stir the ground seeds, kidney beans, chipotles to taste, and chocolate into the stew. Simmer for 10 to 15 minutes. Stir in the cilantro.

SERVING AND MENU IDEAS
The stew is enhanced by finishing each bowl with a dollop of sour cream and a sprinkling of parsley, scallions, or more cilantro. Kale, Jicama, and Orange Salad (page 128) is a good flavor match for this dish.

Five-Spice Tofu with Napa Cabbage and Shiitakes

Tofu braised with spices in a mushroom broth makes a flavorful base for a dish that is quickly stir-fried with fast-cooking vegetables.

Serves 4
Time: 45 minutes

2 cups boiling water
8 dried shiitake mushrooms
2 tablespoons vegetable oil
3 garlic cloves, minced or pressed
2 teaspoons peeled and grated fresh ginger
2 teaspoons five-spice powder
½ teaspoon Chinese chili paste or hot pepper sauce, or more to taste
4 tablespoons soy sauce
6 tablespoons dry sherry
2 tablespoons rice vinegar
1 (15-ounce) block extra-firm tofu, cut into bite-size cubes or triangles
2 teaspoons cornstarch
1 pound napa cabbage, sliced crosswise into 1-inch pieces (about 6 cups)
Rice or noodles, for serving
Chopped scallions

Pour the boiling water over the dried mushrooms, cover, and set aside. Prep the garlic, ginger, tofu, and cabbage, and have the other ingredients close at hand before beginning to cook.

In a large skillet on medium heat, warm 1 tablespoon of the oil and cook the garlic and ginger for a minute before adding the five-spice powder, chili paste, 2 tablespoons of the soy sauce, 2 tablespoons of the sherry, and 1 tablespoon of the rice vinegar. Stir well and cook on medium heat. Drain the mushrooms, reserving all the stock. Add ⅔ cup of the mushroom stock to the skillet along with the tofu pieces. Trim off and discard the stems of the shiitakes, slice the caps, and add them to the skillet. Bring the liquid to a simmer, then reduce the heat to medium-low and cook, stirring often, for about 10 minutes, until most of the liquid has been absorbed by the tofu. Remove from the heat.

Measure the remaining mushroom stock, and if needed, add enough water to yield 1¼ cups of liquid. In a small bowl, whisk this stock into the cornstarch and add the remaining 2 tablespoons soy sauce, 4 tablespoons sherry, and 1 tablespoon of rice vinegar. Set aside.

Heat the remaining 1 tablespoon oil in a wok or large skillet on high heat, add the cabbage, and stir-fry until barely tender and still crisp, 2 to 3 minutes. Add the tofu and shiitakes and heat through. Stir in the cornstarch mixture and cook until the sauce is bubbling and somewhat thickened. Season with more chili paste and/or soy sauce to taste.

Serve on rice or noodles, topped with scallions.

SERVING AND MENU IDEAS
Something refreshing would be nice on the side of this flavorful dish, maybe simply sliced assorted melons. Fresh Pineapple Upside-Down Cake (page 369) or Coconut-Pineapple Sorbet (page 382) would sweetly finish the meal.

Pasta Carbonara with Zucchini

Pasta with Spinach and Apricots

Tagliatelle with Dill Pesto and Roasted Fennel

Bitter Greens Lasagna

Fettuccine with Caramelized Onions and Yogurt

Sweet Potato Gnocchi

Grandma Anne's Pasta with Navy Beans

Fregola with Peas

Spaghetti with Olives and Lemon

Pasta with Avocado Pesto

Pasta Carbonara with Zucchini

This creamy, smoky pasta and zucchini dish is really delicious comfort food you can prepare quickly and easily. The smoked cheddar may be unusual in this Italian-style dish, but it substitutes for the smoky flavor of bacon, and the results are very satisfying. In this recipe, raw eggs are stirred into hot pasta, and the eggs will cook if you have everything ready to toss together just as soon as the pasta has drained, and while it is still piping hot.

Serves 4 or 5
Time: 40 minutes

¼ teaspoon salt, plus more as needed
3 tablespoons extra-virgin olive oil
4 or 5 small zucchini, cut in half lengthwise and
   sliced ¼ inch thick (about 5 cups)
3 garlic cloves, pressed or chopped
1 pound pasta (fettuccine or linguine is nice, but
   any shape is fine)
2 large eggs
Pinch of freshly grated nutmeg
¼ teaspoon freshly ground black pepper, plus more
   as needed
1 cup grated or shredded smoked cheddar cheese
1 cup grated or shredded Parmesan cheese
½ cup finely chopped fresh parsley
½ cup chopped fresh basil

There are a couple of things going on at the same time in this recipe, so prep all the ingredients before you start to cook. What you want is for the zucchini to be cooked and the egg-and-cheese mixture to be at hand when the pasta is done. Have a large serving bowl warmed and ready for the drained hot pasta. Then, as soon as you've drained the pasta, follow the finishing steps and serve immediately.

Bring a large covered pot of salted water to a boil. Meanwhile, heat the oil in a large skillet on medium-high heat. Add the zucchini slices and cook for about 5 minutes, stirring occasionally. Add the garlic to the skillet and cook until the zucchini is golden brown and tender, about 5 minutes. Turn off the heat.

When the water is boiling, stir the pasta into the pot. Cover the pot and when the water returns to a boil, uncover the pot.

Meanwhile, in a bowl, beat the eggs with the nutmeg, salt, and pepper. Stir in the smoked cheddar and half the grated Parmesan. Set aside the remaining ½ cup Parmesan.

When the pasta is al dente, drain it and transfer right away to the warmed serving bowl. Immediately stir the egg and cheese mixture into the hot pasta and toss well to coat the pasta and cook the eggs. Add the cooked zucchini, parsley, and basil and toss well to evenly distribute the flavors. Season with salt and pepper to taste and toss again.

Serve immediately, with the remaining Parmesan cheese sprinkled on top.

VARIATION
Add a few crushed red pepper flakes to the skillet when cooking the zucchini.

SERVING AND MENU IDEAS
A crisp refreshing salad is perfect to accompany this rich, cheesy pasta, perhaps Belgian Endive Citrus Salad with Gremolata (page 129).

Pasta with Spinach and Apricots

Moosewood partner Susan Harville may be the most ardent lover of Italian food among us. She especially likes a quick, uncomplicated pasta with vegetables like this one. As Susan has been preaching for years, most great pasta dishes begin just this way, with garlic sautéed in olive oil. Here, the simple, easy formula is enhanced with lots of fresh baby spinach and bright bits of dried apricots, all held together with melted feta cheese. The topping can be prepped in the time it takes to boil water and cook the pasta.

Serves 4
Time: about 30 minutes

¾ cup sliced or chopped dried apricots
3 tablespoons minced garlic
11 ounces baby spinach (8 cups packed)
1 cup crumbled feta cheese
1 pound whole wheat farfalle or other short pasta
4 tablespoons extra-virgin olive oil
¼ cup pine nuts, toasted (optional)
¼ teaspoon cracked black pepper

Bring a large covered pot of salted water to a boil. Meanwhile, thinly slice or finely chop the apricots and set them aside in a small bowl. Mince the garlic and rinse the spinach in a colander. Crumble the feta cheese and set it aside.

When the water is boiling, ladle out enough water to cover the apricots in the bowl. Stir the pasta into the boiling water and cover the pot so it will quickly return to a boil.

Heat 2 tablespoons of the olive oil in a large heavy skillet. Sauté the minced garlic just until golden. Add the spinach with any water clinging to the leaves, in two batches if necessary to allow the first batch to wilt enough to fit the rest in the skillet. Fold the spinach over itself until it is all wilted but still bright green. Turn off the heat. In a separate small dry skillet, toast the pine nuts until lightly browned.

When the pasta is al dente, reserve ½ cup of the pasta cooking water and drain the pasta. Place the pasta in a serving bowl and toss with the remaining 2 tablespoons olive oil. Stir in the feta and enough of the hot pasta cooking water to make it saucy. Stir in the spinach mixture and the drained soaked apricots. Sprinkle with the pepper. Toss everything together. Sprinkle with toasted pine nuts, if you like, and serve immediately.

VARIATIONS
- If you like a lot of greens, use up to a pound of baby spinach.
- Use arugula in place of spinach.
- Use shredded or grated Parmesan in place of feta.
- Use sliced toasted almonds in place of pine nuts.

SERVING AND MENU IDEAS
While you wait for the pasta to cook, you could nibble on crudités or start with White Bean and Olive spread (see page 83) on baguette rounds. A crisp green salad is a good choice, or pair the pasta with a spring vegetable like Asparagus Cacio e Pepe–Style (page 293).

Tagliatelle with Dill Pesto and Roasted Fennel

Tagliatelle is a rich, but light, egg pasta that perfectly suits simple sauces and easily prepared vegetables. Here we use a very pretty, bright green dill pesto that combines the flavors of Havarti cheese, Dijon mustard, and fennel seeds, and we top the pasta with caramelized and crunchy roasted fresh fennel. Quickly sautéed zucchini rounds are also a good topping for the pasta and pesto.

Yields 1½ cups pesto
Serves 4
Time: 50 minutes

ROASTED FENNEL
½ teaspoon coarse salt
2 fennel bulbs, cut in half end to end and then into ¼- to ½-inch-thick slices
2 tablespoons olive oil

DILL PESTO
¼ teaspoon salt, plus more as needed
2 cups packed chopped fresh dill
½ cup packed chopped parsley
1 garlic clove, minced or pressed
1 teaspoon ground fennel seeds
⅓ cup olive or walnut oil
2 tablespoons fresh lemon juice
½ cup grated Havarti cheese, plus more for garnish
½ teaspoon Dijon mustard
1 pound tagliatelle pasta

Make the fennel: Preheat the oven to 425°F. Line a baking sheet with parchment paper or aluminum foil.

Sprinkle the lined baking sheet with the coarse salt, arrange the fennel slices on top, and drizzle on the oil. Roast for about 30 minutes, turning the fennel over after about 15 minutes. Set aside.

Make the pesto and pasta: Bring a large pot of salted water to a boil. Meanwhile, in the bowl of a food processor, whirl the dill, parsley, garlic, and ground fennel seeds for about 5 seconds. Mix together the oil and lemon juice and, with the food processor running, add it in a steady stream. Turn off the machine and add the grated cheese, mustard, and salt. Whirl for a few seconds until everything is blended. You should have a beautiful bright green paste. Set the pesto aside.

When the water is boiling, add the pasta and cook until al dente. Drain the pasta and divide it among four bowls. Top each serving with some pesto and roasted fennel. Garnish with additional grated Havarti.

VARIATION
For a vegan dish, substitute ½ cup chopped toasted walnuts for the Havarti cheese in the pesto. And it's nice to use walnut oil in place of olive oil. Garnish with toasted walnuts, if you don't think that's overkill.

SERVING AND MENU IDEAS
Serve with Wax Bean and Radish Salad with Buttermilk Dressing (page 121) or Lemony Roasted Beets (page 297).

Bitter Greens Lasagna

This lasagna with its pastel green and cream-colored layers is a lovely dish any time, but we welcome it especially during spring when we crave rejuvenating green plants. Don't hesitate to load your greens mixture with truly bitter greens, such as broccoli rabe; the bite will be tempered by the mild and milky béchamel sauce and the cheeses.

Use whichever lasagna noodles you like; our favorite is Bionaturae whole wheat noodles. If you've never made lasagna without the messy precooking of the noodles, trust that it will work and try it.

Serves 6 to 8
Prep time: 1 hour
Baking time: 45 minutes

1 pound ricotta cheese
6 to 8 ounces goat cheese, crumbled
1 teaspoon finely grated lemon zest
Salt and freshly ground black pepper

2 pounds mixed greens, such as turnip greens, broccoli rabe, mustard greens, collards, escarole, dandelion, spinach (12 to 14 cups prepped)
2 cups minced onions
6 garlic cloves, minced
2 tablespoons olive oil

BÉCHAMEL SAUCE
4 tablespoons (½ stick) butter
¼ cup unbleached white all-purpose flour
2 cups milk or half-and-half, warmed
½ teaspoon salt
Cracked black pepper
Dash of cayenne pepper
Pinch of freshly grated nutmeg
1 (12-ounce) package lasagna noodles
4 ounces Pecorino Romano or Parmesan cheese, grated (about 1½ cups)

Mix the ricotta cheese, goat cheese, lemon zest, and salt and pepper to taste and set aside. Remove any large or tough stems from the greens and chop the greens into bite-size pieces. Rinse the greens well and leave in the sink to drain.

In your largest skillet or a large pot, sauté the onions and garlic in the olive oil until softened. Add the greens, in batches if the pan is too crowded, and sauté until wilted but still bright green, 7 to 8 minutes. Season with salt and pepper to taste and remove from the heat.

Make the béchamel sauce: Melt the butter in a saucepan. Add the flour and whisk until the mixture is smooth and thick. Slowly add the milk, stirring constantly, and bring almost to a boil. Reduce the heat to low and cook, stirring often, until the sauce is thick, about 5 minutes. Remove from the heat and season with salt, cracked black pepper, cayenne, and nutmeg.

(continued)

Preheat the oven to 375°F.

Assemble the lasagna: Coat a 9 x 12-inch baking pan with cooking spray, olive oil, or butter. Drain any excess liquid from the greens. Cover the bottom of the pan with lasagna noodles. Ladle one-quarter of the béchamel over the noodles and spread it gently. Top with one-third of the greens mixture and dot with one-third of the ricotta and goat cheese mixture. Sprinkle with some grated Pecorino Romano. Repeat this layering two more times. Top with noodles. Spread the last quarter of the béchamel over the noodles, trying to coat them completely. Sprinkle with the last of the grated cheese.

Cover the pan with aluminum foil and bake for 25 minutes. Uncover and bake for another 20 minutes, or until you can feel that the noodles are tender when pierced with a sharp knife. Remove the lasagna from the oven and let it rest for 10 to 15 minutes before cutting and serving.

SERVING AND MENU IDEAS

Serve with a side of Beetroot Sticks (page 313) or a little salad with some sweet elements, such as Greens with Citrus-Date Dressing (page 126). You might consider a light dessert such as Coconut-Pineapple Sorbet (page 382).

Fettuccine with Caramelized Onions and Yogurt

This very creamy and satisfying pasta dish is easy and healthful, combining the sweetness of caramelized onions with the slightly sour tang of yogurt. Even nonfat Greek yogurt is thick and unctuous enough to give the illusion and the mouthfeel of an indulgently rich pasta sauce.

Yields 9 cups
Serves 6
Prep time: 35 minutes

6 cups sliced onions
Salt
¼ cup extra-virgin olive oil
1 pound whole wheat fettuccine
2 cups Greek yogurt
1 cup grated Pecorino Romano cheese
Sprinkling of cracked black pepper

To slice the onions, cut off the polar ends and cut in half end to end. Peel. Slice each half from pole to pole into thin slices. (The onion slices hold their shape better when cut this way.)

Put a large covered pot of salted water on to boil.

Heat the olive oil in a large heavy skillet on medium-high heat, add the onion slices and sauté, stirring constantly, until they begin to soften and their color darkens a bit, about 4 minutes. Sprinkle with salt and reduce the heat to low. Cook, uncovered, stirring every few minutes, for about 20 minutes, until the onions are very soft and golden brown. Add a splash of water if the onions stick or begin to brown too fast.

Meanwhile, when the water is boiling, stir in the fettuccine and cover the pot so the water will return quickly to a boil. Uncover the pot and cook the pasta until al dente, 8 or 9 minutes. Reserve ½ cup of the pasta cooking water and drain the pasta.

In a large serving bowl, add ¼ cup of the hot pasta cooking water to the yogurt and stir until smooth. Add the drained pasta, the grated cheese, the caramelized onions, and a sprinkling of cracked black pepper. Toss everything together to coat the pasta. Add a little more pasta water if needed. Serve immediately.

SERVING AND MENU SUGGESTIONS
This creamy, slightly sweet pasta is great with a refreshing green salad on the side, something like Kale, Jicama, and Orange Salad (page 128) or Greens with Citrus-Date Dressing (page 126). Or start with Watercress Toast (page 53) and accompany the pasta with Spicy Roasted Broccoli (page 302) or Beet Greens with Raisins and Pine Nuts (page 290).

Sweet Potato Gnocchi

Gnocchi are comforting, tender little Italian dumplings. Traditionally, white potatoes are used to make gnocchi. But sweet potatoes work as well, and are more nutritious and flavorful. We roast the sweet potatoes because they develop a nicely caramelized flavor and are drier than boiled and mashed sweet potatoes.

Serve gnocchi with Brown Butter Sauce with Sage (see sidebar, page 237), our favorite. Or simply with butter or extra-virgin olive oil and topped with freshly ground black pepper and grated Parmesan cheese. And then there's pesto or tomato sauce or red pepper sauce, Alfredo sauce . . . whatever suits your fancy.

If you have leftover gnocchi, reheat very gently in a pan or microwave.

Serves about 6
Time: 1½ hours, including sweet potato
roasting time and gnocchi cooking time

1 pound sweet potatoes
½ teaspoon salt
½ teaspoon freshly grated nutmeg
2 tablespoons grated Parmesan cheese
1 lightly beaten egg
2 cups all-purpose flour

Roast the whole sweet potatoes in a 425°F oven until soft. Split open and scoop out the flesh into a bowl large enough to accommodate all the ingredients. Discard the skins. Allow the sweet potatoes to cool for a few minutes.

Bring a large pot of salted water to a boil, and then keep it simmering on a back burner until the gnocchi are ready to cook.

Mash the sweet potatoes and stir in the salt, nutmeg, Parmesan, and egg. Add the flour and stir well. You may be tempted to add more flour, but don't; this is a soft dough and too much flour will result in rubbery gnocchi.

Cut the gnocchi dough into 4 equal pieces and, using a rubber spatula, scoop out one-quarter of the dough from the bowl onto a floured surface. Using floured hands, roll out a ½-inch-thick "snake." Repeat with the other pieces of dough. Cut each of these snakes into ½-inch-long pieces. You can leave the pieces as they are, or gently roll each piece between floured fingers or palms to round the edges, or press each piece gently with the back of a fork, making impressions with the tines. Place the pieces on a big tray or baking sheet.

The gnocchi take only a few minutes to cook. Bring the water back to a rolling boil. You may need to cook in a few batches depending on how big your pot is. Drop the gnocchi a few at a time into the boiling water; you want the water to keep boiling. When the gnocchi float to the surface, scoop them out with a mesh strainer, place in a bowl with a bit of butter or olive oil, and cover to keep warm. When they're all done, serve at once.

SERVING AND MENU IDEAS
Serve tender Sweet Potato Gnocchi with the topping or sauce you like (see headnote). And on the side, a salad with some fresh raw texture, like Jason's Fresh Fennel Apple Slaw (page 123), or a vegetable that offers a contrast in sweetness, such as Spicy Broccoli Rabe with Sun-Dried Tomatoes and Almonds (page 288)

BROWN BUTTER SAUCE WITH SAGE

4 tablespoons (½ stick) unsalted butter

8 fresh sage leaves, torn in half (optional)

1 teaspoon balsamic vinegar

In a small pan on medium-low heat, bring the butter to a simmer and cook for 3 to 4 minutes until the solids sink to the bottom of the pan and turn brown. Remove from the heat before the butter burns. Stir in the sage leaves and vinegar.

Grandma Anne's Pasta with Navy Beans

Laura Branca's mother-in-law, Anne (Antonietta) Ricciuti DuCret, grew up in the Bronx during the 1920s. Her parents were Italian immigrants from the small town of Polla in the region of Campania and the tiny village of Crecchio in the region of Abruzzo. They always had a flourishing vegetable garden wherever they lived. Grandma Anne (as Laura's sons Matt and Dan Branca call her) is the Branca family's matriarch in the finest sense of that word, and an outstanding cook with the true gift of making traditional Italian dishes that are both light and incredibly flavorful. Nothing pleases her more than to show the family how to make her great recipes. Laura faithfully shares this one-dish Italian meal; it is inexpensive, nutritious, extremely satisfying, and very easy to make.

It's already stocky enough to serve in soup plates, but if you prefer it as a soup, add 2 cups more stock.

Serves 6 to 8
Time: 30 minutes

½ teaspoon salt, plus more as needed
1 pound of your favorite short chunky pasta, such as penne, farfalle, orecchiette, elbows
3 tablespoons olive oil
1 generous cup chopped onions
1 cup diced celery
1 red or orange bell pepper, seeded and diced
4 garlic cloves, minced
¼ teaspoon freshly ground black pepper, plus more as needed
1 quart vegetable stock
1 (15-ounce) can navy beans
2 to 3 cups chopped baby kale (optional)

2 teaspoons minced fresh oregano, or 1 teaspoon dried
2 tablespoons minced fresh basil leaves, or 2 teaspoons dried

Bring a large covered pot of salted water to a boil for cooking the pasta. When it boils, add the pasta and cook until just al dente. Drain and set aside until ready to add to the soup.

Meanwhile, in a soup pot on medium heat, warm the olive oil. Add the chopped onions and cook for a couple of minutes. Stir in the celery, bell pepper, garlic, salt, and black pepper, cover, and cook for 5 minutes, stirring occasionally. Pour in the stock, cover, and increase the heat to medium-high. When the soup is hot, add the navy beans including the liquid, the kale, if using, and the oregano and basil. Simmer gently until the beans are hot and the kale is soft. Taste and season with additional salt and pepper as needed.

NOTES
- As this dish sits, the pasta absorbs more liquid. Add more stock when you reheat it.
- Grandma Anne freezes 1- or 2-portion leftovers in storage containers; it reheats beautifully.

SERVING AND MENU IDEAS
Serve in soup or pasta bowls with a nice piece of crusty Italian bread with butter or olive oil. Garnish each serving with a few fresh basil and oregano leaves. You don't need anything else to make a fine meal, but Grandma Anne would probably approve of some traditional Italian pickles, such as Giardiniera (page 342), on the table and maybe some Easy Lemon Butter Cookies (page 353) to go with espresso later.

Fregola with Peas

Fregola is a type of toasted pasta from Sardinia that is similar in shape and size to Israeli couscous (which could be substituted if you have trouble finding fregola). This dish is quite attractive because the fregola and peas are handsomely matched in size, and the fresh herbs and cheese cling wonderfully to the pasta and simple sauce. We like petits pois in this dish. Fresh arugula adds another nice note, but if you are in a hurry or tired and can't deal with one more ingredient, the flavor will still be good without it.

Serves 4 as a main dish, 6 as a side
Time: 35 minutes

1 teaspoon salt, plus more as needed
1¼ cups fregola
¼ cup olive oil, plus more for drizzling
2 cups sliced scallions
1 cup dry white wine
2 cups fresh or frozen green peas
½ pound coarsely chopped baby arugula
  (optional)
½ teaspoon ground black pepper
¼ cup chiffonade of fresh mint and/or basil leaves
1 cup grated Parmesan or Pecorino Romano
  cheese

Bring a large covered pot of salted water to a boil. When it boils, add the pasta and cook until al dente. Drain, reserving a cup of the pasta cooking water.

Meanwhile, in a large skillet on medium heat, warm the oil. Add the scallions along with a sprinkle of salt and sauté for about 5 minutes, or until just beginning to brown. Add the wine and allow the liquid to bubble and reduce for a couple of minutes. Stir in the drained fregola, the peas, and the arugula (if using). Add some of the reserved pasta water if needed; it should be saucy, not soupy. Cook for 10 minutes, stirring often, until the sauce thickens. Season with the salt and pepper. Stir in the chiffonade of mint and/or basil and half the cheese.

Drizzle more olive oil over each serving, if you like, and serve with the remaining cheese on the side.

SERVING AND MENU IDEAS
A nice side dish for Fregola with Peas is Romanesco with Green Salsa (page 299).

Spaghetti with Olives and Lemon

With this piquant and delicious pasta in the Southern Italian tradition, the topping will be ready before the water boils and the pasta cooks.

The quality of the ingredients really matters here. Use an assortment of good deli olives, extra-virgin olive oil, and a good, preferably Italian-made pasta; we recommend Bionaturae brand whole wheat spaghetti.

Serves 4
Time: 25 minutes

1 pound whole wheat spaghetti
6 garlic cloves
¼ cup extra-virgin olive oil
2 cups assorted pitted olives★
¾ cup packed chopped fresh parsley
2 teaspoons minced preserved lemon (page 344)
  or finely grated lemon zest
¼ teaspoon crushed red pepper flakes (optional)
Finely grated Pecorino Romano or Parmesan
  cheese (optional)

★Choose a selection of your favorite olives; a mix of black and green is attractive. Include a few rich, briny olives like Kalamatas, and also milder ones like Niçoise, and some meaty green gigantes. Stuffed olives are fine, too; their stuffings add extra little bits of color and flavor.

Bring a large covered pot of salted water to a boil. When it boils, add the pasta and cook until just al dente.

Meanwhile, in a small saucepan on medium-low heat, cook the garlic cloves in the olive oil until golden, 4 to 5 minutes, watching carefully so they don't scorch. Set aside

Put the olives, parsley, preserved lemon or lemon zest, and red pepper flakes (if using), into a food processor. Add the cooked garlic cloves and olive oil. Pulse everything for just a few seconds, until the olives are finely chopped but not pasty.

When the pasta is just al dente (which may happen sooner than the time given on the package), reserve a cup of the cooking water, and then drain the pasta, but not too thoroughly. Place the pasta in a serving bowl and add the olive mixture. Toss, adding some of the cooking water if the pasta needs more moisture.

Serve hot, topped with grated cheese, if you wish.

SERVING AND MENU IDEAS

Spaghetti with Olives and Lemon pairs well with Apulian Fava Beans and Greens (page 255) or with a salad of fresh mozzarella and tomatoes. Or begin the meal with Watercress Toast (page 53) or accompany the pasta with Greens with Apricots Times Two (page 111) or Baby Arugula Salad with Crusted Chèvre and Pears (page 114).

Pasta with Avocado Pesto

If you love all things pesto, this one's a keeper, and it's vegan to boot. Avocados and walnuts are easily available and are so good for you. Avocado Pesto has great mouthfeel and a very pleasant flavor—if you didn't know that it's made with avocados, you might be hard-pressed to identify the base ingredient.

This pesto is perfect on pasta and makes enough for one pound. Gluten-free penne, whole wheat spaghetti or linguine, or any other shape and type of pasta is fine.

Yields 2 cups pesto
Serves 4 to 6
Time: 25 minutes

½ teaspoon salt, plus more as needed
1 pound pasta
2 ripe Hass avocados
1 cup loosely packed fresh basil leaves
½ cup lightly toasted walnuts
3 tablespoons fresh lemon juice
2 garlic cloves, minced or pressed (optional)
⅓ cup extra-virgin olive oil
⅛ teaspoon freshly ground black pepper
1 to 2 tablespoons water

Bring a large covered pot of salted water to a boil for cooking the pasta. When it boils, add the pasta and cook until just al dente.

While the pasta cooks, make the pesto. Slice around each avocado lengthwise down to the pit. Twist the halves apart. Pop out the pit with the tip of a knife. Scoop out the flesh with a spoon. Chop the basil.

In a food processor, combine the avocados, basil, walnuts, lemon juice, garlic (if using), salt, oil, pepper, and water and purée until smooth. Serve immediately, or, if you will serve it later or have leftovers, to prevent discoloration, press plastic wrap directly onto the surface and refrigerate.

Drain the pasta. In a large bowl, stir the pesto into the hot pasta, and *voilà!*

VARIATION
Substitute lightly toasted pine nuts, almonds, or pistachios for the walnuts in the pesto.

SERVING AND MENU IDEAS
Serve this pasta with chopped fresh tomatoes on top. Garnish with parsley or mint. Parmesan cheese can be sprinkled on top for a non-vegan variation. Spicy Roasted Broccoli (page 302) is a good side dish here.

Italian Cannellini Burgers

Black Bean and Quinoa Burgers with Chipotle Ketchup

Roasted Red Pepper, Black Olive, and Tofu Burgers

Cashew-Crusted Chickpea Burgers

Beet Burgers

Apulian Fava Beans and Greens

Chili with Quinoa

Mujadara

Skillet Black Beans with Fruit Salsa and Yellow Coconut Rice

Haitian Rice and Beans with Plantains

Award-Winning Chili with Chocolate and Stout

Italian Cannellini Burgers

Good ol' bean burgers with an Italian twist.

Yields 8 burgers
Prep time: 40 minutes
Baking time: 30 minutes

2 tablespoons extra-virgin olive oil, plus more as
   needed
2 cups diced onions
3 garlic cloves, pressed or minced
1 teaspoon dried basil
1 teaspoon dried oregano
⅔ cup chopped walnuts
½ cup bread crumbs
3 cups cannellini beans (two 15-ounce cans,
   drained)
2 teaspoons tomato paste
1 teaspoon balsamic vinegar
Dash of cayenne pepper
½ cup chopped fresh parsley
Salt, and freshly ground black pepper
Slices of mozzarella cheese (optional)

Warm the olive oil in a large skillet on medium-low heat. Add the onions and cook until soft, about 10 minutes. Add the garlic, basil, and oregano and cook for 5 minutes. Stir in the walnuts and bread crumbs and cook for about 3 minutes. Add the drained cannellini beans and mash (with a fork or a potato masher) and then stir well. Cook for 5 minutes.

Preheat the oven to 375°F. Lightly oil a baking sheet.

Place the bean mixture in a large bowl. Add the tomato paste, vinegar, cayenne, and parsley and stir well. Season with salt and black pepper to taste.

Using a ½-cup dry measuring cup, scoop out the mixture. Place on the baking sheet and slightly flatten each burger. Bake for 30 minutes, until golden brown. If you like, top each burger with a slice of mozzarella and return to the oven for about a minute, until just melted.

VARIATION
Add 1 cup diced bell peppers when adding the onions.

SERVING AND MENU IDEAS
Top each burger with a large tomato slice or some tomato sauce. Round out a meal of Italian Cannellini Burgers (page 245) with Spaghetti Squash with Sage and Parmesan (page 295) and Spicy Broccoli Rabe with Sun-Dried Tomatoes and Almonds (page 288). It will be a colorful plate.

Black Bean and Quinoa Burgers with Chipotle Ketchup

Black beans and quinoa are a perfect partnership of substantial, high-protein foods, and here they are well seasoned with cumin and coriander and very satisfying. The chipotle ketchup is a lusty, spicy inspiration.

This vegan burger mix is very pliable and easy to work with, and the burgers hold together remarkably well. The mixture can be refrigerated for a couple of days, or formed into burgers and frozen for a couple of months. Make a double batch and freeze some for later. When you shape it, the mixture is fully cooked and "meaty," so no need to bake before freezing them; just shape, wrap, and freeze. Then thaw, brush with oil, and bake until heated through.

You can either pan-fry or bake these burgers.

Yields 4 burgers
Preparation time: 40 minutes
Baking or panfrying time: 20 minutes

BURGERS
1 (25-ounce) can black beans (or two 14- or
　15-ounce cans)
¼ cup quinoa
½ cup water
2 teaspoons cumin seeds
1 teaspoon coriander seeds
3 tablespoons vegetable oil
1 cup chopped onions
2 or 3 garlic cloves, chopped
1 cup chopped red bell peppers
¼ teaspoon crushed red pepper flakes (optional)
½ teaspoon smoked paprika (optional)
½ teaspoon salt

CHIPOTLE KETCHUP
½ cup ketchup
1 teaspoon soy sauce
1 teaspoon adobo sauce from canned chipotles

Make the burger mixture: Rinse the beans in a colander and set aside to drain.

Rinse and drain the quinoa in a fine-mesh sieve. Combine with the water in a small pot, cover, and simmer for 10 minutes. Set aside to cool.

Toast the cumin and coriander seeds (see sidebar, page 247) until fragrant but not scorched. Set aside to cool.

Warm 2 tablespoons of the oil in a large skillet and sauté the onions for about 6 minutes. Add the garlic and bell peppers, lower the heat to medium, and cook for about 8 minutes, or until the peppers have softened.

Meanwhile, grind the cooled toasted cumin and coriander seeds and the red pepper flakes (if using), in a spice grinder, and stir into the onions and bell peppers. Add the smoked paprika (if using), and the salt. Turn off the heat. Stir in the drained beans and smash them with the back of a large wooden spoon or a potato masher. Stir in the cooked quinoa. When all the ingredients are well incorporated, set aside until the burger mixture is cool enough to handle, about 10 minutes.

While the burger mixture cools, make the chipotle ketchup: Stir together the ketchup, soy sauce, and adobo sauce in a small bowl. Set aside.

Divide the burger mixture into 4 portions. Press and pat each portion into a patty.

To pan-fry the burgers: In a large skillet, warm the remaining 1 tablespoon oil on medium heat. Fry the burgers, turning once, until hot and a bit crisp, about 20 minutes (longer if the burger mix has been chilled).

To bake the burgers: Preheat the oven to 350°F. Oil a baking sheet or pan. Shape 4 burgers and place them on the baking pan. Brush the tops of the burgers with the remaining oil, and bake until heated through, about 20 minutes (longer if the burger mixture has been chilled).

Serve the burgers on toasted buns with your favorite burger condiments: tomato slices, red onions, lettuce, pickles, mustard. . . . Just be sure to include the chipotle ketchup.

SERVING AND MENU IDEAS

In keeping with its Latin American character, serve this with corn on the cob, Mango-Spinach Salad with Spicy Dressing (page 118), Sweet Potatoes with Bitter Orange (page 303), or Butternut Hash Browns (page 18). But don't overdo it—you may want Cardamom Cookies with Bittersweet Chocolate Drizzle (page 354) at the finish.

HOW TO TOAST SPICES

Toasting releases a spice's aromatic and flavorful oils, bringing out an earthy, rich flavor and fragrance. Toast whole seeds on the stovetop or in the oven, and when cool, grind in a spice grinder or coffee grinder or using a mortar and pestle (with which toasted spices are easier to grind than untoasted). Toast only one spice at a time because spices brown at different speeds. To prevent scorching, which causes bitterness, be sure to remove the spices from the heat as soon as they just begin to brown and transfer them to a plate or bowl to cool. Toasted spices are best used right away, but any extra can be stored in a well-sealed jar or plastic bag.

Stovetop method: Put the whole spice seeds into a cold, dry skillet and warm the pan on medium heat. As the pan heats and the spice becomes fragrant, stir or shake often. The spice seeds might jump a bit and you may hear little popping sounds. As soon as you can really smell the fragrance and the seeds just start to brown, transfer to a bowl or plate to cool.

Oven method: Spread the whole seeds or ground spices on a dry baking sheet and toast at 325°F until fully aromatic and slightly darker in color. Transfer to a cool plate or bowl.

Roasted Red Pepper, Black Olive, and Tofu Burgers

The flavor profile of this tofu burger leans toward the Balkans and Mediterranean. For ease, we use good-quality roasted red peppers in a jar. On a sandwich, we like to pile on the toppings: roasted red pepper mayonnaise, pickled red onions (if you start them first, the pickled red onions will be ready when your burgers come out of the oven), feta cheese, and buttercrunch lettuce, thinly sliced cucumbers or tomatoes, and sprigs of fresh dill.

Use gluten-free bread crumbs and soy sauce, and these burgers can be gluten-free.

Yields 8 small bun-size burgers or 4 larger burgers
Time: about 60 minutes

1 (16-ounce) block tofu

PICKLED RED ONIONS (OPTIONAL)
1 garlic clove
¾ cup apple cider vinegar
½ teaspoon sugar, plus more if you like your pickles less tangy
½ teaspoon salt
1 small red onion, thinly sliced crosswise

BURGERS
2 tablespoons olive oil, plus more as needed
1 cup finely chopped onions
2 teaspoons minced or crushed garlic
½ teaspoon salt
½ teaspoon sweet paprika
¼ teaspoon ground cinnamon
¼ teaspoon freshly ground black pepper
½ cup bread crumbs
¼ cup ground or finely chopped toasted walnuts
¼ cup sliced black olives (Greek, Niçoise, or Kalamata)
½ cup chopped roasted red peppers★
1 large egg
1 teaspoon Dijon-style mustard
1 tablespoon soy sauce
1½ teaspoons dark or roasted sesame oil

ROASTED RED PEPPER MAYONNAISE (OPTIONAL)
½ cup mayonnaise
¼ cup chopped roasted red peppers,★ plus 1 to 2 tablespoons of liquid from the jar
1 teaspoon minced fresh dill (optional)
Splash of vinegar or fresh lemon juice (optional)

½ cup crumbled feta (optional)

★You can find roasted red peppers in a jar or can in the supermarket shelved near Italian products or sometimes near the pickles. Or, of course, you can roast them yourself.

Place the tofu in a shallow-sided baking pan. Balance a cake pan on top of the tofu and place some unopened cans in the cake pan. Press the tofu for 30 minutes. Pour off the pressed water and set the tofu aside.

If making pickled red onions, start them now: Combine the garlic, vinegar, sugar, and salt in a small bowl and stir to dissolve the salt and sugar. Parboil the onions in 2 cups of boiling water for

(continued)

1 or 2 minutes, strain, and transfer to a glass jar or nonreactive bowl. Pour the pickling liquid over the onions. Cover and set aside.

Make the burgers: Preheat the oven to 375°F. Generously oil a baking sheet

Sauté the chopped onions in the olive oil with the garlic and spices for about 10 minutes, or until the onions are soft. In a large bowl, grate or mash the pressed tofu into a fine crumble. Add the bread crumbs, walnuts, olives, and roasted red peppers. Stir in the sautéed onions.

In a smaller bowl, whisk together the egg, mustard, soy sauce, and sesame oil. Pour the egg mixture over the tofu mixture and, using your hands or a spoon, mix until everything is thoroughly combined. The mixture should be firm enough to form into patties.

Form the burgers and place them on the prepared baking sheet. For smaller burgers, use ⅓ cup of the mixture, ⅔ cup for larger ones. Bake for 20 minutes, then flip the burgers and return to the oven for about 10 minutes more.

While the burgers bake, prepare the toppings: If you want to top them with Roasted Red Pepper Mayonnaise, whisk the ingredients together. Crumble the feta. The pickled red onions should be ready to eat when the burgers are done.

Serve in buns or on beds of greens topped with whatever array of extras you like.

SERVING AND MENU IDEAS
This very flavorful burger is complemented by Mashed Potatoes with Lemon and Parsley (page 307) or Mediterranean Potato Salad (page 124). A lovely side dish is Romanesco with Green Salsa (page 299).

Cashew-Crusted Chickpea Burgers

This burger is creamy-soft inside with a crunchy toasted cashew crust. Fragrant garam masala, a roasted spice mix with Indian origins, gives it personality.

Yields 4 burgers
Prep time: 25 minutes
Baking time: 20 minutes

1½ tablespoons vegetable oil, plus more as needed
1½ cups finely chopped onions
1 tablespoon peeled and grated fresh ginger
2 garlic cloves, minced or pressed
2 teaspoons garam masala, less if yours is "hot" (see page 46)
1½ cups grated sweet potatoes★
½ teaspoon salt
Tabasco or other hot sauce (optional)
½ cup toasted cashews
1 (15-ounce) can chickpeas, rinsed and drained
1½ teaspoons apple cider vinegar
2 tablespoons tahini

★1 small sweet potato: grate on the larger-holed side of a box grater.

Warm the oil in a large skillet, add the onions, and sauté for a couple of minutes. Reduce the heat to medium-low and add the ginger, garlic, and garam masala. Stir often for a minute or two to prevent the mixture from sticking to the pan, then add the grated sweet potatoes and salt. Cover and cook, stirring often, until the sweet potatoes are tender, about 8 minutes. Add a little water if necessary to prevent sticking.

Preheat the oven to 375°F. Lightly oil a baking sheet.

In a food processor, whirl the cashews until coarsely ground. Transfer to a plate and set aside. To the same bowl of the processor (no need to clean), add the chickpeas, vinegar, and tahini and process until fairly smooth. Stir this mixture into the cooked sweet potatoes. Season with salt to taste, and a splash or two of hot sauce if you like.

Form the mixture into 4 burgers. Gently press both sides of each burger into the ground cashews to coat, and place on the prepared baking sheet. Bake for 20 minutes until firm.

SERVING AND MENU IDEAS
Serve with a fruit chutney, minted yogurt, or Lemon-Tahini Sauce (page 325). Monsoon Pickles (page 339) will add a delicious piquancy to this burger. Something green on the side would be welcome, perhaps Southeast Asian Green Beans (page 300) or Collards with Coconut Milk, Pineapple, and Peanuts (page 285).

Beet Burgers

These mildly flavored burgers are vegan, gluten-free, and nightshade-free, and they make a great vehicle for all the extras that make burgers delicious. They are simple, easy to prepare, and cook on the stovetop. The burgers are fine reheated after a day or two in the refrigerator or up to several weeks in the freezer.

It's surprising how much the moisture content of beets and carrots varies: sometimes this burger mix is very wet and we add more cornmeal, other times we've added up to ⅓ cup water to make the mix moist enough to form patties. Because there are no eggs or flour to bind the mix—the patties are raw—you may wonder if they'll hold together as burgers, but once they're cooked, they're firm patties. The first flip of the burgers can be messy, but follow our directions and you'll end up with firm burgers that are so moist inside.

Yields 8 burgers
Prep time: 25 minutes
Stovetop cooking time: about 25 minutes

2 cups packed shredded peeled raw beets
1 cup packed shredded carrots
⅓ cup minced onions
1 cup rolled oats
1 teaspoon salt
¼ cup chopped fresh cilantro
1 cup packed shredded kale or other greens★
2 garlic cloves, minced (optional)
¼ cup finely ground cornmeal (more if the mix is too wet)
2 to 4 tablespoons olive oil, for pan-frying

★To shred kale, strip the leaves from the large central stems. Pile the leaves on a cutting board. Gather the kale into a tight mass and, using a sharp knife, thinly slice it.

In a bowl, mix the beets, carrots, onions, oats, and salt. Stir in the cilantro, kale, garlic, if using, and cornmeal. Set aside for 15 minutes or up to a couple of days in the refrigerator.

When you're ready to cook, if the mixture is too wet to easily shape into patties, stir in more cornmeal a tablespoon at a time. If the mixture is too dry, add water, a tablespoon at a time, until it holds together.

Warm 2 tablespoons of olive oil in a large skillet on low heat. Using a dry measuring cup, scoop out ½-cup portions of the mix and shape into burger patties with your hands, placing each patty in the skillet as you go. Tidy up the edges and if a burger cracks when you put it in the skillet, press it back together.

Cook the patties for about 10 minutes on the first side. The heat should be quite low: check the bottoms and lower the heat if scorching begins. Flip the burgers, tidy the edges if they crumble, press down on the top with the spatula to compress, and cook for about 8 minutes until the bottom is becoming crisp. Flip over onto the first side (this time the burgers should hold together well) and cook for about 5 minutes to brown. Let the burgers rest for a few minutes before serving.

The burgers will keep in the refrigerator for up to 3 days or in the freezer for several weeks. Reheat frozen burgers in a lightly oiled skillet on low heat, a few minutes each side.

SERVING AND MENU IDEAS

Make a delicious Beet Burger sandwich with Minted Mayo or Herb-packed Mayo (see sidebar), mustard, or Russian dressing; plus thinly sliced cucumbers, avocados, or tomatoes; and baby greens, arugula, or shredded lettuce.

Beet Burgers alone, without the bread and all the extras, are good next to Mushroom Barley Salad (page 147) or Orzo Risotto (page 322), perhaps with a vegetable side of Asparagus Cacio e Pepe–Style (page 293) or Shredded Brussels Sprouts with Apples (page 314).

FLAVORED MAYONNAISE

MINTED MAYO

½ cup mayonnaise

2 tablespoons minced fresh mint

1 tablespoon minced fresh chives or scallions (optional)

HERB-PACKED MAYO

½ cup mayonnaise

¼ cup minced fresh basil

¼ cup minced fresh cilantro

1 tablespoon minced fresh chives or scallions

Stir the mayonnaise and mint or herbs together in a small bowl or a jar. Refrigerate for at least an hour before serving. The mayonnaise will keep, refrigerated, for about a week.

Apulian Fava Beans and Greens

This is a simple recipe for a classic Pugliese way of cooking favas with some potatoes and serving them with fresh greens. We think that the buttery, mild-tasting mashed beans and potatoes are enlivened by a combination of greens that have a bit of a bite, such as mature arugula or sharp chicory, and mildly flavored greens, such as endive or escarole. But you may prefer collards, chard, broccoli rabe, or whatever is your favorite.

Fresh fava beans are not easy to find and their season is short. Ned Asta remembers when her family would get them the one time of year they were available in Glendale, Queens. Removing the pods first and then shelling each large bean was a laborious time-consuming project she did with her mother, Palma. We have found a year-round source of dried skinless fava beans, packed by Goya foods in 1-pound bags.

Serves 4 to 6
Prep time: 20 minutes
Total time: 1 hour, 20 minutes

FAVA BEANS
2 cups dried skinless fava beans (about 11 ounces)
1 medium red or gold potato, peeled and sliced
1 bay leaf
Crushed red pepper flakes
½ teaspoon salt
1 tablespoon extra-virgin olive oil
Freshly ground black pepper

GREENS
2 tablespoons extra-virgin olive oil
6 garlic cloves, minced or pressed
4 cups chopped escarole, curly endive, or other mild greens★
4 cups arugula, chicory, or other sharply flavored greens★
½ teaspoon salt

Lemon wedges, for garnish

★Or 8 cups of a single green or a combination of greens that you like most.

Make the fava beans: Put the beans, potato slices, and bay leaf into a pot with water to cover. Bring to a boil on high heat, add a pinch of red pepper flakes and the salt, cover, and simmer gently for about 1 hour. Check a couple of times during cooking and add just enough water to prevent sticking.

After about an hour, the beans should be getting tender and starting to fall apart. Remove the bay leaf, and if the mixture is very soupy, discard some of the liquid. Add the olive oil and use a potato masher to mash the beans and potatoes. Season with additional salt to taste and some black pepper.

While the beans are cooking, prep the garlic and greens. You'll need a large pot; the greens are bulky to start but cook down dramatically. When you've mashed the beans, cook the greens, so they will be bright green and hot when you serve them—this takes only a few minutes. Warm the olive oil and sauté the garlic for just a moment before adding the greens and salt. If the greens are still damp from washing them, that's all the moisture needed; if

(continued)

the greens are dry when you add them to the pot, add a couple tablespoons of water. If you're using a combination of greens, first add the greens that take longer to cook. Stir until they wilt, and then add quicker-cooking greens. Escarole takes 4 to 5 minutes, while arugula may take only 2 minutes. Stir the greens frequently; cook until just tender and still bright green.

Serve the beans and greens side by side on a platter, or make a bed of the favas and top with the greens. Arrange lemon wedges on the side of the platter.

SERVING AND MENU IDEAS

Apulian Fava Beans and Greens can be the centerpiece of a casual Mediterranean meal. Put some good crusty bread on the table with a couple cheeses, a bowl of olives, a cruet of olive oil, sliced tomatoes, and maybe some melon wedges or grapes and enjoy an easy feast. Other dishes in this book that pair well with beans and greens are Raspberry-Carrot Pickles (page 340), Summer Squash and Tomato Tian (page 306) and Za'atar Yogurt and Cucumber Salad (page 122).

Chili with Quinoa

We combine red quinoa, orange sweet potatoes, multicolored peppers, and bright green cilantro to create this richly hued and healthful chili. It can feed a hungry crowd and is gluten-free and vegan. Of course you can also offer grated cheese and sour cream as a garnish, if you wish.

Yields 10 to 11 cups
Serves 6 to 8
Time: about 1 hour

2 tablespoons olive oil
1 large sweet potato, peeled and diced (¾-inch cubes, about 3½ cups)
¾ teaspoon salt
1 teaspoon dried basil
½ cup red quinoa
1 cup water
2 tablespoons olive oil
1 large onion, chopped (about 2 cups)
2 large garlic cloves, minced or pressed
1 teaspoon salt, plus more as needed
1 red or orange bell pepper, seeded and diced
1 medium zucchini, diced
1 teaspoon chili powder
1½ teaspoons ground cumin
¼ teaspoon cayenne pepper
1 teaspoon dried oregano
1 (28-ounce) can diced tomatoes
2 (15-ounce) cans pinto beans, undrained
½ cup water
2 tablespoons fresh lime juice
¼ cup chopped fresh cilantro

Preheat the oven to 425°F. Lightly oil a baking sheet.

In a large bowl, toss the diced sweet potatoes with the olive oil, ½ teaspoon of the salt, and the basil. Spread out on the prepared baking sheet and roast until tender, about 20 minutes, stirring once after about 10 minutes.

Meanwhile, cook the quinoa. Rinse it in a fine-mesh sieve under cold running water. Bring the rinsed quinoa and the water and remaining ¼ teaspoon salt to a boil. Lower the heat and simmer, covered, for about 25 minutes, or until all the water has been absorbed and the quinoa is tender.

While the quinoa cooks, make the chili: Warm the oil in a soup pot on medium heat. Cook the chopped onions and garlic along with the salt until the onions begin to soften. Stir in the bell peppers and zucchini and cook for 3 minutes. Stir in the chili powder, cumin, cayenne, and oregano and cook for a minute or so to open up the spices. Add the tomatoes, pinto beans, and water and bring to a low boil, stirring occasionally. When the quinoa and sweet potatoes are done, add them to the pot. Cover and simmer for about 20 minutes.

Five minutes before serving, stir in the lime juice and cilantro and season with additional salt to taste.

SERVING AND MENU IDEAS
Chili with Quinoa is a thick, hearty dish, so a crisp refreshing salad, like Kale, Jicama, and Orange Salad (page 128) is nice with it. Cornbread is the first thing we think of to go with chili. Golden Cornbread (page 280) is also gluten-free, just like this chili. Watermelon is the best dessert we can imagine with this meal.

Mujadara

Still one of the most well-loved comfort dishes of the Middle East, *mujadara* seems to have first appeared in the tenth century. Many variations exist in Greece, India, Syria, Iran, Iraq, and Egypt, where it is called *kosheri*.

While the recipe calls for a number of ingredients, the preparation is simple and straightforward. We encourage you to seek out pomegranate molasses in the Middle Eastern section of the grocery store; it adds a wonderful taste and rich color.

Any leftover red pepper sauce will keep for weeks in the refrigerator, and can be used to enhance steamed or roasted vegetables, or as a topping for an omelet.

Yields 3 cups Red Pepper Sauce
Serves 6
Time: 1 hour, 15 minutes

1½ cups green or brown lentils
3½ cups water or vegetable stock

RED PEPPER SAUCE

4 roasted red peppers (homemade, or one
  28-ounce can, drained and rinsed)
¼ teaspoon crushed red pepper flakes, or 1 small
  hot pepper, minced (seeded for a milder hot)

1½ cups chopped walnuts
1 large garlic clove, minced
1 teaspoon ground cumin
¾ teaspoon salt
2 tablespoons fresh lemon juice
1 teaspoon sugar
¼ cup extra-virgin olive oil
¼ cup chopped fresh cilantro
3 tablespoons pomegranate molasses (see
  headnote) or balsamic vinegar

1¼ cups white basmati rice
2 tablespoons butter or coconut oil
2 teaspoons cumin seeds
½ teaspoon ground turmeric
1¾ cups water
½ teaspoon salt

3 tablespoons olive oil
2 large Spanish onions, thinly sliced (about 6 cups)

Freshly ground black pepper
½ cup chopped fresh cilantro, for sprinkling

Rinse the lentils in a sieve. In a saucepan, bring the lentils and water or stock to a boil. Lower the heat, cover, and simmer for about 35 minutes. When tender but not mushy, drain off any excess liquid and set aside.

Make the red pepper sauce: Whirl all the sauce ingredients in a food processor or blender. Set aside for the flavors to marry while you cook the rice and onions.

Rinse and drain the rice. In a saucepan, warm the butter or coconut oil, stir in the cumin seeds and turmeric, and cook for 30 seconds. Stir in the drained rice, water, and salt. Bring to a boil, cover, and simmer for 15 to 20 minutes until the rice is tender. Remove from the heat, place a clean kitchen towel over the top of the saucepan, and replace the lid. Allow the rice to sit for 10 minutes and then fluff with a fork.

In a large skillet on medium-low heat, cook the onions in the olive oil with a sprinkling of salt until they're a rich brown color, 20 to 30 minutes. Stir frequently.

In a large serving bowl, combine the cooked lentils, rice, and onions. Season with additional salt and black pepper to taste and sprinkle chopped cilantro on top. Serve the red pepper sauce alongside, to ladle about ½ cup over each portion.

SERVING AND MENU IDEAS

Add a dollop of yogurt on top and pita bread on the side. Or serve Mujadara with Za'atar Yogurt and Cucumber Salad (page 122) or another crisp salad, such as Greens with Citrus-Date Dressing (page 126), which features kumquats, radishes, and almonds. Turkish Coffee Brownies (page 358) are good for dessert.

Skillet Black Beans with Fruit Salsa and Yellow Coconut Rice

Here's a great recipe for when you need a fast, easy, and super-flavorful lunch or supper. All three elements—salsa, rice, and beans—are useful as stand-alone recipes. The salsa recipe is versatile, because you can mix and match fruits and customize it to your own taste.

This recipe is an example of the way we develop and test and retest dishes. A couple of us had worked on this recipe and it was good, just not yet perfect. So we called in Linda Dickinson, who we call LD, to taste and make suggestions. LD has one of the most discerning palates at Moosewood and has served as the final arbiter of recipes for a number of our cookbooks. She added coconut milk, tweaked the seasonings, and created the yellow coconut rice, improvements that upgraded this dish to *superlatively* excellent.

The hotness of curry pastes varies in intensity from brand to brand, so start cautiously and add more to taste. We like the balance of flavors in Thai Kitchen Red Curry Paste.

Serves 4
Time: 40 minutes

FRUIT SALSA
2 cups diced fresh fruit★
2 tablespoons fresh lime juice or vinegar
1 teaspoon minced fresh hot peppers or hot sauce, or ⅛ teaspoon cayenne pepper
½ teaspoon salt
1 tablespoon chopped fresh cilantro, basil, Thai basil, or scallions
Brown sugar (optional)

YELLOW COCONUT RICE
1½ cups white, white basmati, or jasmine rice, rinsed and drained
1 teaspoon ground turmeric
½ teaspoon salt
1 teaspoon vegetable oil or olive oil
1½ cups water
¾ cup coconut milk★★

BLACK BEANS
⅔ cup minced shallots
2 large garlic cloves, minced
1 tablespoon peeled and grated fresh ginger
2 tablespoons olive oil
4½ cups drained cooked black beans (three 15-ounce cans, drained)
2 teaspoons red curry paste (see headnote)
¼ cup fresh lime juice
¾ cup coconut milk★★
Brown sugar (optional)
Salt or soy sauce

★Use one fruit or a mix, whichever you like or have on hand: mangoes, pineapple, peaches.
★★One 13.5-ounce can coconut milk is the right amount for both the rice and beans.

Make the salsa: Stir together all the ingredients for the fruit salsa and set aside to allow the flavors to meld while the rice cooks and you prepare the beans.

Make the rice: Rinse and drain the rice in a fine-mesh sieve. In a saucepan on medium-high heat, sauté the rice, turmeric, and salt in the oil for a minute or two, stirring constantly. Add the water and coconut milk and bring to a boil. Cover, reduce the heat to low, and simmer until the rice is tender and the liquid has been absorbed, 15 to 20 minutes. Turn off the heat and fluff the rice with a fork.

(continued)

Cover the saucepan with a clean kitchen towel, and replace the lid. Let sit until ready to serve.

Make the black beans: Meanwhile, in a large skillet on medium heat, cook the shallots, garlic, and ginger in the olive oil for a few minutes, until the shallots are lightly browned. Add the beans, curry paste, lime juice, and coconut milk and stir well. Simmer, stirring often, for 10 to 15 minutes. Mash some of the beans right in the skillet if you want a thicker consistency. Add additional curry paste, a teaspoon or two of brown sugar if you want a little sweetness, and salt or soy sauce to taste.

Serve the beans on rice with a generous dollop of the fruit salsa.

SERVING AND MENU IDEAS

This dish has a lot going on, but a crisp side salad, such as Sugar Snap Peas with Coconut and Lime (page 113) would be welcome. For a more expansive meal, add Latin American Peppers and Corn (page 296) or Sweet Potatoes with Bitter Orange (page 303). Rich Vegan Chocolate Pudding (page 380) is the perfect dessert.

Haitian Rice and Beans with Plantains

For several years, Moosewood's Nancy Lazarus has enjoyed working with the Coalition for Healthy School Food's Cool School Food project in the Ithaca City School District with Executive Director Amie Hamlin to develop plant-based dishes to serve in the cafeterias. Nancy developed this Haitian rice and beans recipe for home cooking, based on a popular dish created for the New York City Cool School Food program by chefs Angel Ramos, Jorge Pineda, and Joy Pierson of Candle Café. In the schools, it's called Black Bean and Rice Casserole, a favorite of students and cooks alike. Clearly, school lunch has gotten a lot better!

The rice and beans are mildly flavored with cumin and fresh ginger, and somewhat sweet with ripe plantains cooked in. Toppings make this dish really delicious. Fresh Pineapple-Mango Relish (page 327) will add sweetness and tang—a refreshing, fruity, and not-too-spicy choice. If you like a little heat, make zesty Sos Ti-Malice (page 332), a traditional Haitian tomato-onion hot sauce. Fastest of all would be to simply top it with salsa or chopped tomatoes and scallions and wedges of lime.

Yields 8 cups
Serves 6 to 8
Time: about 50 minutes

1 cup uncooked short-grain brown rice
3½ cups water
1½ cups chopped onions
2 garlic cloves, minced or pressed
1 teaspoon salt
1 tablespoon olive oil
1 tablespoon ground cumin
1 tablespoon peeled and grated fresh ginger
½ teaspoon freshly ground black pepper

4½ cups drained cooked black beans, pintos, or small red beans★
2 ripe plantains, peeled and cut into pieces about the size of black beans

★Cook dried beans or use canned: Three (15-ounce) cans = 4½ cups drained beans; 1 pound dried beans makes 6 to 7 cups drained cooked beans.

Bring the rice and 2½ cups of the water to a boil in a small saucepan. Reduce the heat to low, cover, and simmer until done. Most brown rice takes about 40 minutes.

While the rice cooks, in a soup pot on low heat, cook the onions, garlic, and salt in the oil, covered, stirring occasionally, for about 15 minutes. When the onions are very soft, increase the heat to medium, add the cumin, ginger, and black pepper and cook, stirring, for a minute or so. Stir in the beans, plantains, and remaining 1 cup water. Reduce the heat to low, cover, and cook for at least 15 minutes, stirring every 5 minutes. If it starts to stick, add a little more water. The plantains will soften but remain little nuggets of flavor.

Stir the cooked rice into the beans.

You can serve this as soon as it is done, but if you turn off the heat and let the rice and beans sit, covered, for 15 minutes, the flavors will intensify.

Serve with toppings (see headnote) and lime wedges.

SERVING AND MENU IDEAS

You could begin a meal of Haitian Rice and Beans with little cups of Chilled Pineapple-Mango Soup (page 104) or serve Winter Chopped Salad (page 130), which is colorful with radicchio, avocado, and pomegranate seeds, alongside. A platter of melon wedges is a stellar dessert.

Award-Winning Chili with Chocolate and Stout

Every February in Ithaca there is Chili Fest, often in the coldest week of the year. Cafés, caterers, and cooks vie to warm and win the taste buds of intrepid festival-goers. We set up a long table in our café and decorate with brightly colored tablecloths, bouquets of flowers, bowls of red, yellow, and green peppers, and hundreds of chili pepper lights. Out comes the hot chili, and the crowds pour in.

In 2015, we served our chef Tim Mooney's innovative recipe: certainly spicy and rich with chocolate, hot peppers, and stout, but also with ingredients and seasonings not usually found in most chilis. The creamy cilantro topping finishes it perfectly, however this chili tastes great completely unembellished. We hope you enjoy it—the crowd did. We took our fourth first prize in the Vegetarian category.

Yields 10 cups
Serves 6 to 8
Prep time: 45 minutes
Simmering time: 30 minutes
Total time: 1 hour 15 minutes

1 (15-ounce) can lentils, or ½ cup dried lentils and 1½ cups water
2 tablespoons extra-virgin olive oil
1½ cups chopped onions
1 tablespoon diced jalapeño
1½ teaspoons salt
1 cup diced celery
1 cup diced carrots
1 cup diced mushrooms
1 teaspoon dried oregano
1 teaspoon dried thyme
1 tablespoon apple cider vinegar
1 teaspoon crushed red pepper flakes
1 teaspoon sweet paprika
1 cup vegetable stock
1 ounce bittersweet, semisweet, or sweet chocolate (about 2 tablespoons)
1 tablespoon vegetarian Worcestershire sauce
1 tablespoon Dijon mustard
1 (15-ounce) can black beans, drained and rinsed
1 (15-ounce) can white navy beans, drained and rinsed
1 cup dark beer (porter or stout)
1 (28-ounce) can diced tomatoes

CILANTRO CREME TOPPING
(optional)
1 cup plain yogurt or sour cream
3 tablespoons chopped fresh cilantro, or more if desired

If you're using dried lentils, put the lentils and water in a small saucepan. Bring to a boil, then cover and simmer for at least 10 minutes. Reserve.

Meanwhile, in a soup pot on medium heat, warm the olive oil. Add the onions, jalapeños, and salt and cook until the onions are soft, about 10 minutes. Stir in the celery, carrots, mushrooms, oregano, thyme, vinegar, red pepper flakes, paprika, and vegetable stock and bring to a boil. Lower the heat to a simmer and cook until the vegetables are just tender. Stir in the chocolate, Worcestershire sauce, mustard, black beans, white beans, lentils, beer, and tomatoes. Simmer for 30 minutes.

Meanwhile, if desired, in a small bowl, stir together the yogurt or sour cream and the cilantro. Set aside.

Serve each bowl of chili topped with a dollop of cilantro creme, if you like.

SERVING AND MENU IDEAS
This big generous chili is ideal for a celebration meal. You might want plain rice or even dramatic, glossy Black Rice Pilaf (page 319) to go with it. Beautiful Tomatillo Pickles (page 343) would add a tart note. And then Carrot Cornbread (page 281) seems just right, too. End the feast sweetly with Pumpkin Cheesecake (page 370) or Coconut-Pineapple Sorbet (page 382).

Pizza Crust

Gluten-Free Pizza Crust

Pizza Rosso e Verde

Pizza with Arugula Salad

Pizza with Roasted Eggplant and Plum Tomatoes

Pizza with Greens

Focaccia Pugliese

Bialys

Golden Cornbread

Carrot Cornbread

Pizza Crust

Here is a useful pizza dough with a relatively short rising time and a tasty, medium-thick crust. We like a balance of whole wheat and unbleached white flours; all whole wheat would give a chewier texture and heavier density that lacks some of the crispness and lighter appeal of our blend.

Top with one of our pizza toppings (pages 271-275), or if you're rolling out both crusts, have a party and choose two.

Yields 2 pizza crusts
Prep time: 15 minutes
Rising time: 2 hours
Baking time: 10 to 15 minutes

2½ cups unbleached white all-purpose flour★
1 cup whole wheat bread flour
1 (¼ ounce) package active dry yeast (2¼ teaspoons)
2 teaspoons salt
1½ cups warm (110°F) water
1½ tablespoons olive oil, plus more for the bowl
Cornmeal, for dusting
14-inch round or 10 x 14-inch rectangular baking sheets
Baking stone or tiles★★

★If using a bread-making machine to mix and rise the dough, add an additional ¼ cup flour.
★★Baking stones are ceramic and produce a crisp crust in a shorter time. Available at kitchenware stores or online, they come in round or rectangular shapes. Baking tiles, less expensive than baking stones, are 6-inch unglazed quarry tiles from any building-supply store. Four or six tiles will suffice as a baking surface. It's important to place baking stones or tiles in the oven before preheating. Use a pizza peel or an upside-down baking sheet to transfer the pizza on and off the stone or tiles.

Mix and knead the dough by hand or in a food processor.

To work by hand in a large bowl: Start with the dry ingredients and then add the wet. Using first a large spoon and then your hands, combine the ingredients to form a ball of dough. Knead the dough by pressing the ball flat with the heels of your hands, folding it over, and pressing it down again until flat; continue kneading for about 8 minutes. It will be a moister dough than the typical bread dough, but add a little flour if needed to prevent stickiness.

To make in the bowl of a food processor: Whirl the flours, yeast, and salt for a couple of seconds. Add the water and olive oil and pulse for just 12 seconds or so until a rough mass of dough forms. If it's not forming a ball, sprinkle it with 1 to 2 tablespoons water and pulse again. Let the dough rest for 5 minutes, then process again for 30 seconds to knead it.

With either method, put the kneaded dough in an oiled bowl large enough to allow it to double in volume. Cover the bowl with plastic wrap and place in a warm spot until doubled in size, about 1½ hours. Punch it down and divide it into 2 balls. Let the dough rest, covered, for 10 minutes.

Make pizza right away, or refrigerate the balls of dough for up to 24 hours, or freeze it for up to a couple of months (see Note).

To shape the pizza crust(s): Lightly dust the baking sheet(s) with cornmeal to keep the dough from sticking. Place the ball of dough in the center of the pan and flatten it a bit first. Then, using your fingers or a rolling pin and starting at the center, stretch it to the sides of the pan. If it springs back a lot, let it rest a minute or two before continuing. Cover the crust with a damp towel and let it rise for 15 minutes. Preheat the oven to 450°F.

Top the pizza and bake for 10 to 15 minutes until the crust edge is golden brown and firm and the topping is done.

NOTE: It takes about 2 hours at room temperature to thaw a ball of dough. After briefly re-kneading (add flour if necessary), press the dough to the desired shape and let it rise for about 30 minutes before baking.

Gluten-Free Pizza Crust

We played with several recipes for a gluten-free pizza crust and then tried one from a good resource in the baking world: King Arthur Flour. Here's our variation of their recipe, and a tip of the chef's hat to King Arthur. We recommend it thanks to its excellent flavor and texture and ease of preparation.

When putting together Moosewood's Gluten-Free All-Purpose Flour Mix for this recipe, make enough for 2 cups. You'll need ⅔ cup for proofing the yeast and another cup for the dough.

Yields one 12-inch pizza crust
Hands-on time for prepping the yeast mixture:
  5 minutes
Yeast activating time: 30 minutes
Hands-on time for prepping the dough:
  8 minutes
Dough rising time: 30 minutes
Hands-on time for shaping the crust: 8 minutes
Pizza crust resting time: 15 minutes
Baking time: 8 to 10 minutes for initial baking;
  additional 10 to 12 minutes for topped pizza
Total time: 1 hour, 45 minutes

1⅔ cups Moosewood's Gluten-Free All-Purpose
  Flour Mix (page 351)
1½ teaspoons instant or fast-acting yeast★
1 tablespoon sugar
1 cup warm water (ideally between 100°F and
  115°F)
4 tablespoons olive oil
1 teaspoon baking powder
1 teaspoon xanthan gum
¾ teaspoon salt

★This is less than a full packet, so it's important to measure.

In a small bowl, mix together ⅔ cup of the gluten-free baking mix, the yeast, sugar, water, and 2 tablespoons of the olive oil. Set aside to rest for about 30 minutes, or until bubbling. In a large bowl, combine the remaining 1 cup baking mix, the baking powder, xanthan gum, and salt.

When the yeast mixture is ready, add it to the dry ingredients and mix with an electric mixer until very well blended, 4 to 5 minutes. Cover the bowl and set aside for 30 minutes.

Preheat the oven to 425°F. Brush the remaining 2 tablespoons olive oil on a baking sheet to cover a circle about 12 inches in diameter.

To shape the pizza crust: Using a flexible spatula, turn the dough onto the baking sheet and use your moistened fingertips to spread it to a 12-inch circle (see Note). Let the crust rest for 15 minutes. This time plus the initial baking period is a good interval to get the toppings together.

Bake the crust for 8 to 10 minutes until just set and firm. To finish the pizza, add toppings and bake for 10 to 12 minutes more, until the crust is lightly browned and the topping is nicely cooked.

NOTE: Try to make the thickness of the crust as uniform as possible. This is a sticky dough and it requires some patience to press it out evenly. Because it doesn't have the elasticity of a gluten dough, it breaks, and so it is important to push together the dough to repair the splits. Don't make the crust thicker around the outside edges than in the center, because when the center is topped with wet ingredients, it won't crisp as well as the uncovered edges of the pizza, and it's more likely to stick to the pan and may break when you serve the pizza.

Pizza Rosso e Verde

Impress your friends; they've probably never had a pizza layered with a puttanesca-flavored pesto.

Yields one 14-inch pizza
Prep time, with crust and pesto ready:
**   10 minutes**
Baking time: about 10 minutes

1 (14-inch) Pizza crust (page 269, or for
   gluten-free pizza, opposite page)
10 ounces spinach leaves
½ to ¾ cup Pesto Rosso★ (page 328)
¾ cup shredded mozzarella cheese

★If your pesto is intensely olive-flavored you may want to use the lesser amount, and if it's mild, the greater amount.

Preheat the oven to 450°F. (If making a gluten-free crust, preheat the oven to 425°F, and follow the recipe directions for prebaking the crust before adding the topping.) To shape the crust, follow the directions in the pizza dough recipe.

Rinse the spinach and quickly sauté it in a dry pan until just barely wilted. Top the crust with the spinach first, then the pesto, and the mozzarella on top. Bake for 8 to 12 minutes until the crust is lightly browned and the cheese has melted.

VARIATION
For an extra bit of "tang," try ½ cup mozzarella and ¼ cup crumbled feta.

SERVING AND MENU IDEAS
Serve with crudités and a dip like Edamame Hummus (page 65) or Roasted Carrot Hummus (page 67).

Pizza with Arugula Salad

Fresh and delicious, this warm cheesy pizza crust topped with lemony fresh arugula is to die for.... We want some right now! You won't get a pizza like this from a pizzeria, and with a pizza crust ready, it's quicker than delivery.

Yields topping for one 13-inch round pizza, two 9-inch round pizzas, or a 10 x 13-inch rectangular pizza
Prep time, with crust ready: 10 minutes
Baking time: 10 to 15 minutes

Pizza Crust (page 269 or for gluten-free pizza, page 270)
1 cup grated mozzarella cheese
⅓ cup grated Parmesan cheese
2 tablespoons olive oil
4 ounces baby arugula (about 4 loose cups)
1 tablespoon fresh lemon juice

Preheat the oven to 450°F, or for a gluten-free crust, to 425°F. To shape and prebake a gluten-free crust, follow the instructions in the pizza dough recipe.

Sprinkle the crust with the mozzarella and Parmesan and drizzle 1 tablespoon of the olive oil across the top. Bake for 10 to 15 minutes until the crust edge is golden brown and firm and the cheese is bubbling. Meanwhile, toss the arugula with the remaining 1 tablespoon olive oil and the lemon juice.

Spread the dressed arugula on the cooked pizza crust. Some of us put the arugula-topped pizza back in the oven for just a minute, to wilt the arugula, but many others of us like the arugula less wilted, so we serve the pizza as soon as it's topped with the arugula.

SERVING AND MENU IDEA
Serve this lighter-than-usual pizza with a side of Tofu Fillets with Onion and Fresh Herb Relish (page 77).

Pizza with Roasted Eggplant and Plum Tomatoes

Fragrant herbs and balsamic vinegar give depth to Mediterranean favorites, roasted eggplant and tomatoes. This topping is succulent, hearty, and perfect on a thin, crisp crust topped with sharp, melted Italian cheeses.

Yields topping for one 13-inch round pizza, two 9-inch round pizzas, or a 10 x 13-inch rectangular pizza
Prep time, with crust ready: 15 minutes at start, 10 minutes to top pizza crust
Topping roasting time: 25 minutes
Pizza baking time: 10 to 15 minutes
Total time: about 1 hour

3 tablespoons olive oil, plus more for the pan
1 tablespoon balsamic vinegar
3 garlic cloves, minced or pressed
1 teaspoon chopped fresh rosemary, or ½ teaspoon dried
1 teaspoon dried oregano
1 teaspoon salt
Pinch of crushed red pepper flakes
1 medium eggplant
3 or 4 plum tomatoes
Pizza Crust (page 269 or for gluten-free pizza, page 270)
¾ cup grated Asiago cheese (about 3½ ounces)
½ cup grated Parmesan cheese (about 3 ounces)

Preheat the oven to 425°F. Oil a rimmed baking sheet.

In a small bowl, mix together the olive oil, vinegar, garlic, rosemary, oregano, salt, and red pepper flakes and set aside. Peel the eggplant and cut horizontally into ½-inch-thick slices. Cut the plum tomatoes lengthwise into quarters, then cut the quarters in half. Place the vegetables on the prepared baking sheet, drizzle the marinade over them, and toss with a rubber spatula to coat.

Roast for 12 minutes. Remove the pan from the oven, turn over the eggplant slices, and return to the oven until both the eggplant and tomatoes are tender and nicely browned, about 10 minutes. Remove from the oven and set aside to cool for a few minutes.

Raise the oven temperature to 450°F. (If making a gluten-free crust, maintain the oven temperature at 425°F, and follow the recipe directions for prebaking the crust before adding the topping.) To shape the crust, follow the directions in the pizza dough recipe.

Arrange the roasted eggplant and tomatoes to cover the pizza crust and sprinkle with the cheeses. Bake for 10 to 15 minutes, until the crust is browned and the cheeses have melted.

SERVING AND MENU IDEAS
A simple green salad with an easy dressing, like the one featured in Baby Arugula Salad with Crusted Chèvre and Pears (page 114), is just right.

Pizza with Greens

The sweetness of golden onions joins piquant olives, slightly bitter greens, and rich cheeses in this delicious pizza.

Yields topping for one 13-inch round pizza, two 9-inch round pizzas, or a 10 x 13-inch rectangular pizza
Prep time, with crust ready: 30 minutes
Baking time: 10 to 15 minutes
Total time: 45 minutes

Pizza Crust (page 269, or for gluten-free pizza, page 270)
2 tablespoons olive oil
2 cups chopped onions
¼ teaspoon salt
2 garlic cloves, minced or pressed
6 packed cups chopped escarole (about 10 ounces)
⅓ cup chopped pitted olives (Kalamata, Niçoise, and Gaeta are nice)
1 cup grated Fontina Valle d'Aosta cheese (see headnote, page 14)
⅓ cup grated Pecorino Romano cheese

Preheat the oven to 450°F. (If making a gluten-free crust, preheat the oven to 425°F, and follow the recipe directions for prebaking the crust before adding the topping.) To shape the crust, follow the directions in the pizza dough recipe.

In a skillet on medium heat, warm 1 tablespoon of the olive oil and cook the onions, sprinkled with the salt, until lightly golden, about 10 minutes.

Meanwhile, in a pot large enough to hold all the greens, warm the remaining 1 tablespoon olive oil, add the garlic and briefly sauté, then add the escarole. Cook on medium heat, adding a couple of tablespoons of water if needed to prevent scorching or sticking, until the escarole is tender but not soggy. Add the onions. Remove from the heat and set aside to cool for a few minutes.

Spread the escarole mixture on the pizza crust, sprinkle on the olives, and top with the cheeses. Bake for 10 to 15 minutes until the crust is browned and the cheeses have melted.

VARIATION
In place of the escarole, use other greens, such as kale, Swiss chard, radicchio, or spinach.

SERVING AND MENU IDEAS
Lemony Roasted Beets (page 297) or Roasted Winter Squash Agrodolce (page 309) are tasty accompaniments to this pizza.

Focaccia Pugliese

Moosewood Collective member David Hirsch's partner John Campione, grew up with his family's version of this nicely textured flat bread, moist yet crusty. His grandfather, Frank Rotolo, a native of Puglia in Southern Italy, was a baker who followed the regional tradition of adding mashed potatoes to the yeasted dough for focaccia. The result is worth the extra effort—yeasty and spongy with a delicious tenderness and crusty edge.

Yields one 14-inch round or 10 x 15-inch rectangular flatbread
Prep time: 40 minutes
Dough rising time: 60 to 90 minutes
Focaccia rising time: 15 minutes
Baking time: 20 to 25 minutes

2 cups peeled and diced potatoes (about ½ pound)
1 (¼-ounce) packet active dry yeast (2½ teaspoons)
5 tablespoons extra-virgin olive oil, plus more as needed
1 teaspoon salt
1 cup whole wheat bread flour
2½ to 3½ cups unbleached white all-purpose flour
¾ cup sliced red onions
12 cherry or grape tomatoes, halved
⅓ cup pitted and halved Kalamata, jumbo green, Sicilian oil-cured, or similar olives

In a small saucepan, cook the potatoes with water to cover until very tender. Drain, reserving the liquid. In a small bowl, combine ½ cup of the potato-cooking liquid with ½ cup cool water to yield 1 cup liquid between 105°F and 115°F. Stir in the yeast and set aside.

In a large bowl, mash the potatoes with 3 tablespoons of the olive oil and the salt until smooth and creamy. Stir in the yeast mixture. Add the whole wheat flour, ½ cup at a time, mixing well after each addition, and then add enough white flour, ½ cup at a time, to make a smooth dough; a large wooden spoon works well here.

Place the dough on a floured board and knead with floured hands for 7 to 8 minutes, adding more flour as needed. The finished dough should be soft and just a little bit sticky.

Place the kneaded dough in an oiled bowl and cover loosely with plastic wrap or a moist kitchen towel. Set in a warm place until doubled in size, 1 to 1½ hours. (While the dough is rising, prepare the toppings and set them aside.)

When the dough has doubled, punch it down in the bowl. Preheat the oven to 450°F. Lightly oil a 10 x 15-inch baking sheet or a 14-inch round pan.

Spread the dough over the prepared baking pan, using oiled fingers to gently stretch it to the pan edges. Arrange the onion slices, tomatoes (cut side down), and olives on top. Drizzle the remaining 2 tablespoons olive oil over all. Cover and let rest for 15 minutes.

Bake for 20 to 25 minutes until the focaccia is browned and firm.

Remove from the oven and let the focaccia sit in the pan for a couple of minutes, and then slide it onto a wire rack. Cool until warm or room temperature.

VARIATIONS

- Add minced fresh rosemary, oregano, or thyme or sautéed garlic to the mashed potatoes.
- Use minced fresh herbs in addition to, or instead of, the tomatoes, onions, and olives.

SERVING AND MENU IDEAS

Foccacia Pugliese is great with one of the soups made with Italian Cheese Broth (page 94). For a casual meal, serve it with Hummus with Preserved Lemon (page 66), crudités, a couple of cheeses, and a bowl of fresh fruit. Or it's a natural with Apulian Fava Beans and Greens (page 255).

Bialys

Many of the foods that evoke nostalgia are simple pleasures with uncomplicated ingredients. Flour + water + yeast + onions + salt = bialys. Moosewood's David Hirsch's childhood love of a toasted bialy was fostered by his father's weekly Saturday-morning trips to a bialy factory in Bayside, Queens, for the best, freshest bialys. Most others were frozen, because even freshly baked, they have a short shelf life.

David's maternal grandmother came from Volkovysk, a town in Belarus not far from Bialystok—maybe that fresh warm chewy onion bread evoked an ancestral memory? If you go to Bialystok today, there are no longer any bialys baked there. The food writer Mimi Sheraton wrote *The Bialy Eaters* about her worldwide search in New York, Poland, Paris, and Argentina to learn what she could. Guess David's not alone in his quest!

Yields 9 bialys
Prep time: 15 minutes
First rising time: about 2 hours
Second rising time, after punch-down: about 2 hours more
Baking time: about 10 minutes

3 cups unbleached white bread flour★
1 teaspoon active dry yeast
1½ teaspoons salt
1 cup plus 2 or 3 tablespoons room temperature water
1 tablespoon vegetable oil, plus more for the bowl
¾ cup chopped onions
Cornmeal (optional)
Salt and freshly ground black pepper

★Use 1 cup whole wheat bread flour and 2 cups white flour for a more whole-grain, but less traditional, bialy.

You can mix this dough with a food processor or an electric mixer. Combine the flour, yeast, and salt. Gradually add 1 cup of the water while mixing. Process or mix at medium speed for a couple of minutes. If the dough seems dry and isn't forming a ball, add 2 or 3 tablespoons more water. Continue to process or mix for about 3 minutes to knead the dough. Place the dough in a lightly oiled bowl and turn it over to coat all sides. Cover the bowl with plastic wrap and put in a warm place until the dough has doubled in volume, 1½ to 2 hours.

Punch down the dough and cut it into 9 equal pieces. Sprinkle cornmeal or flour on a baking sheet for the next rising of the bialys. Form each piece into a disk 2 to 3 inches in diameter and place on the baking sheet. Lightly sprinkle with flour and cover loosely with plastic wrap. Put in a warm place to rise for 1½ to 2 hours until the dough doesn't bounce back when pressed with a finger.

Meanwhile, sauté the onions in the oil until lightly golden. Sprinkle with salt and pepper and set aside.

About 20 minutes before baking, preheat the oven to 475°F. To enhance crustiness, consider putting a baking stone or upside-down skillet in the oven. Since it's a fairly short baking time, if you have only one stone or skillet, you can bake the bialys in batches. Or just bake them on baking sheets.

Line two baking sheets with parchment paper for the formed bialys. Using both hands, gently stretch each disk of risen dough to a larger round 4½ to 5 inches in diameter. With your thumb, make a depression in the center of each disk. Put a teaspoon or so of the cooked onions in each depression. Bake the sheet on the baking stone or skillet for 8 to 10 minutes until the bialys are firm with lightly browned bottoms. If you don't use a stone or skillet, add a couple of minutes to the baking time. Using a spatula, transfer the cooked bialys to a cooling rack. Freeze any you won't eat that day.

Bialys warm from the oven are tasty, but they're at their best when toasted to a crisp, butter- or cream cheese–melting goodness, kind of like an English muffin. Slice them in half crosswise before toasting, and eat over a plate to retrieve any falling onions!

VARIATION
Traditionalists would never do this, but onion bialys are delicious. Sauté 1½ cups onions, and work half the sautéed onions into the dough. Use the rest of the sautéed onions to fill the little indentations. *Ochen vkusno!* ("Very tasty!" in Russian).

SERVING AND MENU IDEAS
Usually bialys are for breakfast with butter or cream cheese and coffee or tea. But if you were to toast one to serve beside Smoky Split Pea Soup (page 96) or Mushroom Barley Salad (page 147), what could be wrong?

Golden Cornbread

This moist, golden cornbread has universal appeal. It is completely whole grain without any refined flours or starches. We considered calling this cornbread Corny Cornbread, but decided that was way too corny. However, our recipe is unusual in the world of gluten-free baking in that the only starch used is corn. Not only does it not include a gluten-free flour blend, but there are also no gums or enhancers.

To arrive at the rustic texture we like, we combine medium-grind cornmeal with more finely ground corn flour. Yellow or white is up to you. Our preferred baking pan is a preheated cast-iron skillet. The cornbread is best eaten right out of the oven.

Yields one 10-inch round cornbread
Prep time: 10 minutes
Baking time: 15 to 25 minutes

Oil, for the pan
3 tablespoons unsalted butter, melted
1 cup corn flour★
1 cup stone-ground cornmeal, medium grind
2 teaspoons baking powder
1 teaspoon baking soda
1 teaspoon salt
2 large or 3 medium eggs
1 cup buttermilk
⅓ cup packed brown sugar★★

★Corn flour is finely milled cornmeal.
★★We prefer light brown sugar in this cornbread, but only because of color; the flavor is fine with dark brown sugar.

Preheat the oven to 400°F. Lightly oil a 10-inch cast-iron skillet or 9-inch square baking pan. Place the skillet or pan in the oven to heat.

Melt the butter and set aside to cool. Sift the corn flour, cornmeal, baking powder, baking soda, and salt into a large bowl. In a separate bowl, whisk together the eggs, buttermilk, brown sugar, and cooled melted butter. Stir the wet ingredients into the dry until the batter is smooth.

Carefully remove the hot skillet or pan from the oven, pour in the batter, and return the skillet or pan to the oven. Bake until the cornbread pulls away from the sides of the pan and a toothpick inserted into the center comes out clean, 15 to 25 minutes (the baking time varies depending upon how hot the preheated baking pan is).

Cut into wedges and serve warm.

SERVING AND MENU IDEAS
Hot cornbread with butter and jam is mighty nice with eggs or a tofu scramble or simply a smoothie. It is also a really good bread to serve with a soup like Sopa Verde de Elote (page 90) or a stew like Winter Squash and Red Bean Mole (page 225).

Carrot Cornbread

High-rising, golden Carrot Cornbread is quick, tasty, coarse-textured, moist, and slightly sweet with some extra vitamins and orange color from the addition of carrots. Squash or pumpkin purée can be used instead of carrots. Whole wheat pastry flour works great in this cornbread, but you can substitute a combination of white and whole wheat flour.

**Yields one 10-inch round or 9-inch square
  cornbread**
Prep time: 25 minutes
Baking time: 25 to 30 minutes

1 large or 2 medium carrots
Oil, for the pan

WET INGREDIENTS
2 large eggs, beaten
1⅓ cups buttermilk
½ cup packed brown sugar or pure maple syrup
4 tablespoons butter, melted

DRY INGREDIENTS
1 cup stone-ground yellow cornmeal
1⅓ cups whole wheat pastry flour
1 tablespoon baking powder
1½ teaspoons baking soda
1 teaspoon salt

Peel the carrots and cut into thin slices. Steam or cook in water to cover until soft. Purée in a food processor or blender. For this recipe, you need ½ cup packed carrot purée.

Preheat the oven to 400°F. Oil a 10-inch cast-iron skillet or 9-inch square baking pan.

In a medium bowl, whisk together the eggs, buttermilk, sugar or maple syrup, butter, and ½ cup carrot purée until well blended. In a separate mixing bowl, sift together the dry ingredients. Make a well in the dry ingredients and pour in the wet ingredients. Mix together until just combined; do not overmix.

Pour the batter into the prepared skillet or pan. Smooth the top and bake until golden brown, 25 to 30 minutes.

Allow the cornbread to cool for 10 minutes before cutting. Serve warm or at room temperature.

VARIATION
Bake the cornbread in a preheated pan: Place the oiled skillet or pan in the oven to heat while you make the batter. Then, carefully remove the hot pan from the oven, pour in the batter, and return the pan to the oven. Bake until the cornbread pulls away from the sides of the pan and a toothpick inserted into the center comes out clean, 15 to 25 minutes (the baking time varies depending upon how hot the preheated baking pan is).

SERVING AND MENU IDEAS
Hot Carrot Cornbread with lots of butter and some peach jam is the best. But it's also pretty great with Green Tomato Omelet (page 13) or Stuffed Poblano Peppers (page 179). If you were to make a Southern vegetable garden spread with Wilted Greens with Blue Cheese and Walnuts (page 289), Butternut Hash Browns (page 18), and Beetroot Sticks (page 313), this would be the proper bread to serve.

Collards with Coconut Milk, Pineapple, and Peanuts

Ethiopian Greens

Spicy Broccoli Rabe with Sun-Dried Tomatoes and Almonds

Wilted Greens with Blue Cheese and Walnuts

Beet Greens with Raisins and Pine Nuts

Yu Choy with Stir-Fried Onions

Snow Peas with Seaweed

Asparagus Cacio e Pepe–Style

Spice-Crusted Roasted Carrots with Harissa-Yogurt Sauce

Spaghetti Squash with Sage and Parmesan

Latin American Peppers and Corn

Lemony Roasted Beets

Romanesco with Green Salsa

Southeast Asian Green Beans

Fennel Gratin

Spicy Roasted Broccoli

Sweet Potatoes with Bitter Orange

Red Cabbage with Blueberries

Summer Squash and Tomato Tian

Mashed Potatoes with Lemon and Parsley

Roasted Winter Squash Agrodolce

Mashed Rutabaga with Fried Red Onions

A Hash of Spuds, Beets, and Greens

Beetroot Sticks

Shredded Brussels Sprouts with Apples

Collards with Coconut Milk, Pineapple, and Peanuts

We made this creamy-seeming vegan dish the first time simply because we thought the combination of tropical flavors would be delicious—and they are. If it has a regional influence, that would be East African. The sauce is smooth, and within the sauce, the tender deep green collards have a smooth, somewhat slippery mouthfeel. Chopped roasted peanuts sprinkled on top add a little crunch.

Collards and kale are highly rated nutritionally. They are good sources of calcium, more so than other greens.

Serves 4
Time: about 35 minutes

2 cups water
¼ teaspoon salt
4 firmly packed cups chopped collard leaves

COCONUT MILK, PINEAPPLE, AND PEANUT BUTTER SAUCE

⅓ cup peanut butter
⅓ cup coconut milk
⅓ cup chopped scallions
1 cup pineapple chunks (fresh or canned)
2 tablespoons white or apple cider vinegar
½ teaspoon salt
1 to 3 teaspoons hot sauce (optional)

½ cup chopped roasted peanuts (optional)

In a covered 2-quart saucepan, bring the water and salt to a boil. Meanwhile, rinse the collards and strip the leaves off the stems (sometimes that's easiest done by laying each leaf flat on a cutting board and cutting close along each side of the main stem). Stack the leaves and roughly chop. When the water boils, add half the chopped collards and stir until just wilted, then add the rest of the collards and stir until you can poke all the leaves into the water. Simmer for about 5 minutes, or until just tender.

Meanwhile, make the sauce: Purée all the sauce ingredients in a blender. If the mixture is too stiff to blend easily, add a tablespoon or two of hot water from the cooking collards.

When the collards are tender, drain them, reserving about a cup of the pot liquor. In the saucepan, combine the collards and the sauce and bring to a simmer. If it becomes too thick and might scorch, add some of the collard cooking water. Simmer for 5 minutes.

Serve topped with chopped peanuts, if you like.

VARIATION
Use kale in place of collards.

SERVING AND MENU IDEAS
To make a meal, these saucy collards are excellent on a bed of rice, millet, or other grain and topped with roasted Sweet Potatoes with Bitter Orange (page 303). Or have them with Jamaican Jerk Tempeh Patties (page 200) or Black Rice Pilaf (page 319).

Ethiopian Greens

This dish is redolent with the fragrance and flavors of traditional Ethiopian cooking where *niter kebbeh*, a spiced ghee (clarified butter), and dry pot cheese are used. We think ghee is best to create authentic taste and texture for this dish, but butter works and coconut oil adds another dimension of flavor.

If you prefer to make this recipe vegan, just skip making the spiced cheese, use coconut oil, and add all the spices to the sautéing onions.

Serves 4
Time: 30 minutes

SPICED CHEESE
1 cup farmer's cheese or drained cottage cheese★
½ teaspoon ground cardamom
½ teaspoon ground cinnamon
¼ teaspoon ground cloves (less to taste)
1 large garlic clove, pressed or minced
½ teaspoon salt

GREENS
10 cups chopped kale, collards, and/or chard leaves
2 tablespoons ghee, butter, or coconut oil
2 cups diced onions
Salt
2 large garlic cloves, pressed or minced
1 tablespoon peeled and grated fresh ginger
⅓ teaspoon minced fresh habanero, or ½ teaspoon jalapeño, or more to taste
¼ cup water
Freshly ground black pepper

★Farmer's cheese, made on farms all over the world, especially in the Middle Eastern and European countries, is a mild-flavored fresh cheese that can be eaten almost immediately after it is made and dried. Friendship brand Farmer's Cheese comes in 7.5-ounce packages and is a delicious product, often shelved near cottage cheese, yogurt, or specialty cheeses. If you can't get farmer's cheese, drain cottage cheese in a sieve for about 20 minutes (discard the liquid) before making the spiced cheese.

Make the spiced cheese: Mix together the cheese, cardamom, cinnamon, cloves, garlic, and salt and set aside while you prepare the greens.

Make the greens: In a large skillet or pot on medium-low heat, warm the ghee and cook the onions with a sprinkling of salt for about 10 minutes, or until softened. Add the garlic, ginger, and hot pepper and cook for a couple of minutes. Increase the heat to medium and add the chopped greens in batches: toss frequently and as the leaves wilt, add more. Add the water, cover, and cook until the greens are soft but still bright green. Season with additional salt and black pepper to taste.

Combine the greens and spiced cheese in a serving bowl, or serve by spreading the spiced cheese on a platter and piling the greens on top.

SERVING AND MENU IDEAS
Ethiopian Greens makes a wonderful meal with Simple Seasoned Tofu (page 346) and Cracked Freekeh with Dried Cherries and Almonds (page 137), or serve it with Cashew-Crusted Chickpea Burgers (page 251) and Jeweled Rice (page 321).

GHEE

Ghee is a type of clarified butter made by long simmering. During the simmer, the milk solids caramelize, making ghee nutty-tasting and aromatic. Simmering removes the moisture, and straining removes the residue of solids, giving ghee a high smoke point (482°F). Ghee originated in India and is used in the cuisines of India, Nepal, the Middle East, and North Africa.

Ghee doesn't need to be refrigerated, but light and moisture degrade it, so store it in an airtight container in the dark; it will keep for a couple of months at room temperature. Unopened in the refrigerator, ghee will keep for up to a year, but if you'll use it often, don't keep it in the fridge because when you open the container to warm air, water will condense on the ghee.

It is purported to have many health benefits and is high in vitamins A, D, and E, antioxidants, medium- and short-chain fatty acids, and butyric acid. Many people who are lactose- or casein-intolerant do not react to ghee because the milk solids and imperfections have been removed.

Spicy Broccoli Rabe with Sun-Dried Tomatoes and Almonds

Moosewood's Ned Asta was developing this recipe in her kitchen. Her son Tazio was helping and said, "Hey, I usually don't like broccoli rabe, but this is delicious!" Yeah, Taz, we agree! Broccoli rabe or rapini is one of those slightly bitter old-world greens bursting with nutrition and strong character that your Italian grandma couldn't live without. The sun-dried tomatoes and crushed red pepper are intensely flavorful and stand up to the assertive greens. The slivered almonds or pine nuts sautéed with garlic are just a fabulous, elegant inspiration. Thanks, Neddie!

Serves 3 or 4
Time: 20 minutes

Salt
1¼ pounds broccoli rabe
3 tablespoons slivered almonds (or pine nuts)
4 garlic cloves, minced
¼ teaspoon crushed red pepper flakes
3 tablespoons extra-virgin olive oil
8 sun-dried tomatoes packed in oil, drained and
  sliced thinly
Freshly ground black pepper

Bring a pot of salted water to a boil. Trim the hard stems from the broccoli rabe, leaving the leafy parts intact. Add the broccoli rabe to the boiling water and simmer until just tender, 2 to 3 minutes. Run cold water over the broccoli rabe in a colander and set aside to drain well.

In a skillet, sauté the almonds, garlic, and red pepper flakes in the olive oil for a couple of minutes. Add the sun-dried tomatoes and cook for a minute longer. Add the drained broccoli rabe and stir constantly until hot.

Season with salt and black pepper to taste and serve immediately.

SERVING AND MENU IDEAS
This full-flavored side dish will complement a creamy entrée, such as Fettuccine with Caramelized Onions and Yogurt (page 235) or Cheesy Risotto with Grapes (page 176). It also makes a good pizza topping with mozzarella.

Wilted Greens with Blue Cheese and Walnuts

This recipe is adapted from a dish that is served at Just a Taste, our favorite Ithaca tapas bar. It is quick, easy, and delicious and will induce anyone to eat their greens and really enjoy them. Use just one kind or a combination of several greens—whatever is freshest in your market or garden.

Serves 4
Prep time: 15 minutes

1 tablespoon butter
2 tablespoons extra-virgin olive oil
1 tablespoon minced garlic
¼ cup walnuts
1 tomato, diced
8 cups chopped greens (kale, mustard greens, chard, escarole, curly endive, collards, or a mixture)
½ teaspoon salt
½ teaspoon freshly ground black pepper
1 tablespoon red wine vinegar
¼ cup crumbled blue cheese

In a large skillet on medium-high heat, brown the butter until it smells nutty. Add the olive oil, garlic, and walnuts. Cook, stirring, until the garlic is golden; do not allow it to burn. Add the tomatoes and greens and stir well so the greens wilt evenly. Season with the salt and pepper and stir again. When the greens are almost completely wilted, sprinkle with vinegar and stir. Cook until all the greens are tender. Depending on the maturity and freshness of your greens, you may need to lower the heat and cook them, covered, to achieve the tenderness you like. Add more salt and/or vinegar to taste.

Serve topped with crumbled blue cheese.

VARIATION
Also delicious topped with the crumbled feta or goat cheese.

SERVING AND MENU IDEAS
Wilted greens are perfect as a starter course followed by a creamy soup, such as Celery or Celeriac Soup Two Ways (page 100). You'll probably want some good crusty bread and a glass of red wine, too. Or serve the greens as a side dish with Sweet Potato Gnocchi (page 236).

Beet Greens with Raisins and Pine Nuts

Little bits of sweet raisins and nutty pine nuts make these Italian-style beet greens (*biete da orta*) an interesting way to eat your greens. They're dense with flavor and a special treat. Beet greens are loaded with vitamins and you will love their earthy, sweet flavor in this traditional dish.

Beet leaves still attached to the bulbs draw moisture from the roots, so if you aren't going to eat them right away, cut the greens off near the top of the bulbs and store them in a plastic bag for up to 3 days. If you can't find beet greens, Swiss chard or spinach can be substituted in this recipe.

Serves 4
Time: 15 minutes

3 tablespoons raisins or currants
8 cups coarsely chopped beet greens with
   the stems
3 tablespoons olive oil
2 large garlic cloves, minced or pressed
3 tablespoons pine nuts
Salt and freshly ground black pepper

In a small bowl, cover the raisins or currants with hot water and set aside to soften.

Put the greens into a large pot and cover with water. Bring to a boil, remove from the heat, stir, and let sit until the greens are wilted. Drain in a colander. (Save the liquid to add to a soup or smoothie.) When cool enough to handle, thoroughly squeeze out excess liquid. Drain the raisins.

In a large skillet on medium heat, warm the oil and briefly cook the garlic and pine nuts until both are lightly golden. Stir in the softened raisins. Add the greens and stir until coated with oil and hot. Season with salt and pepper to taste and serve.

VARIATION

Beet greens are loved all over the Mediterranean and are a traditional ingredient in many Sephardic Jewish recipes. For a delicious Jewish-Italian twist, add the juice and zest of half of a lemon to the finished greens.

SERVING AND MENU IDEAS

Beet Greens with Raisins and Pine Nuts is a natural with Mediterranean foods, such as Spaghetti with Olives and Lemon (page 241). But a dish this easy and healthful can complement many cuisines. Try it next to Beet Burgers (page 252), Scalloped Potatoes and Mushrooms (page 202), or Mushroom-Stuffed Winter Squash (page 180).

Yu Choy with Stir-Fried Onions

For this quick *yu choy* dish, we stir-fry some onions and garlic first and then cook the yu choy in the same wok or skillet. The platter of yu choy is topped with the onions and drizzled with a simple sauce that can be made a little spicier if you like. Passing some rice vinegar and hot sauce at the table is an easy alternative to making the whole dish spicy or tangy. A sprinkle of toasted nuts is a nice garnish.

Serves 4 to 6
Time: 20 minutes

SAUCE
1 tablespoon vegetable oil
1 tablespoon soy sauce
1 teaspoon toasted sesame oil
2 teaspoons vegetarian Worcestershire sauce
½ teaspoon Chinese chili paste or hot sauce (optional)

1 tablespoon vegetable oil
1 large sweet onion, peeled, sliced in half crosswise, then sliced lengthwise
4 large garlic cloves, thickly sliced
1 pound yu choy, rinsed and drained★

OPTIONAL GARNISHES
Chopped toasted almonds and/or cashews
Rice vinegar
Sriracha or other hot sauce

★Yu choy is a Chinese cabbage with slender stalks, flat green leaves, and little yellow flowers, and a slightly sweet flavor. It is usually 10 to 12 inches long. Some yu choy has such slender stalks and tender leaves that it cooks in a minute or two, and other yu choy, still very delicious, has larger leaves and thicker stalks that may have tough ends that should be trimmed, and it becomes tender with 4 to 5 minutes of cooking.

Make the sauce: In a small bowl, mix together the vegetable oil, soy sauce, sesame oil, Worcestershire sauce, and chili paste (if using). Set aside.

Heat the vegetable oil in a large skillet or wok. Add the onion and garlic and stir-fry until soft and beginning to brown, about 5 minutes. Remove from the wok and set aside.

Cover the bottom of the wok or skillet with an inch of water and bring to a boil. Add the yu choy, cover, and cook until the stems are tender and the leaves are dark green, 1 to 5 minutes. With tongs or a large slotted spoon, move the yu choy to a platter. Drain off any water that accumulates on the platter.

Top with the stir-fried onions and garlic and drizzle on the sauce. Serve immediately, garnished with nuts, vinegar, and/or hot sauce, if you like.

SERVING AND MENU IDEAS
Serve Yu Choy alongside Rainbow Carrot Stir-Fry (page 221) on rice, or mix it with some Simple Seasoned Tofu (page 346) and pile it on top of buckwheat noodles.

Snow Peas with Seaweed

This is a simple, fast, and flavorful accompaniment to any Asian entrée or spread. The vivid green snow peas and black strands of hijiki really stand out in the glossy dressing. It is best served soon after preparation, before the vinegar discolors the lovely green of the snow peas.

Serves 4 to 6
Hijiki soaking time: 30 minutes
Prep time: 20 minutes

1 tablespoon plus 1 teaspoon dried hijiki seaweed
6 ounces snow peas
2 tablespoons vegetable oil
1 tablespoon rice vinegar
1 tablespoon plus 2 teaspoons honey or agave
   syrup
½ teaspoon salt
1 teaspoon peeled and grated fresh ginger

In a small bowl, cover the hijiki with 1 cup cool water. Set aside to soak for 30 minutes.

While the hijiki soaks, rinse and string the snow peas, slice them crosswise into thin pieces, and place in a heatproof bowl. Bring 2 to 3 cups water to a boil. Pour the boiling water over the snow peas to immerse for 3 minutes. Drain in a colander and run under cold water to cool. Drain and return them to the bowl.

Whisk together the oil, vinegar, honey, salt, and ginger and set aside.

When the hijiki is hydrated and soft, drain it and add to the snow peas. When ready to serve, pour the dressing over the snow peas and seaweed and toss to combine.

SERVING AND MENU IDEAS
This fresh colorful dish is a welcome addition to any Asian meal. It's also really good beside Tomato-Sesame Tofu Scramble (page 21).

Asparagus Cacio e Pepe–Style

Cacio e pepe, a traditional Italian Pecorino-and-black pepper preparation for pasta, was the inspiration for this recipe for asparagus simply prepared, quick, and delicious. And look at the other vegetables you can make this way: spaghetti squash; chopped, spiralized, or sliced zucchini or summer squash; broccoli, broccoli rabe, or broccolini; braised kale or other greens; green beans; cauliflower; potatoes, small, whole, or chunks; steamed, boiled, or roasted carrots or winter squash. . . . You name it. Kids love this lovely side dish with its speckled coating of tasty cheese.

Serves 2 to 6
Time: about 10 minutes

1 pound fresh asparagus
Salt
2 teaspoons extra-virgin olive oil
¼ cup grated or finely shredded Pecorino
  Romano cheese
½ teaspoon coarsely ground black pepper

Snap off the fibrous tough ends of the asparagus spears. Rinse the spears and cut them into 1-inch-long pieces (about 2 cups). Bring 2 cups of salted water to a boil in a covered saucepan. Add the asparagus and cook until just tender (still a little dot of white visible in the middle of a cut end). Drain or remove the asparagus with a slotted spoon, and put it in a serving bowl. Drizzle on the olive oil, sprinkle with the cheese, and top with the pepper. Toss well.

VARIATIONS

- For a more elegant presentation, leave the asparagus spears whole, sprinkle on the oil, cheese, and pepper, and roll them a bit to coat.
- Steam or boil almost any vegetable and toss with extra-virgin olive oil; grated or finely shredded Parmesan, Pecorino Romano, or other hard Italian cheese; and lots of ground black pepper.
- Or roast vegetables and toss with grated cheese. Grind pepper right onto the steaming-hot vegetables. If you use a cheese less salty than pecorino, add salt to taste.

SERVING AND MENU IDEAS

Here's a nice meal: Asparagus Cacio e Pepe–Style with Roasted Red Pepper, Black Olive, and Tofu Burgers (page 249) and Orzo Risotto (page 322). Or serve with Aigo Bouido (page 102) and Apulian Fava Beans and Greens (page 255). No matter what you serve it with, you'll want a hunk of crusty bread to mop up the tasty oil and cheese left when you've finished every piece of asparagus.

Spice-Crusted Roasted Carrots with Harissa-Yogurt Sauce

Dip these spicy roasted carrots into the Harissa-Yogurt Sauce—delicious! If you can find super-thin carrots, that's good, but this recipe also works fine with only moderately thin carrots. Long thin carrots just roast well, look good on the plate, and are fun to eat.

Make your own harissa (page 338), a thick, spicy North African condiment made from puréed roasted red peppers, or find it in jars or tubes on the international shelves of well-stocked supermarkets. This recipe features roasted carrots for their color and sweet contrast to the spicy sauce, but you can add potatoes, onions, parsnips, turnips, or winter squash (see Variations). Harissa can really vary in heat and intensity, even if homemade, depending on the hotness of the peppers you use.

Serves 4 to 6
Prep time: 15 minutes
Roasting time: 25 to 45 minutes, depending on the thinness of the carrots

2 pounds thin carrots with green tops
¼ cup olive oil, plus more for the pan
Laura's Spice Rub (page 333)
Salt and freshly ground black pepper
2 teaspoons fresh thyme or ½ teaspoon dried thyme (optional)

HARISSA-YOGURT SAUCE
1 cup plain Greek yogurt
1 tablespoon harissa (page 338)
1 teaspoon finely grated lemon zest

Preheat the oven to 400°F. Oil a baking pan.

Scrub and rinse the carrots, and peel them if you think it's necessary. Trim the green tops, leaving on 1 to 2 inches. Trim off most of the roots, leaving about ¾ inch if the root looks edible. Coat the prepped carrots with the olive oil and arrange them in the prepared baking pan. Sprinkle with the spice rub, turn the carrots over, and sprinkle the other side. Season with salt and pepper, and the thyme (if using). Roast for 25 to 45 minutes until the carrots are tender and look crusty.

Make the sauce: In a small bowl, swirl the harissa into the yogurt and top with the lemon zest.

Arrange the roasted carrots on a platter and serve with the harissa-yogurt sauce alongside. Or spoon the sauce into individual condiment dishes, or put a tablespoon or two on each plate for dipping the carrots into.

VARIATIONS
- Roast potatoes and onions with the carrots. Use 1 pound carrots, plus 1 or 2 large white potatoes, peeled and sliced into wedges, and 1 large onion, sliced into wedges or chunks.
- Roast chunks or sticks of winter squash or parsnips.

SERVING AND MENU IDEAS
Serve this deeply flavorful carrot side dish with something milder, perhaps Persian Kuku (page 192), Farro Pilaf with Cannellini and Arugula (page 317), or Mujadara (page 258). Skip the yogurt on top of mujadara and serve Harissa-Yogurt Sauce (page 294) with both dishes. Try it with Burmese Tohu Thoke (page 194).

Spaghetti Squash with Sage and Parmesan

On a chilly day, warm up your house for an hour and have this simple and delicious version of spaghetti squash for lunch or as a side dish. The bright yellow-orange of the squash with flecks of green sage looks as good as it tastes, and we think the sage, olive oil, and grated cheese are a tasty match for the squash.

Serves 4 to 6
Prep time: 10 minutes before baking,
   10 minutes after baking
Baking time: 1 hour

1 spaghetti squash (about 3 pounds)
3 tablespoons minced fresh sage leaves
¼ cup extra-virgin olive oil
½ cup grated Parmesan or Pecorino Romano
  cheese
Salt and freshly ground black pepper

Preheat the oven to 400°F.

Make slits all around the squash with a paring knife to allow steam to escape. Place the squash on a baking sheet and bake for about 1 hour. Test for doneness by seeing if a paring knife can be inserted easily.

While the squash bakes, in a small skillet on medium-high heat, sauté the sage in the olive oil until a little darker in color and the flavor is released, not more than a minute.

Slice the baked squash in half lengthwise. Scoop out the seeds with a spoon. Using a fork, drag through the stringy part of the squash, remove, and put into a bowl. Add the sage, olive oil, and the cheese and toss together. Season with salt and pepper to taste, and serve.

VARIATIONS
- Add minced garlic and crushed red pepper flakes when sautéing the sage.
- Instead of spaghetti squash, roast butternut or other winter squash chunks, or bake cubed butternut squash.

SERVING AND MENU IDEAS
Serve as a side dish alongside a bean burger, such as Italian Cannellini Burgers (page 245), or serve it as your main dish, as you would spaghetti, perhaps with Walnut-Cheddar-Herb "Meatballs" (page 204) and a salad.

Latin American Peppers and Corn

This is a colorful side dish for any Latin meal. You might say it's our homage to Frida Kahlo's palette and palate. It's quick, it's easy, and it's beautiful.

Yields 3 cups
Serves 2 or 3
Time: 35 minutes

1½ teaspoons minced or pressed garlic
2 tablespoons vegetable oil, plus more for the pan
1½ teaspoons ground cumin
1 teaspoon salt, plus more as needed
¼ teaspoon freshly ground black pepper
2 cups fresh corn kernels, or 12 ounces frozen and thawed
1 poblano pepper, seeded and diced
1 red bell pepper, seeded and diced
⅓ cup chopped scallions
2 teaspoons finely grated lime zest
2 tablespoons chopped fresh cilantro

Whisk the garlic, oil, cumin, salt, and black pepper in a large bowl. Add the corn and poblano and bell peppers and toss well.

Spread the vegetables on a lightly oiled baking sheet. Broil for about 10 minutes, stirring twice, until the corn is slightly brown and beginning to crinkle.

Remove from the broiler and transfer the vegetables to a bowl. Add the scallions, lime zest, and cilantro and mix well. Season with additional salt to taste. Serve warm.

SERVING AND MENU IDEAS
Latin American Peppers and Corn will add color and zest to many Latin meals, for example Winter Squash and Red Bean Mole (page 225), Pozole Verde (page 223), or Haitian Rice and Beans with Plantains (page 263). It's also really good next to a Green Tomato Omelet (page 13) or even a Mexican Toasted Cheese Sandwich (page 84).

Lemony Roasted Beets

Orange beets often peek out shyly among the vegetables at farmers' markets these days, and they are a lucky and delicious find. When cooked, these beets turn golden yellow with a pink hue around the edges. A little lemon and salt brightens their color and delicate sweetness in this well-balanced dish.

Serves 4
Prep time: 15 minutes
Roasting time: 45 minutes
Cooling time: 15 minutes

5 medium-size orange beets
Sprinkling of coarse salt
½ teaspoon finely grated lemon zest
2 tablespoons fresh lemon juice
1 tablespoon olive oil
Salt and freshly ground black pepper

Preheat the oven to 425°F.

Rinse the beets. Sprinkle with coarse salt and wrap in aluminum foil. Roast in the oven for about 45 minutes, or until a knife will easily pierce each beet. Unwrap the beets and place them on a cutting board until cool enough to handle, 10 to 15 minutes. Remove the skins by rubbing them off with your hands; they will rub off more easily if you cut off the stem end to get them started. Cut the beets into 1-inch chunks and place in a bowl. Add the lemon zest, lemon juice, and olive oil and toss. Season with salt and pepper to taste.

SERVING AND MENU IDEAS

Lemony Roasted Beets are perfect alongside Kale and Walnut Risotto (page 173), Bitter Greens Lasagna (page 233), or Pizza with Arugula Salad (page 273).

Romanesco with Green Salsa

Romanesco is that beautiful green, fractal-looking vegetable shaped something like a cauliflower but building to a pointed dome. We see it off and on at our farmers' market and in supermarkets. It even comes in both green and orange varieties.

The beauty of this dish is all the different green colors. It is also nice, for a change, to have a steamed vegetable. Of course, this recipe would work with ordinary cauliflower (white, green, or orange), but romanesco is the most beautiful and has a mild flavor that's a good foil for the salsa.

Serves 4 to 6
Time: 30 minutes

GREEN SALSA
1 cup lightly packed chopped fresh parsley
2 tablespoons chopped fresh tarragon
½ cup chopped pitted green olives
¼ teaspoon crushed red pepper flakes
1 tablespoon capers
3 garlic cloves
1 tablespoon finely grated lemon zest
½ cup extra-virgin olive oil
Salt and freshly ground black pepper

1 large or 2 small heads romanesco cauliflower
Shaved Manchego, Parmesan, or Pecorino
  Romano cheese

Make the salsa: Stir together all the ingredients for the salsa. Season with salt and black pepper to taste. Set aside.

Cut the cauliflower apart into bite-size florets and stem pieces (which also have lots of flavor). Steam the cauliflower until tender, 5 to 7 minutes. Drain.

Place in a serving dish, top with the green salsa, and sprinkle with shaved cheese.

VARIATIONS
- For the salsa, try substituting fresh basil for the tarragon.
- Add hot sauce if you'd like a little more heat.

SERVING AND MENU IDEAS
Romanesco with Green Salsa is a lovely side dish for Fregola with Peas (page 239), Pizza Rosso e Verde (page 271), or Pasta Carbonara with Zucchini (page 229).

Southeast Asian Green Beans

This outstanding sweet and spicy dressing bursts with flavor and is easy to make. We love it on crisp, still brightly colored green beans, and also on thinly sliced cabbage, summer squash, winter squash, broccoli, bok choy, yu choy, snow peas, even corn.

Serves 4 to 6
Time: 20 minutes

Salt
1½ pounds green beans, ends trimmed

SOUTHEAST ASIAN DRESSING
1 teaspoon chili paste with garlic★
3 tablespoons finely chopped fresh cilantro
3 tablespoons thinly sliced scallion greens
1 (1-inch) piece fresh ginger, peeled and finely grated
3 tablespoons fresh lime juice
2 tablespoons sunflower, grapeseed, or other vegetable oil
1 large garlic clove, minced or pressed
2 tablespoons brown sugar
3 tablespoons soy sauce

★We like Lan Chi brand, which is made without additives and can be found in Asian markets or specialty aisles at the grocers. If you like, substitute minced fresh hot pepper, seeded or not, to taste.

Put a few inches of water with some salt into a large pot and bring to a boil. Add the green beans and cook until just tender, 3 to 4 minutes. When the beans are tender, using a slotted spoon, transfer them to a large bowl of ice water. When the beans have cooled, drain and pat dry.

Whisk together the dressing ingredients, or whirl briefly in a blender or mini food processor. Toss the cooked green beans with the dressing and serve.

SERVING AND MENU IDEAS
Of course this is a good side dish with Asian meals, but also, it would liven up a simple supper of rice, baked or mashed sweet potatoes, and baked tofu. Or scrambled eggs and toast. Or macaroni and cheese. Try it and you'll think of lots of things. Take it to a potluck dinner.

Fennel Gratin

Meltingly tender, this braised fennel dish is finished with a deliciously crunchy, cheesy topping. A fine vegan version can be prepared without the cheese.

Serves 6
Prep time: 35 minutes
Baking time: 20 minutes

3 or 4 medium fennel bulbs (about 2 pounds, whole)
1 medium onion
2 tablespoons olive oil, plus more as needed
½ teaspoon salt
¼ teaspoon freshly ground black pepper
1 tablespoon dried thyme
⅓ cup dry white wine
¼ cup water

BREAD-CRUMB TOPPING

2 tablespoons olive oil (or use 1 tablespoon butter, 1 tablespoon oil)
2 garlic cloves, minced
¾ cup bread crumbs
½ teaspoon salt
¼ teaspoon freshly ground black pepper
1 tablespoon dried thyme
1½ teaspoons finely grated lemon zest
⅓ cup grated Parmesan cheese (optional)

Slice off the tops of the fennel bulbs. Remove any bruised outer layers. Halve the bulbs lengthwise and remove the inner core by cutting a V-shaped wedge. Slice each half lengthwise into ¾-inch wedges. Peel the onion and cut it in half lengthwise and then into ½-inch wedges.

In a large skillet on medium heat, warm the olive oil and cook the fennel, onion, salt, pepper, and thyme for about 5 minutes. Add the wine and bring to a low boil for a minute, add the water, cover, and simmer for about 15 minutes, or until the vegetables are just tender.

Preheat the oven to 425°F. Oil a baking dish.

While the fennel cooks, make the bread crumb topping: In a heavy skillet, heat the olive oil and sauté the garlic until golden. Add the bread crumbs, salt, pepper, thyme, and lemon zest. Stir for about 5 minutes, until crunchy. Remove from the heat, stir in the cheese (if using), and set aside.

Transfer the cooked fennel and onions to the baking dish and sprinkle evenly with the bread crumb topping. Bake, uncovered, for about 20 minutes until the topping is golden brown.

SERVING AND MENU IDEAS

For an easy, delightful Italian-style meal, pair with a simple pasta such as Spaghetti with Olives and Lemon (page 241) or farfalle with Power Pesto (page 329) and chopped tomatoes. Or serve Fennel Gratin (page 301) alongside Mushroom-Stuffed Winter Squash (page 180).

Spicy Roasted Broccoli

Here is another lovely way to serve broccoli. It is simple and easy with just the right level of mild heat. The strips of red jalapeños look pretty. If you don't want spicy-hot, use sweet red bell peppers in place of the hot. This dish remains good-tasting at room temperature. Take it to your next potluck!

Serves 4 to 6
Prep time: 10 minutes
Roasting time: 20 to 30 minutes

1 pound 6 ounces broccoli crowns (about 6 cups prepped)
2 large fresh hot peppers (we like red jalapeños or other red hot peppers)
3 tablespoons olive oil
Coarse salt

Preheat the oven to 400°F.

Cut the broccoli crowns into florets with long stems. Peel off any tough skins.

Stem and seed the hot peppers. Slice lengthwise into strips. Cut the strips in half.

In a bowl, toss the prepped broccoli and hot peppers with the olive oil. Spread out on a baking sheet. Sprinkle with coarse salt. Roast until tender, 20 to 30 minutes, stirring every 10 minutes. The roasting time will depend on the size of the florets. When you can easily pierce a broccoli stem with a fork, remove the broccoli from the oven.

Serve warm or at room temperature.

SERVING AND MENU IDEAS
This quick and easy and very versatile side dish goes well with many different ethnic cuisines and is good any time of year. Try it with Scalloped Potatoes and Mushrooms (page 202), Pasta with Spinach and Apricots (page 230), or Burmese Tohu Thoke (page 194).

Sweet Potatoes with Bitter Orange

Sweet potatoes are wonderful. We love to dress them up or down. For this recipe we wanted a showstopper that could perform as an elegant small plate or as a main event.

We began by creating a complex-tasting, spicy-sweet glaze using some simple ingredients. See if you can find Hero brand Bitter Orange Marmalade, as it adds just the right balance of bitter with the sweet. Or you can use regular orange marmalade and add some fresh orange zest—that will work fine, too. This dish is perfect for Thanksgiving or any harvest meal.

Serves 4 as a small plate, 2 as a main dish
Prep time: 20 minutes
Roasting time: about 60 minutes

GLAZE
2 tablespoons butter or natural butter substitute
  like Earth Balance
2 tablespoons honey
½ cup fresh orange juice
½ cup bitter orange marmalade (or orange
  marmalade with zest of one orange stirred in)
¼ cup apple cider vinegar
½ teaspoon salt
1 teaspoon dried sage
1 teaspoon dried thyme
Dash of cayenne pepper

2 large sweet potatoes (about 3 pounds)
½ teaspoon salt, plus more as needed

¼ teaspoon freshly ground black pepper
2 large garlic cloves, minced
½ cup crumbled feta or goat cheese (optional)

Make the glaze: In a saucepan on medium heat, melt the butter, stir in the rest of the ingredients for the glaze and bring to a low boil. Turn down the heat and simmer for about 10 minutes; the glaze will bubble and thicken.

Meanwhile, preheat the oven to 400°F. Lightly oil a baking sheet.

Peel the sweet potatoes and cut into 2-inch chunks. In a large bowl, toss with the salt, black pepper, and garlic. When the glaze has thickened enough to coat a spoon, toss it with the sweet potatoes.

Spread out the coated sweet potatoes in a single layer on a baking sheet. Roast for about an hour, gently stirring every 15 minutes, until the glaze has been absorbed into the potatoes and they are soft and browned and crisp around the edges. Season with salt to taste.

For an added layer of flavor, serve topped with crumbles of creamy feta or goat cheese.

SERVING AND MENU IDEAS
These bittersweet roasted sweet potatoes are a pleasant surprise next to Baked Eggs with Spinach and Frizzled Sage (page 16) for a special brunch. Their distinctive flavor goes well with Quinoa Tabouli with Pomegranates and Pistachios (page 145) or Pineapple-Lime Glazed Tofu with Spicy Cucumber Salad (page 190). They lend some warm heft to a salad meal, such as Spring Greens and Vegetables with Shallot Vinaigrette (page 139).

Red Cabbage with Blueberries

This beautiful deep purple dish delivers a double dose of purple with all its beneficial phytonutrients. Blueberries add sweetness and an interesting tart-sweet flavor. Leftovers are just as good as the first time around.

Serves 8
Time: 35 minutes

1 generous cup red onions cut into strips
2 tablespoons olive oil
8 cups thinly sliced red cabbage (about one 1½-pound head)
¼ cup water
1 teaspoon salt, plus more as needed
2 cups blueberries, fresh or frozen
¼ cup pure maple syrup, agave syrup, or brown sugar
¼ cup apple cider vinegar

In a soup pot or large saucepan on medium-high heat, sauté the onions in the oil for 3 minutes. Add the cabbage and stir for a couple of minutes until the cabbage is glistening and beginning to wilt.

Add the water and salt, reduce the heat to low, cover, and cook for 10 minutes, stirring once or twice.

Add the blueberries. If they're frozen, increase the heat and stir for a couple of minutes to maintain the temperature of the cabbage, and then lower the heat. If the water has evaporated, add a little more, just a tablespoon or two. Stir in the maple syrup and vinegar and cook, uncovered, on medium heat until the cabbage is tender yet firm and the blueberries retain their shape, 5 to 10 minutes. Season with additional salt to taste.

NOTE: With leftovers, you can make a delicious hash: fry some onions and potatoes, and when they're done, stir in Red Cabbage with Blueberries and cook just long enough to heat through.

SERVING AND MENU IDEAS
Red Cabbage with Blueberries is a sweet-and-sour counterpoint to Scalloped Potatoes and Mushrooms (page 202) or Autumn or Winter Potpie (page 163 or page 166). Add a dessert, such as Custard and Pear Pie (page 376) or Pumpkin Cheesecake (page 370) to one of these meals and you have a feast.

Summer Squash and Tomato Tian

Tian, a Provençal-style delight, is the name of both the gratin and the earthenware dish that it is traditionally baked in. All the vegetables reduce and caramelize, resulting in a juicy, flavorful mélange of summer goodness. So succulent, and well worth the wait for it to come out of the oven.

Summer squash varieties abound and any can be used in this tian. We use dried herbs instead of fresh for their concentrated flavor. The flavor of fresh herbs would be lost in the extended baking time.

Serves 4 as a main dish, 6 as a side
Prep time: 25 minutes
Baking time: 90 minutes

4 tablespoons olive oil, plus more for the pan
4 cups thinly sliced onions
Salt
2 garlic cloves, minced or pressed
4 medium summer squash (we like a mix of
  yellow squash and zucchini), thinly sliced on
  the diagonal, about 8 cups
1½ teaspoons dried thyme
1½ teaspoons dried basil
3 ripe tomatoes, thinly sliced
½ teaspoon freshly ground black pepper
½ cup grated cheese (mixture of Fontina Valle
  d'Aosta and Parmesan, or all Parmesan)

Preheat the oven to 400°F. Oil a 3-quart baking dish or 9 x 13-inch baking pan.

In a large skillet on medium-high heat, warm the oil. Add the onions, sprinkle with salt, and cook, stirring often, for about 10 minutes. Stir in the garlic.

Spread half the cooked onions on the bottom of the prepared baking dish, then half the squash. Sprinkle with ¾ teaspoon each of thyme and basil. Layer half the tomatoes and sprinkle with ½ teaspoon salt and ¼ teaspoon of the pepper. Repeat the layers: the remaining onions, squash, herbs, tomatoes, salt, and pepper. Drizzle the remaining 2 tablespoons olive oil over the top and then sprinkle with the grated cheese.

Bake for about 90 minutes, pressing down on the vegetables with a spatula after about 45 minutes. The finished tian should be well browned, with the vegetables meltingly soft, bubbling in the juices.

SERVING AND MENU IDEAS
Serve this tian next to a burger, a pasta with pesto, such as Garlic Scape Pesto (page 331), or Pizza with Greens (page 358). Serve it as a main dish in a light meal with a green salad. Pair it with Spinach Salad with Blueberries and Corn (page 148) and a good crusty bread for a late summer feast.

Mashed Potatoes with Lemon and Parsley

Mashed potatoes are always good. These are kind of new and interesting—fresh tasting and special while still providing a favorite comfort food, no pools of butter needed.

Serves 4 to 6
Time: 25 to 30 minutes

Salt
2 pounds Yukon Gold potatoes
3 tablespoons chopped fresh parsley
Finely grated zest of 1 lemon
2 tablespoons snipped fresh chives
4 ounces cream cheese
¼ cup extra-virgin olive oil
2 tablespoons fresh lemon juice
1 teaspoon Dijon mustard
Cracked black pepper

In a large covered pot, bring several inches of salted water to a boil. Peel (or not, as you wish) and dice the potatoes and add them to the pot. When the water is boiling, reduce the heat to a simmer, cover, and cook until the potatoes are tender, 10 to 15 minutes.

Meanwhile, put 1 tablespoon of the chopped parsley and the lemon zest, snipped chives, and cream cheese into a serving bowl.

In a blender, whirl the remaining 2 tablespoons chopped parsley and the olive oil, lemon juice, and mustard for a few seconds until smooth.

When the potatoes are soft, drain them in a colander and add them to the serving bowl. Using a potato masher, crush the potatoes and distribute the cream cheese as it melts into the hot potatoes. When the potatoes are mashed to your liking, pour in the vinaigrette from the blender and stir well. Season with salt and cracked black pepper to taste. Serve hot.

SERVING AND MENU IDEAS
Not that we couldn't make a whole meal of just mashed potatoes, but serve them next to Simple Seasoned Tofu (page 346) and a side vegetable, such as Asparagus Cacio e Pepe–Style (page 293), Spicy Roasted Broccoli (page 302), or Beet Greens with Raisins and Pine Nuts (page 290), and you'll feel better about yourself.

Roasted Winter Squash Agrodolce

Flavorwise, this dish kind of has it all—earthy, sweet, tangy, and hot. Visually, it's gorgeous enough for a holiday platter. But all those layers of flavor and color are constructed with just one easy step after another.

Serves 6 to 8
Prep time: about 40 minutes

Cooking spray or oil, for the pans
3 pounds delicata or butternut squash
4 shallots, quartered lengthwise
2 tablespoons extra-virgin olive oil
½ teaspoon salt, plus more as needed
2 teaspoons ground coriander
¼ teaspoon ground black pepper, plus more as needed
⅓ cup honey
⅓ cup apple cider vinegar
1 cup Greek yogurt
1½ teaspoons hot sauce
½ cup pomegranate seeds*
¼ cup chopped fresh mint, parsley, or cilantro

*An easy way to separate pomegranate seeds without mess is to cut the whole pomegranate in half lengthwise and submerge it in a large bowl of warm water. Use your thumbs to push the seeds out of the spongy pith. The seeds sink and the pith floats and your fingers and countertops remain unstained. (A large pomegranate yields about 2 cups of seeds. Reserve the rest for sprinkling on salads or oatmeal.)

Preheat the oven to 425°F. Lightly coat two rimmed baking sheets with cooking spray or oil.

Halve the squash lengthwise and scoop out the seeds. Cut delicata squash, the skin of which is edible, crosswise into 1-inch-thick slices. Peel butternut squash and cut into 1-inch wedges. In a large bowl, toss together the squash slices, quartered shallots, olive oil, salt, coriander, and pepper. Spread the mixture on the baking sheets. Roast, turning over once after 15 minutes, until tender and caramelized in spots, 25 to 35 minutes. (Delicata squash requires less time to roast than butternut.)

Meanwhile, in a small saucepan, combine the honey, vinegar, and a pinch of salt. Bring to a boil, then lower the heat and simmer until reduced by about half, 5 to 6 minutes. Set aside.

Stir together the Greek yogurt and hot sauce, and season with salt and pepper to taste. Set aside.

When you take the squash from the oven, pour the honey-vinegar syrup over it and stir to coat.

Arrange the squash prettily on a platter. Drizzle the yogurt sauce decoratively on top. (Use a small squeeze bottle or put it in a plastic sandwich bag with a corner cut off.) Sprinkle with pomegranate seeds and chopped fresh mint, parsley, or cilantro.

SERVING AND MENU IDEAS

Roasted Winter Squash Agrodolce's sweet-and-sour goodness is the perfect foil for Lentil Salad with Baby Greens and Oranges (page 142) or Herbed Quinoa Salad (page 133), which features chickpeas, apricots, and green olives. It's also a hit on the Thanksgiving table.

Mashed Rutabaga with Fried Red Onions

Rutabaga is a large root vegetable with a mild, delicious taste and a lovely golden yellow color. Try this simple mashed rutabaga mixed with fried onions. Yellow or white onions are fine to use, but we like the color contrast of red onions.

Serves 4
Time: 30 minutes

1 large rutabaga (about 1¾ pounds), peeled and
   chopped (4 generous cups)
2 tablespoons olive oil
1 large red onion, chopped (about 1½ cups)
2 tablespoons butter, plus more as needed
Salt and freshly ground black pepper

Put the chopped rutabaga in a saucepan with water to cover and bring to a boil. Reduce the heat, cover, and simmer until soft, 20 to 30 minutes.

Meanwhile, warm the olive oil in a skillet on medium-high heat, and fry the chopped onions, stirring often, until golden brown and crisp around the edges.

Drain the cooked rutabaga and mash thoroughly by hand with a potato masher or in the bowl of a food processor. Stir in the butter and the fried onions. Season with salt and pepper and more butter to taste.

SERVING AND MENU IDEAS
Rutabaga may not be in your usual repertoire of vegetable side dishes, but give this simple recipe a try and you may be pleasantly surprised. For a fall or winter meal, serve this dish with a burger or with Jamaican Jerk Tempeh Patties (page 200) along with a green vegetable, such as Shredded Brussels Sprouts with Apples (page 314).

RUTABAGA

The rutabaga, also called swede, yellow turnip, or neep, is a member of the Brassica family. Bigger and sweeter than turnips, it has edible greens and yellow flesh.

Each December for twenty years, the Annual International Rutabaga Curling World Championship has been held at the Ithaca Farmers Market on the last day the market is open outdoors. In recent years, there is also a Turnip Toss for children. Registration fees include "your very own rutabaga to take home and turn into soup." We mash ours.

A Hash of Spuds, Beets, and Greens

When you're gazing at this week's CSA allotment of greens and root vegetables and feeling stymied, think hash! It's a satisfying and tasty choice for breakfast, brunch, or a no-frills supper.

We like to use a mixture of greens (don't overlook the greens from the beets, a delicious *and* virtuous option), but any single variety of greens works just as well. If mixing your greens, try a combo of a sharp one like broccoli rabe, turnip greens, or escarole and a mild variety like beet greens, chard, or kale. Feta cheese is a nice tangy counterpoint.

Serves 4
Time: 30 minutes

8 cups packed chopped greens
2 cups peeled and diced potatoes
1 cup peeled and diced beets
2 tablespoons olive oil
1½ cups chopped onions
1 tablespoon minced or crushed garlic
1 teaspoon salt, plus more as needed
¼ teaspoon freshly ground black pepper
½ teaspoon ground fennel seeds
⅓ cup crumbled feta cheese (optional)

Bring 3 quarts water to a boil. Immerse the greens and cook until tender, about 5 minutes. Cooking time will vary with the tenderness of the greens. Drain the greens in a colander positioned over a large bowl to reserve the cooking water. Return the greens water to the pot you cooked the greens in, add the potatoes and beets, bring the water back to a boil, and cook until tender. While the potatoes and beets cook, transfer the greens to the now empty bowl used to reserve the cooking water. Set aside. The colander is now free for draining the potatoes and beets.

Heat the olive oil in a 10-inch heavy skillet. Sauté the onions and garlic with the salt, pepper, and ground fennel until the onions begin to brown. Stir in the drained potatoes, beets, and greens, lower the heat, cover, and cook for 8 to 10 minutes. Stir occasionally to prevent sticking. Season with salt to taste.

Spoon the hash into bowls and top with the feta, if desired.

SERVING AND MENU IDEAS

This hash is perfect with simple fried or scrambled eggs or with Green Tomato Omelet (page 13). At lunch or dinner, you could serve it with A Big Fat Tomato Sandwich (page 85) or a bowl of Purée of Parsnip, Carrot, and Celeriac (page 91).

Beetroot Sticks

This dish seems to grow on people. While chewing the first bite: "Nice flavor. I like the crunch." After four or five mouthfuls: "This is great! Are there more?"

The beets should be cooked to the "not raw, yet still crunchy" stage. The size you've cut the beets determines how long to stir-fry them, so think of wooden "strike-anywhere" match sticks. The beets turn glossy, retain their deep magenta color, and taste sweet, zingy, and very flavorful.

Serves 4 to 6
Time: 20 minutes

1 tablespoon olive oil
3 to 4 cups raw beets peeled and cut into
    matchsticks
1 tablespoon apple cider vinegar or white vinegar
3 tablespoons Dijon, brown, or whole-grain
    mustard
1 tablespoon honey, agave, or pure maple syrup

Heat the oil in a wok or large skillet on high heat, add the beets, and stir-fry for 2 to 5 minutes, depending on the size of the beet pieces: if you cut into matchsticks the size of actual wooden matchsticks, 2 minutes will do it; with larger pieces, stir-fry up to 5 minutes. When the beets are tender but still crunchy, add the vinegar and cook for another minute. Add the mustard and honey and toss well to evenly coat the beets. Season with salt to taste.

Serve hot out of the pan, warm, at room temperature, or chilled.

SERVING AND MENU IDEAS
Garnish Beetroot Sticks with chopped fresh dill or parsley, a sprinkle of capers or roasted almonds, or some red onions. Serve on the side of Mushroom Barley Salad (page 147), Spring Risotto (page 174), Mediterranean Potato Salad (page 124), or Squash Polenta with Mushroom and Kale Stew (page 196). Or almost anything else.

Shredded Brussels Sprouts with Apples

Some stores carry ready-shredded Brussels sprouts, but you can make this little side dish using whole sprouts by thinly slicing them or shredding them in a food processor. The basic recipe is tasty as a simple side, but it can also be seasoned in a couple of different directions. A sprinkle of dill and/or ground caraway gives the dish an Eastern European, Hungarian accent. Add parsley and butter, or a flavorful oil such as olive or walnut oil, for a Mediterranean style.

Serves 4 to 6
Time: 20 minutes

1 crisp, sweet red apple
2 tablespoons vegetable oil
4 cups shredded Brussels sprouts★
¼ teaspoon salt
2 teaspoons apple cider vinegar

★If you don't have packaged preshredded Brussels sprouts in your store, prepare the sprouts by thinly slicing them with a sharp knife or shredding them in a food processor.

With a large-holed box grater, shred the unpeeled apple into a bowl and to prevent discoloration, press plastic wrap directly onto the surface.

In a large skillet on medium heat, warm the oil and cook the Brussels sprouts until tender. Stir in the grated apple and heat until just warm. Stir in the salt and vinegar and serve.

ADDITIONS
Add any of these to the finished dish:
- 1 to 2 teaspoons butter or flavored oil (walnut oil, extra-virgin olive oil, sesame oil, herbed basting oil, or chili-spiced oil)
- 2 tablespoons minced fresh flat-leaf parsley
- 2 teaspoons minced fresh dill
- ½ to 1 teaspoon finely ground caraway seeds

SERVING AND MENU IDEAS
Here's a fall or winter feast: start with Dilly Deviled Eggs (see page 57), then serve Mushroom-Stuffed Winter Squash (page 180) with Lemony Roasted Beets (page 297) and these very delicious Shredded Brussels Sprouts with Apples. For dessert, Vegan Apple-Blueberry Crumble (page 378).

Farro Pilaf with Cannellini and Arugula

Basmati Rice Pilaf

Black Rice Pilaf

Bulgur and Pomegranate Pilaf

Jeweled Rice

Orzo Risotto

Farro Pilaf with Cannellini and Arugula

Considered an ancient grain, farro has been found in Egyptian tombs and was apparently a staple food of the legions of Rome and both the peasantry and royalty of the Fertile Crescent. Farro is a high-fiber food rich in iron, zinc, vitamin B3, magnesium, and protein. Farro is not a single grain but a name for three different types of hulled wheat—einkorn, emmer, and spelt—that cannot be threshed. Pearled farro has some of the bran removed and cooks without soaking. It works well in risottos or as a hearty addition to soups or salads.

Cooked farro grains are tan, plumper than rice, have a tender-chewy consistency and an earthy, nutty flavor, and look somewhat like barley. Cannellini beans have a creamy melt-in-your mouth consistency and thin skin. Seasoned with olive oil and garlic, they are a nice contrast to the bright green of gently wilted arugula and basil in this hearty dish bursting with flavor and nutrition.

Serves 4 to 6
Time: 30 minutes

2¼ cups water
¼ teaspoon salt, plus more as needed
1¼ cups pearled farro★
2 tablespoons olive oil
1 red onion, cut lengthwise into thin slices
3 garlic cloves, minced or pressed
¼ teaspoon crushed red pepper flakes
1 (15-ounce) can cannellini beans, drained
4 to 5 cups loosely packed baby arugula
2 tablespoons fresh basil chiffonade

½ cup sherry or ¼ cup fresh lemon juice
Freshly ground black pepper
Grated Parmesan, Provolone, Asiago, or Pecorino Romano cheese (optional)

★Farro is either whole grain or pearled. If you use whole grain, it should be soaked overnight and cooked for 45 minutes.

In a covered saucepan, bring the water and salt to a boil. Stir in the farro and simmer, covered, until the water has been absorbed and the grains are plump and tender, about 25 minutes.

While the farro cooks, warm the oil in a large skillet. Add the onion, garlic, red pepper flakes, and a sprinkle of salt, and cook, covered, until slightly caramelized, 10 to 15 minutes. Stir in the beans and arugula and cook for about 5 minutes, or until the arugula wilts. Remove from the heat.

When the farro is done, stir it into the beans and arugula with the fresh basil and sherry or lemon juice. Season with salt and black pepper to taste.

Serve topped with cheese, if you like.

VARIATION
Use 2 teaspoons dried oregano in addition to, or in place of, the basil. Add it to the cooking onions.

SERVING AND MENU IDEAS
Garnish with chopped fresh herbs, such as basil, chives, and/or oregano. We like to serve this pilaf with Tofu Fillets with Onion and Fresh Herb Relish (page 77), or Roasted Fennel and Leek Tomato Soup (page 98).

Basmati Rice Pilaf

This pilaf has it all: nutty brown rice, aromatic herbs, and fruit and nuts in a sweet, tart, and salty balance of flavors and textures. It is a colorful side dish and easily doubles as a stuffing for grilled or roasted vegetables.

You may be familiar with the more widely used white basmati rice, but there's also the healthier, equally fragrant, and fluffy whole-grain choice.

Serves 4
Rice cooking time: about 40 minutes
Hands-on time: 15 minutes
Total time: 50 minutes

2 tablespoons butter
1½ cups brown basmati rice
1¼ teaspoons salt
2¼ cups water
½ cup dried cranberries
2 tablespoons fresh lemon juice
1 tablespoon plus 2 teaspoons chopped fresh
   tarragon
½ cup chopped fresh parsley
½ cup chopped toasted almonds or pistachios
Freshly ground black pepper

Melt the butter in a heavy-bottomed pan on medium heat. Add the rice and salt and cook, stirring constantly, until the rice is fragrant. Add the water, stir once, increase the heat to high, and bring to a boil. Reduce the heat to low, cover the pot, and cook for 40 minutes.

While the rice cooks, in a small bowl, toss the dried cranberries with the lemon juice. Set aside. Prepare the herbs and the nuts.

When the rice is done, fluff with a fork and transfer to a large bowl. Stir in the cranberries with lemon juice, tarragon, parsley, and the nuts. Season with black pepper to taste.

Serve warm or at room temperature.

SERVING AND MENU IDEAS
Serve with Mushroom-Stuffed Winter Squash (page 180), Roasted Red Pepper, Black Olive, and Tofu Burgers, hold the bun (page 249), or Wilted Greens with Blue Cheese and Walnuts (page 289).

Black Rice Pilaf

This mélange of simple flavors and textures is a dramatically colorful pilaf. Impress your friends. Treat yourself.

Serves 6 to 8
Prep time: 25 minutes
Total time: about 1 hour

3 cups water
½ teaspoon salt
2 cups raw black rice (see sidebar, page 136)
1 cucumber, peeled, seeded, and diced
1 mango, peeled, pitted, and diced (see sidebar, page 118)
½ red onion, minced
¼ cup minced fresh cilantro

ORANGE VINAIGRETTE
⅓ cup fresh orange juice
2 tablespoons white vinegar
¼ teaspoon salt
½ cup olive oil

1 cup toasted pepitas (pumpkin seeds)

Cook the rice: In a saucepan, bring the water and salt to a boil. Add the rice and when the water returns to a boil, reduce the heat to low. Stir well, cover, and cook for about 45 minutes. Check at about 35 minutes to see that the water hasn't completely evaporated, and if it has, add a little more hot water. When the rice is almost tender, turn off the heat (if there's any water in the bottom of the pan, drain it off) and let the rice sit, tightly covered, for about 10 minutes. Fluff with a fork.

While the rice is cooking, prep the cucumber, mango, red onion, and cilantro. Put into a serving bowl, cover, and set aside until the rice is done.

Make the dressing: In a blender, whirl together the orange juice, vinegar, and salt. With the blender running, slowly pour in the oil. Set aside.

When the rice is done, toss it with the prepped cucumbers, mangoes, red onions, and cilantro. Add the dressing and toss well. Just before serving, stir in the pepitas.

SERVING AND MENU IDEAS
Pair with Black Bean and Quinoa Burgers (page 246), or Simple Seasoned Tofu (page 346), or Spicy Roasted Broccoli (page 302).

Bulgur and Pomegranate Pilaf

Bulgur and pomegranates are both beloved foods of the Middle East, Western Asia, North Africa, and India. Fragrant, naturally sweet, and healthful, this unusual pilaf has an interesting chewy, nutty texture and is easy and quick to make. Pomegranate juice and bits of red onion give the bulgur a purplish-brown color, and with fresh crunchy pomegranate seeds, the finished pilaf looks like it's studded with little jewels. Minced fresh parsley sets off the whole affair.

Serves 4 to 6
Time: 35 minutes

2 tablespoons extra-virgin olive oil
1½ teaspoons fennel seeds
1½ cups finely chopped red onions
½ teaspoon salt, plus more as needed
2 cups fine- to medium-grade bulgur
2 cups pomegranate juice★
1 pomegranate
Freshly ground black pepper
½ cup minced fresh parsley (optional)

★If using pomegranate juice concentrate, be sure to dilute according to the directions, or the pilaf will be way too sticky.

In a saucepan or large skillet with a good lid on medium-low heat, warm the olive oil and cook the fennel seeds until they start to sizzle, about a minute. Add the onions and salt and cook until soft and somewhat transparent, about 7 minutes. Add the bulgur and stir for a minute. Stir in the pomegranate juice, cover, and bring to a boil. Lower the heat and simmer for a couple of minutes, then set aside for about 15 minutes.

While the bulgur sits, rinse the pomegranate and cut it into quarters. Place the quarters in a bowl of comfortably warm water in the sink. Gently remove the seeds with your fingers, separating them from the white membrane. The seeds will sink to the bottom and the membrane will rise to the top. Skim off and discard the bits of membrane, then drain the seeds and set aside.

When the bulgur is chewy, no longer hard or crunchy, stir it to make sure all the juice has been absorbed. If not, cover and set aside for a few more minutes. When ready, season with additional salt and pepper to taste and stir in the pomegranate seeds and parsley. Serve warm.

VARIATION
This pilaf is satisfying on its own, and also good garnished with a little crumbled feta cheese, or lightly toasted pine nuts, or chopped walnuts (but be judicious: a small amount of feta or nuts is delicious with this pilaf; more can easily dominate the other flavors).

SERVING AND MENU IDEAS
Serve with one or more of Za'atar Yogurt and Cucumber Salad (page 122), marinated artichokes, and Roasted Carrot Hummus (page 67).

Jeweled Rice

We're forever fans of whole grains, but once in a while, fluffy, quickly cooked white rice feels like a reward. Colorful, festive, studded with sautéed vegetables and luscious dried fruits, aromatic Jeweled Rice is beautiful, substantial, and bursting with chewy textures, savory notes, and sweet flavors of orange and cinnamon.

Other combinations of dried fruits will work, but we highly recommend crimson-colored cranberries, dried sweet cherries, and chopped apricots. You could add a pinch of fragrant saffron or healthful turmeric when cooking the rice if you'd like yellow-colored rice. This dish is gluten-free, vegan if made with olive oil, and a total treat.

Serves 4 as a main dish; 6 as a side dish
Time: 45 minutes

1¼ cups white basmati or jasmine rice
1¾ cups plus 2 tablespoons water or vegetable stock
2 tablespoons butter or olive oil, or a mixture
1 leek, thinly sliced, or 1 medium onion, chopped
Salt
¾ cup grated carrots
1 teaspoon ground cinnamon
Pinch of cayenne pepper
½ red or orange bell pepper, seeded and cut into small dice
¾ cup mixture of dried cherries, cranberries, currants, and/or diced dried apricots
Finely grated zest and juice of 1 large orange (½ cup juice)
Freshly ground black pepper
Olive oil, for drizzling (optional)

Place the rice and 1¾ cups water in a saucepan with a tight-fitting lid and bring to a boil. Cover, reduce the heat to a simmer, and cook for about 15 minutes, or until all the water has been absorbed. Remove from the heat, cover with a clean dish towel, replace the lid, and set aside for about 10 minutes. Fluff the rice with a fork.

While the rice cooks, in a pan on medium-high heat, warm the butter or oil. Add the leek along with a sprinkle of salt, and sauté for about 3 minutes, until softened. Stir in the carrots, lower the heat to medium, and cook for a few minutes. Add the cinnamon, cayenne, bell pepper, remaining 2 tablespoons water, and dried fruit. Cover and cook on low heat for a few more minutes.

In a large serving bowl, toss the cooked rice and the leek-and-spices mixture. Toss thoroughly with the orange zest and juice. Season with additional salt and black pepper to taste, and drizzle a little olive oil on top if you like.

SERVING AND MENU IDEAS
Serve warm alongside Spicy Filo Samosas with Spinach, Mint, and Cilantro (page 44), Two Potato Tomato Curry with Yellow Split Pea Dal (page 210), or Cashew-Crusted Chickpea Burgers (page 251).

Orzo Risotto

The small, rice-like shape of orzo pasta makes a quick, simply prepared risotto-like side dish that has a nice golden color. This is a side dish, but could also be a satisfying lunch.

We like to use whole wheat orzo for its nutritional benefits as well as its flavor. Onions, herbs, and sharp Italian cheese make it yummy. If you have a good nonstick saucepan, this dish is a good reason to put it to use.

Serves 4
Time: 20 minutes

2 tablespoons butter
1 generous cup diced onions
½ teaspoon dried thyme
¼ teaspoon salt
3 cups water
1½ cups whole wheat orzo
¼ cup grated Parmesan or Pecorino Romano cheese
2 tablespoons chopped fresh basil
1 tablespoon minced fresh parsley
Freshly ground black pepper

Melt the butter in a 1-quart saucepan on medium-high heat. Add the onions, thyme, and salt and cook, stirring often, for about 5 minutes. When the onions are lightly browned and softened, add the water and the orzo and bring to a boil. Lower the heat to a simmer and cook, uncovered, for about 15 minutes, or until most of the liquid has been absorbed, but the pasta is still creamy. Stir in the cheese, basil, and parsley. Season with additional salt and pepper to taste.

VARIATION
For a vegan dish, use olive oil instead of butter, vegetable stock instead of water (we like the flavor of no-chicken stock), and omit the cheese.

SERVING AND MENU IDEAS
This mildly flavored orzo is good with more assertive dishes such as Spicy Broccoli Rabe with Sun-Dried Tomatoes and Almonds (page 288), Persian Kuku (page 192), or Ethiopian Greens (page 286).

SAUCES,
PICKLES
& OTHER
GOOD
THINGS

Lemon-Tahini Sauce

Fresh Pineapple-Mango Relish

Pesto Rosso

Power Pesto

Garlic Greens Pesto

Garlic Scape Pesto

Sos Ti-Malice

Laura's Spice Rub

Za'atar

Gingered Radish Pickles

Harissa

Monsoon Pickles

Raspberry Vinegar

Raspberry-Carrot Pickles

Pickled Sweet Peppers

Giardiniera

Tomatillo Pickles

Spiced Preserved Lemons

Cashew-Coconut Butter

Simple Seasoned Tofu

Lemon-Tahini Sauce

People have been enjoying lemon-tahini sauces for centuries in the Near East where sesame seeds and lemon trees flourish. Many folks like to keep it simple and make dressings with just tahini and lemon juice; others add yogurt. But to make it irresistible, go a little further. To us, the combined flavors of tahini, olive oil, garlic, fresh lemon juice, vinegar, cumin, and salt are almost addictive. It's not quite a dip, but this sauce is thicker than a typical dressing for green salad or to squirt on a falafel pita. If you find that you like this sauce, make a double recipe next time; if covered tightly, it will last a long time in the fridge.

Yields 1 cup
Time: 10 minutes

2 tablespoons olive oil
½ cup tahini (sesame seed paste)
2 garlic cloves, minced or pressed
¼ cup fresh lemon juice
¼ teaspoon ground cumin
2 tablespoons water
1 teaspoon vinegar (white, cider, or red wine vinegar), plus more as needed
¼ teaspoon salt, plus more as needed

In a blender, combine the olive oil, tahini, garlic, lemon juice, cumin, water, vinegar, and salt and blend until very smooth and thick, adding more water if needed. Add more vinegar and/or salt to taste.

SUGGESTIONS FOR USE

Of course you can serve this on a green salad, but it's also great on simply roasted or steamed vegetables or your favorite vegetable burger. Try it on Roasted Eggplant Salad with Chermoula Sauce (page 125), just hold the chemoula!

Fresh Pineapple-Mango Relish

Perhaps because she grew up in Santiago, Chile, or because of her abiding fondness for mangoes, our esteemed Moosewood partner Eliana Parra has a flair for salsas—and also a flair for efficient and fast! These few ingredients go into a food processor, and in a flash, you have a sweet and refreshing, fine-textured condiment. You'll relish this relish when your mango and pineapple are beautifully ripe, juicy, and sweet, and you'll be dreaming up excuses to put it on the table again and again.

Yields about 3 cups
Time: 15 minutes

1 ripe mango
½ ripe pineapple, cut into chunks (about
  2 cups)
¼ cup chopped fresh cilantro
3 scallions, chopped
¼ teaspoon salt
2 tablespoons apple cider vinegar

Cut the mango into cubes (see sidebar, page 25). Whirl all the ingredients in a food processor until chopped, but not yet puréed. Stored in a jar in the refrigerator, the relish will stay fresh-tasting for up to 3 days.

SERVING AND MENU IDEAS
Serve on Sweet Potato Croquettes (page 35), Jamaican Jerk Tempeh Patties (page 200), enchiladas, falafels, beans and rice, or burgers. Or dip into it with baked tofu, spring rolls, tempura, sweet potato fries . . . you name it.

Pesto Rosso

If a blend of assertive Greek olives and richly concentrated tomato appeals to you, you've found your bliss. Toss this pesto with any type of pasta for a satisfying vegan meal. It's also good topped with small dollops of chèvre or sprinklings of another soft, fresh cheese.

Yields about 1½ cups
Time: 15 minutes

¾ cup lightly packed sun-dried tomatoes
¼ cup almonds
2 garlic cloves, minced or pressed
⅓ cup pitted Mediterranean black and/or green
    olives
⅔ cup chopped fresh tomatoes★
3 tablespoons extra-virgin olive oil
Salt and freshly ground black pepper

★Simply chop plum tomatoes or grape tomatoes, but if you use a regular tomato, before chopping it, halve it and scoop out most of the seeds and some of the juice. You don't have to be too thorough, just get most of the seeds out for a firmer pesto.

Soak the sun-dried tomatoes in boiling water to cover for 10 minutes and then drain.

Whirl the almonds in the bowl of a food processor until chopped. Add the garlic, olives, fresh tomatoes, and soaked and drained sun-dried tomatoes to the processor. Pulse until all the ingredients are well chopped. While the processor blade is whirling, add the oil in a steady stream and process until the pesto is fairly smooth. Season with salt and pepper to taste.

SERVING AND MENU IDEAS
Toss the pesto with pasta and garnish with a chiffonade of basil and/or finely chopped fresh parsley. Spread some on crostini and top with a slice of fresh mozzarella. Add some to mayonnaise for flavorful sandwich enrichment. Make a pizza (see Pizza Rosso e Verde, page 271).

Power Pesto

What we have here is a nutritious pesto recipe that features healthful greens along with protein from nuts. We all need recipes that can be thrown together in an instant, so to make this even more convenient, look for a packaged blend of baby spinach, kale, and chard. Any combination of dark greens will do; if you have a garden full of greens, just pick your favorites and power up the pesto!

If you leave out the cheese, this pesto will freeze quite well. Cheese can be added at serving time.

Yields 1½ cups
Time: 15 minutes

4 cups packed baby spinach, kale, and chard★
½ cup toasted chopped walnuts or almonds, or toasted pine nuts
2 large garlic cloves, minced or pressed
¾ cup grated Parmesan cheese (or ½ cup Parmesan and ¼ cup Pecorino Romano)
¼ cup extra-virgin olive oil
½ teaspoon salt

★A 5-ounce package of "power blend" or "deep green blend" is just right.

In a food processor, whirl half of the greens so that you can then fit in the rest of the greens and all the other ingredients. Add the remaining greens and the nuts, garlic, cheese, oil, and salt. Whirl to a rough paste. If you prefer a smoother pesto, don't add the oil with the other ingredients. Rather, after you have a rough paste, with the machine running, add the olive oil in a steady stream and process until the mixture is smooth.

VARIATIONS
- This recipe can be made vegan by omitting the cheese and increasing the nuts to 1 cup. Add 2 tablespoons each of fresh lemon juice and water.
- The addition of 1 to 2 tablespoons milk or half-and-half mellows the flavor.
- If you want to create an even richer taste, try using grated Fiore Sardo Pecorino for some of the cheese.

SERVING AND MENU IDEAS
This makes enough pesto to generously dress a pound of pasta. It's delicious in a sandwich of roasted vegetables, fresh mozzarella, and tomatoes. Or top Mediterranean-style soups with a dollop. It's also good on a burger, pizza, plain green beans, or new potatoes.

Garlic Greens Pesto

If you've ever grown garlic in your garden, you've noticed the lovely blades of green that spring up in clumps unbidden the next year from last year's self-seeded garlic. Your garlic patch grows and spreads without any help from you. If you don't have a garden, in early spring ask at the farmers' market or your CSA for the greens. These nutrient-rich greens are much milder in flavor than the garlic bulbs that form later, but they still have a hint of the pungent sharpness of garlic, and they make a vivid green pesto that satisfies our bodies' cravings for fresh plant life in early spring.

Yields 1¼ cups
Time: 10 minutes

2 cups lightly packed snipped or sliced garlic
   greens
½ cup extra-virgin olive oil
½ cup chopped toasted walnuts
Pinch of salt
½ cup grated Pecorino Romano or Parmesan
   cheese★

★This pesto can be made without cheese. If you're making a batch to freeze, don't include the cheese.

Using scissors or a knife, cut the garlic greens into ½-inch pieces until you have 2 cups, lightly pressed down. In the bowl of a food processor, whirl the greens for about 10 seconds. Add the rest of the ingredients and process to a rough paste. Add a couple tablespoons of water, if needed, to keep things moving.

SERVING AND MENU IDEAS

This recipe makes plenty of pesto for a pound of pasta. Reserve about ½ cup of the hot pasta cooking water to use if necessary to thin the pesto a bit so that it coats the pasta smoothly. Top the pasta with chopped fresh tomatoes and/or cubed fresh mozzarella.

Garlic Greens Pesto is also good spread on pizza or sandwiches or crostini and to give a flavor punch to soups or stews. A little coating of pesto enhances steamed or boiled vegetables, such as green beans, potatoes, cauliflower, and zucchini. To make a delicious dip for crackers and crudités, add a few tablespoons of Greek yogurt to the pesto.

Garlic Scape Pesto

Garlic scapes are the long stems with seed pods that shoot up from the tops of garlic plants in early summer. Their color is springtime green, and the shoots can be thick or thin, curved or corkscrewed, and vary in height. Garlic scapes have a mild garlic fragrance and a mellow garlic flavor. Gardeners prune them so the garlic plant will pour all its energy into forming the bulb and not the seeds. When the scapes are harvested, you'll likely find them at your farmers' market and then you're in for a delicious treat—garlic scape pesto.

Yields about 1½ cups
Time: 20 minutes

¼ cup almonds, toasted
1 cup chopped garlic scapes
1 cup fresh basil leaves
Salt and freshly ground black pepper
⅓ cup olive oil
1 to 2 tablespoons chopped preserved lemon rind
  (page 344, optional)

In the bowl of a food processor, whirl the almonds until coarsely ground. Add the garlic scapes and basil along with a little salt and pepper. With the processor running, slowly pour in the olive oil and purée until well mixed and mostly smooth. Stir in the preserved lemon, if using. Season with additional salt and pepper to taste.

The pesto will keep in the refrigerator for about 2 weeks. Or you can freeze it in small plastic bags for later use. It will keep in the freezer for about 6 months.

SERVING AND MENU IDEAS

This recipe makes plenty for a pound of pasta. Or spread on sandwiches, bruschetta, or crostini. A satisfying simple supper is pesto tossed on whole wheat orzo with a side of sautéed asparagus.

Sos Ti-Malice

There may be as many ways to make *sos Ti-Malice*, the widely popular traditional Haitian hot sauce, as there are Haitian cooks. Many include tomato paste, but here's one of our favorite ways using only fresh tomatoes. We leave the amount of hot peppers up to you. It's a good fresh hot sauce, brightly pungent, piquant, and spicy hot that contrasts well with the mild, savory sweetness of Haitian Rice and Beans (page 263).

Malice is only a name in Spanish. One of the stories about the origin of this hot sauce involves a man named Ti-Malice.

Yields about 2 cups

1 cup chopped onions
2 garlic cloves, pressed or minced
1 to 3 habanero, Scotch bonnet, jalapeño, or other fresh hot pepper*
1 fresh tomato, chopped
2 tablespoons olive oil
½ teaspoon salt
¼ teaspoon freshly ground black pepper
1 tablespoon apple cider vinegar
2 tablespoons fresh lime or lemon juice
1½ cups water

*How many depends on how hot you like it and how hot your particular peppers are. Remove the stems, remove the seeds (or don't, if you like it fiery), and chop.

In a food processor, whirl the onions, garlic, hot peppers, and tomato until there are no large pieces and the mixture is smooth but not fully puréed. In a saucepan, warm the oil on medium-high heat. Carefully add the purée. Add the salt and black pepper, stir for a minute, and cook, uncovered, on low heat for about 15 minutes, or until very soft. Stir frequently, and if too much liquid evaporates and it's in danger of sticking or browning, add a little water. When the onions and peppers are very soft, but not browned, add the vinegar, lime juice, and water. Simmer, uncovered, for 10 to 15 minutes.

Cool to room temperature. The sauce will keep, refrigerated, in a well-covered container up to a week.

SUGGESTIONS FOR USE
Use as you do any hot sauce or salsa: on enchiladas, beans and rice, and scrambled eggs; to dip tortilla chips into; to add extra spark to soups, other sauces, casseroles . . . you get the picture. Once you've had some on hand for a while, you might find yourself making it regularly.

Laura's Spice Rub

Your kitchen will be wonderfully fragrant if you toast and grind whole spices. It takes a little longer than just using purchased ground and roasted spices, but the richness and depth of freshly toasted spices is hard to beat.

It's fitting that we titled this Laura's Spice Rub, and not only because Moosewood's Laura Branca developed it for this cookbook. The Moosewood Collective cooks have done a lot of cooking, tasting, and eating together, in both the restaurant and our home kitchens. Intense and interesting flavor is one of the qualities that Moosewood fans say is what they like about our food. Laura is the queen of "make it more flavorful." She can take a perfectly acceptable, but somewhat ho-hum, stew (or whatever) to the next level, so that we say, "Now that's *really* tasty."

Yields 3 tablespoons
Prep time: 10 minutes; 20 minutes if toasting and grinding the spices from scratch

1 teaspoon ground toasted cumin★
1 teaspoon ground toasted coriander★
½ teaspoon ground toasted fennel seeds★
1 teaspoon smoked paprika★★
⅛ teaspoon ground black pepper
1 teaspoon sugar
1 teaspoon salt
⅛ teaspoon cayenne or roasted cayenne pepper (optional)
1 to 2 teaspoons fresh or dried thyme leaves (optional)

★To toast whole cumin, coriander, and fennel seeds, spread out the seeds on a toaster oven tray and toast at 325°F for 4 to 5 minutes until they begin to darken and become richly aromatic. Or, toast them in a dry skillet for 2 to 3 minutes, tossing or stirring once or twice. Do not allow the seeds to scorch. Grind the toasted seeds in a spice grinder or with a mortar and pestle. At home, many of us label one coffee grinder for spices and another for coffee.

★★Smoked paprika has a distinctive flavor and aroma. It's made of peppers dried by smoking. Available at most supermarkets.

Mix the ground spices with the smoked paprika, black pepper, sugar, and salt. For a hotter flavor, add the cayenne. Stir in thyme if you like its flavor.

A spice jar with a shaker top is an ideal way to store the mix and will allow you to evenly sprinkle on as much as you like.

SUGGESTIONS FOR USE

In this cookbook, we use this spice rub for Spice-Crusted Roasted Carrots (page 294) and Spiced Nuts (page 59). It's also good on other roasted or grilled vegetables, and grilled or baked tofu. The aromatic spices used are favorite seasonings in parts of the Middle East and North Africa.

Za'atar

Za'atar is a spice mixture made of sumac, sesame seeds, and herbs used as a table condiment and in cooking. All over the Middle East and Mediterranean, people bake flatbreads and pitas brushed with olive oil and sprinkled with za'atar. It is used to season roasted vegetables, salads, stews, rice, pasta, and more. A classic simple dish is chickpeas simmered in olive oil, garlic, and za'atar.

Experiment with one or more of the optional additions to find the combination you like best.

Za'atar is commercially available in international foods aisles in well-stocked markets and specialty spice stores.

ZA'ATAR SEASONING MIX WITH DRIED HERBS

This is the traditional za'atar that is used as a condiment—put it on your table and you might find yourself sprinkling it on all sorts of dishes!

Yields ½ cup

¼ cup sumac powder (see sidebar)
3 tablespoons toasted sesame seeds★
2 teaspoons dried thyme
½ teaspoon salt (coarse salt is best)

OPTIONAL ADDITIONS

2 teaspoons dried marjoram
2 teaspoons dried oregano
1 tablespoon ground cumin seeds

★In a dry cast-iron skillet on the stovetop, or on a lightly oiled baking sheet at 350°F in a conventional oven or toaster oven, toast the sesame seeds until fragrant, 2 to 3 minutes.

Mix everything together. Store in a small covered jar at room temperature.

ZA'ATAR WITH FRESH HERBS

The flavor of za'atar made with fresh herbs is more subtle, and nuanced with that brightness that only fresh herbs can lend. The aromatic qualities of fresh thyme and oregano are rounded out in a most delicious way by nutty toasted sesame seeds and lemony sumac.

Yields ¾ cup

¼ cup sumac powder (see sidebar)
2 tablespoons toasted sesame seeds
1 tablespoon minced fresh oregano
½ teaspoon salt (coarse salt is best)

OPTIONAL ADDITIONS

1 tablespoon minced fresh thyme
1 tablespoon minced fresh marjoram

Combine all the ingredients. Za'atar will keep in the refrigerator in a covered jar or in a plastic bag for a week or two.

SUGGESTIONS FOR USE

We use this delightful seasoning in several recipes in this book: Za'atar Yogurt and Cucumber Salad (page 122), Roasted Cauliflower Salad (page 127), Za'atar Pita Chips (page 60), Easy Labneh Dip (page 70).

SUMAC

Sumac powder is ground from the deep red berries of a shrub (*Rhus coriaria*) that grows wild in high plateau areas throughout the Middle East and Mediterranean regions. Sicily is especially known for growing sumac in its wild, rocky lands. Sumac's sour and fruity astringency brings out natural flavors similar to the way salt does. A small sprinkle adds a beautiful maroon-red color to any dish.

You can find sumac powder in the Mediterranean or Middle Eastern sections of supermarkets, or at Middle Eastern markets and specialty foods stores, or online.

The staghorn sumac (*Rhus typhina*) growing in yards and along roadways in North America is a related, but different, plant. It is often seen in beautiful little groves that create a smooth canopy. The red conical fruit (drupes) of staghorn sumac that develop in late summer are sometimes used to make a beverage called "rhus juice," "Indian lemonade," and "sumac tea." This drink is made by soaking the drupes in cool water, rubbing them to extract the essence, straining the liquid through a cotton cloth, and sweetening it.

Gingered Radish Pickles

These crisp little sweet-hot-tangy pickles are easy to make and are ready to eat the next day. The red radish skins turn the brine a lovely pink, and as each day passes, the flavors deepen.

Yields 1 pint
Prep time: 15 to 20 minutes
Pickling time: at least 8 hours

¾ cup rice vinegar
1 tablespoon salt
3 tablespoons sugar
¼ teaspoon crushed red pepper flakes
1 cup sliced red globe radishes (¼-inch-thick rounds)
1 cup sliced white globe radishes (¼-inch-thick rounds)
1 tablespoon peeled and slivered fresh ginger
2 or 3 garlic cloves, sliced

In a small saucepan, bring the vinegar, salt, sugar, and red pepper flakes to a simmer, stirring to dissolve the salt and sugar. Set aside to cool.

Spread the radish slices between paper towels and press lightly to absorb some of the moisture.

Layer the radish slices, ginger, and garlic in a clean pint jar with a lid, packing them densely by shaking the jar and lightly tapping it on a hard surface. Set aside.

When the vinegar mixture is tepid, pour it over the radish mix, topping off with water if needed to cover the radishes. You may need to press down on the radishes to submerge them. Cap the jar and refrigerate for at least 8 hours before serving.

Stored in the refrigerator, these pickles will keep for a month.

VARIATION
Substitute daikon radish for white globe radishes. If the daikon is large, cut it in half lengthwise and then slice into ¼-inch-thick half-moons.

SUGGESTIONS FOR USE
Enjoy these pickles for picnics, with appetizers, or as a condiment with Indian and Asian dishes.

Harissa

This bright vermilion hot chili paste is a traditional Moroccan seasoning. Harissa is aromatic and flavorful, not just hot. The fire-roasted peppers, smoked paprika, and toasted cumin give it smoky undertones.

The dried hot peppers we call for are ones we think are readily available, but if you have other dried red-colored hot peppers you like, use them. We recommend that when you're handling hot peppers you use latex gloves and be careful not to touch your face.

Yields about 2 cups
Time: 45 minutes

2 cups water
3 dried red New Mexico hot peppers or darker red Pulla hot peppers
6 dried àrbol hot peppers (small, bright red)
2 red bell peppers
1 tablespoon crushed garlic
½ teaspoon salt, plus more as needed
¾ teaspoon ground roasted cumin
¾ teaspoon ground coriander
1 teaspoon sweet or smoked paprika
¼ teaspoon ground cinnamon
1 tablespoon fresh lemon juice
2 tablespoons chopped preserved lemon (page 344) or 2 teaspoons lemon zest
⅓ cup extra-virgin olive oil

Bring the water to a boil. Remove the stems and gently squeeze the edges of the dried hot peppers to split them open. Shake out all the seeds and discard. Heat a dry skillet (nonstick is good) and toast the hot peppers for 3 to 5 minutes, until they begin to darken and give off a strong fragrance. Stir or shake to make sure they don't burn. Don't deeply inhale the aroma or you'll irritate your throat and start coughing; it's OK to cover the skillet. Put the toasted hot peppers in a bowl and pour the boiling water over them. Cover the bowl and set aside to soak for 20 to 25 minutes.

Fire-roast the bell peppers on a grill or directly over a stovetop burner until the skins are blackened and blistered. Put them in a bowl, cover, and set aside to steam and cool down. When the peppers have cooled, scrape off the blackened skin and then halve the bell peppers and remove the stems and seeds.

In a food processor or blender, combine the roasted peppers, garlic, salt, spices, lemon juice, preserved lemon or zest, and olive oil. Drain the soaked hot peppers well and add them. Purée until smooth. Add more salt to taste.

Store harissa in a glass jar or bowl with a tight-fitting lid in the refrigerator. The paste thickens as it cools. Each time after you've spooned out some harissa, to preserve it, drizzle a little olive oil on top, cover tightly, and return to the refrigerator.

SUGGESTIONS FOR USE
Add some harissa to any dish that needs a bit of excitement. It can be stirred into soups, stews, sauces, and dips, and drizzled or spooned over vegetables, and used as a garnish.

Monsoon Pickles

These pickles play all over your tongue with their spicy, hot, tangy, citrusy, and salty elements. Their crunch adds a bright surprise to softer textured dishes. You can store them in the refrigerator for at least 2 months.

You can use more or less of each of the sliced vegetables as long as you have about 4 cups altogether.

Yields 1 quart

VEGETABLES
¾ cup sliced carrots
¾ cup thickly sliced sweet onions
¾ cup trimmed and halved green beans
¾ cup thickly sliced red bell peppers
¾ cup trimmed cauliflower florets

PICKLING LIQUID
2 teaspoons vegetable oil
½ teaspoon mustard seeds
½ teaspoon whole black peppercorns, lightly crushed
½ teaspoon coriander seeds, lightly crushed
1 teaspoon cumin seeds
3 or 4 cardamom pods
½ cup water
½ cup fresh lime juice
¾ cup plus 2 tablespoons white vinegar
¼ cup packed light brown sugar
1½ teaspoons salt
3 garlic cloves, sliced
1 (1-inch) piece fresh ginger, peeled and sliced
¼ teaspoon ground turmeric
¼ to ½ teaspoon crushed red pepper flakes

Prepare the vegetables: Parboil the carrots in about a pint boiling water for 30 seconds. Drain and douse with cold water. Put the drained carrots in a large ceramic or stainless steel bowl with the rest of the prepared vegetables.

Make the pickling liquid: Warm the vegetable oil in a small heavy skillet on medium heat. Add the mustard seeds and roast until they pop. Add the peppercorns, coriander, cumin seeds, and cardamom pods and roast for about 30 seconds. Remove from the heat and scrape the spices into a small nonreactive saucepan on medium heat. Add the water and the remaining ingredients to the saucepan and bring to a simmer. Simmer for 2 to 3 minutes.

Pour the hot pickling liquid over the vegetables in the bowl. To keep the vegetables submerged, cover with a plate that fits inside the bowl and if necessary, top the plate with a heavy can. Set aside to cool to room temperature. When cool, pack the pickles into a clean quart glass jar. Fill the jar to the brim with brine and spices, cover with a lid, and refrigerate.

These pickles may be eaten as soon as they are cool, but they develop a richer flavor when marinated for at least 24 hours. They will keep in the refrigerator for at least 2 months.

SUGGESTIONS FOR USE
These are delicious with Indian dishes that echo the spices imbued in the pickles. Try them with sandwiches and as a condiment with mild or medium-sharp cheeses.

Raspberry Vinegar

A fruity and tangy splash of this fragrant, ruby red vinegar will brighten both vegetables and palate.

Yields 1½ cups
Prep time: 15 minutes
Steeping time: 1 week

1 pint raspberries, fresh or frozen
1 cup red wine vinegar

Pack a clean, dry pint jar with a lid with raspberries, but do not crush the berries. Pour the vinegar over the berries, cover the jar, and set aside in a dark place where it will not be disturbed for 1 week or a little longer.

At the end of a week, strain the berries and vinegar through a fine-mesh strainer. Press the berries to release all the liquid, but do not press pulp through the strainer. Discard the berry mash. Pour the vinegar into a clean, dry glass jar with a lid and store as you would other vinegar.

SUGGESTIONS FOR USE

Use raspberry vinegar for making Raspberry-Carrot Pickles (this page) and raspberry dressings and vinaigrettes. As well as being a special addition to salad dressings, raspberry vinegar is great to splash on simply cooked beets, carrots, cabbage, or parsnips or sautéed beet greens or turnip greens.

Raspberry-Carrot Pickles

Quick to make and delicious, these crunchy raspberry-soaked carrot pickles are pretty additions in salads and on hors d'oeuvre plates. They will keep in the fridge for a couple of weeks, but are best if eaten within one week.

Yields 1 pint
Prep time: 20 minutes
Cooling time: about 1 hour

1 quart water
2 cups sliced carrots (⅛-inch-thick rounds)
¾ cup raspberry vinegar (page 340)
1½ teaspoons sugar
¾ teaspoons salt
¼ cup water
3 or 4 slices of lemon peel

Bring a quart of water to a boil. Parboil the carrots for 15 seconds, drain, and place in a heatproof bowl. In a small saucepan, bring the vinegar, sugar, salt, water, and lemon peel to a simmer. When the sugar and salt have dissolved, pour the liquid over the carrots. Cool to room temperature.

Serve right away or store in a covered jar and refrigerate for up to 2 weeks.

SUGGESTIONS FOR USE

These will perk up savory sandwiches and grain salads as well as platters of cheese and crackers.

Pickled Sweet Peppers

This mild, colorful, and tart-sweet pickle is the perfect condiment for a variety of savory dishes, as well as a zesty ingredient in salads and sandwich fillings. In fact, you may find this little "extra" an indispensable ingredient to have on hand. This recipe can be doubled or quadrupled for larger batches.

Yields 1 pint
Prep time: 20 minutes
Cooling time: about 1 hour

2 bell peppers (red, yellow, and/or orange), seeded and cut into wide strips★

2 sprigs fresh thyme, tarragon, or oregano (optional)

½ cup olive oil

½ cup apple cider vinegar

½ teaspoon whole black peppercorns

3 garlic cloves, sliced

2 bay leaves

2 teaspoons salt

3 tablespoons sugar

★You can also use halved mini peppers.

Pack the bell peppers and herb sprigs, if using, into a clean, dry pint jar with a lid.

Heat the oil, vinegar, peppercorns, garlic, bay leaves, salt, and sugar in a nonreactive saucepan and simmer for 2 minutes. Pour this hot brine over the peppers. The brine should cover the peppers; if it doesn't, squeeze in another pepper strip or two. Put the lid on the jar. Allow the peppers to cool at room temperature and then refrigerate.

The pickled peppers will be ready to eat the next day and will keep in the refrigerator for about 3 months. Olive oil coagulates when cold, so before using, remove the jar from the refrigerator and allow the olive oil to warm to room temperature.

SUGGESTIONS FOR USE

A simple everyday sandwich like cheese and mayo will transcend the usual with chopped pickled sweet peppers. Use as a colorful and perky garnish on savory dishes that need a bit of a lift.

Giardiniera

A jar of this colorful array of pickled vegetables is pretty enough to give as a gift. These pickles are always part of the antipasto platters served in American Italian restaurants. The recipe is easy and it's a good way to use up small amounts of raw vegetables that may be left over from other recipes—a pepper half, single carrot, chunk of cauliflower, wedge of onion—pieces that might otherwise die in the fridge.

We decided to modify this classic by tilting its flavor decidedly toward fennel and by using more mellow white wine vinegar in place of the standard white vinegar. Or try white balsamic vinegar for an even sweeter pickle.

Yields 1 quart
Prep time: 45 minutes, plus 10 to 15 minutes to cool the brine
Pickling time: at least 3 hours

A mix of vegetables to fill 4 cups; we suggest:
1 cup cauliflower florets
1 cup green beans (cut into 2-inch pieces)
¾ cup sliced carrots (½-inch-thick coins)
½ cup thinly sliced red bell peppers
½ cup thinly sliced fresh fennel
¼ cup thinly sliced red onions
3 garlic cloves, smashed
1 sprig fresh rosemary

BRINE
1 teaspoon fennel seeds
1 teaspoon whole black peppercorns
¼ teaspoon crushed red pepper flakes
1½ cups white wine vinegar
1 cup water
1 tablespoon sugar
½ tablespoon coarse salt

Bring a large pot of water to a boil. Parboil the cauliflower, green beans, and carrots separately just until they can first be pierced with a fork, about 4 minutes. Remember, this is a crisp pickle. When each vegetable is done, use a slotted spoon or skimmer to transfer it to a bowl of ice water, swirl to cool, and then spoon into a dry bowl. Add the bell peppers, fresh fennel, red onions, garlic, and rosemary to the bowl of cooked vegetables and stir gently to combine. Pack the vegetables into a clean glass quart jar.

Make the brine: In a small dry skillet, toast the fennel seeds and peppercorns until aromatic, 1 to 2 minutes, and transfer to a small nonreactive saucepan. Add the red pepper flakes, vinegar, water, sugar, and salt and bring to a boil. Lower the heat and simmer for 3 minutes. Cool the brine completely; 10 to 15 minutes in the freezer will do the trick.

Pour the cooled brine over the jarred vegetables, making sure to include the fennel seeds or peppercorns. If you have more brine than you need, strain it and add the seeds to the jar.

Tightly cover the jar and refrigerate. Giardiniera is ready in about 3 hours, but gets even better with time. Refrigerated, it will keep for 4 weeks.

VARIATION

If you prefer a crunchier pickle, don't parboil the vegetables. Pack them in the jar raw and pour the hot brine over them. Leave the jar open until cooled to room temperature. Cover with a tight lid and refrigerate.

SUGGESTIONS FOR USE

Perfect as part of a Mediterranean platter of roasted vegetables, olives, dips or spreads, and chunks of coarse bread or wedges of pita. Use as a contrasting, attractive side for any rich entrée. Top a green salad with Gorgonzola or other blue cheese, chèvre, or feta and these pickles.

Tomatillo Pickles

Last summer Moosewood partner Joan Adler started three small tomatillo plants, never imagining the vitality and fertility of those unassuming seedlings. By summer's end she was trawling every food medium imaginable for ways to use tomatillos. Initial castings about landed her in the world of pickles. After trying a few recipes, she struck out on her own to produce a simple, clean-tasting pickle with tones of coriander and lime. She aced it, and here's her recipe.

It takes at least 12 hours in the brine for the flavor to saturate these tomatillo pickles, but assembling is so easy that you can pop them into the fridge the night before or even in the early morning of an evening meal. Use these pickles as a tart little counterpoint to creamy, milder dishes.

Yields 1 pint
Prep time: 15 minutes
Pickling time: at least 12 hours

½ pound fresh firm tomatillos
6 sprigs fresh cilantro
½ teaspoon coriander seeds
3 garlic cloves, smashed
1 or 2 strips of lime peel★
½ small fresh jalapeño hot pepper, seeded for
    milder "hot" (optional)
⅓ cup white wine vinegar, plus more as needed
⅓ cup water, plus more as needed
¾ teaspoon salt
¾ teaspoon sugar

★We use a potato peeler to shave a shallow strip of peel about 2 inches long and ½ inch wide. Be careful not to cut too deeply, because the white pith can be bitter.

Have a clean pint jar with a lid ready.

Remove the papery husks of the tomatillos. Rinse the tomatillos and cut them into wedges ¾ to 1 inch thick. Put the cilantro sprigs and the coriander seeds in the bottom of the jar. Closely pack the tomatillo wedges into the jar, inserting the garlic cloves between the wedges and the lime peel and jalapeño along the inside wall of the jar.

In a small bowl, combine the vinegar, water, salt, and sugar. Whisk until the salt and sugar dissolve. Pour the mixture into the jar of tomatillos. Top off with equal amounts of water and vinegar. Cover tightly, invert once or twice, and refrigerate. These pickles are ready in 12 hours. They'll keep in the refrigerator for up to 4 weeks.

SUGGESTIONS FOR USE

Serve with any dish in the Hispanic canon. They are particularly suited to creamy enchiladas, stuffed chilies, frittatas, and tortillas. To add zing and interest, chop them into a salsa, pico de gallo, or guacamole, or sprinkle on top of tostadas in place of tomatoes.

Spiced Preserved Lemons

Preserved lemons, a common ingredient in North African dishes, make their salty, tangy, citrusy presence into many cuisines around the globe. Kip Wilcox first tasted this delicious condiment in a mouthwatering tagine served at Flor da Laranja, a small Moroccan bistro in Lisbon, where the lively and intrepid restaurateur, Rabea Esserghini, gave her a tour of her tiny kitchen. There, perched above the counter, was Rabea's jar of homemade preserved lemons, which she added liberally to many of her signature dishes.

Preserved lemons can be found in the international section of well-stocked supermarkets and specialty stores, and they are quite pricey. However, they can be easily prepared at home, cured for 4 to 6 weeks, and kept in the refrigerator for 6 months or longer.

Use organic lemons with thin rinds for quicker curing.

Yields 1 quart
Prep time: 20 minutes
Special equipment: quart canning jar

2 teaspoons coriander seeds
2 teaspoons cumin seeds
2 teaspoons fennel seeds
1 teaspoon whole black peppercorns
4 to 6 organic lemons★
¼ cup kosher salt
3 bay leaves
1 to 2 cups fresh lemon juice (from 6 to 8 lemons)

★Thin-skinned lemons work best. According to the size, use the number needed to fill the canning jar.

Wash a quart canning jar and lid in very hot soapy water, rinse with boiling water, and set aside to drain.

In a small heavy skillet on medium heat, toast the coriander, cumin, fennel, and peppercorns for about a minute. While the spices cool, quarter the lemons, leaving the stems intact. Briefly grind the cooled spices in a spice grinder, just to crush (not to a powder) and then mix with the salt. Cover the lemons with the spice-salt mixture and press them into the jar so that some of the juice emerges. Slide the bay leaves into the jar alongside the lemons.

Pour lemon juice over the salted lemons until they are covered. The amount will vary according to the size and juiciness of the lemons. Cap and store in a dark, cool place.

Shake the jar several times a week for 4 to 6 weeks. The salt will extract juice from the lemons and soften the rinds. After 4 weeks, taste a snippet of lemon. Cured lemons should be soft and pliable throughout the rind: "cured."

Refrigerate the preserved lemons and use within 6 months.

SUGGESTIONS FOR USE

To use, remove the fruit from the rind and add chopped preserved lemon rind to spreads and dips ranging from hummus to simple cheese spreads. Add to grain dishes like tabouli or pilafs, as well as soups, stews, and sauces. In dishes that are cooked, Spiced Preserved Lemons have more "punch" when added just a few minutes before finishing, but will still add flavor if simmered for a while.

Cashew-Coconut Butter

Cashew-Coconut Butter is easily made with a food processor. We want the flavor of freshly roasted nuts to shine through, so there's only a modest amount of spices. When you taste the nut butter while it's being processed, add more spices to your taste.

Enjoy this butter just as you would peanut butter—on bread or toast, or with fruit. Nut butter should be refrigerated if not eaten within a few hours. Cold nut butter is hard to spread; try brief microwaving, about 20 seconds, just to soften and make it spreadable, but not cooked.

Yields 1 cup
Time: 15 minutes

1¼ cups cashews
⅓ cup unsweetened shredded coconut
¼ teaspoon salt
1 tablespoon agave syrup
1½ tablespoons coconut oil
1 tablespoon water
¼ teaspoon coconut extract (optional)
¼ teaspoon ground ginger (optional)

Preheat a conventional or toaster oven to 350°F. Place the cashews on a baking sheet in a single layer and bake until lightly browned, but not too dark, 7 to 12 minutes. The timing also depends on whether the nuts are whole or chopped.

Whirl the cashews in the bowl of a food processor until they're finely chopped. Add the coconut, salt, agave syrup, coconut oil, water, and the coconut extract and ginger, if using. Continue to process until the nut butter is fairly smooth, but still has some texture.

SUGGESTIONS FOR USE
Cashew-Coconut Butter is good on graham crackers and dabbed on fruit such as strawberries, pineapple chunks, and mango. Or make a sandwich with thin apple slices. Spread it on toast at breakfast with a Sweet Fruit Smoothie (page 24) or at lunch with Chilled Pineapple-Mango Soup (page 104).

Simple Seasoned Tofu

This is such a useful, tried-and-true recipe that we're reprinting it unrevised from *Moosewood Restaurant Favorites*. When these tasty little nuggets are around, people can't resist coming back again and again to help themselves to a salty, savory protein fix—and we're talking both at the restaurant and at home—so we're confident saying that it's a great snack. We put seasoned tofu on stir-fries, salads, stews, pasta, sandwiches . . . everything!

We make it both in the oven and on the stovetop; each method is useful and produces different results. At the restaurant, we usually bake tofu because we make a lot of it and we like the chewy skin it gets in the convection oven. That can also be achieved in a regular oven. But if it's hot outside, or you don't want to turn the oven on, try the faster pan-fried method.

You can serve seasoned tofu hot, cold, or at room temperature. The basic marinade is fine alone, but one or two additional options are great, too. We're fond of adding chili paste and fresh grated ginger to baked tofu. Young folks love a ketchup version (big surprise!). The tofu can be made soft, moist, chewy, or crisp, depending on the heat, timing, and which marinade you choose.

Serves 4
Prep time: 10 minutes
Baking time: 30 to 60 minutes
Stovetop time: 10 to 15 minutes

1 (14- to 16-ounce) block firm tofu, pressed or not

BASIC MARINADE

1 tablespoon vegetable oil, plus more for the pan
1 tablespoon dark sesame oil
3 tablespoons soy sauce
¼ cup oil, for frying (optional)

OPTIONAL ADDITIONS

1 tablespoon peeled and grated fresh ginger
2 teaspoons Chinese chili paste or Tabasco
2 tablespoons ketchup
2 tablespoons fresh lemon juice
1 tablespoon white or apple cider vinegar
1 to 2 tablespoons minced chipotles in adobo sauce (omit the sesame oil and increase the vegetable oil to 2 tablespoons)

Baked Tofu: Preheat a conventional oven to 400°F, convection to 375°F. Lightly oil a baking pan large enough to hold the tofu in a single layer; 9 inch square, 7 x 9-inch, 9 x 11-inch, and 9 x 13-inch pans all work well.

Cut the tofu into cubes, triangles, or strips. In the baking pan, stir together the marinade ingredients. Put the tofu pieces in the baking pan and gently turn to thoroughly coat with the marinade. Bake, uncovered, until firm, browned, and chewy. To expose all sides to the hot air, turn gently every 10 to 15 minutes. It will take 30 to 60 minutes, depending on the size of the tofu pieces and how browned and chewy you like it.

Pan-Fried Tofu: Cut the tofu into small cubes, about ¾ inch. Mix together the marinade. Use a 10-inch or larger skillet or other heavy-bottomed pan.

For crisp tofu nuggets, heat oil on medium-high heat. Add the tofu cubes and cook for 6 to 7 minutes, stirring every minute or so. Add sesame oil and soy sauce and any other marinade ingredients (except more oil) and stir well. Cook, stirring frequently, for a couple of minutes.

To make softer tofu cubes, marinate the tofu cubes for 5 minutes or longer. Warm about 2 tablespoons of oil in the skillet on medium-high heat. When the oil is warm, add the tofu and marinade and cook, stirring often, for 10 to 15 minutes, until the tofu is firm and browned. Depending on your skillet, you may need to lower the heat after a couple of minutes.

NOTE: Unless you are using a nonstick skillet and lower heat, we don't recommend adding grated ginger or ketchup to pan-fried tofu until the last couple of minutes because it may scorch.

SERVING AND MENU IDEAS

Just a sample of dishes that Simple Seasoned Tofu would nicely accompany: Nori Rolls with Kale and Egg (page 38), Scallion Crepes with Chinese Greens (page 186), Sugar Snap Peas with Coconut and Lime (page 113), Mediterranean Potato Salad (page 124), Asian Filo Rolls (page 198), Basmati Rice Pilaf (page 318).

Moosewood's Gluten-Free All-Purpose Flour Mix

Peanut-Ginger Cookies

Easy Lemon Butter Cookies

Cardamom Cookies with Bittersweet Chocolate Drizzle

Espresso Shortbread

Orange-Oatmeal Cookies with Dark Chocolate Chips

Sara's Surprise Chickpea Brownies

Turkish Coffee Brownies

Whole-Grain Blondies

Our Favorite Chocolate Cake

Fresh Ginger Gingerbread

Lemon-Zucchini Cake with Thyme

Orange-Pistachio Cornmeal Cake

Cherry Tomato Upside-Down Cake

Texas Italian Cream Cake

Erma Mabel's Rhubarb Cake

Fresh Pineapple Upside-Down Cake

Pumpkin Cheesecake

Orange-Carrot-Almond Torte

Piecrust

Apple and Fig Galette with Rosemary

Custard and Pear Pie

Apricot Frangipane Tart

Vegan Apple-Blueberry Crumble

Coconut Rice Pudding with Mangoes

Rich Vegan Chocolate Pudding

Tropical Bread Pudding

Coconut-Pineapple Sorbet

Date-Walnut Shake

Moosewood's Gluten-Free All-Purpose Flour Mix

You can buy several ready-made gluten-free flour mixtures in supermarkets, but we've had the best results with this unique combo developed by Moosewood dessert maker, John Lenz. We use this mix in our gluten-free pastries, and we can proudly say that they don't have the sandy mouthfeel that many gluten-free cakes, cookies, and breads do. You can substitute this flour mix in most recipes calling for wheat flour.

3 cups white rice flour
3 cups brown rice flour
3 cups potato starch
3 cups tapioca flour

Stir all the ingredients together well until evenly distributed. Store the mix in a cool, dry place in a closed canister or plastic bag. Keeps best refrigerated or frozen.

NOTE: Xanthan gum (or ground chia seeds or flaxseeds) is used in much gluten-free baking because it adds a binding, thickening, emulsifying quality to the dough or batter. We don't add it to our flour mix because each recipe using a gluten-free flour mix is different. In this book, Our Favorite Chocolate Cake (page 361) calls for xanthan gum, Fresh Pineapple Upside-Down Cake (page 369) includes chia seeds or flaxseeds, and Texas Italian Cream Cake (page 367) and Erma Mabel's Fresh Rhubarb Cake (page 368) have neither.

Peanut-Ginger Cookies

These cookies are lightly sweet with a roasted peanut flavor and surprising little hits of ginger. These mounded peanut cookies (after baking from a ball to start) are quite delicate and tender with a crumbly texture.

Yields at least 24 to 32 cookies, depending upon how you portion the dough
Prep time: 20 minutes
Baking time: 20 minutes

2 cups roasted peanuts
½ to 1 teaspoon salt (less if the roasted peanuts are salted)
1¼ cups packed brown sugar
2 cups unbleached white all-purpose flour
¾ teaspoon baking soda
1 large egg
1 tablespoon dark sesame oil
¾ cup vegetable oil
⅓ cup minced crystallized ginger (3.5 ounces)
24 to 32 whole peanuts, for topping each cookie

Preheat the oven to 325°F. Line two baking sheets with parchment paper.

In a food processor, pulse the peanuts for just a few seconds, until the texture of coarse crumbs. Add the salt and brown sugar and pulse again briefly, until the texture of fine crumbs. Don't overprocess or you'll make peanut butter.

Put the flour and baking soda into a mixing bowl and stir until well combined. Add the peanut mixture and stir to incorporate.

In a small bowl, beat the egg with a fork. Add the dark sesame oil and vegetable oil and mix together. Stir in the minced crystallized ginger. Add the wet ingredients to the dry ingredients and mix until the dough has the texture of wet sand.

Using a small scoop or a soupspoon, dish out rounded 2-tablespoon portions of dough for each cookie. In your hand, squeeze the portions of the cookie dough together to form balls about 1½ inches in diameter. Place on the prepared baking sheets. Lightly press a whole peanut (or a half) into the top. If the raw cookie crumbles, just press it back together on the baking sheet (in a sort of dome shape).

Bake the cookies for about 20 minutes until browned and dry looking. Let sit for a couple of minutes on the baking sheets before removing with a spatula.

SERVING AND MENU IDEAS

Sandies-type cookies like this are at their best served with a hot beverage.

Peanut-Ginger Cookies are excellent little sweet treats after an Asian or Southeast Asian meal.

Easy Lemon Butter Cookies

One really nice thing about Moosewood is that we often hear from lots of people: people who have our cookbooks, people who used to live in Ithaca or work at Moosewood, people who have simply noticed our website. Sometimes they tell us about a new restaurant or a new cookbook they've discovered, or they just talk about food, but best of all is when someone sends a recipe they think we should try—and usually they're right. This recipe came to us from longtime friend and talented cook David Gershan, who lives in San Francisco.

We pass it on to you because it makes a simple, homey butter cookie that is very easily and quickly made in a food processor. A log of this cookie dough can wait in the freezer for a couple of weeks until the perfect time comes along for an almost instant warm and fragrant batch of cookies.

Yields 24 cookies
Prep time: 15 minutes
Chilling time: at least 30 minutes
Baking time: 18 to 22 minutes

2 cups flour (pastry flour preferred)
1 cup confectioners' sugar
1 cup (2 sticks) butter, at room temperature
½ teaspoon salt
Finely grated zest of 1 lemon
2 teaspoons pure vanilla extract
½ cup raisins

Place all the ingredients except the raisins in the bowl of a food processor. Process until a dough forms, about 30 seconds. Add the raisins and process for just a couple of seconds to distribute them evenly. Lay a 20-inch length of waxed paper on the countertop. Scrape the dough out of the processor bowl along one of the long sides of the waxed paper and form a log about 14 inches long and 2½ inches in diameter. Roll up the log in the paper and twist the ends closed. Place in the freezer to firm up for at least a half hour (or up to 2 weeks, tightly wrapped).

Preheat the oven to 325°F. Line a baking sheet or two with parchment paper.

Carefully unwrap the log of chilled dough; if the log has been in the freezer for days, give it a few minutes to warm slightly. Cut the log into ½-inch rounds; you should get about 24 slices. Place the rounds flat on the prepared baking sheet(s) at least 2 inches apart. Bake for 18 to 22 minutes until the edges of the cookies are brown and the centers are firm. Using a spatula, transfer the cookies to a wire rack or the countertop to cool.

VARIATIONS
- Add 2 tablespoons cornmeal to the flour.
- Try using orange zest instead of lemon, and dried cranberries instead of raisins.
- Use almond extract instead of vanilla, and chopped dried apricots instead of raisins.
- Add ¼ cup finely chopped candied ginger instead of dried fruit.

Cardamom Cookies with Bittersweet Chocolate Drizzle

Made in the tradition of "slice 'n bake," these spicy, crisp, not-too-sweet cookies topped with a Jackson Pollock drizzle of bittersweet chocolate can be eaten up immediately, stored for several days in an airtight container, or frozen. The dough can be made ahead and kept in the fridge for up to a week before baking.

Yields about 48 cookies
Prep time: 20 minutes
Chilling time: at least 1 hour
Baking time: 25 minutes

¾ cup (1½ sticks) butter, at room temperature
¾ cup sugar
2 large eggs
1 teaspoon pure vanilla extract
1 teaspoon cardamom seeds, freshly ground
½ teaspoon ground cinnamon
½ teaspoon whole black peppercorns, freshly ground
2 cups unbleached white all-purpose flour
½ teaspoon salt
4 ounces bittersweet chocolate

In a large bowl, beat the butter until fluffy. Add the sugar and continue to beat until light and soft. Add the eggs, vanilla, cardamom, cinnamon, and pepper and beat until creamy.

In a separate bowl, sift together the flour and salt. Add the flour to the butter mixture in three additions, mixing briefly after each. Scrape the dough onto a countertop, divide in half, and roll into two logs, each about 8 inches long and 1½ inches in diameter. Wrap with plastic wrap and refrigerate for at least 1 hour or up to a week.

When you're ready to bake, preheat the oven to 350°F. Line two baking sheets with parchment paper. Cut the dough into ¼-inch-thick slices and arrange on the baking sheets. Bake until golden around the edges, about 25 minutes. Transfer the cookies to a wire rack to cool.

In a small heatproof bowl over a pan of hot water (or in a double boiler), melt the chocolate. Drizzle the melted chocolate over the cookies. Allow the chocolate to cool and harden before storing the cookies in an airtight container.

Espresso Shortbread

Buttery shortbread has a unique, homey charm that satisfies so nicely. The optional topping adds some chocolate to the espresso flavor of the light brown, crisp cookies. . . . What could be bad? Our food processor method is easy, and no rolling of the dough is required.

Yields twenty-four 2-inch squares
Prep time: 30 minutes
Baking time: 25 to 30 minutes
Cooling and cutting time: 10 minutes cooling;
  5 minutes to cut

1 cup (2 sticks) unsalted butter, at room
  temperature
½ cup sugar
½ teaspoon salt
2 tablespoons espresso powder, dissolved in
  1 teaspoon hot water
1 teaspoon pure vanilla extract
2¼ cups unbleached white all-purpose flour
⅔ cup bittersweet chocolate chips or chunks
  (optional)

Preheat the oven to 350°F. Line a baking sheet or 9 x 13-inch baking pan with parchment paper. Or, if the pan is heavy, it will be fine bare and unoiled.

Whip the softened butter in the bowl of a food processor for a minute, then add the sugar, salt, dissolved espresso powder, and vanilla. Continue to process for a couple of minutes until the mixture is fluffy. Add the flour all at once and pulse briefly. Using a flexible spatula, scrape down any butter stuck to the sides and bottom of the processor bowl. Pulse until the dough is uniform in consistency, but do not overmix.

Scrape the dough onto the baking sheet or pan and press it into a rectangle about 8 x 12 inches and no more than ¼ inch thick. Using your fingertips, push the dough to an even thickness and tidy the edges so they aren't ragged or thin. Bake for 25 to 30 minutes until the shortbread is just firm and the edges are beginning to darken a bit.

Place the baking sheet on a wire rack and allow the shortbread to cool for about 10 minutes. Using a thin, sharp knife, cut the shortbread into 24 pieces (4 rows of 6). Don't wait too long to cut; do it while the shortbread is warm, or it will become too brittle to cut nicely. Separate the pieces and place them on a rack to cool completely.

If you'd like a topping, melt the chocolate in a small pan or a microwave. Stir well. Spoon a little dollop onto each cooled cookie.

Store the shortbread in an airtight container.

SERVING AND MENU IDEAS

Enjoy shortbread with tea, coffee, or hot chocolate and you may feel positively "Jane Austenish." Or serve them for high tea along with Kip's Favorite Scones (page 31) and/or Radish and Herbed Chèvre Spread (page 69) on crustless bread.

Orange-Oatmeal Cookies with Dark Chocolate Chips

Moosewood partner Dave Dietrich, who single-handedly repairs everything at Moosewood, includes in his job description quality control over cookies. Though he's not highly discriminating when it comes to cookies, this is one of his favorites; a rather compelling version of good old oatmeal cookies. At Moosewood we make large cookies to qualify as dessert or a takeaway snack, but you can make them smaller (and eat more) if you prefer.

**Yields about 30 large cookies (or about sixty
  3-inch cookies)**
Prep time: 25 minutes
Baking time: 15 to 20 minutes per batch

2 cups (4 sticks) butter, at room temperature,
  plus more for the pans
1 cup granulated sugar
1 cup packed brown sugar
2 large eggs
Finely grated zest of 3 oranges
⅔ cup fresh orange juice
1 tablespoon orange extract
4 cups unbleached white all-purpose flour
1 teaspoon salt
1 teaspoon baking powder
1 teaspoon baking soda
2 cups rolled oats
3 cups dark chocolate chips or chunks

Preheat the oven to 350°F. Lightly butter baking sheets or coat them with cooking spray.

In a large bowl, thoroughly cream the butter, granulated sugar, and brown sugar. Add the eggs, orange zest, orange juice, and orange extract and beat well. In a separate bowl, stir together the flour, salt, baking powder, and baking soda. Add the flour mixture along with the oats to the mixing bowl and blend well. Fold in the chocolate chips.

Drop ping-pong-ball-size clumps of dough onto the baking sheets, placing them several inches apart. Using the palm of your hand, flatten each piece of dough slightly. Bake until golden, 15 to 20 minutes (less time for smaller cookies).

Using a spatula, transfer the cookies to a wire rack. Cool completely before storing in an airtight container.

SERVING AND MENU IDEAS
These are quite sturdy cookies, so they are good for picnics and lunch boxes and for packing into tins and mailing off to faraway friends.

Sara's Surprise Chickpea Brownies

Moosewood's Sara Robbins's brownies are yummy and as easy as can be. The flourless brownie batter is mixed together in a blender in under 5 minutes and then baked for 30 minutes. What holds it all together? Eggs and . . . chickpeas!

Yields one 9-inch pan of brownies
Prep time: 10 minutes
Baking time: 30 minutes

Butter, for the pan
4 large eggs
1 (15-ounce) can chickpeas, drained and rinsed
1 cup sugar
1 teaspoon pure vanilla extract
½ teaspoon salt
1 teaspoon baking powder
1½ cups semisweet chocolate chips or bits

Preheat the oven to 350°F. Butter an 8 inch square or 9 inch round baking pan.

Blend the eggs, chickpeas, and sugar in a blender until smooth. Add the vanilla, salt, baking powder, and chocolate chips. Blend everything together until smooth and thoroughly mixed. The batter should be chocolaty brown.

Pour the batter into the prepared pan and bake for about 30 minutes, or until a knife inserted into the center comes out clean. Do not overbake.

Turkish Coffee Brownies

These easy-to-make brownies are not too sweet and have a marked dark chocolate presence with a jolt of espresso.

Moosewood kids, siblings, nieces, nephews, and, for some time now, grandchildren have developed deep attachments to Moosewood. Back in the early '70s, partner Joanie Adler's much younger sister, Melanie, spent a lot of her middle school and high school breaks with her big sister in the Moosewood kitchen. After each shift, with no parent in sight, Joanie would indulge her with a big brownie à la mode. This recipe is dedicated to Mel, who has never stopped eating brownies, and has gone on to become an accomplished baker specializing in all things chocolate—and who even served chocolate milk at her wedding!

Yields 16 squares
Prep time: 20 minutes
Baking time: 25 to 30 minutes

½ cup (1 stick) butter, plus more for the pan
⅔ cup unbleached white all-purpose flour, plus more for the pan
3½ ounces dark chocolate (72% or 85% cacao)
3 large eggs
¾ cup packed brown sugar
2 teaspoons instant espresso powder
½ teaspoon ground cinnamon
1 teaspoon pure vanilla extract
½ teaspoon salt
⅔ cup chocolate chips

Preheat the oven to 325°F. Butter an 8-inch square baking pan and dust with cocoa or flour.

In a small saucepan, melt the butter. Turn off the heat and add the dark chocolate.

Meanwhile, in a bowl, whisk together the eggs and brown sugar. Stir in the espresso powder, cinnamon, vanilla, and salt. Stir in the flour until the batter is evenly colored. Stir the melted butter and chocolate to combine, and then stir it into the batter.

Pour the batter into the prepared baking pan and bake for 25 to 30 minutes until firm and pulling away slightly from the sides of the pan. As with other brownies, if you like your brownies moist and fudgy, remove from the oven while the center is still shiny, and if you like drier cakey brownies, give it a few more minutes in the oven, until a knife inserted into the center really does come out not gooey.

Sprinkle the chocolate chips evenly over the top of the hot brownies. Place the pan on a wire rack to cool. After about 5 minutes, using a spatula or the back of a spoon, spread the melted chocolate chips over the top. When cool, cut into 16 squares.

SERVING AND MENU IDEAS

Turkish Coffee Brownies are a fine dessert after a Middle Eastern meal, such as Smoky Split Pea Soup (page 96), Quinoa Tabouli with Pomegranates and Pistachios (page 145), or Middle Eastern Grain Bowl (page 152). Or, these intense chocolate and coffee treats are perfect at the end of an adult pizza party, after Pizza with Roasted Eggplant and Plum Tomatoes (page 274) and Pizza with Greens (page 275).

Whole-Grain Blondies

Chewy, butterscotchy, full of little bits of fruit, nuts, and chocolate, *and* whole-grain . . . what's not to like? In this recipe, the butter is melted and then cooled; it's most efficient to prep the chopped fruit and nuts while waiting for it to cool.

Yields 16 to 24 squares
Prep time: 15 minutes
Baking time: 20 minutes

½ cup (1 stick) butter, plus more for the pan
1 cup packed light brown sugar
2 cups chopped nuts, dried fruit, and/or
  chocolate★
1½ cups whole wheat white flour
1 teaspoon baking powder
½ teaspoon salt
2 large eggs
2 tablespoons pure vanilla extract

★Dried fruit such as figs, dates, apricots, or mangoes, cut into small pieces; raisins or dried cranberries, whole or roughly chopped; coconut flakes. Nuts such as walnuts, pecans, almonds, hazelnuts, or salted roasted peanuts, chopped. Bittersweet, dark, or white chocolate in chunks or chips. (See Variations for our favorite combinations.)

Preheat the oven to 350°F. Butter, oil, or spray a 9 x 13-inch baking pan.

In a small saucepan on medium heat, melt the butter, swirling often, until it begins to brown. Pour the hot butter into a mixing bowl and stir in the brown sugar until moistened. Set aside to cool. Combine the chopped fruit, nuts, and/or chocolate and set aside. In a separate bowl, whisk or stir together the flour, baking powder, and salt to evenly distribute.

When the butter-sugar mixture has cooled, add the eggs and vanilla and beat until smooth. Add the flour mixture and beat just until well combined; the batter will be quite stiff. Set aside about ⅓ cup of the chopped fruit, nuts, and/or chocolate, and fold the rest into the batter. Spread the batter into the prepared baking pan. Sprinkle the reserved fruit-nuts-chocolate pieces on top.

Bake for 20 to 22 minutes until turning brown around the edges and a bit puffy in the middle. Remove the pan from the oven and put it on a wire rack to cool. The blondies will firm up as they cool. When cool, cut into 16 to 24 squares or bars.

VARIATIONS
Our favorite blondie additions:
  • chopped figs and pecans with bittersweet
    chocolate chunks
  • chopped toasted cashews and dried mango
    with coconut flakes
  • chopped walnuts and dark chocolate chips

SERVING AND MENU IDEAS
Whole-Grain Blondies are welcome at the end of many casual meals. Try them with Mexican Toasted Cheese Sandwich (page 84), Italian Cheese Broth (page 94), or Middle Eastern Grain Bowl (page 152). Pack them in the kids' lunch boxes for a special treat.

Our Favorite Chocolate Cake

The origin of this quick-and-easy, moist, dark, vegan chocolate cake goes back to World War II butter and egg rationing. For years at Moosewood, we've referred to it as Vegan Chocolate Cake, but the overwhelming opinion of our customers is that this cake isn't just for vegans. It's so popular that we have it on our menu every day. This new gluten-free version topped with chocolate ganache can be enjoyed by everyone.

Yields one 9 x 13-inch cake or two 9-inch round cakes
Serves 12 to 15
Prep time: 20 minutes
Baking time: 35 to 50 minutes

Cooking spray or oil, for the baking pan
⅔ cup unsweetened cocoa powder, plus more for dusting the baking pan
3 cups Moosewood's Gluten-Free All-Purpose Flour Mix (page 351)★
1½ teaspoons xanthan gum
2 cups sugar
1 teaspoon salt
1 teaspoon baking soda
1 cup vegetable oil (we use ½ cup olive oil and ½ cup canola oil)
2 cups hot water or brewed coffee
2 teaspoons pure vanilla extract
¼ cup apple cider vinegar

SIMPLE GANACHE
2 cups semisweet chocolate chips or chunks
1¼ cups boiling water or brewed coffee

★To make only enough for this recipe, mix ¾ cup white rice flour, ¾ cup brown rice flour, ¾ cup potato starch, and ¾ cup tapioca starch. You can also use a commercial gluten-free flour mix, such as Bob's Red Mill. And if you want to use wheat flour, use 3 cups and omit the xanthan gum.

Preheat the oven to 350°F. Coat a 9 x 13-inch baking pan with cooking spray or oil and dust with cocoa powder. Or spray or oil two round layer cake pans, line the bottoms with parchment paper, spray or oil the paper, and dust with cocoa powder.

In a medium bowl, stir together the cocoa, flour mixture, xanthan gum, sugar, salt, and baking soda. Add the vegetable oil, hot water or coffee, and vanilla, and using an electric mixer or a whisk, mix well until thick and smooth with no lumps. Add the vinegar and stir briefly, just until the batter is evenly colored. Without wasting any time, scrape the batter into the prepared baking pan(s).

Bake a 9 x 13-inch pan for about 45 minutes; round cake pans for 35 to 40 minutes. Turn the pan midway if your oven heats unevenly. When the top feels springy and the cake pulls away slightly from the sides, remove from the oven. Cool on a wire rack.

While the cake bakes, make the ganache: Place the chocolate chips in a blender and pour in the boiling water or coffee so the chocolate is just covered. Wait a couple of minutes and then blend until smooth. Pour the chocolate mixture into a wide, shallow pan or large plate and let cool to a spreadable consistency. When the cake is cool, spread the chocolate over the top, or between the layers and on top for a layer cake.

SERVING AND MENU SUGGESTIONS
Our Favorite Chocolate Cake is our go-to dessert when some of the guests at a dinner party avoid gluten. It's not a rich, heavy cake, but it is a wonderful chocolate indulgence after a light salad meal. Baked as a layer cake, it's a perfect birthday cake with a dark glossy icing.

Fresh Ginger Gingerbread

Adapted from a recipe by renowned pastry chef Claudia Fleming, whose work was an award-winning feature at Gramercy Tavern and North Fork Table and Inn, and who doesn't do frou-frou desserts. This gingerbread is dark, spicy, moist, and springy, and not too sweet because of the addition of stout. We like to use Wolaver's organic oatmeal stout, but any rich, roasted malt stout will do.

Accompanied by a billowing bowl of whipped cream and some poached pears, this is a spectacular winter holiday dessert. Or serve it after a tropical meal in summer, accompanied by fresh tropical fruits.

Yields one 9 x 13-inch gingerbread
Serves 12
Prep time: 20 minutes
Baking time: about 1 hour

1 cup stout
1 cup molasses
1½ teaspoons baking soda
Butter or cooking spray, for the pan
¾ cup vegetable oil★
½ cup granulated sugar
½ cup packed brown sugar
3 large eggs
one 6-inch piece fresh ginger
2 cups white flour, plus more for the pan★★
1½ teaspoons baking powder
2 tablespoons ground ginger
1 teaspoon ground cinnamon
¼ teaspoon freshly grated nutmeg
¼ teaspoon ground cardamom

★We usually use half canola and half extra-virgin olive oil.
★★We usually use pastry flour.

Combine the stout and molasses in a large saucepan and bring to a boil. Remove from the heat and stir in the baking soda. The mixture will foam up and expand. Set aside to cool to room temperature.

Preheat the oven to 325°F. Butter or spray a 9 x 13-inch baking pan. Dust with flour.

In a large bowl, using an electric mixer, beat together the oil and granulated and brown sugars. Add the eggs and beat well.

Peel the fresh ginger. On the large holes of a box grater, grate the ginger to yield about ½ cup. In your hand, squeeze the grated ginger over the beer and molasses mixture to release the juice into the pan. Discard the squeezed-out ginger pulp.

In a separate bowl, stir together the flour, baking powder, and all the dried spices. Add the stout-molasses mixture to the oil-sugar mixture and beat until smooth. Add the flour mixture and beat until well incorporated.

Pour the batter into the prepared baking pan and bake for about 1 hour, or until the top feels springy and firm to the touch and the whole kitchen is fragrant.

Serve warm or at room temperature.

SERVING AND MENU IDEAS
In cold weather, serve this spicy gingerbread after a meal of Mushroom-Stuffed Winter Squash (page 180) and Red Cabbage with Blueberries (page 305). When it's hot, it's a perfect dessert with Chilled Pineapple-Mango Soup (page 104) and Kelp Noodle Salad (page 143).

Lemon-Zucchini Cake with Thyme

A perfect ode-to-summer cake, this green-speckled one is not the usual dense spicy zucchini bread–like version; instead, think summery with a touch of thyme and lemony sweetness. Serve it warm and glazed, with peaches or raspberries and ice cream, or just simply on its own with a glass of iced tea or lemonade.

Serves 8 to 10
Prep time: 30 minutes
Baking time: about 50 minutes

¾ cup olive oil or vegetable oil, plus more for
  the pan
2 cups grated zucchini
1 tablespoon chopped fresh thyme
2 cups unbleached white all-purpose flour,
  plus 2 tablespoons
1½ teaspoons baking powder
¼ teaspoon salt
½ teaspoon baking soda
¾ cup sugar
2 tablespoons fresh lemon juice
½ lemon (not peeled), chopped and seeded
3 large eggs

LEMON GLAZE
1 cup confectioners' sugar
2 tablespoons fresh lemon juice

Preheat the oven to 350°F. Oil the bottom and sides of a 9-inch round or 8-inch square cake pan. Line the bottom with parchment paper, brush with a little oil, and set aside.

Press the grated zucchini between layers of paper towels to extract most of the moisture. In a small bowl, toss the zucchini with 2 tablespoons of the flour and the thyme. Set aside. Sift the remaining 2 cups flour, the baking powder, salt, and baking soda together in a large bowl, and set aside.

In a food processor, whirl the sugar, lemon juice, and chopped lemon for about 20 seconds. Add the oil and eggs and whirl briefly. Add half the flour mixture, pulse for a few seconds, and then pulse in the rest of the flour mixture.

Scrape the batter into a bowl. Stir in the grated zucchini mixture. Fill the prepared cake pan. Bake until the top is golden and the center is firm to the touch, about 50 minutes. Cool for about 15 minutes before removing the cake from the pan.

Make the glaze: Stir the confectioners' sugar into the lemon juice with a fork. Brush the glaze over the warm cake.

SERVING AND MENU IDEAS
Serve as a snack, breakfast, with tea, or as a dessert.

Orange-Pistachio Cornmeal Cake

A gorgeous young woman from Spain got a job at Moosewood a few years ago. Pilar Molina quickly impressed us with her bubbly enthusiasm, her cheerful work ethic, and her knowledge of European cuisines. She really distinguished herself when she began making sophisticated Mediterranean-style desserts for the restaurant. Soon, customers were saying, "Mmmm, delicious. Did Pili make this?"

Drizzled with a fragrant orange syrup and laden with toasted pistachios and that certain distinctive something that fruity extra-virgin olive oil gives a sweet pastry, this Spanish-style cake is dense and moist with a rustic look and "grown-up" appeal. It's simple to put together and is great for a last-minute dinner party.

Yields one 9-inch round cake
Serves 6 to 8
Prep time: 30 minutes
Baking time: 45 minutes

¾ cup extra-virgin olive oil, plus more for the pan
1 cup sugar
3 large eggs
1 tablespoon finely grated orange zest
½ cup fresh orange juice
1½ cups unbleached white all-purpose flour
½ cup cornmeal
½ teaspoon salt
2 teaspoons baking powder
¾ cup coarsely chopped toasted pistachios

SYRUP
2 teaspoons finely grated orange zest
¼ cup fresh orange juice
¼ cup sugar

Preheat the oven to 350°F. Cut a piece of parchment paper to fit the bottom of a 9-inch cake pan. Lightly oil the bottom and the sides of the pan before putting in the parchment paper. Oil the top of the parchment paper as well.

In a large bowl, thoroughly beat together the olive oil and sugar. Add the eggs one at a time and beat after each addition. Beat in the orange zest and orange juice.

In a separate bowl, sift together the flour, cornmeal, salt, and baking powder. Add to the wet ingredients and stir until just blended. Stir in the pistachios.

Pour the batter into the prepared pan. Bake until the top is set and the sides begin to separate from the pan, about 45 minutes.

While the cake is baking, make the syrup: Put the orange zest, orange juice, and sugar in a small saucepan. Cook on low heat until the sugar has dissolved. Set aside.

When the cake is done, put the pan on a wire rack and cool for 10 minutes. Remove the cake from the pan and remove and discard the parchment paper. Put the cake back on the wire rack and place a serving plate or baking sheet beneath the cooling rack, to catch any excess syrup. Poke small holes here and there in the cake with a sharp thin knife or a thin skewer. Drizzle the syrup evenly over the cake. Serve warm or at room temperature.

VARIATION
In place of pistachios, use coarsely chopped toasted almonds or hazelnuts.

SERVING AND MENU IDEAS
This cake is a lovely dessert after Summer Stir-Fry with Halloumi Cheese (page 215) or Bitter Greens Lasagna (page 233).

Cherry Tomato Upside-Down Cake

Kip Wilcox ordered this unusual, very attractive upside-down cake topped with glistening fruit at Hazelnut Kitchen, a wonderful restaurant in Trumansburg, New York. Then she developed this simple version that lends itself to many other fruits, as you can see in the variations below. While the cake bakes, the juices of the fruit seep into the topping and batter, creating a moist, fruity cake that is even more tantalizing topped with a scoop of vanilla ice cream. Easily made and portable, it is perfect for brunch, summer picnics, potlucks, or just dinner at home.

Yields one 9-inch cake
Serves 6 to 8
Prep time: 20 to 25 minutes
Baking time: 35 to 40 minutes

3 tablespoons butter
¾ cup packed brown sugar
2 cups halved cherry tomatoes

CAKE
⅔ cup butter, at room temperature
½ cup packed brown sugar
1 teaspoon pure vanilla extract
1 large egg
1½ cups unbleached white all-purpose flour
½ teaspoon baking soda
½ teaspoon baking powder
½ teaspoon salt
¾ cup buttermilk

Ice cream or whipped cream, for serving

Preheat the oven to 375°F.

In a 9-inch ovenproof skillet, melt the butter on low heat. Stir in the brown sugar until well mixed and remove from the heat. Arrange the tomatoes, cut side down, in the pan, close together or overlapping; they'll shrink as they bake. Set aside.

Make the cake batter: In a large bowl, beat the butter and brown sugar with an electric mixer or by hand until creamy. Beat in the vanilla and egg. In a separate, smaller bowl, sift together the flour, baking soda, baking powder, and salt.

Alternating, add the flour mixture and the buttermilk to the butter mixture in three additions, mixing between each just until the flour is incorporated. Do not overmix. Scoop the batter onto the tomatoes in small spoonfuls. Try not to leave gaps, although the batter will smooth out in the oven.

Bake until a knife inserted into the center of the cake comes out clean, 35 to 40 minutes. Allow the cake to sit in the pan for 15 to 20 minutes before inverting onto a plate.

Serve warm, topped with ice cream or whipped cream.

VARIATIONS
- Replace tomatoes with 2 cups sliced pitted peaches, nectarines, plums, apples, or mangoes, or pitted cherries.
- Add the zest of 1 lemon or lime to the cake batter.
- Add 1 teaspoon ground cinnamon to the batter.

SERVING AND MENU IDEAS
Cherry Tomato Upside-Down Cake is a beautiful addition to a brunch alongside Herbed Baked Eggs in a Ramekin (page 11). Make it for dessert after Asparagus with Fried Eggs and Sizzled Shallots (page 183) or Award-Winning Chili with Chocolate and Stout (page 264).

Texas Italian Cream Cake

This cake is a favorite throughout the southern United States and has its origins in Texas, where, for reasons we can't possibly guess, it is always called Italian Cream Cake. At Moosewood, it became one of our first adaptations to gluten-free. Always popular, the coconut-pecan cake frosted with a fluffy cream cheese frosting is luscious for special occasions. A foolproof cake, it bakes up big for a dramatic presentation.

Yields one double-layer 9-inch round cake
Cake prep time: about 15 minutes
Cake baking time: 30 to 35 minutes
Cake cooling time: about 20 minutes
Frosting prep time: about 10 minutes
Frosting the cake time: about 10 minutes

1 cup (2 sticks) butter, at room temperature, plus more for the pans
2 cups Moosewood's Gluten-Free All-Purpose Flour Mix (page 351), plus more for the pans
1¼ teaspoons baking soda
¼ teaspoon salt
½ cup unsweetened shredded coconut
2 cups granulated sugar
4 large eggs
1 teaspoon pure vanilla extract
1 teaspoon pure coconut extract
1 cup buttermilk
1 cup chopped toasted pecans

CREAM CHEESE FROSTING

4 tablespoons (½ stick) butter, at room temperature
6 ounces cream cheese, at room temperature
1 tablespoon pure vanilla extract
3 cups confectioners' sugar

Preheat the oven to 350°F. Butter two 9-inch round cake pans and lightly dust them with some of the flour mix.

In a bowl, sift together the flour mix, baking soda, and salt. Add the shredded coconut and mix well. Set aside. In a large bowl, cream the butter and sugar with an electric mixer. Add the eggs, one at a time, beating well after each addition. Stir in the vanilla and coconut extracts. Alternate adding the buttermilk and the dry mixture to the butter mixture, beating well after each addition, to form a smooth batter. Stir in the toasted pecans. Divide the batter evenly between the two prepared pans.

Bake until the cakes begin to pull away from the edges of the pans and a knife inserted into the center comes out clean, 30 to 35 minutes. Cool the layers in the pans for about 5 minutes and then turn them out onto a wire rack to cool completely before frosting.

Make the frosting: In a food processor or using an electric mixer, cream the butter and cream cheese until well blended and light. Beat in the vanilla, and gradually add the sugar until the frosting is smooth and thick.

To frost the cake, first spread frosting between the two layers and then on the sides and top.

NOTE: *MAKE IT PRETTY*

Sprinkle shavings of fresh or toasted coconut on top, or press flakes of dried coconut into the frosting all over. Decorate the top with pecan halves. Or go all out: a few edible nasturtium blossoms would be the icing on the cake.

Erma Mabel's Fresh Rhubarb Cake

Moosewood's Lisa Wichman shares a family recipe from her grandma Erma Mabel, who taught her how to make this light, simple, and delicious vanilla cake with a sweet-tart fruity layer of fresh rhubarb in the middle. The recipe originated years ago in the hills of north central West Virginia. We've enjoyed this easy, old-fashioned cake for years, and now we've developed a gluten-free version using a gluten-free wheat flour substitute that is rice flour–based. We recommend Bob's Red Mill One-to-One Flour, or try making a supply of Moosewood's Gluten-Free All-Purpose Flour Mix (page 351).

Serves 8
Preparation time: 30 minutes
Baking time: 35 to 40 minutes

½ cup (1 stick) butter, at room temperature, plus
    more for the baking dish
1 cup sugar
3 large eggs
1½ cups white gluten-free flour mix
1 tablespoon baking powder
¼ teaspoon salt
½ cup milk
1 teaspoon pure vanilla extract
2½ cups ¾-inch pieces rhubarb stalks (about
    12 ounces)★

★Be sure to discard the leaves of the rhubarb, which are poisonous, and the tough fibrous ends of the stalks.

Preheat the oven to 350°F. Butter a 10-inch round or 7 x 11-inch baking dish.

Using an electric mixer, cream the butter and sugar until light. Add the eggs one at a time, beating well after each addition. In a separate bowl, sift together the flour mix, baking powder, and salt. In a small bowl, mix together the milk and vanilla.

Add some of the flour mixture to the creamed butter-sugar mixture and beat until incorporated. Alternate mixing in the milk and the dry ingredients, beating well after each addition. Beat until the batter is fluffy.

Spread about two-thirds of the batter into the prepared baking dish, and gently and evenly distribute the chopped raw rhubarb pieces over the entire surface. Then spread the remaining batter evenly over the rhubarb, being careful not to press the rhubarb into the bottom layer of batter.

Bake for 35 to 40 minutes, until a knife inserted into the center comes out clean and the top is golden brown. The rhubarb will cook thoroughly inside the cake.

SERVING AND MENU IDEAS
A good dessert after Spring Greens and Vegetables with Shallot Vinaigrette (page 139) or Spring Pot-pie (page 168). Erma Mabel's cake is so delicious that you may want it for breakfast, if there's any left over.

Fresh Pineapple Upside-Down Cake

This homespun classic is no less delicious because it is gluten-free. It calls for fresh pineapple and that makes all the difference.

If following tradition, slice your pineapple into rings, but it's also fine to use pineapple chunks instead of rings. The cake will look lovely with pineapple chunks arranged in concentric circles or whatever design you come up with.

We use ground chia seeds or flaxseeds in this cake. They act the same way that xanthan gum does in gluten-free baking. Many people who experience digestive problems with xanthan gum are fine with chia seeds and flaxseeds.

Yields one 9- or 10-inch cake
Prep time: 20 minutes
Baking time: 30 to 35 minutes

1 fresh, ripe pineapple
4 tablespoons (½ stick) butter
½ cup packed brown sugar
1 cup chopped walnuts
1⅓ cup Moosewood's Gluten-Free All-Purpose Flour (page 351)
¾ cup granulated sugar
2½ teaspoons baking powder
¾ teaspoon ground chia seeds or flaxseeds
½ teaspoon salt
¼ cup vegetable oil
¾ cup milk
2 large eggs, beaten
1 teaspoon pure vanilla extract
Finely grated zest of 1 lemon
1 tablespoon reserved pineapple juice or bottled pineapple juice

Cut off both ends of the pineapple and stand it upright on a cutting board. Using a sharp knife, cut off the peel from top to bottom. Either use a pineapple corer to remove the core and then cut the pineapple into six or seven ¼-inch-thick rings, or cut the pineapple into rings and then use a paring knife to cut the core out of each ring. Place the pineapple in a bowl for a little while and most likely some juice will accumulate in the bowl. Reserve this juice. In the unlikely event that your pineapple doesn't yield any juice, you can substitute bottled pineapple juice.

Preheat the oven to 350°F. Put the butter in a 9- or 10-inch cast-iron skillet, 9-inch round cake pan, or 10-inch pie plate and place in the preheated oven to melt. When the butter has melted, remove the pan from the oven and sprinkle the brown sugar evenly across the bottom. Arrange the pineapple rings in a single layer (a 10-inch pan usually accommodates 6 rings around the pan and 1 in the middle, but it depends on the size of the rings). Evenly sprinkle the walnuts over the pineapple.

In a mixing bowl, sift the flour mix with the sugar, baking powder, ground chia or flaxseeds, and salt. Add the oil and milk and stir to combine. Add the eggs, vanilla, lemon zest, and pineapple juice and mix until smooth.

Pour the batter evenly over the pineapple rings in the skillet or pan. Bake for 30 to 35 minutes until the cake is golden brown and begins to pull away from the sides of the skillet. Remove from the oven and cool on a wire rack for 5 to 10 minutes. While the cake is still warm, invert it onto a serving plate.

SERVING AND MENU IDEAS
Pineapple Upside-Down Cake works well at the end of a tropical meal, after a casual outdoor meal in summer, and as a winter coffee break treat, and it has a certain nostalgic appeal, perfect for your next '50s-themed dinner party.

Pumpkin Cheesecake

Easier to make than a pumpkin pie, this attractive, pastel orange–colored cheesecake is a crowd-pleaser, especially for fall and winter holiday occasions. The delicious crust is gluten-free when made with gluten-free oats. When cooking for someone who has celiac disease, be sure to use oats processed in a gluten-free facility; look in the gluten-free section of the supermarket.

Yields one 10-inch cheesecake
Prep time: 25 minutes
Baking time: 45 minutes
In-oven cooling time: 20 minutes to 1 hour
Room temperature cooling time: a couple of hours
Chilling time: at least 3 hours

CRUST
Butter or cooking spray, for the pan
1 cup rolled oats
1 cup walnuts or pecans
½ cup packed brown sugar
4 tablespoons (½ stick) butter, melted

FILLING
1 (15-ounce) can pumpkin purée (1¾ cups)
1½ pounds cream cheese, at room temperature
1 cup sugar (white or brown)
1 teaspoon ground cinnamon
½ teaspoon freshly grated nutmeg
½ teaspoon ground ginger
½ teaspoon salt
4 large eggs

Make the crust: Preheat the oven to 325°F. Generously butter or spray a 10-inch springform pan. (See Note.)

In a food processor, whirl all the ingredients for the crust until crumbly. Spread the mixture evenly over the bottom of the prepared pan and press it to form an even layer. Bake for 15 minutes while you prepare the filling.

Make the filling: In a food processor, whirl the pumpkin, cream cheese, sugar, cinnamon, nutmeg, ginger, and salt. Run a rubber spatula around the sides and if there are any lumps of cream cheese, break them up and process again briefly until smooth. Add the eggs and process for a few seconds, just until smooth and evenly colored.

When the crust has baked for 15 minutes, remove it from the oven and turn the oven temperature down to 300°F. Pour the filling into the pan and bake the cheesecake for 45 minutes, until the sides are firm and the center still moves a bit when gently shaken. Turn the oven off, open the oven door a couple of inches, and leave the cheesecake in the oven to cool for at least 20 minutes and up to 1 hour.

Remove the cheesecake from the oven and cool it in the pan to room temperature. Cover it with a plate and refrigerate in the pan until firm, at least 3 to 4 hours, or overnight.

Remove the cheesecake from the pan when you're ready to serve it. Release the clasp slowly and run a knife around the edges if necessary. Using a long, offset spatula, you'll probably be able to slide the cheesecake from the pan bottom onto a serving plate, but if it sticks, warm the bottom by holding it over hot water for about 15 seconds to melt the butter just enough to release the crust from the pan.

NOTE: You can use two smaller (7- or 8-inch) springform pans; the baking time is still 45 minutes. If you use one 9-inch springform pan, bake for 55 to 60 minutes. The height of the cheesecake, not the diameter, is what influences the baking time: the deeper the filling in the pan, the longer the time.

SERVING AND MENU IDEAS
Pumpkin Cheesecake is simply and beautifully garnished with a sprinkling of spiced nuts (page 59). Arrange some fresh apple or pear slices on the side, or if you'd like a more elaborate topping, try a chunky apple or pear sauce, or a cranberry sauce made with whole cranberries.

CHEESECAKE TIPS

Cheesecakes have a tendency to crack, but they don't have to. Avoid overbeating the batter, because overbeating incorporates additional air. Mix the batter well and eliminate cream cheese lumps before you add the eggs. To help with this, bring the cream cheese to room temperature or soften it by unwrapping it and placing it in a glass or ceramic bowl and microwaving for 30 to 45 seconds until slightly softened. Eggs hold air in the batter, so add them last, and mix the batter as little as possible once they are in.

Another cause of a cracked surface is a too-rapid temperature change. If you heat a cheesecake too fast or cool it down too fast, it's likely to crack. So, bake the cheesecake at a low oven temperature and don't overbake. When perfectly done, there will still be a 2- to 3-inch wobbly spot in the middle of the cheesecake. The texture will smooth out as it cools.

Cheesecake shrinks as it cools. Hence the directions for a slow, gentle cooling down. And generously butter the sides of the baking pan before pouring in the batter to allow the cake to pull away from the pan as it cools and shrinks instead of pulling apart from the middle.

If, after all this, you still have a crack, and you care what your cheesecake looks like, spread on a topping or a sauce to camouflage the crevasse.

Baked cheesecakes freeze well. First, freeze the cheesecake, uncovered, on the level, and then wrap it securely in plastic wrap and then heavy-duty foil. Do not freeze cheesecakes with garnishes or toppings. Defrost in the refrigerator.

Orange-Carrot-Almond Torte

This torte (or it could be called a cake) is rich, dense, and spongy, with lots of almonds and orange zest and a lovely moistness from the orange syrup drizzled over the cake after baking. Served with fresh peaches, strawberries, raspberries, or blueberries, it makes a perfect summer dessert. It's not bad in the winter, either, topped with a dollop of whipped cream.

Yields one 8-inch round cake
Serves 8 to 12
Prep time: 30 minutes
Baking time: about 45 minutes
Cooling and finishing time: 15 minutes

CAKE
Oil, for the pan
1 cup unbleached white all-purpose flour
1 teaspoon baking powder
½ teaspoon salt
1 teaspoon ground cinnamon
¼ teaspoon freshly grated nutmeg
4 large eggs, at room temperature, separated
½ cup sugar
½ teaspoon pure vanilla extract
1 teaspoon almond extract
1 teaspoon finely grated orange zest
1½ cups grated carrots
1 cup ground toasted almonds

ORANGE SYRUP
⅔ cup water
⅓ cup sugar
1 teaspoon finely grated orange zest
¼ cup fresh orange juice

Preheat the oven to 350°F. Oil the bottom and sides of an 8-inch round cake pan. Line the bottom with parchment paper, brush a little oil over the parchment, and set aside.

In a large bowl, sift together the flour, baking powder, salt, cinnamon, and nutmeg. Set aside.

In a medium bowl, using an electric mixer, beat the egg whites until foamy. Then slowly sprinkle in 2 tablespoons of the sugar as you continue to beat until the whites turn glossy and stiff. Scrape the whites into a smaller bowl and set aside. Again in the medium bowl, beat the egg yolks while gradually adding the remaining sugar. Beat for 2 to 3 minutes until the yolks are pale and thick. Beat in the
vanilla and almond extracts, and the orange zest. Stir in the carrots and almonds. Using a spatula, alternately stir in half the flour mixture and egg whites and then half again and fold until almost no whites are visible. Scoop the batter into the prepared baking pan and smooth the top. Bake for 40 to 50 minutes, until light brown and springy on top.

While the cake is baking, make the syrup: Place the water and sugar in a small saucepan and boil until the liquid has reduced to ⅓ cup. Stir in the orange zest and orange juice. Set aside to cool.

When the cake has baked, cool it on a wire rack for about 10 minutes, then transfer it from the pan onto a plate. With a skewer, poke holes down through the top of the cake. Pour the orange syrup evenly over the top; the syrup will drizzle down the holes and the sides of the cake and be soaked up at the bottom.

Cool completely before serving.

SERVING AND MENU IDEAS
Serve with fresh fruit, sorbet, ice cream, or whipped cream, or all by itself.

Piecrust

This recipe comes from Betty Harville, mother of Moosewood Collective members Susan Harville and Nancy Lazarus. During the 1950s and '60s, Betty made hundreds of pies for her five children, always with tender, flaky crusts. Now, Susan, a Moosewood dessert maker, makes many different sorts of piecrusts, but when Nancy wants to make a pie, she digs out the handwritten index card that Betty gave her in the '70s. Still always tender and flaky.

Yields a single or double crust for one 9½- or 10-inch pie plate
Time: 15 minutes

SINGLE CRUST
1½ cups unbleached white all-purpose flour
3 tablespoons water
½ cup (1 stick) cold butter
¼ teaspoon salt, if using unsalted butter

Put the flour into a mixing bowl. In a cup or small bowl, make a paste of ¼ cup of the flour and the water. With a pastry cutter or two table knives, cut the butter into the dry flour until the pieces are the size of small peas. Add the flour paste and mix (with a spoon or your hands) until the dough comes together and can be shaped into a ball.

DOUBLE CRUST
2½ cups unbleached white all-purpose flour
⅓ cup water
¾ cup (1½ sticks) cold butter
Scant ½ teaspoon salt, if using unsalted butter

Use the same procedure as for single crust, except make the flour paste with ½ cup of the flour and ⅓ cup water.

If you want to hold the pie dough to roll out later, wrap it well in plastic wrap and keep it in the refrigerator.

Apple and Fig Galette with Rosemary

This rustic pie is delectable, especially if you love rosemary. Maple syrup, vanilla, and rosemary are a tasty combo of flavors with apples and figs. Peel the apples, or don't peel, as you wish. We call for dried figs, but you can certainly use fresh figs—just slice them and add to the apple sauté for the last couple of minutes.

Yields one 10-inch galette
Serves 6 to 8
Prep time: 40 minutes
Baking time: 30 to 40 minutes

½ cup pure maple syrup
1 or 2 sprigs fresh rosemary
½ cup dried figs, coarsely chopped
1 cup water
dough for one double piecrust (page 373)
1½ teaspoons minced fresh rosemary leaves
6 cups sliced apples
2 tablespoons butter
1 teaspoon pure vanilla extract
1 large egg

On the stovetop or in a microwave, heat the maple syrup and rosemary sprigs until the syrup foams. Set aside to steep for 30 minutes.

Bring the dried figs and water to a boil and simmer for 15 minutes. Remove the figs with a slotted spoon and set aside.

Prepare the pie dough. Form into a ball and set aside, loosely covered.

Preheat the oven to 375°F.

Sauté the apple slices with 1 teaspoon of the minced rosemary, stirring frequently, for 5 minutes. If the apples are juicy and release liquid, cook until the liquid has evaporated. Remove from the heat and stir in the vanilla and the plumped figs. Remove the rosemary stem from the maple syrup, and stir the syrup into the apples and figs.

Roll the pie dough out into a rough circle about 14 inches in diameter (see Note). When the circle is about 12 inches in diameter, sprinkle it evenly with the remaining ½ teaspoon minced rosemary and continue rolling. Drape the pie dough over a 10-inch pie plate with the extra crust hanging over the sides. Or place the dough on a baking sheet lined with parchment paper and make a free-form galette.

Spread the filling in the dough. Fold the extra dough over the filling (in the middle of the top, there will be a roughly circular area of filling not covered). Whip the egg until evenly colored. Brush the top of the exposed dough with the egg wash. Bake the galette for 30 to 40 minutes, until the crust is golden.

Serve warm or at room temperature.

NOTE: You can make two or more smaller galettes; just roll out the dough to fit smaller pie plates or baking pans with about 3 inches draping over the sides, or make several small free-form galettes.

SERVING AND MENU SUGGESTIONS

Apple and Fig Galette with Rosemary is a wonderful dessert to serve after a rustic Mediterranean meal, such as White Bean Stew with Rosemary on Orecchiette with Goat Cheese Toast (page 217) or Aigo Bouido (page 102) with Lentil Salad with Baby Greens and Oranges (page 142).

The galette is also an impressive addition to a special brunch, perhaps after Mushroom Tofu Scramble with Truffle Oil (page 19) or Baked Eggs with Spinach and Frizzled Sage (page 16).

Custard and Pear Pie

Here's how a new pie can happen at Moosewood. On Super Pi Day in 2015 (3/14/15), we of course wanted to serve pie, both savory dinner tarts and toothsome desserts. We had some particularly flavorful pears on hand, and we were thinking of milk tert, a South African comfort-food treat, and its wonderful triad of flavors: cinnamon, vanilla, and almond. Our customers loved the pie and so do we, so here it is.

Yields one 10-inch pie
Serves 8
Prep time: 30 minutes, with already prepared pie shell
Baking time: about 1 hour

dough for one 10-inch single piecrust (page 373)

CUSTARD

⅓ cup butter, melted
½ cup half-and-half
⅓ cup white all-purpose flour
3 large eggs
1 cup granulated sugar
1 tablespoon pure vanilla extract
1 teaspoon almond extract

TOPPING

¼ cup turbinado sugar or packed brown sugar
1 teaspoon ground cinnamon

3 or 4 not-quite-ripe pears

Roll out the pie dough and fit it into a 10-inch pie plate. Trim the overhang to about 1 inch all around. Save the trimmings, because they may come in handy to patch sparse spots around the edge. Roll the overhang under and crimp to make a traditional fluted edge. Set aside.

When the pie shell is ready, make the custard: Put all the ingredients in a blender and process until smooth.

Make the topping: Stir the sugar and cinnamon together and set aside.

Preheat the oven to 350°F.

Peel and core the pears. Cut lengthwise (from stem end to blossom end) into slices about ⅓ inch thick. Arrange the slices in a spoke pattern, thin ends toward the center and wider ends almost touching the outside edges. Make two layers of pear slices, using the smaller pieces of pear to fill in empty spots and the middle. Briefly whirl the custard in the blender and pour it evenly over the pears. Sprinkle the topping over the pie.

Bake for about 1 hour, until the middle is just set. When the middle is set, remove the pie from the oven.

Cool to room temperature before serving. Store this pie in the refrigerator, but before serving, let the pie sit at room temperature; the flavors are more vibrant when the pie isn't cold from the refrigerator.

Apricot Frangipane Tart

If you're a fan of pastries with the appetizing richness and fragrance of almond paste, that's what frangipane is all about. It's happily combined here with a favorite shortbread-like crust and apricots. Apricots and almond paste are a beautiful partnership.

For years, dessert maven David Hirsch has been employing this recipe for Sweet Pastry Crust, originally published in our *Moosewood Restaurant Book of Desserts*, to provide the shell for all manner of tarts. It's put to perfect use here.

Yields one 9- or 10-inch tart
Serves 8
Prep time: 30 minutes
Dough chilling time: 30 minutes
Baking time: 30 to 35 minutes

¾ cup dried apricots (about 14 apricots)

SWEET PASTRY CRUST
¼ cup sugar
¼ teaspoon salt
1½ cups unbleached white all-purpose flour
½ cup (1 stick)/cold butter, cut into small chunks
1 large egg, separated
1 teaspoon pure vanilla extract
2 to 3 tablespoons cold water

FILLING
½ cup apricot preserves
7 to 8 ounces almond paste★
½ cup thinly sliced or slivered almonds

★We like Odense-brand almond paste because it has no preservatives.

In a bowl, soak the dried apricots in boiling water to cover. Set aside.

Make the crust: In the bowl of a food processor, whirl together the sugar, salt, and flour. Add the butter and pulse briefly, until the mixture is crumbly. Put the egg yolk in a small bowl and reserve the white for the filling. Add the vanilla and 2 tablespoons of cold water to the egg yolk and add it to the dough in the food processor; pulse briefly. With your fingers, push the dough together and if it doesn't hold, add an additional tablespoon of cold water and pulse again. Remove the dough, form into a disk, cover with plastic wrap, and refrigerate for 30 minutes.

While the dough is chilling, make the filling: Drain the apricots, reserving the soaking liquid. Finely chop the soaked apricots and combine them with the preserves. Set aside.

In the bowl of the food processor, whirl the almond paste, reserved egg white, and 3 tablespoons of the apricot soaking liquid until smooth. Set aside.

When the dough has chilled, preheat the oven to 375°F. On a lightly floured surface, roll the dough into a circle and fit it into the bottom of a 9½-inch tart pan with a removable rim or into a 9- or 10-inch pie plate.

Spread the almond paste mixture evenly on the dough. Spread the apricots and preserves evenly over the almond paste. Sprinkle the almonds on top. Bake for 30 to 35 minutes until the crust is lightly browned. Cool before serving.

SERVING AND MENU IDEAS
A dollop of whipped cream on the side would not be amiss. Such a succulent tart would be a fine dessert after a meal of Watercress Toast (page 53) or Scalloped Potatoes and Mushrooms (page 202) and Red Cabbage with Blueberries (page 305).

Vegan Apple-Blueberry Crumble

Crumbles are extremely popular at the restaurant all year . . . blueberry and apple, apple and raspberry, peach and cherry, mango and strawberry, pear and cranberry, whatever fits the season. Both fresh and frozen fruits work.

Susan Harville, our dessert maker for forty-plus years, developed this vegan crumble topping that features the warm, sweet taste and pleasantly nubbly texture of cornmeal that complements soft-baked fruit so well. The topping can be made in double or quadruple batches to keep in the freezer, making it quick and easy to pop a luscious, wholesome dessert into the oven.

Yields one crumble in a 10-inch deep-dish pie plate, 9- or 10-inch square baking pan, or 8 x 11- or 9 x 12-inch baking pan, or in six to eight 12-ounce baking cups
Serves 6 to 8
Hands-on time: 20 minutes
Baking time: 1 hour, 30 minutes

FRUIT FILLING

5 or 6 tart, crisp apples, peeled and sliced (about 6 cups)
1 pint (12 ounces) fresh blueberries or 1 pound frozen blueberries (about 2½ cups)
½ cup sugar
1 tablespoon ground cinnamon
2 tablespoons cornstarch

CRUMBLE TOPPING

1½ cups unbleached white all-purpose flour
1 cup cornmeal
1 cup sugar
1 teaspoon salt
1½ teaspoons ground cinnamon
¼ cup vegetable oil
¼ cup olive oil

Preheat the oven to 375°F.

Make the fruit filling: In a large bowl, stir together all the filling ingredients until the fruit is evenly coated with the dry ingredients. Put the fruit filling into the baking dish(es). If you are using individual cups, place them on a baking sheet to catch drips. (If you're using a baking dish and it seems really full, put it on a baking sheet, too.) Bake for about 45 minutes until the fruit seems soft and juices have thickened.

While the fruit bakes, make the crumble topping: Stir together all the dry ingredients in a bowl. Add the oils and stir to distribute evenly. Rub the mixture between your fingers for a minute or two until it has a crumbly texture.

When the first stage in the oven is done, spoon the crumble mixture on top of the fruit and return it to the oven to bake for another 35 to 45 minutes until the topping is nicely browned.

Fruit crumbles are good warm, at room temperature, or chilled.

NOTES: We usually combine a couple of fruits in a crumble, but a single fruit is fine, too. Juicier fruits may need a little more cornstarch; apples alone may not need any. The amount of sugar needed depends upon the sweetness of the fruit. Cranberries, for instance, we cook on a stovetop with enough sugar to make them tart-sweet before adding to other fruit and baking. Peaches don't take as long to bake as apples. Nutmeg is tasty in addition to or instead of cinnamon, especially with peaches and cherries. If you have fresh apricots, try a little cardamom in the crumble.

SERVING AND MENU IDEAS

Fruit crumble is a beloved classic American dessert, good in every season and with all sorts of fruit. For those of you who aren't vegan, a little whipped cream, ice cream, or yogurt on top is delicious. Crumble is also appropriate for breakfast, brunch, an afternoon pick-me-up, or a midnight snack.

Coconut Rice Pudding with Mangoes

This simple-to-make, sweet-and-satisfying vanilla rice pudding is yummy all by itself, and outstanding when studded with chunks of refreshing mango.

Arborio rice makes an exceptionally creamy pudding. Arborio is the rice most often used to make risotto, which entails adding small amounts of very hot liquid to raw rice and stirring it constantly. In this dish, just simmering the rice and liquid over low heat and stirring occasionally will make the grains very plump and moist. As the pudding sits, the rice may absorb more of the liquid, and if so, stir in a little more coconut milk to restore the right consistency.

Serves 4 to 6
Time: 65 minutes

1 cup Arborio rice
4 cups water
1 cinnamon stick (optional)
1 (13.5-ounce) can unsweetened coconut milk
½ teaspoon salt
1 tablespoon pure vanilla extract
½ cup agave syrup or sugar, more to taste
1 fresh, ripe mango, for garnish

In a 2-quart pan, combine the rice, water, cinnamon stick (if using), about 1 cup of the coconut milk, and the salt. Cover and bring to a boil. Reduce the heat to low and simmer, covered, until the rice grains are very plump and the liquid has thickened and coats a spoon, about 45 minutes. Stir frequently to prevent sticking.

Stir in the vanilla, agave syrup or sugar, and the remaining coconut milk. Cover and cook on very low heat until the mixture is thick and the rice is sticky and soft, about 20 minutes. The consistency should be very thick and very creamy but not runny.

While the rice is cooking, peel, pit, and slice or chop the mango (see sidebar, page 118).

Serve warm or chilled, topped with the mango.

NOTE: To keep the pudding from drying out, press plastic wrap directly onto the surface and store refrigerated.

SERVING AND MENU IDEAS

Make it beautiful by garnishing with a small sprig of spearmint and/or strawberries, blueberries, or red or black raspberries. Toasted coconut and finely chopped toasted almonds are also nice garnishes. The pudding is delicious with banana slices. One way to serve this is to put a little pudding in a wine or parfait glass, add a layer of mango, then another layer of pudding, and top with a few pieces of mango and a spearmint leaf.

Rich Vegan Chocolate Pudding

Using avocados as the basis of a pudding has become one of the best-loved recipe sensations of recent years. In minutes you can whip up this creamy, rich, dark, glossy, and a little fruity vegan treat. And if you didn't know, you might not guess that avocado is the main ingredient. Surely this will be a special after-school treat for kids who don't realize, or particularly care, that it's more healthful than they think.

Yields 2 cups
Serves 4
Prep time: about 10 minutes

PUDDING
2 large ripe Hass avocados
¼ cup unsweetened cocoa powder
½ cup pure maple syrup★
½ cup water
1 teaspoon pure vanilla extract
⅛ teaspoon salt

★A mild, pourable honey also works, as does agave nectar.

GARNISHES
Flaked toasted coconut
Toasted chopped nuts
Espresso beans
Fruit such as raspberries, or sliced strawberries or bananas

Halve and pit the avocados. Scoop the flesh into the bowl of a food processor. Add the cocoa powder, maple syrup, water, vanilla, and salt and process until smooth and creamy. Chill before serving.

Serve plain or topped with one of the garnishes.

VARIATIONS
Mexican: Add ⅛ teaspoon ground cinnamon.
Mocha: Add 1 to 2 tablespoons brewed coffee or espresso.

SERVING AND MENU IDEAS
Serve as a seemingly indulgent dessert for a vegan meal, such as Lentil Salad with Baby Greens and Oranges (page 142), Award-Winning Chili with Chocolate and Stout (page 264), or Black Bean and Quinoa Burgers with Chipotle Ketchup (page 246).

Tropical Bread Pudding

While this dairy-free, vegan pudding bakes, the coconut milk and sugar caramelize and thicken to create a tropical taste and a custardy texture punctuated with sweet, gooey chunks of pineapple.

Serves 4 to 6
Prep time: 30 minutes
Baking time: 45 minutes

Oil, for the pan
4 cups loosely packed 1-inch bread cubes★
3 tablespoons vegan margarine or melted coconut oil
½ cup packed brown sugar★★ or coconut sugar
1 (13-ounce) can unsweetened coconut milk
2 teaspoons pure vanilla extract
1 teaspoon ground cinnamon
¼ teaspoon freshly grated nutmeg
½ teaspoon salt
1 (20-ounce) can crushed pineapple or pineapple chunks
¼ cup unsweetened shredded coconut

GLAZE
1 cup sifted confectioners' sugar
2 tablespoons dark rum

★Use day-old or stale bread, or lightly toast fresh bread cubes or spread them out on a tray and let them sit overnight.
★★We prefer light brown sugar in this pudding, but if dark is what you have on hand, use it.

Preheat the oven to 350°F. Lightly oil an 8- or 10-cup baking pan or an 8-inch square baking dish.

In a large bowl, toss the bread cubes with the margarine or coconut oil. In a separate bowl, whisk together the brown sugar, coconut milk, vanilla, cinnamon, nutmeg, and salt. Pour over the bread cubes, stir to coat, and allow to sit for 20 minutes. Drain the pineapple and reserve ¼ cup of the juice.

Add the drained pineapple and the coconut to the bread cubes and toss lightly. Spread the mixture in the prepared baking pan or dish. Bake until the top is lightly browned and the pudding feels firm to the touch, about 45 minutes.

Make the glaze: Stir together the confectioners' sugar, reserved ¼ cup pineapple juice, and rum.

Serve the bread pudding warm, with a drizzle of glaze on top.

SERVING AND MENU IDEAS
Serve after a mostly salad meal (salad without grains), such as Kelp Noodle Salad (page 143) or Lentil Salad with Baby Greens and Oranges (page 142).

Coconut-Pineapple Sorbet

It is a snap to make refreshing, delicious sorbet at home. This delightful Coconut-Pineapple Sorbet is fun to make and has a sweet, happy piña colada flavor. We recommend a ripe, organic pineapple for optimal flavor. The cost will be so much less than a premium store-bought, organic sorbet. The instructions below for preparing the pineapple work very well. For the creamy texture it lends, we use regular coconut milk, but "lite" coconut milk also works.

This recipe yields close to a half gallon of sorbet, so it's great to serve at a dinner party, but in a good container it keeps well in the freezer for a surprisingly long time. Solidly frozen sorbet can be loosened by placing it in a microwave on low power for 15 to 20 seconds.

Yields 6 to 8 cups
Prep time: 20 minutes
Freezing time: 2 hours or overnight

1 ripe pineapple
1 (13-ounce) can unsweetened coconut milk, chilled
3 tablespoons fresh lime juice
⅓ cup sugar

To prepare the pineapple, twist off the crown, and cut lengthwise in half and then into quarters. Cut off and discard the ends and the core. With the fruit-side up, run a sharp knife between the fruit and the peel and remove the fruit from the shell. Cut the pineapple fruit into small chunks; you

should have about 6 cups. Spread out in a single layer on a baking sheet or in a baking dish and put into the freezer for at least 2 hours, or overnight.★

When you're ready to prepare the sorbet, in a bowl, whisk the coconut milk until smooth.

Make the sorbet in two batches (which is not necessary if your food processor is large enough to contain and process all the ingredients together). Put half the coconut milk, lime juice, sugar, and frozen pineapple chunks into the bowl of the food processor and pulse. Scrape down the sides of the processor bowl and continue to process until smooth. Repeat with the remaining ingredients. Put the sorbet into a freezer-safe container with a cover. Serve immediately, or if necessary to get a firm texture, put the sorbet into the freezer for a bit before serving.

★Once pineapple chunks are frozen, if you won't use them right away, freeze them in a sealed freezer bag, and they'll keep for months.

SERVING AND MENU IDEAS
Serve Coconut-Pineapple Sorbet by itself in a brightly colored bowl. Or serve it topped with toasted coconut or lime or orange zest. Garnish it with fresh blackberries or serve it with Espresso Shortbread (page 355). It's beautiful served in a parfait glass with layers of sorbet and layers of fresh fruit, such as strawberries, mangoes, or papaya. You could drizzle some rum on top, or apricot brandy, cherry liqueur, or amaretto.

It's the perfect refreshing dessert after a meal that was a bit spicy, or rich, or served in hot weather.

Date-Walnut Shake

Here in Upstate New York, we occasionally find ourselves indulging in good old California dreaming. We know that our friends who live in California also have similar fantasies, so it probably doesn't really have much to do with the actual place but with an imagined state of mind. Date-Walnut Shake is one result . . . or could be a cause of dreaming.

With vegan ice cream, this creamy and thick shake is vegan.

Yields 2½ cups
Serves 2
Time: 15 minutes

1 cup crushed ice (or more)
¼ cup walnuts, toasted
⅔ cup chopped pitted Medjool dates
½ cup boiling water
Pinch of ground cinnamon
Pinch of salt
1 cup vanilla or coconut ice cream, or vegan ice "cream" or sorbet

Put the dates into a small bowl and pour the boiling water over them. Set aside to soak for 10 minutes.

In a blender, crush ice cubes to yield at least 1 cup of well-crushed ice. (You may want a bit more if you prefer a thinner shake). Remove the crushed ice and set it aside. In the blender, whirl the walnuts, soaked dates and their soaking liquid, the cinnamon, and salt until a coarse thick paste forms. Add the ice cream and the crushed ice, and purée. You may need to poke and stir the mixture to get it moving freely. Blend until smooth. We like this shake so thick it will support a straw upright, but if you prefer a thinner shake, add more crushed ice or a little cold water.

Pour (or spoon) the shake into two glasses and serve immediately.

SERVING AND MENU IDEAS
Whip up this shake when you want a quick, special treat for two. For a meal with retro appeal, serve Date-Walnut Shake as a beverage to go with one of our burgers (pages 245–253). Or serve it as a frosty dessert after Quinoa Tabouli with Pomegranates and Pistachios (page 145) or Mujadara (page 258).

THE MOOSEWOOD COLLECTIVE

Joan Adler, Ned Asta, Michael Blodgett, Laura Branca, Tony Del Plato, Linda Dickinson, Dave Dietrich, Penny Goldin, Susan Harville, David Hirsch, Nancy Lazarus, Neil Minnis, Eliana Parra, Sara Robbins, Wynelle Stein, Maureen Vivino, Jenny Wang, Lisa Wichman, Kip Wilcox

Moosewood Collective members who are the authors of *The Moosewood Restaurant Table* (first row, left to right) Nancy Lazarus, Laura Branca, Ned Asta (back row, left to right) David Hirsch, Wynnie Stein, Susan Harville, Kip Wilcox, and Joan Adler.

INDEX